AF575924

THE SCULPTING BOOK

Élisabeth Bonvalot

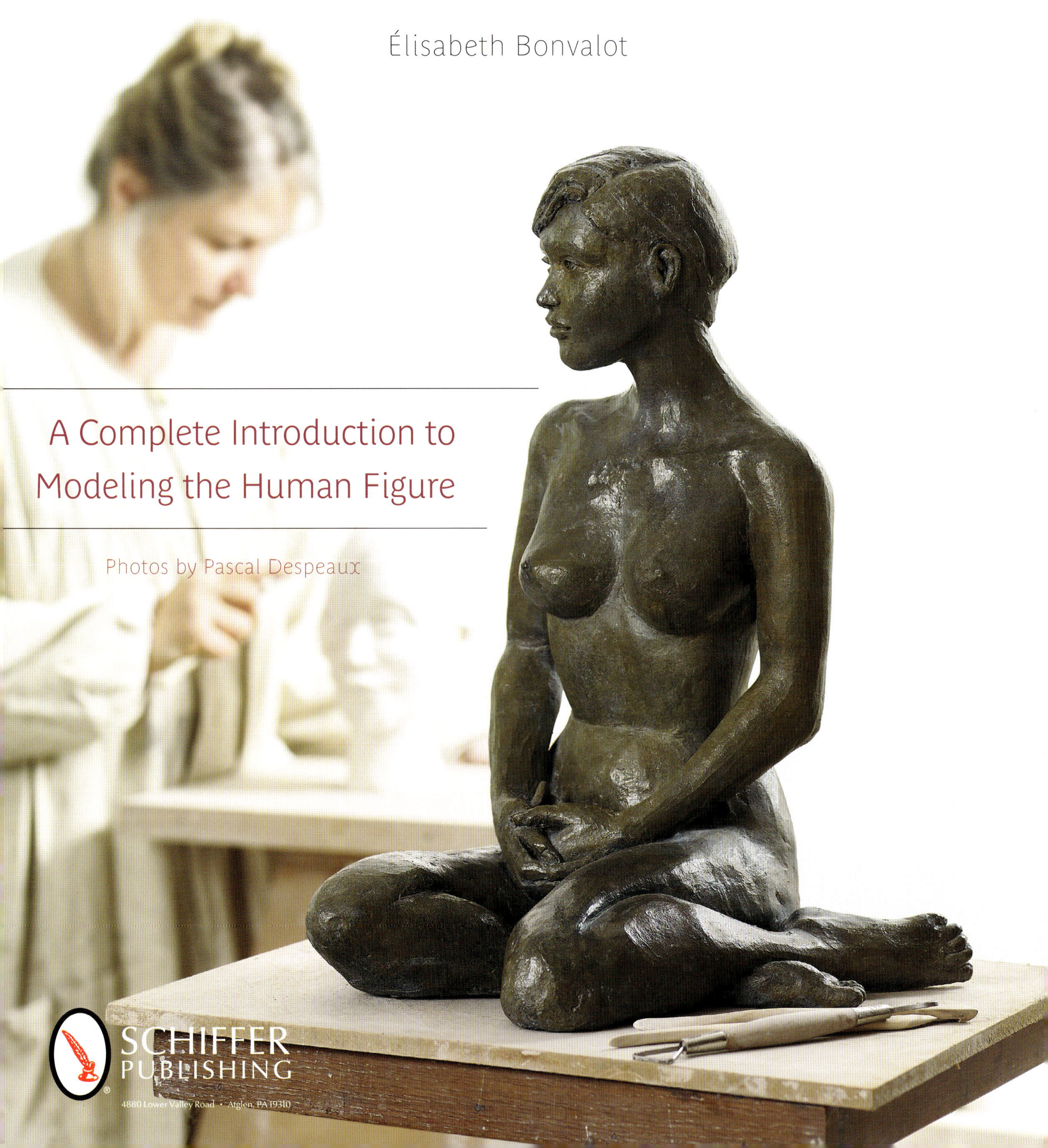

A Complete Introduction to Modeling the Human Figure

Photos by Pascal Despeaux

SCHIFFER PUBLISHING
4880 Lower Valley Road • Atglen, PA 19310

Originally published as *Le grand livre du modelage* by Mango, Pologne © 2017 Mango
Translated from the French by Omicron Language Solutions, LLC

Library of Congress Control Number: 2019934843

ISBN: 978-0-7643-5857-9
Printed in China

Published by Schiffer Publishing, Ltd.
4880 Lower Valley Road
Atglen, PA 19310
Phone: (610) 593-1777; Fax: (610) 593-2002
E-mail: Info@schifferbooks.com
Web: www.schifferbooks.com

For my parents, who always believed in me.

For my teachers:

Jean Gilles (Ecole des Beaux Arts, Besançon)

Eliane Chiron, Eva Eyquem, and Bernard Teyssèdre (faculté d'Arts plastiques, Paris 1), who guided my first steps and who awakened the critic and sense of rigor that resides in me even today.

With thanks to François Raoult: Etablissement Raoult et fils (Calvados, France)

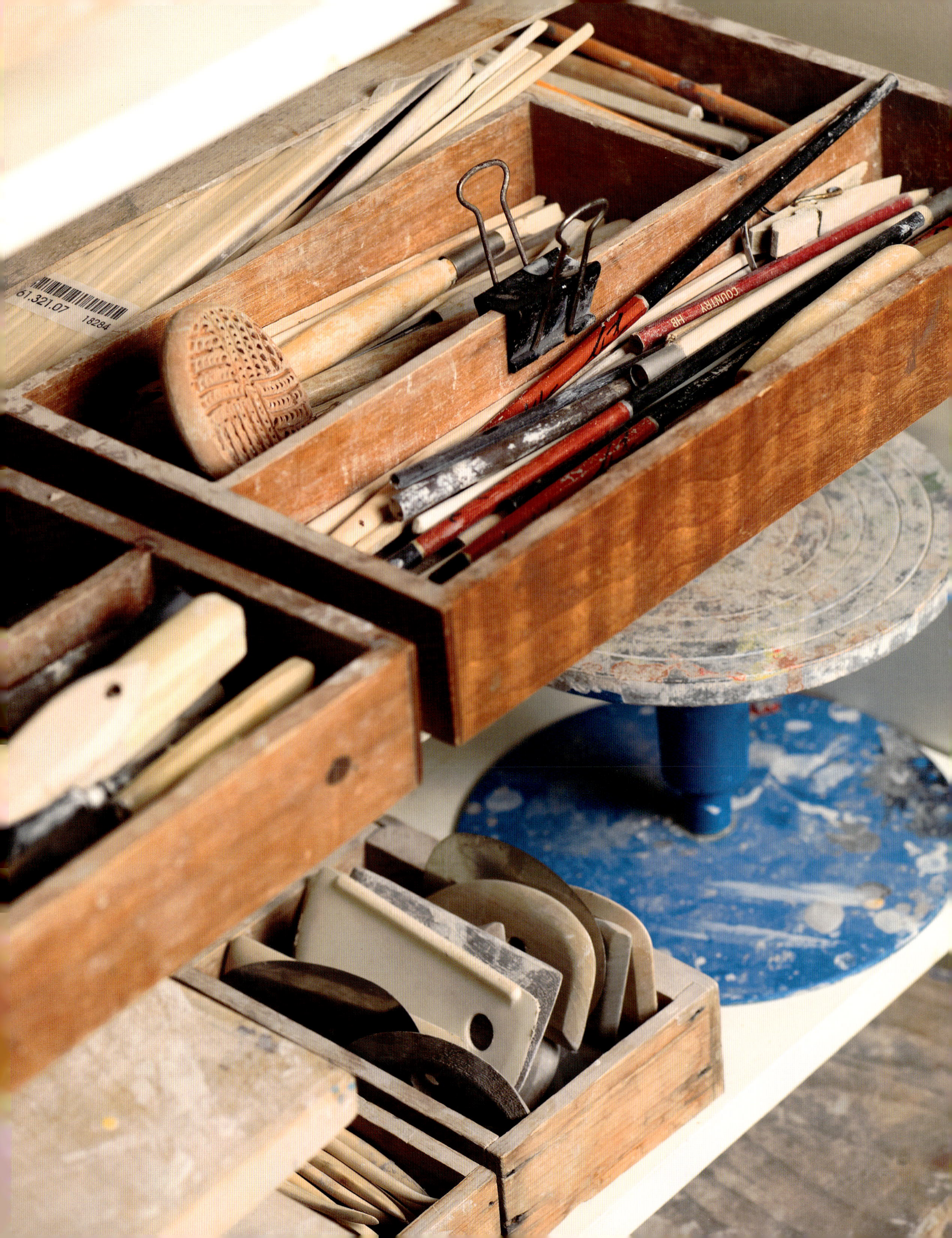
61.321.07
18284
COUNTRY
HB

Contents

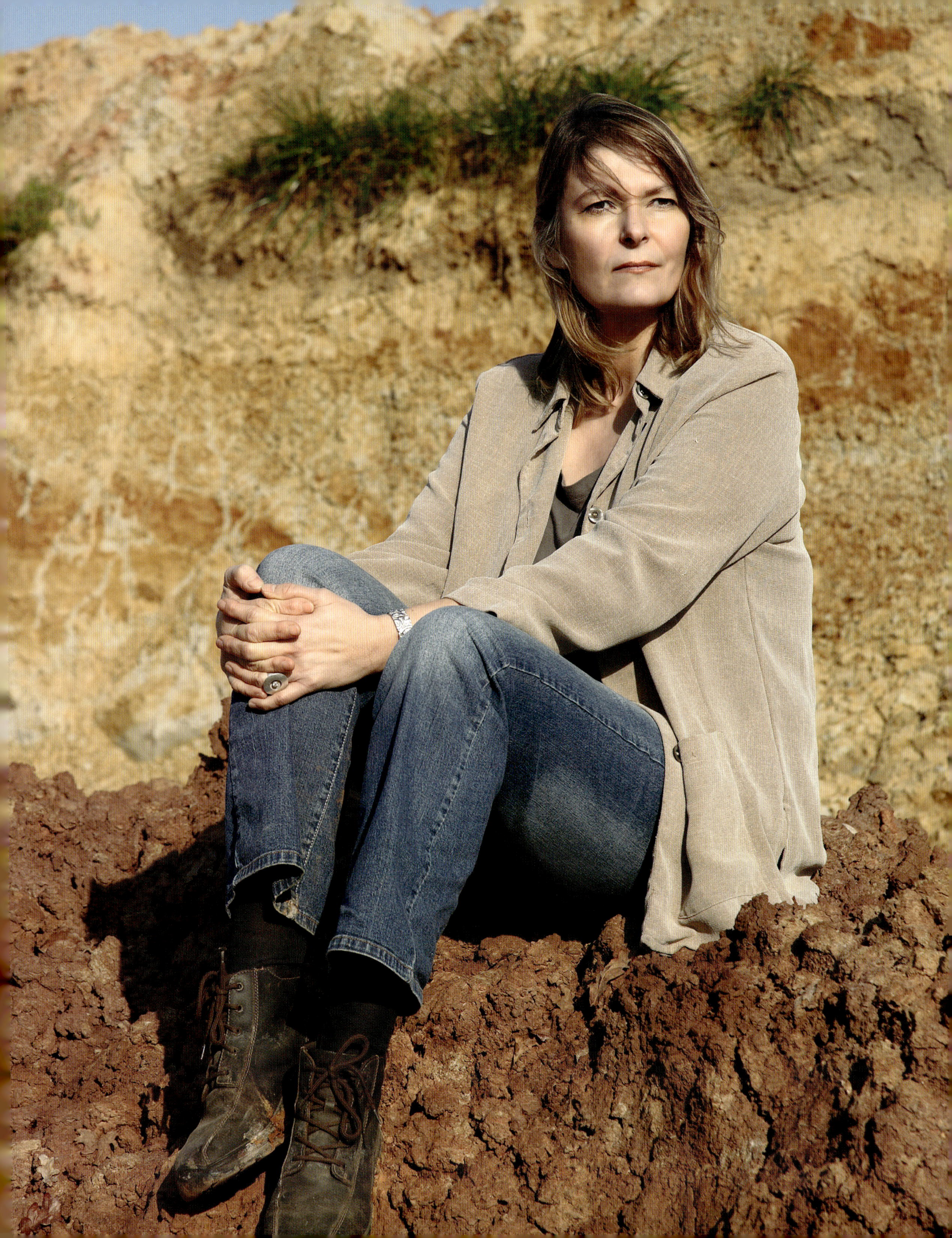

Sculpture Opened My Eyes

The combinations that I shape, among thousands of others, have walked hand in glove with a predisposition for fine arts since my early childhood. Fascinated by reality, I wanted to touch everything, to understand everything, and explain to everyone what I felt, but I was blocked by my hypersensitivity. Drawing and painting became my only outlets. I lived with colors deep inside me that were both intense and ecstatic. I expressed myself through a graphic representation of all I saw, dreamed, or felt.

When I was only three years old, my deepest dream was to be a painter. My godmother, an artist herself who admired my talent, offered me my first book about art: Picasso's works. Whenever I had free time, I spent it drawing. I thought that being an artist would be the best thing in the world, and I wanted to be one when I grew up.

I was twelve years old when my parents signed me up for drawing lessons at the Beaux-Arts de Besançon. Two years later, I started drawing and painting living things.

At age nineteen, I started at the faculty of fine art in Paris, where over the years I developed a very expressive graphic technique. I had fallen in love with the works of the painter Egon Schiele.

When I was twenty-five, I wrote my thesis on the representation of the image of the female body. However, the irrepressible desire to touch, to dig into the matter, to grasp reality through my sketches was so strong that I began to feel the need to approach volume . . .

The apprenticeship of representation in three dimensions wasn't easy, in spite of my ability to draw, and I needed a lot of humility. My eye had relearned to look and to see, not understanding what my hand had to do. It couldn't see the depth of the reality, or its true structure, because it was used to calculating and representing an illusory space on a two-dimensional plane. I was lost, but I persevered and tried to understand why I couldn't do it.

So every day I kneaded clay, made objects, experimented with techniques, built sculptures, and unmade those I found lacking interest, and four years later I finally stopped my education. My artwork had taken a different direction, and I needed to orient myself. Above all, I found that clay gave me a feeling of serenity. Sculpture calmed me, while drawing had the opposite effect. I spent a few years working around clay in different workshops, even going as far as learning pottery to better understand clay's chemistry and nature. But I eventually turned to ceramic sculpture and the representation of modern or classical figures. Doubtless I was and still am influenced by my irrepressible desire to capture the magic of living things, the instant, and the very breath of a person posing naturally.

My work as a sculptor was built little by little, even if volume always seemed difficult to see precisely. I became interested in the works of Jean-Baptiste Carpeaux (nineteenth century). His style, both classical and alive, made me want to improve my work, and I quickly sought to breathe life into my earthen characters.

When I was thirty-five, after organizing courses in Ireland, I finally opened my own workshop in Paris so that I could develop my work and also give sculpting lessons and courses for adults—either beginners or confirmed sculptors wishing to improve their technique. I structured my work thanks to a living model and produced forty pieces—four of which were large—in the space of three months: for example *Serenity* (page 61) and *Sensuality* (page 137). At the end of those three intensive months, I realized that I was finally seeing in terms of volume. There had been an irreversible exchange of perception between my eye and my hand: my eye touched while my hand saw. My gestures became precise; it became obvious where each piece of clay should be placed because I could see exactly where it should go. Previously, this step took a lot of time and intermediary stages, using a mirror and photos as reminders.

I could finally pass on the approach toward volume to my students, along with working with clay, and I could now advance in my personal work.

Today, at nearly fifty years of age, I find that happiness is being able to enter my personal creative space every day and find peace through working with clay and sharing magical instants with my students. I love teaching my passion for sculpture and watching my students progress; I am fulfilled thanks to the way they interpret reality through their work.

Élisabeth Bonvalot

Before Starting

The Material

Clay is a living matter that we find in abundance in nature, since it forms all the time. It is, in fact, one of the principal components of the soil covering the earth's crust. Clay minerals result from the decomposition of igneous rocks and sedimentary rocks over millions of years and can form in and remain in one place (primary clay) or be transported for long distances by alluviums (secondary clay).

Depending on the mother rock and climate, the resulting clay minerals differ: illites, chlorites, kaolinite, smectite, and vermiculite. You don't need to learn their names by heart before modeling them. On the other hand, you should remember that clay is composed of aluminum oxide, silicon oxide, and water. The chemical formula for the purest clay is represented by two molecules of silica—a molecule of aluminum and two molecules of water—which means that this earth is white before and after firing (kaolin).

Clay particles, invisible to the naked eye, are flat and surrounded by water. Even when clay is "dry" it still contains 6 percent water. Colored clays (red, black, ocher, green, gray) contain small quantities of minerals that can either be present in their natural state or added during fabrication (iron oxide, manganese, etc.). These are called impurities.

Clay contains multiple particularities, exploited since time immemorial:

Absorption: Dry clay eagerly soaks up water. It is used naturally and purified in medical treatments (poultices, alimentary detoxification, beauty products, etc.).

Insulation and preservation: Clay has always been used in the conception of culinary utensils, construction material, interior decoration, etc., either naturally or fired.

Abrasion: Clay polishes and cleans without scratching. It is found in household products for cleaning metal or glass, in toothpaste, etc.

Resistance and accumulation: At very high temperature, clay tolerates thermal shock because it becomes very hard. It's used in industry (a composite of engines), in orthodontics (dental prosthesis), and as a heat accumulator for heaters or spatial engines (refractory clay).

Cutting: In its hardest and finest form, clay is used to make knives and very sharp tools.

Fusibility and impermeability: At very high temperatures, clay vitrifies (sandstone, porcelain) and can be used to enamel crockery, and it can be made into highly resistant ceramic tiles (stoneware) or even glossy paper.

Handling clay can hold some surprises, giving it a reputation for being capricious and sometimes unpredictable and requiring attention, observation, and experimentation beforehand.

Like the richness of its components in its natural state, there are a plethora of different clays for sale in stores. They can be put into six main categories. For sculpture, it's possible to choose one quality or another according to the desired result and to your preferences (see the following page).

Modeling or ceramic sculpture is more concerned with the first three categories, which are firing clays (earthenware, stoneware, porcelain). Modeling clay is used as an intermediary stage for molding or can be used as teaching or exercising material, with the understanding that each exercise will be broken up afterward, since the clay doesn't fire.

Self-hardening clays can be used to make small decorative objects. They are ideal when working with children but don't inspire the same interest that "ceramic" clays do, since throughout their transformation to the final result they give us enormous satisfaction and offer an infinite variety of interventions and questions that we will touch on in this book.

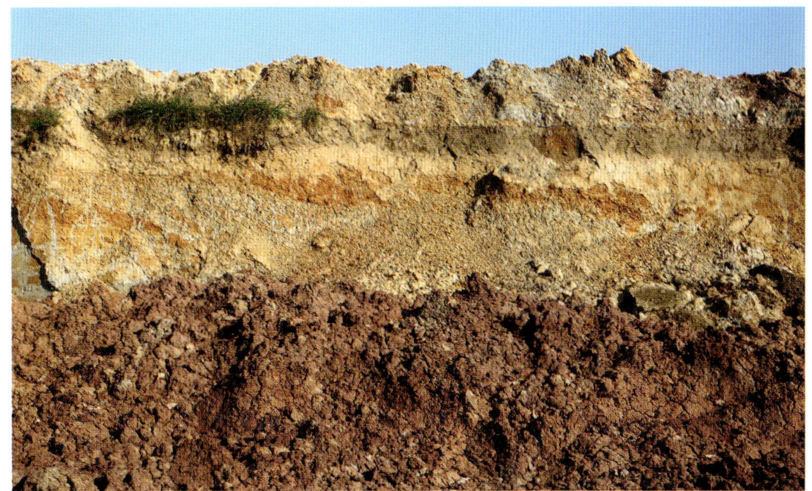

Earthenware is fired at a low temperature (1,796°F) and presents a certain fragility because of its softness (even fired, a fingernail can leave a scratch mark, and impacts can easily crack or smash your work). But the ceramic colors fired in earthenware, or at a low temperature, are prettier and livelier than those fired in stoneware (see "Engobe or Colors on Unfired Clay," page 32).

Be careful! Earthenware clay should never be fired at high temperatures—more than 1,832°F—because it will melt and damage the kiln's tray and electrical components, as well as stick to other pieces of work. Read the manufacturer's instructions concerning the maximum firing temperature. If you don't have your own kiln, show the instructions to the person who will fire your pieces. If you are in doubt, fire a very small piece at 1,796°F, which corresponds to the minimum temperature.

Stoneware is fired and vitrifies at a high temperature (2,192°C–2,372°C). Its hardness gives it great solidity. Sometimes it is fired at lower temperatures if, for example, it is going to be enameled afterward. In this case, since its surface hasn't closed completely, a layer of enamel can cover the half-fired object, which passes at a high temperature during the second firing.

No matter what, always check the manufacturer's instructions for the maximum firing heat, because some stoneware (or clays that resemble stoneware) can "blister" if it is too closed, or if it contains certain minerals such as manganese. In this case the manufacturer will mark a lower firing temperature (e.g., 2,264°C maximum).

Porcelain is also fired at a high temperature (2,192°C–2,678°C). Its hardness ensures great solidity, but it is also fragile because of the fineness required in shaping it. Entirely fabricated using several clays that give it its whiteness (kaolin), fineness, and plasticity (ball clay), porcelain is used mostly in pottery. Some ceramic sculptors use it for its delicacy and translucency to sculpt flowers, for example. Personally, I use it for making slips on stoneware, because its substance and its whiteness magnify colors, and it produces a satiny aspect at high temperatures (see "Making Slip for 'Gluing' the Clay Together," page 26).

Refractory clay (fire clay) is rough clay that is fired at very high temperatures (2,732°C). It is used to make trays, tripods, or other supports for ceramic kilns. In sculpture it is used to make large pieces.

Modeling clay (or oily clay) isn't fired. It is used as a mold to preserve the identical shape of the prototype and will then be unmade after molding. This clay can be reused, since each time the model is taken apart after molding. To keep it supple, make sure to remove any bits of plaster that might cling to it after molding.

Self-hardening clay is more expensive but can be sculpted without having to be hollowed out or fired. It solidifies definitively as it dries out. It contains hardening agents (resins or other substances) that allow it to solidify without firing.

The Production of Blocks of Clay

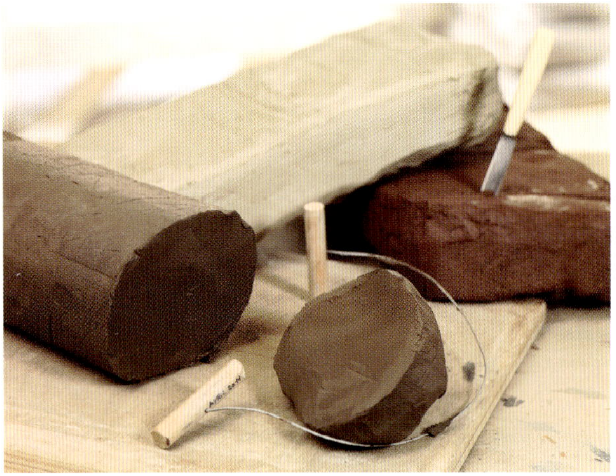

The ceramic clays found on the market come from open quarries where different layers of clay are superimposed. The clay is analyzed and can be mixed with other clay or mineral elements that give it greater plasticity, fusibility, resistance, or a different color . . . the clay is ground and put into settling tanks filled with water, and left for several days. It is then sieved to remove impurities. It is then dried on plaster (or another absorbent material) or sent in a liquid form between layers of canvas, which drains the water away until the clay is malleable to the touch. It is then mechanically mixed and packaged to be stored in blocks in plastic wrapping. Some manufacturers* store them for up to two years in cellars, until they have entirely absorbed their own organic elements. They can also be used immediately for modeling and sculpting work.

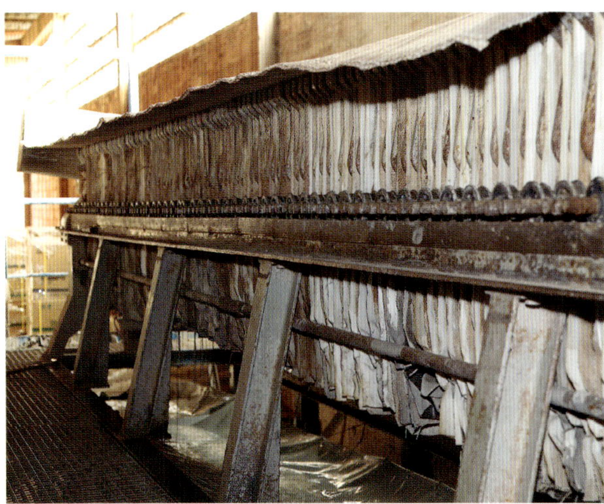

Clay drying between canvases at clay manufacturers "Etablissements Raoult," Calvados, France

Shrinkage

When clay is soft and easy to model—that is to say, when it is plastic—it presents a shrinkage of between 2 and 8 percent while drying and shrinks again between 5 and 7 percent during firing. When mixed with grog, shrinkage is less important (see below).

Before starting on a piece, you should take these figures into account so that your work, once it has been fired, corresponds to the size desired. Check on the shrinkage percentage of the clay before you buy it. It's better to do some experimenting with a flat piece of clay 4" × 4" to find out the exact shrinkage percentage of your clay according to the firing heat of your kiln. Personally, I have tested a great number of clays and still do so from time to time, since each manufacturer has its own references.

A Variant: Paper Clay (or Fiber Clay)

You can make your own clay mixed with cellulose (very fine paper). All ceramic clays—except those with a high concentration of grog—can be used. First of all, the mixture should be done by weighing dry material (60–70% of dry clay, 10% of grog, and 20–30% of cellulose). The mixture is then sieved and well kneaded to make it homogenous. It is then left to repose to become plastic. The dry mixture can be kept indefinitely.

ADVANTAGES	DISADVANTAGES
The mixture has almost no shrinkage percentage and the material can be restuck at any given moment. The cellulose adds a complementary element as well as solidity to the material, which is therefore less capricious.	The clay/cellulose mix can't be kept damp for long, because over a period of time it gets moldy due to the presence of cellulose. However, you can add a little diluted bleach to give it a long life span. Because of this, it's impractical to make great quantities of paper clay in advance; it's best to make it as you need it. It's an operation that is best left for those who have time to spare.

* I've always heard that a potter prepares the clay for his successor. This is probably because settling and absorption of the organic elements occurs over several months or years, giving the clay greater plasticity.

Choosing the Clay

In sculpture, it is best to choose earthenware or stoneware clay mixed with grog and to adapt the quality and quantity of this latter element according to the size and quality of the piece you are going to make. You should remember that the larger the piece, the higher the quantity of grog in the clay.

If your piece is intended for exterior use, it is better to choose stoneware clay, which is more resistant to climate changes. Don't forget that stoneware needs to be fired. When your piece is small, with fine details, you should work with grog that is impalpable to the touch but will ensure the protection of your work during firing.

The Composition and Role Played by Grog

Grog is composed of grains of fired clay or grains of sand (quartz)—more or less fine and in greater or lesser quantities—added to raw clay at the moment of fabrication. When it comes to grains of sand, these are either added or naturally present in the clay. Grog has several functions:

- First, solidity: it reinforces the clay's resistance.
- Plasticity: it makes the clay more malleable.
- Ventilation: it creates a multitude of canals in the clay, which allow contained air to escape more easily during the first 100 degrees of firing.
- Cleaning: the clay becomes drier and more malleable to the touch.
- Texture: it allows the creation of granular material.

Because the clay is subjected to a lot of manipulation during the creation of a piece of sculpture, grog is important. For any modeling work (for small pieces) you can choose impalpable grog, which will have a lot of plasticity and allow you to do all the details you require. For medium-sized work that doesn't exceed 3 feet, medium grog that is more or less dense will allow you to work in greater thickness when hollowing out. Finally, for very large pieces (over 3 feet) you should use large quantities of grog.

Personally, at first I was attracted to smooth clay, soft to the touch but difficult to handle due to the close bond—not very plastic and rather oily. I now prefer to use grog, even for small pieces. I'm now used to working with large grains, which add texture to the clay and facilitate construction. It gives more expression to my work. My students experiment daily, and those who began working with smooth clay have pointed out to me that grog is easier to use for construction.

Test the Clay

You should always test clay before buying it in large quantities. Some clays are oily, while others close up too much during firing and can't be enameled properly afterward, or take a patina of certain substances that need to penetrate (e.g., wax or stain made with India ink). Some clays also produce a lot of cracks due to overmanipulation either before or after firing.

My Preferences

Earthenware clays found on the market are often made "chemically" because they have a lot of added elements, while stoneware clay is pretty much the same as when it came out of the ground and is simply settled in water and sieved to remove impurities. The manufacturer might add a few elements to make the material more comfortable to work with. Personally, I prefer clays that are fired like stoneware. More natural and more resistant, they offer two possibilities: low fired or high fired.

For a few years now I have used two types of clay:

- Raku clay (PRAF or Fuji), which contains more or less fine, dense grog. It hydrates very quickly and tolerates all retouches and ballooning by hydration, as well as shrinkage during successive dryings. Porous after firing (even at high temperatures), it has a rather pleasant "stone" aspect that means you can preserve its natural off-white, slightly yellow color.
- I use clay that is considered as stoneware par excellence for building large pieces in complete safety. This stoneware—totally impermeable after firing at very high temperatures in spite of the presence of grog—can be smooth or gritty. I used it to make the sculpture *Sainte Anne et Marie enfant* in Asnières, Normandy, in 2009.

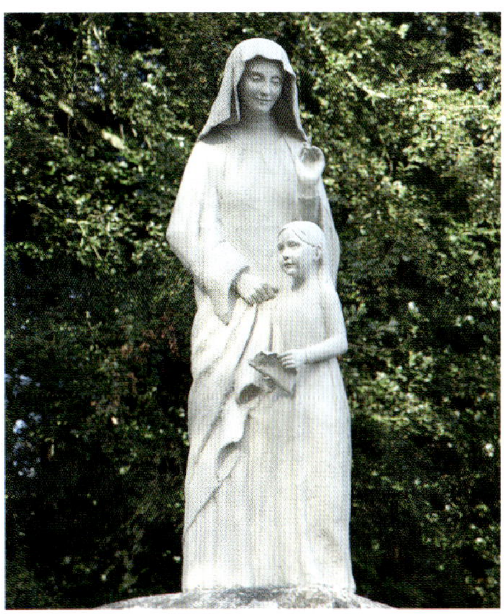

Sainte Anne et Marie enfant, *Asnières, 2009. Height: 5 ft.*

How Clay Reacts

Clay is a living, capricious material that evolves throughout the creation of a sculpture, from a very soft, malleable stage to a firmer one called "green" or "leather hard." It is at that moment that it can be hollowed out and engobed (see pages 27 and 32). After this the clay evolves into a harder state (before completely drying out, where it can be restored with precaution) and then reaches a dry state when it is the most fragile: the water has mostly evaporated, and the material is breakable and should be manipulated with extreme care.

Porosity

When drying, the clay particles bond but can leave spaces between themselves, because they stop bonding once the clay is completely hard. The spaces left by the evaporation of these water particles make the clay porous if it doesn't retract or vitrify during firing. For example, this is the case with earthenware. Grog can accentuate porosity because it creates microconduits of ventilation in the clay.

Clay's Hydration

The earth molecules are very small (about the size of a micron). However, clay has pores like human skin that allow it to react by capillarity. It therefore hydrates itself from the exterior to the interior and dries out in the same way—from the outside toward the inside. If you want to thoroughly hydrate a block of clay, it will take a certain amount of time and contact with water for the cells to transmit water by contact or capillarity (from cell to cell) from the exterior to the interior. The best way is to envelop the block in a damp cloth and then put it into a plastic bag to make sure the water doesn't evaporate. Depending on the hydration desired, you will see (several hours later or the following day) that the cloth is dryer and the clay is softer because it has absorbed the water to the heart of its mass (see "Preservation" and "Reconditioning").

Accidents

If clay isn't treated properly, you could say that it gives as good as it takes. If you twist it to give it a certain shape, or if you don't follow the principle of construction by progressively adding pieces and collage by score and slip, it will reward your mistreatment with accidents: multiple cracks will form; the added pieces that haven't been joined by score and slip will fall off during or after firing; bits will break or deform due to too much or not enough hollowing out in places; the piece will crumble entirely if it has dried out too much and you hydrate it to work on it again; or the piece will explode into thousands of bits if it hasn't dried out enough, bursting into several pieces if the air inside hasn't been able to escape or if you have forgotten to leave a hole where the air can escape . . .

Taking Care of Your Clay

Preservation

While you are working, protect the block of clay you aren't using in its wrapping to keep it moist.

Before storing the piece you are working on, take care to wrap it up properly to isolate it from the air:

- Place your piece on a plastic-covered support so that the water in the clay isn't absorbed by the wooden support, which will eventually warp or get moldy.
- Dampen your piece often and cover it with a plastic bag, taking care to flatten it against the clay to leave as little room for air to pass as possible, so that the clay doesn't dry out. Don't hesitate to cover the first bag with a second one just to be on the safe side.

Reconditioning

What to do if your block of clay is dry:

- If it is just a little harder, all you need to do is hydrate it with damp cloth and wrap it in plastic for a few hours until it is sufficiently malleable to the touch.
- If it is really hard but not completely dry, cut it into small cubes, which you will then put in a plastic bag; spray the lot with water for a couple of minutes, then knead the mass of clay inside the bag until you feel the cubes getting softer. With it still in the bag, compress the mass of clay, which will recover its original plasticity.
- If your clay has completely dried out, put it in a bucket of water. Let the molecules soak up the water and turn into mud. Remove the surface water and leave the clay to evaporate the surplus water. After a couple of days the clay will be plastic again, and you can remove chunks from the bucket and leave them to dry a little on a piece of wood or plaster before beating them into a single block. Reconditioning is long and laborious.

ADVICE

As soon as your clay starts getting too dry, hydrate it and, above all, remove it from its wrapping as and when you need it, to stop the entire block from drying out.

Basic Tools and Material

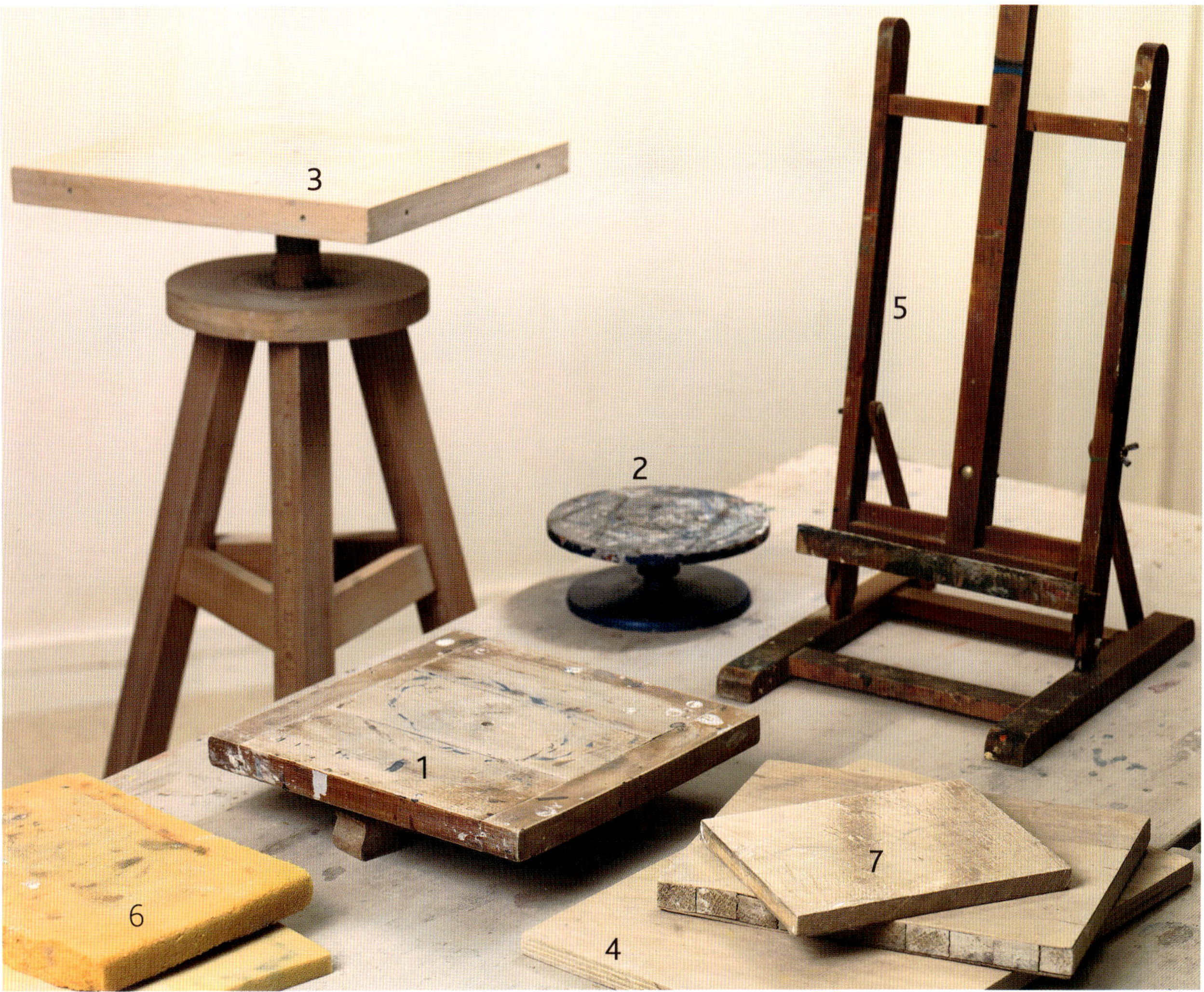

Supports

The first piece of equipment you need is a potter's wheel (1)—preferably a wooden one, but you can also find a metal one (2), which is usually used mainly for pottery. If you don't have a great deal of room, you could use a tabletop wheel or a wooden (or wooden and metal) sculpting stand (3) with an adjustable top.

Plywood boards that are ¾ inch thick (4) are useful because they are very resistant. An ordinary wooden board will eventually warp and crack because of dampness. Your piece will be placed on one of these boards while you are working on it, which means you will be able remove to it from the wheel and store it on a shelf.

You will need an easel for working on bas-relief tablets (5).

Squares of sponge (6) will be needed to place and protect the clay removed when hollowing.

Don't forget to have a supply of plastic bags in different sizes to cover your pieces when you aren't working on them, and plastic cling wrap (7) for covering the wooden board.

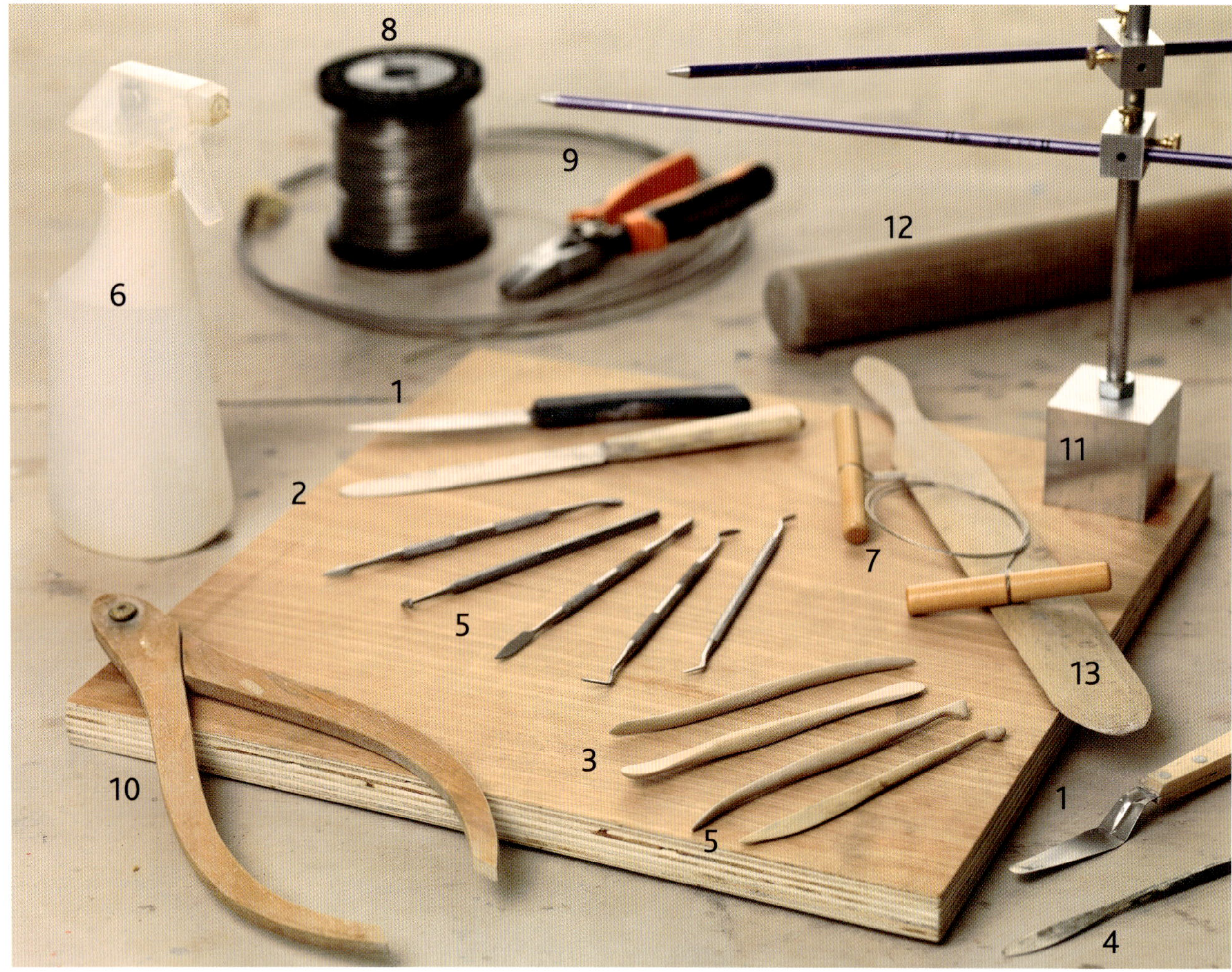

For Creating the Piece

Sculpting knives (1) or old kitchen knives (2) and wooden (3) or metal (4) spatulas that can replace the knives.

A wooden clay knife set (5, preferably boxwood) for sculpting details. A set contains different forms (slightly slanting or curved) that fit the hollows, guide the clay, etc.

A water-filled spray bottle (6) to help moisten the clay when it starts to dry out and for spraying your piece before wrapping it in its plastic bag.

A wire clay cutter (7) for cutting clay off the block and removing pieces of your work before hollowing out. You can make your own with fine metal wire or fishing line composed of metal covered by a thin layer of plastic, adding two small pieces of wood at each end for gripping.

A spool of nickel and chrome wire (8)—which resists high temperatures—to reinforce the structure of your piece during its creation and for guiding the volume. A spool is sold by the foot, and you should have different thicknesses. It's rather expensive but lasts a long time because you can pull it out when the clay starts to dry out, or when hollowing, and use it again.

Cutting pliers (9) for cutting the metal wire.

A wooden compass (10) for checking proportions, plans, and alignment.

A metal or wooden back iron (11) for keeping figures upright, and for more-complex pieces with parts that need exterior support in addition to the inner structure. It's possible to make your own if you are something of a handyman.

You will also need a wooden rolling pin (12), wooden calipers for measuring and guiding, and a wooden scraper (13) to regularize flat surfaces.

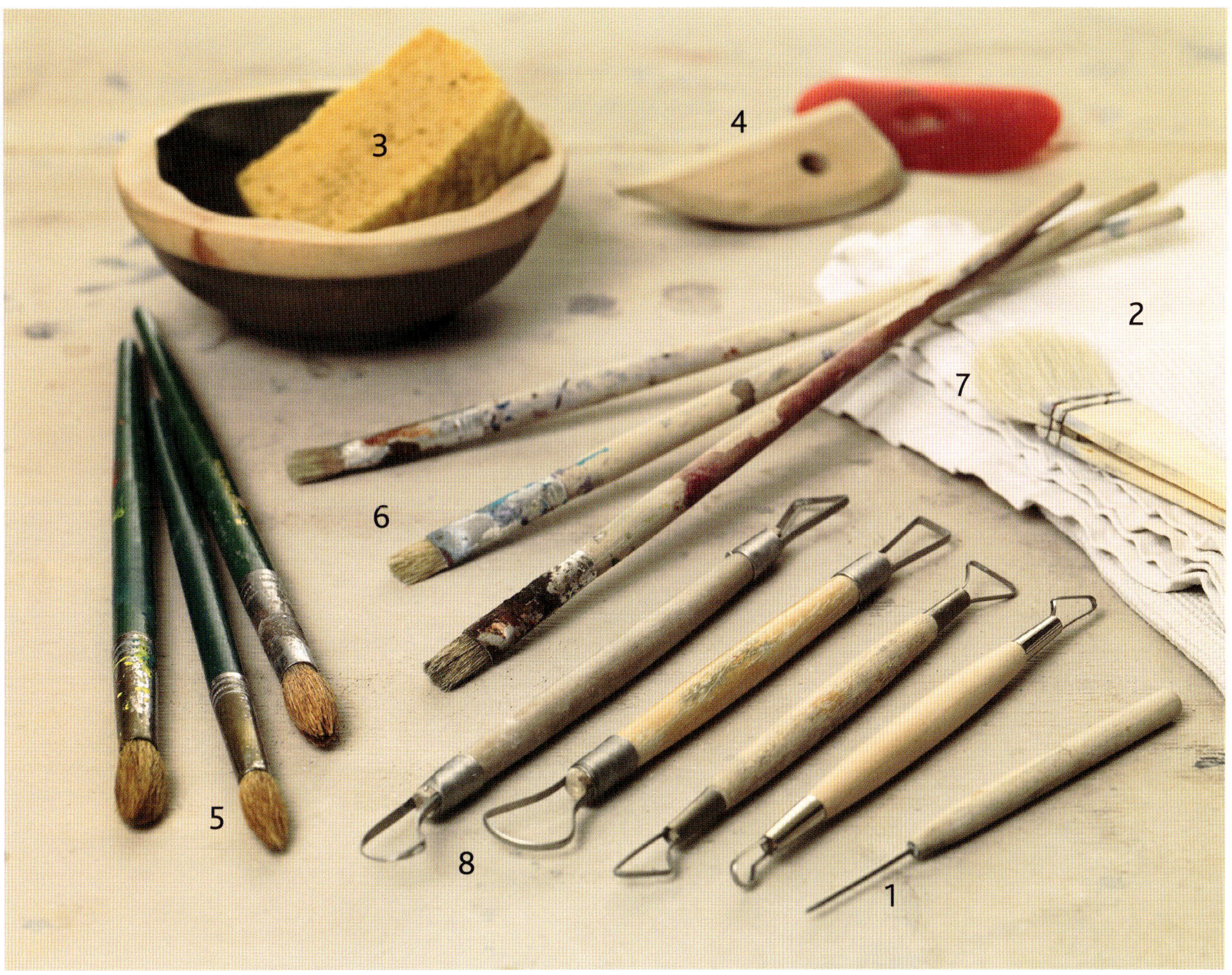

For Refining, Trimming, Retouching, Hollowing Out, and Smoothing

A potter's needle (1) has several functions: hollowed-out writing, tracing, or marking; cutting finely; testing the thickness of the clay; making holes, etc.

Cotton cloths (2) for hydrating the clay.

A sponge and a cup of water (3) for sponging the clay to moisten it, and for smoothing it once the piece is finished.

Wooden or plastic ribs (4) for scraping, regularizing, and smoothing the surface.

Fine-haired brushes (5) for hydrating, smoothing, and engobe work.

Stiff-haired brushes (6) for painting on slip, and for shellac patina, wax, or mediums such as Caparol.

A large, supple brush (7) for slipping large areas.

Loop tools (8) in different shapes for hollowing out, or for removing small imperfections.

Main Sculpting Principles

The Eye, Observation

Before starting on a piece of sculpture—whether you choose a sample in a photo, a living model, or a still life—don't rush into starting on it. Take the time to really look at it and understand its volume. You can use a sheet of paper or tracing paper to mark references. These orthogonal references help you to understand the direction of your volume in space. Make a graphic schema of the volume by looking for the key points; see "Standing Nude," page 82.

The Function of the Eye's Haptic Perception

After a few years of practice it's easy to develop a see/touch facility, which Gilles Deleuze calls the "function of the eye's haptic perception" (from the ancient Greek *hapto*, "to touch"). With time, a bond is created between the hand and the eye: each time the hand reaches out it's because the eye understands and sees exactly what the hand should do, and it guides it with great precision. Effectively, the eye immediately spots what is missing or what is superfluous in the constructed volume, as if it could touch the material. With experience the eye understands the concept of depth better and better and immediately transmits the necessary adjustments to the hand. The hand becomes the eye and the eye the hand until they reach a point where they merge to become one. At this point, sculpture becomes child's play; each portion of placed clay is clear, and you see in terms of volume.

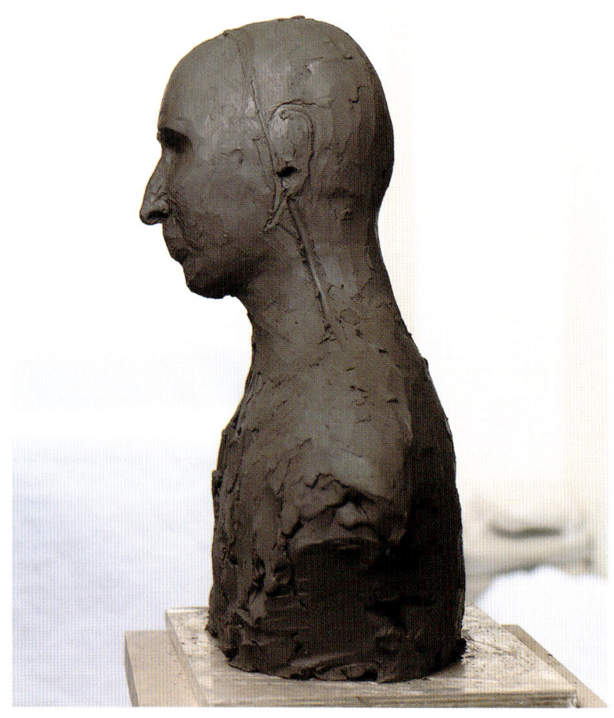

Starting the Construction of a Three-Dimensional Volume

The third dimension is produced through depth. It is very difficult to feel and understand the depth of an object when it is facing you. If you turn it so you see its profile, you will see the volume in the third dimension. To avoid miscalculating depth, it is best to begin an object in profile, to continue with it facing you to get its width, and then to refine it with a three-quarter view.

Once this is done, looking down on it will help you correct any asymmetries between the left and right sides. In the same way, when the piece is hollowed out and nearly finished, looking down on it will show any areas that lack a little thickness.

Proportions

Proportions are the dimensional relationship between the different parts of a volume. They are essential for creating a resemblance to the subject. The relation of height, width, gaps, and gradient between the elements of a volume can be measured by eye, with a compass, with string, etc., to reproduce it properly.

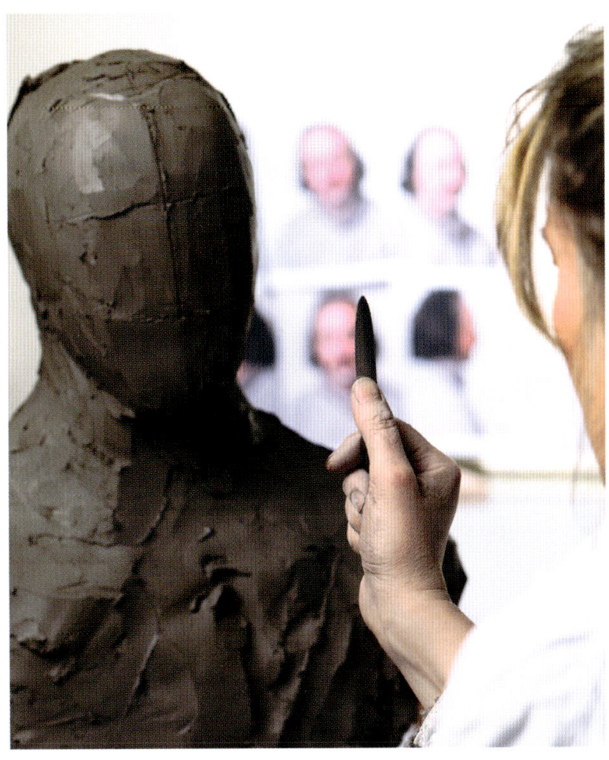

Planes

A volume is composed of a multitude of planes that can be tiny (the size of a pinhead) or very large (as in flat surfaces). In sculpture, a plane can be defined by a thin, flat space comprising at least three nonaligned points: vertical, horizontal, or slanting. A plane ends at the point where another plane begins. Therefore, their intersection allows us to localize the structure of a volume. When the planes are too small, we speak of points directed in space in relation to the others, in a manner that forms a singular volume. A round volume is made up of a myriad of minuscule points, whereas a cube is composed of six identical sides or planes.

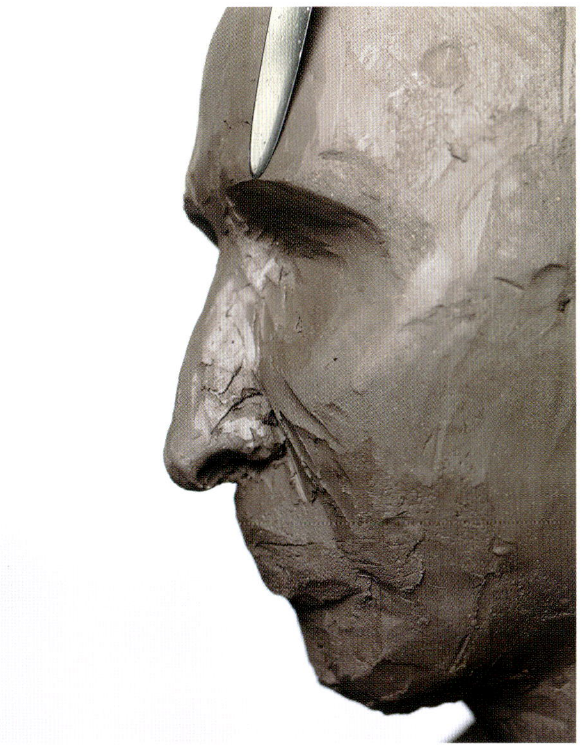

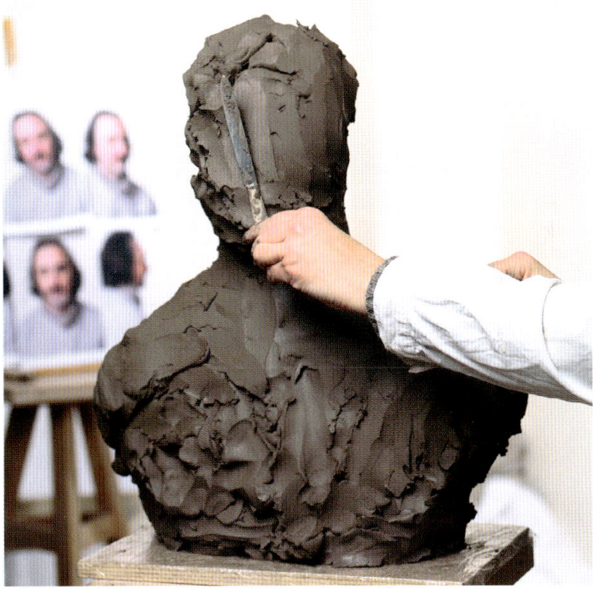

In this part of the face, the eyebrow arch delimits two distinct planes: the eye socket at the bottom and the forehead at the top.

When you start to work on a volume, after carefully looking over your model and noting the proportional elements, try to spot the planes without going into the volume's details. For example, the face can be schematically represented as a flat surface once you have abstracted the nose, the eye sockets, and the mouth.

Later, while working on the details, you gradually reach an understanding of the complexity of the planes while simplifying and refining them as you go along. This means that at first you must synthesize the volume and represent it as large planes and large masses. After this you can progressively trace on each plane (or mass) the marks you have carefully noted that will allow you to enter into the details little by little.

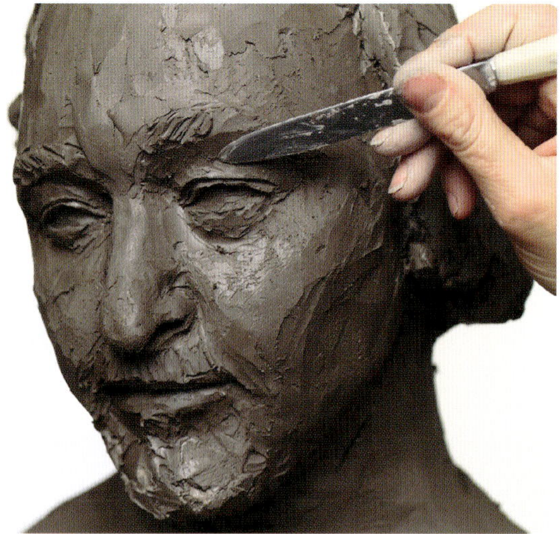

Structure

A body's skeleton is subjacent and can be found if you take the time to look for it. The knowledge of a body's structure enables you to locate and understand, or to feel the model better. Thus, you will be able to find the main points that structure the body of your model, the main areas the structure rests upon, and the forms and proportions of the different parts that direct the volume and serve as supports for muscles and masses of soft tissue and the organs.

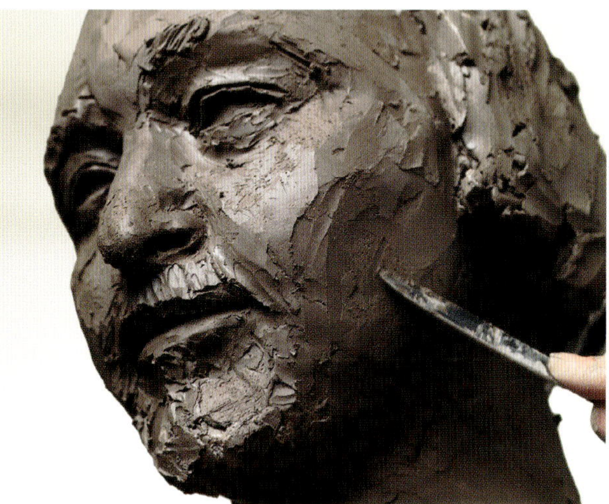

Contour

You can also imagine a volume by its contours. By slowly turning the model we obtain a multitude of views (profile, three-quarter, face, back), and we can progressively adjust its representation so that the contours of the volume match it. The three-quarter contour is often used to show the roundness of the cheeks, since a profile or face-on view won't show this detail.

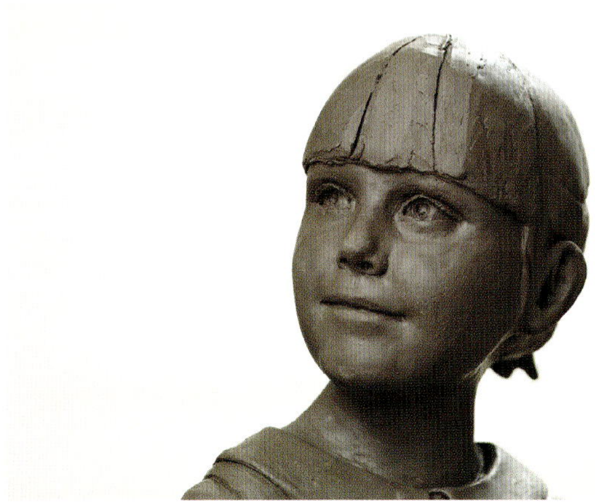

The View from Different Angles

To put things into perspective in relation to any constructed volume, you should walk around it to see it from different angles—head on, in profile, from the back of it, and also from above—to be able to correct the volume's symmetry (e.g., on its face) and to complete things that can't be seen from any other point of view. Looking up at your model is a little more difficult but remains important, particularly if the volume is imposing and is intended to be set on a high pedestal.

ADVICE

Don't stay too close to your work; stand back from time to time, especially when the item starts to take shape, because from a distance you'll see places needing to be corrected that you won't notice when you are close up.

A Mirror, a Photo

Using a mirror while you are working can be very useful for correcting the symmetry of your work; for example, to simply put things into perspective in relation to the representation of your work. Look at the sculpture's reflection in a mirror from different angles. You can also take photos of different stages of your work and look through them later to better understand anything that might be wrong regarding the model.

Physical Constraints: The Weight of the Clay

Clay is very heavy materiel. If it is too soft, it will settle throughout your work and you'll have to go back several times to correct the proportions that have been modified by settling. It's a bit discouraging to see your sculpture settle or slump and become misshapen! It's best to advance calmly without rushing your work. The first thing to do is beat your clay to make it firmer and get rid of any bubbles. Then, throughout your construction—if you have chosen to work by adding successive lumps—reinforce your piece with metal rods (large ones if your work is large, medium if the piece is narrower, and fine ones if your work isn't wide). These will allow you to build your piece by guiding and reinforcing the clay until it hardens a little, at which time you should remove the rods. If you are using nickel and chrome wire, you can leave it in the clay during firing if the reinforced part is suspended in the air (e.g., an upraised arm).

Shrinkage

Clay shrinks between 2 and 8 percent while it is drying out, and then between 5 and 7 percent during firing (see "Shrinkage," page 10). Counting drying out and firing, the overall average is 10 percent. Avoid leaving too much metal inside your piece when it is fired. When the clay retracts and encounters an object (the rod), it continues its shrinkage—both during drying out and firing—by following the shape of the rod, which causes small cracks during drying out and larger and larger cracks during firing. These cracks can be repaired after firing when you can't remove the rods from a suspended part.

To prevent the piece from cracking, I advise you to make sure all the metal has been removed when you hollow out your work, even in the slim parts that aren't hollowed out. Certain extremely fine wires can be used that don't cause cracks and that reinforce fragile or suspended parts.

ADVICE

Wait for the clay to stabilize when drying out a little before continuing your work.

So that your piece slumps as little as possible, it is best to build it slowly by adding on lumps of clay, leaving the mass to settle and dry a little and then progressively adding more clay. You can also let the clay dry out a little before using it, or use hardened clay to build the heart of the sculpture. In this case you will then be working with fresher, softer clay on the surface, being sure to add slip to the dry clay each time before adding fresh clay. Another possibility: place wedges of clay or wood under certain parts to maintain them at their starting level until the clay has set.

Basic Techniques

Here we will be building a freestanding cubic volume with 4" sides, using four different techniques: two with a mass of clay that will be hollowed out (cutting away and adding on) and two "hollow" techniques with a space inside the assembled (or modeled) object. The goal of these exercises is to familiarize you with the different possibilities open to you when sculpting. It is necessary to know how to create an object by cutting away or by adding on, to build an object in coils, and to make a more-or-less thick slab (certain elements are easier to make "in slabs"; for example, a base or architectures that allow you to expose your work). With cutting away, it's entirely possible to create a piece by adding on and then cutting parts away to adjust the size, especially if the clay has dried out too much. With the "coil" technique, certain aerial and delicate parts

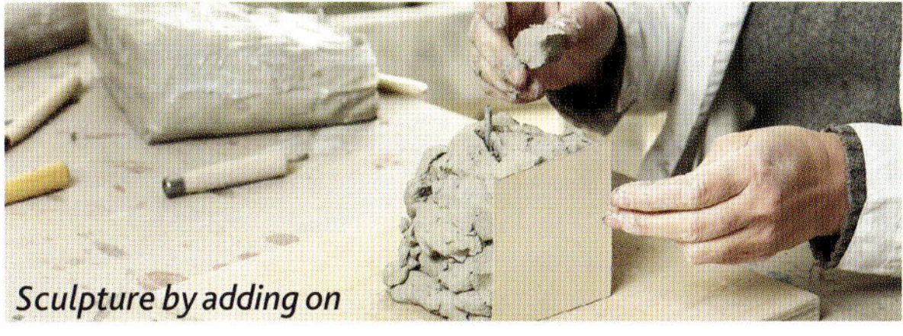

Sculpture by adding on

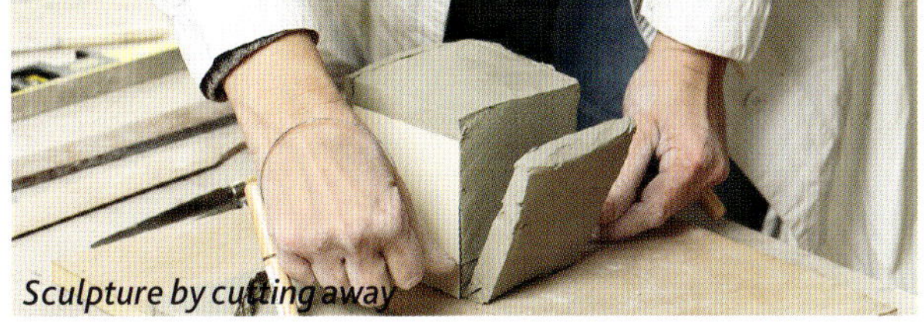

Sculpture by cutting away

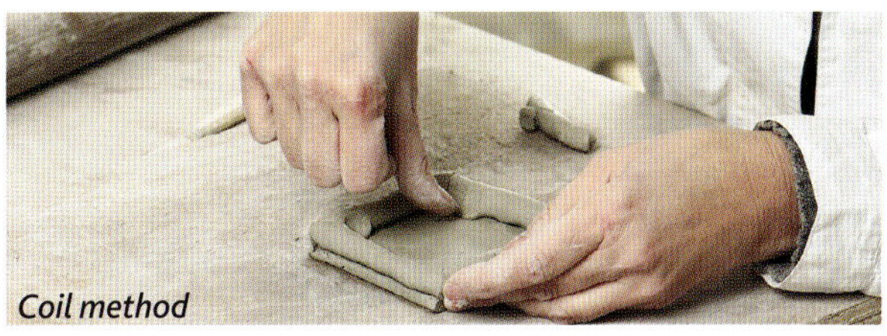

Coil method

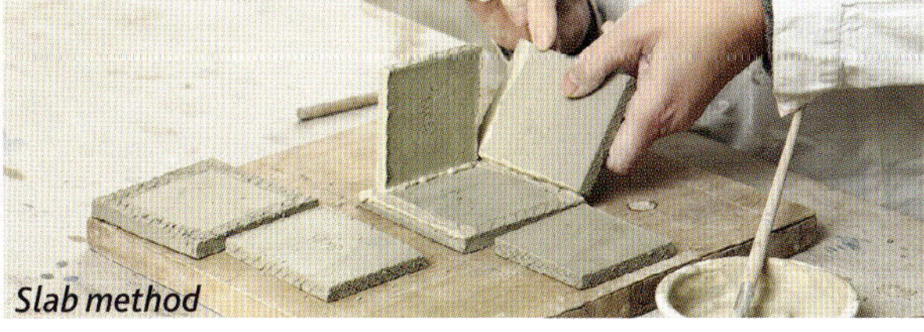

Slab method

Sculpture by Adding On (Constructive Technique)

The volume is built from lumps of clay placed and stuck together by squashing them, starting from the center and working outward.

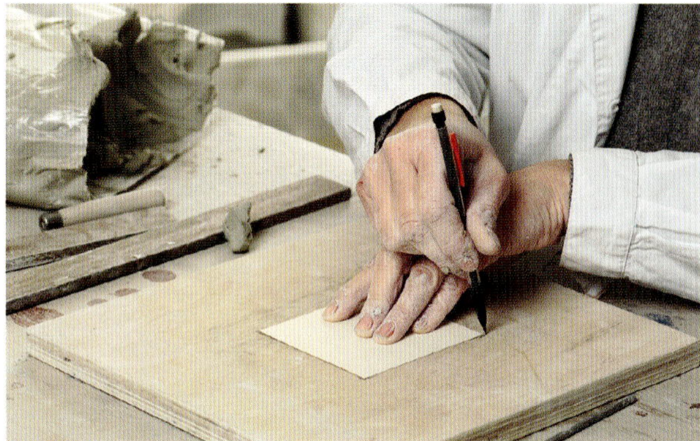

1 Using a thick piece of paper, trace a 4" × 4" square (the base of the cube) on the unpolished surface of the wood that will hold the cube while it's being made.

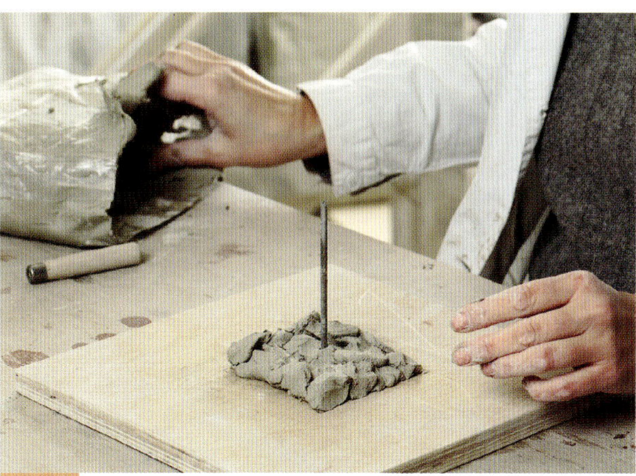

2 Once the base has reached a height of $^{3}/_{4}$", plant a slim metal rod in the center; it will eventually be removed. It is merely there for the clay to stick to, and as a guide to mark the center of the cube.

NOTE

For safety reasons, it is better to use metal inside the sculpture that can support firing at a very high temperature. Even though metal rods or wires are removed before firing, it stops the piece breaking into pieces if a small piece of metal hasn't been removed beforehand.

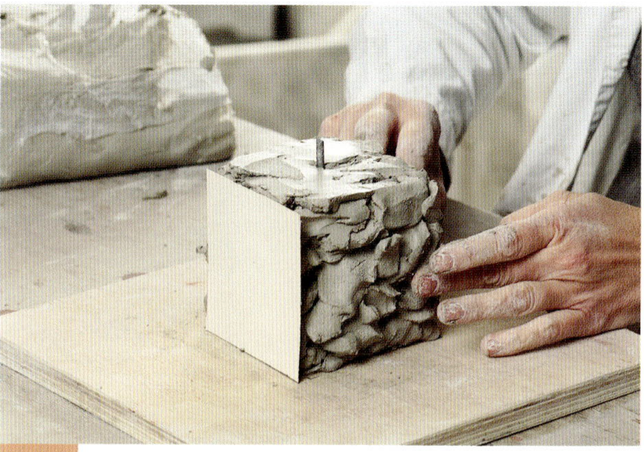

3 Continue your sculpture by adding on lumps of clay and using the thick paper as a guide for shaping the cube.

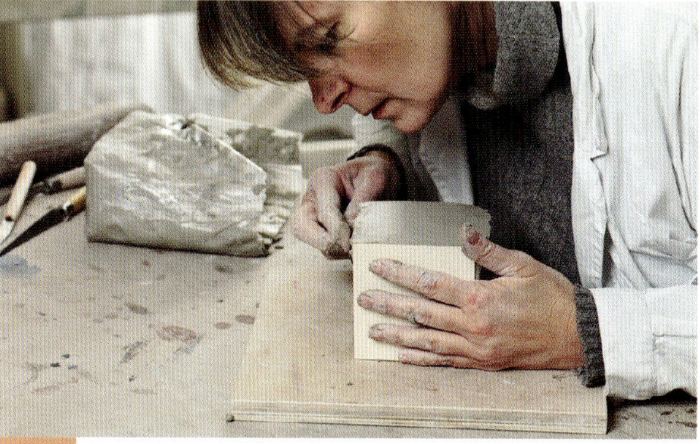

4 The cube will have facets due to the amalgamated clay. You can either leave it as is, or smooth it entirely by adding a little clay in the hollows and smoothing the surface with your knife. Remove the metal rod and stop up the hole.

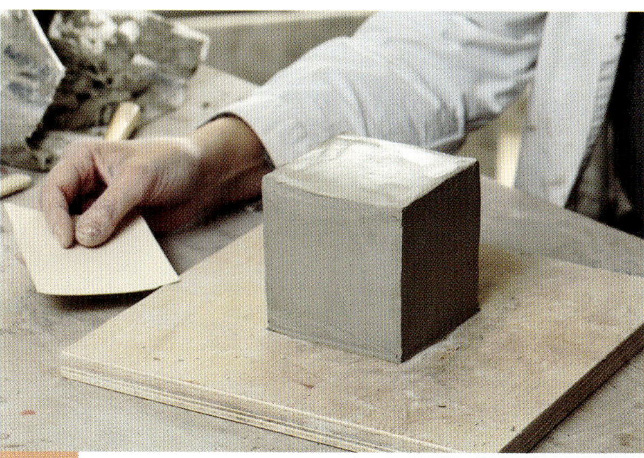

5 Use the thick piece of paper to align the edges and check it with a wooden slide rule. Your cube is finished.

Cutting Away—Destructive Techniques

This means destroying a piece of clay to obtain a cube that is identical to the first. This technique is the opposite of the first, since we will be working from the exterior toward the interior.

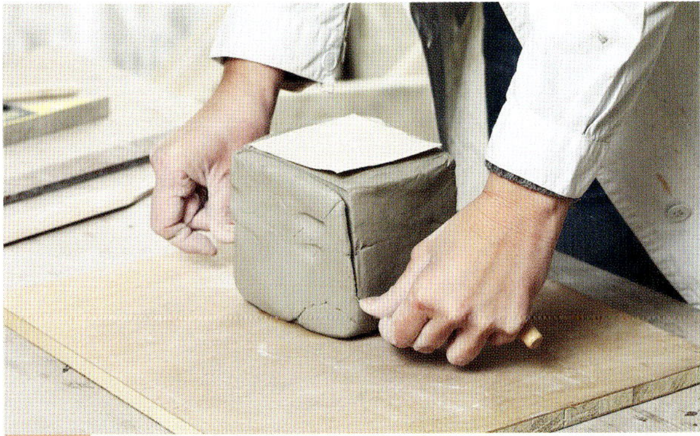

1 Rough out a large square of clay and place your thick square of paper on top of it. Cut the first side vertically with cheese wire, using the square of paper as a guide to get a straight plane.

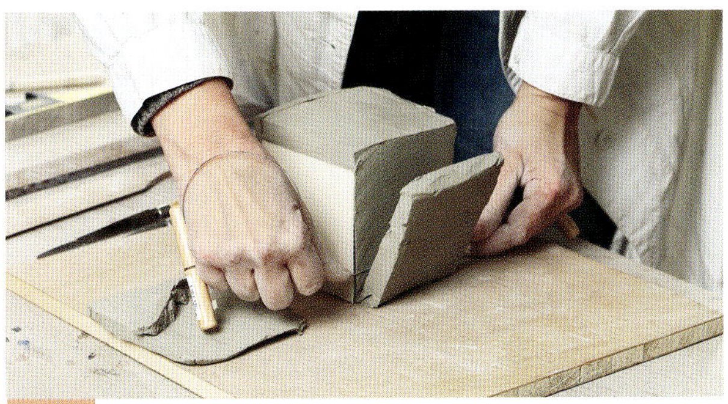

2 Trace a square on this smooth side, using your paper as a guide, and then cut away the other sides, using the paper as a guide.

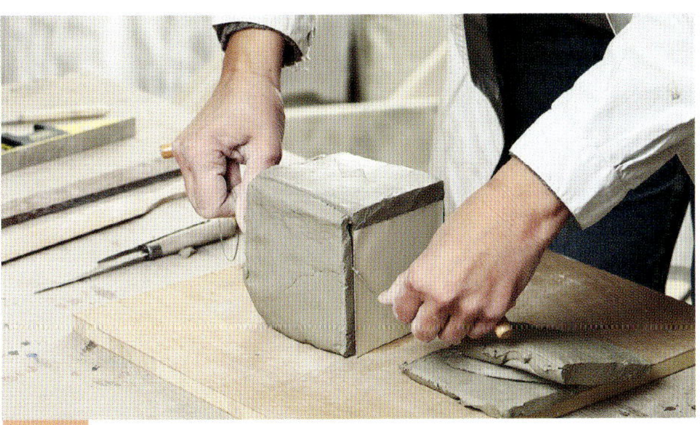

3 Finish cutting vertically, with the paper as a guide.

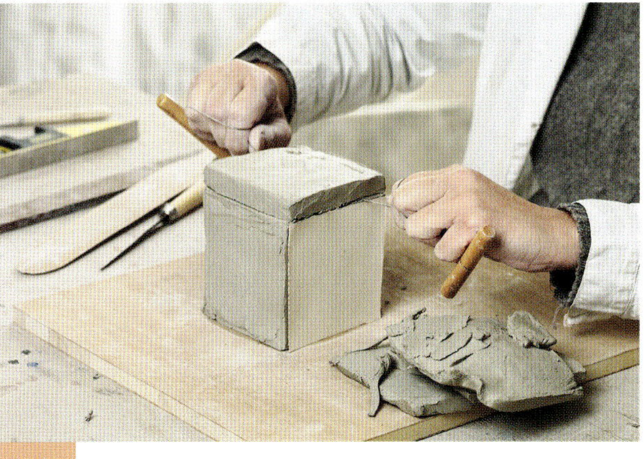

4 All you need to do now is cut the top of the clay horizontally to obtain your cube.

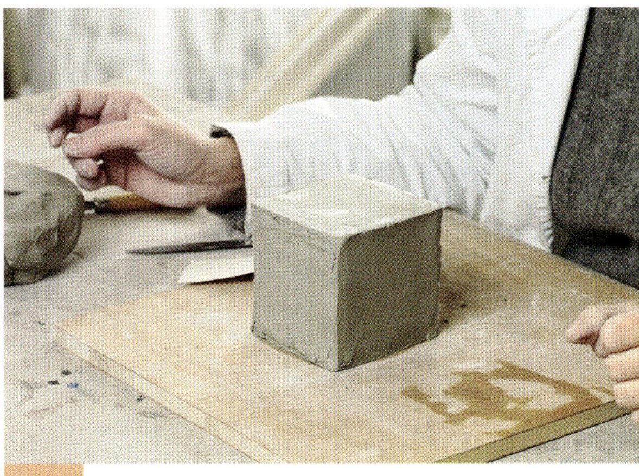

5 Your cube is finished; it just needs to be smoothed out.

NOTE

When making a geometrical object such as a cube, this method is very easy. But a complex piece is more complicated, because you have to know the exact volume that needs to be cut away and where to stop. You need to calculate the cut—leaving a margin for maneuvering—to succeed. Luckily, because clay is malleable you can always add more if you have cut too much away.

Hollow Sculpting: Coil Method

This is an ancient technique that comes from Colombia and allows you to build—by superimposing coils—sides that can be given any shape. The finished object is already hollow. This technique enables you to make large pieces, notably in pottery, but also in sculpture.

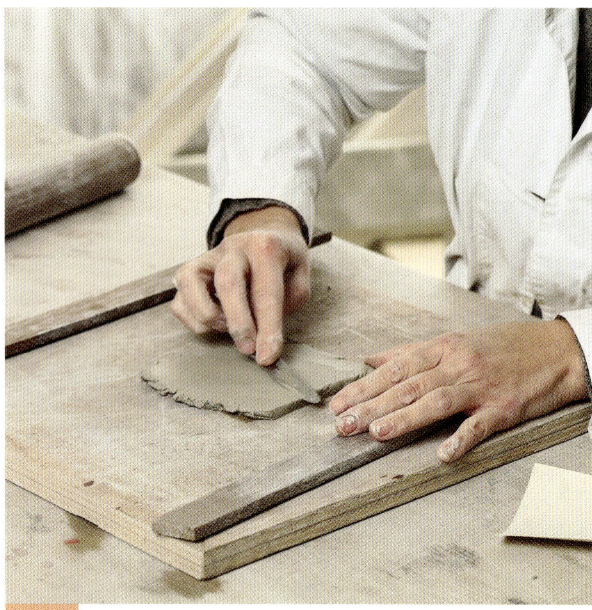

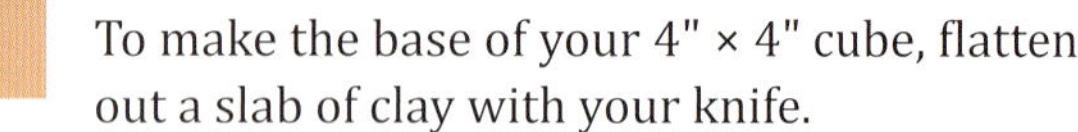

1 To make the base of your 4" × 4" cube, flatten out a slab of clay with your knife.

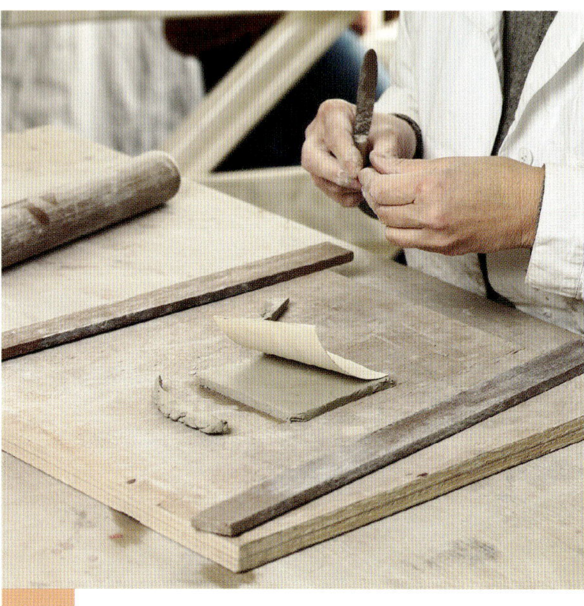

2 Using your thick piece of paper, trace out a square in the clay and cut it out with your knife.

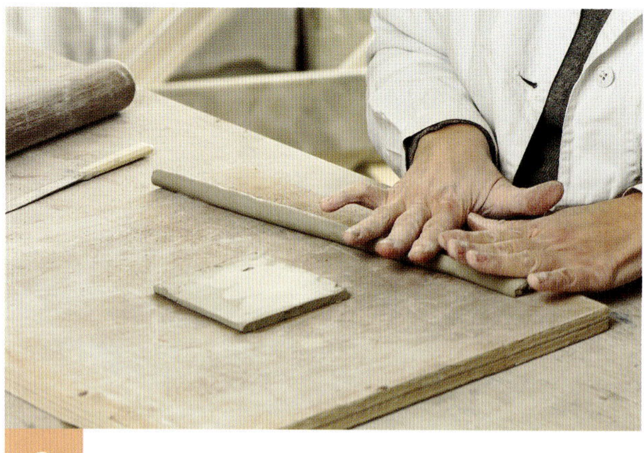

3 Model "sausages" with the palm of your hand, rolling the clay on a table. Continue (putting on a little pressure with your fingers) in a rocking movement from the center toward the outer edges to make your coil as even and as round as possible. Pressing down too hard will flatten it.

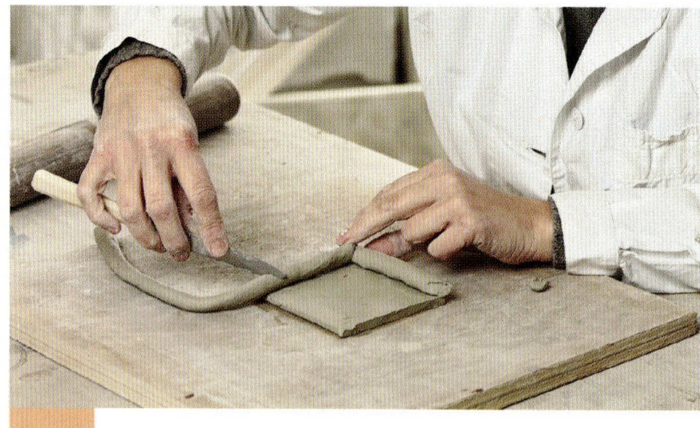

4 Cut the coils into lengths that go around the border of the base of your cube.

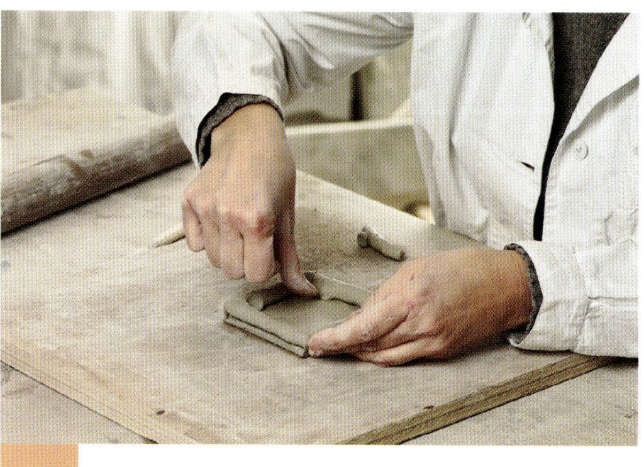

5 Join the first coil to the slab by squashing it with your finger.

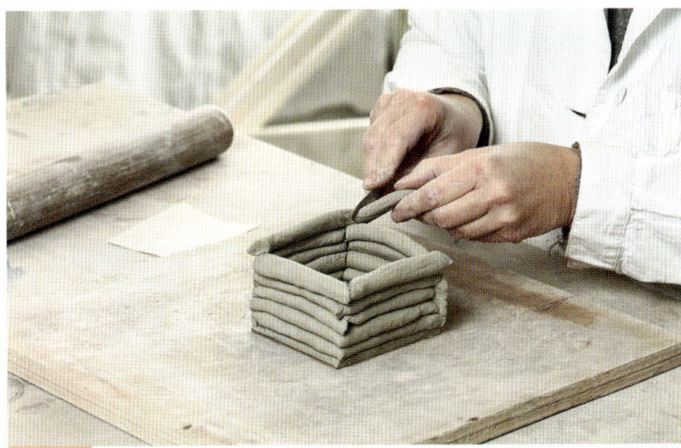

6 Build the volume of your cube by placing the coils one on top of the other, being careful to stay vertically aligned.

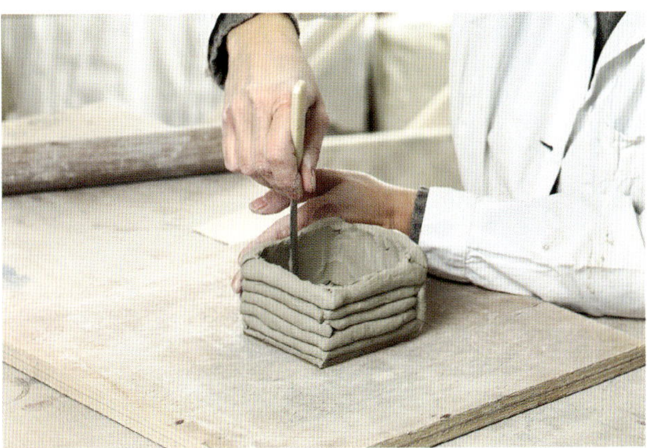

7 Use your fingers to join the coils on the inside and then smooth them out with your knife, with your other hand keeping the outside in place (because the clay is soft).

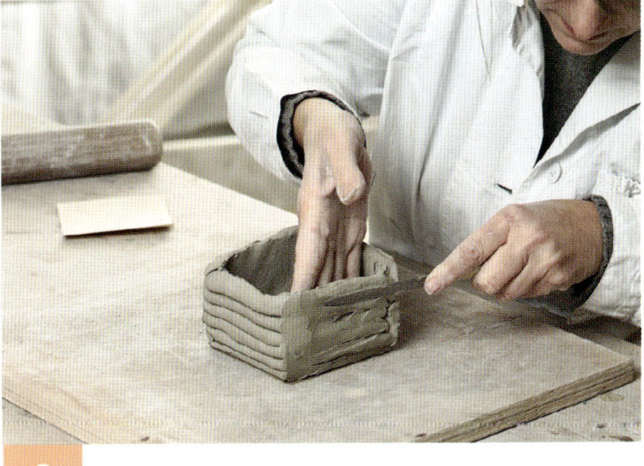

8 Smooth the exterior in the same way. Continue until your sides are $3^{1}/_{2}$" high (because the lid is $^{1}/_{3}$" thick).

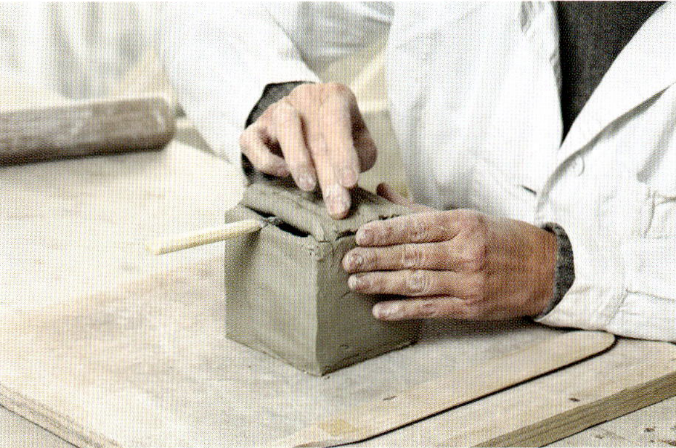

9 To close the cube, place the coils horizontally to make the top. Join them together by smoothing out the clay, keeping them in place with the blade of your knife.

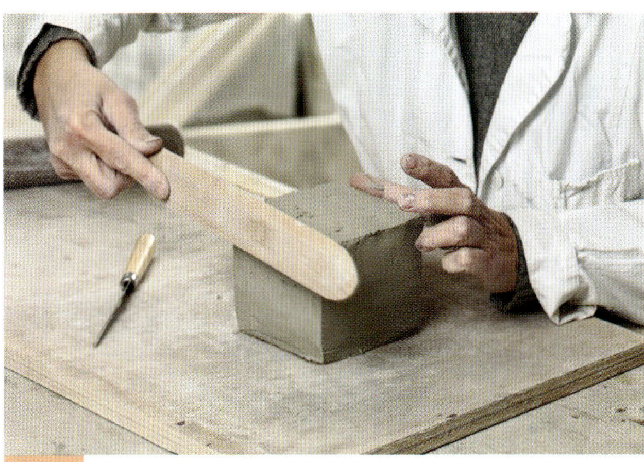

10 Smooth out the top and remove the knife. Then align the angles by using a wooden scraper.

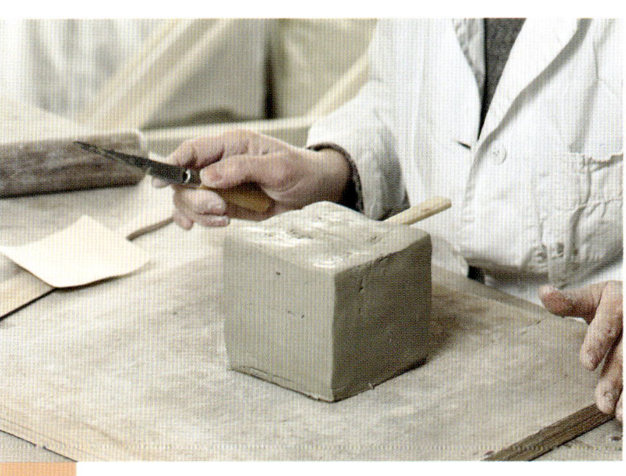

11 Your "coil" cube is almost finished; smooth it out a little more to obtain a more regular surface. You can leave it to dry out prior to doing the finishing touches with your knife.

Slab Method—Assembly Techniques

This exercise is done in two sessions, because to assemble the slabs, the clay needs to dry out beforehand. To make a large slab 12" × 8¹/₄" and ¹/₃" thick, you will need two wooden battens ¹/₃" thick (called rulers or guides) and an unpolished plywood board that the clay won't stick to.

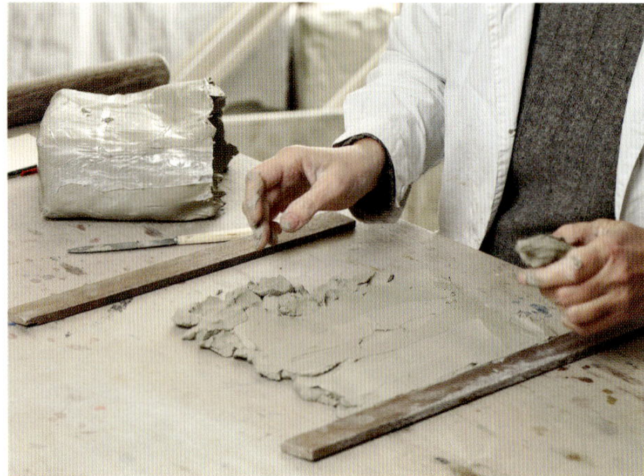

1 Place the guides at least 12" apart and start the slab by joining lumps of clay together along the edges of the battens, being careful not to create air bubbles. Smooth the clay with your knife as you go along.

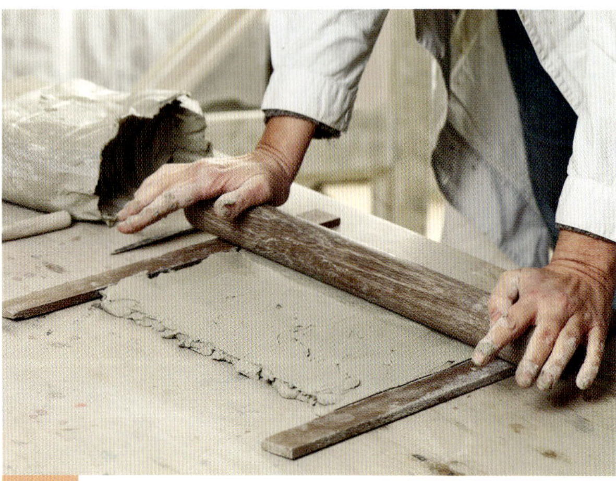

2 Once the clay has reached the depth of the guides, or even a few millimeters more, squash the slab with an unpolished rolling pin, pressing down on the guides.

ADVICE

You should have a nice smooth surface. If you see air bubbles, pierce them with a pointed object, add a little clay, and smooth it out with your knife.

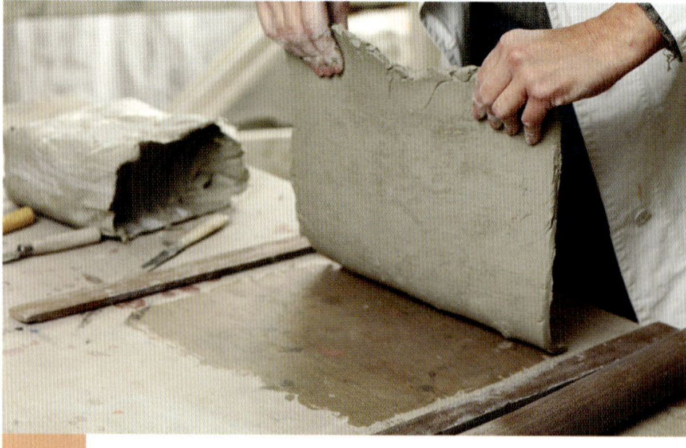

3 Turn the slab over. This should be easy because the clay hasn't stuck to the plywood.

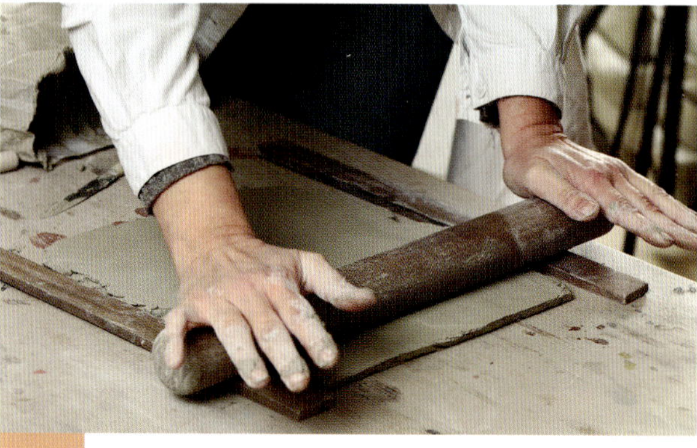

4 Even out the surface with your knife, put the guides back in place, and go over the clay with a rolling pin.

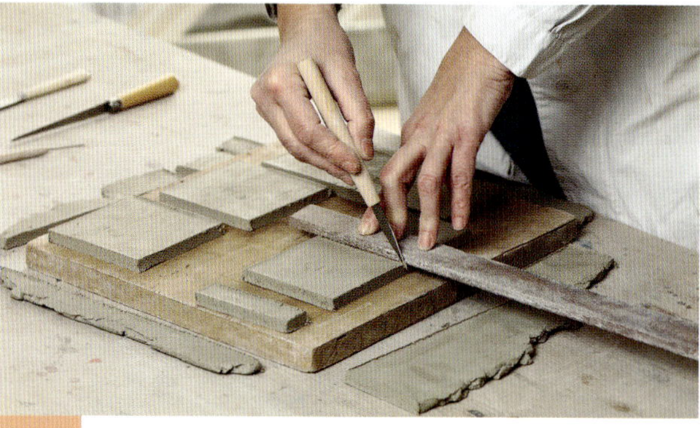

5 Leave the slab on the board to dry out for an hour of two. Then trace out the six sides of your cube, using a slide rule: two slabs 4" × 4", two 3¹/₄" × 4", and two 3¹/₄" × 3¹/₄". Cut them out with a bevel-edged knife, using a batten as a guide. Leave the clay to dry out another hour. During this time, prepare the slip (see page 26).

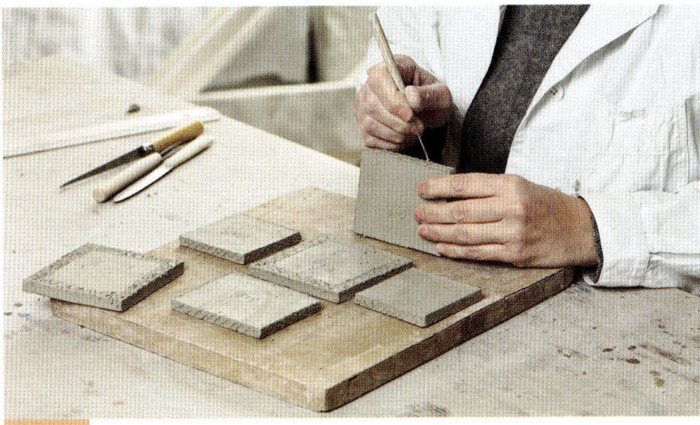

6 Now that the slabs are hard, you can start to assemble them. Score the edges of the slabs where they will be in contact when building the cube, using a potter's needle (see "Scoring" on page 27).

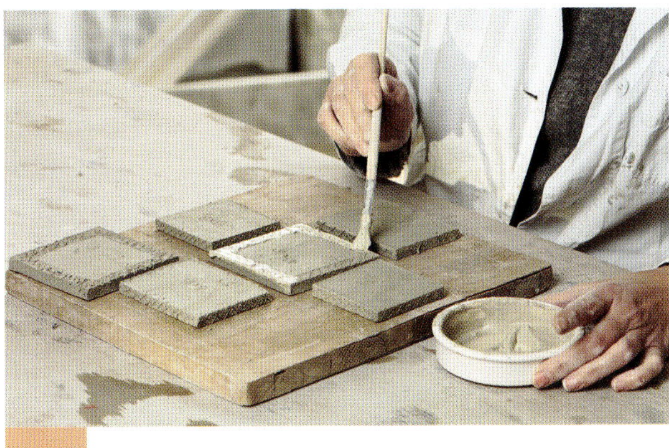

7 Cover the scored edges with slip by using a paintbrush, starting with the slab that will be the base of the cube.

8 Assemble the vertical sides of the cube onto the base, scoring the edges that will be in contact as you go along. Press each side gently so that the slip seeps out, making sure the edges are in contact with each other. Check that the slip hasn't been absorbed by the clay; if this is the case, add more so that the slabs stick to each other properly.

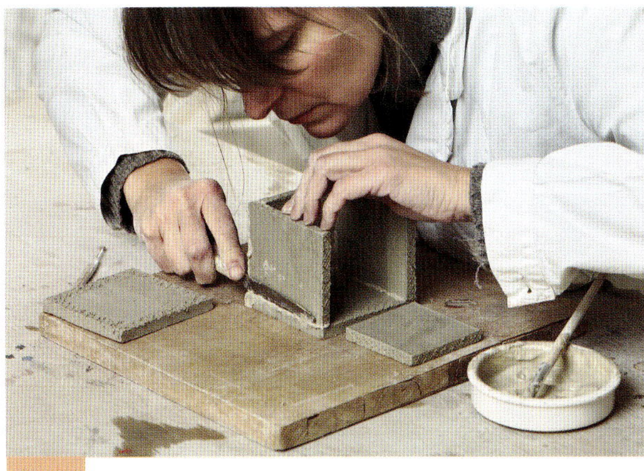

9 If parts of the clay overlap, cut them away with your knife.

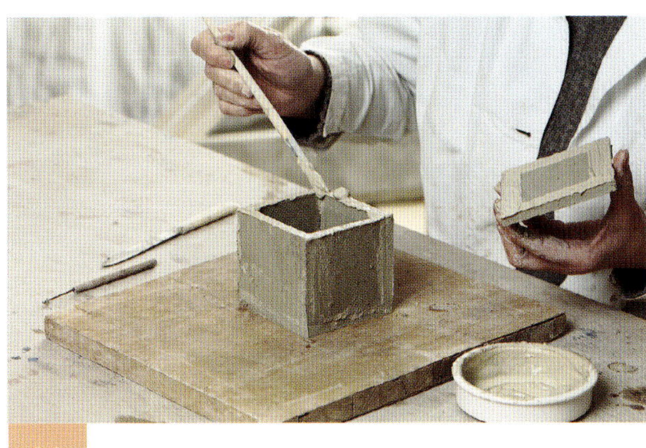

10 Once the sides are finished, paint on some slip and put the top in place.

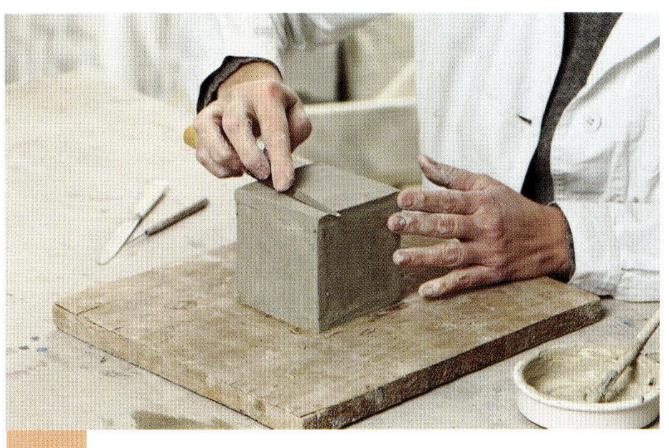

11 Once the cube is finished, you can score and then smooth out the places where the slabs have stuck together so that the seams don't show.

Making Slip for "Gluing" the Clay Together

Slip is used like glue. It is made up of a little clay and a lot of water. It is made with the same clay as the piece you are working on, so that the glue is invisible. You should make it at the start of each session and have it permanently at hand. This liquid matter is used as soon as the clay has dried out a little, to glue each added piece. There are two ways of making it:

Using Dry Clay Sanded Down

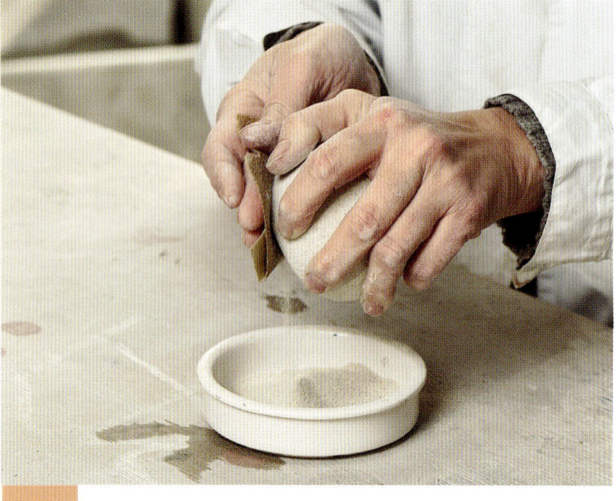

1 Sand the dry clay into a dish, using sandpaper.

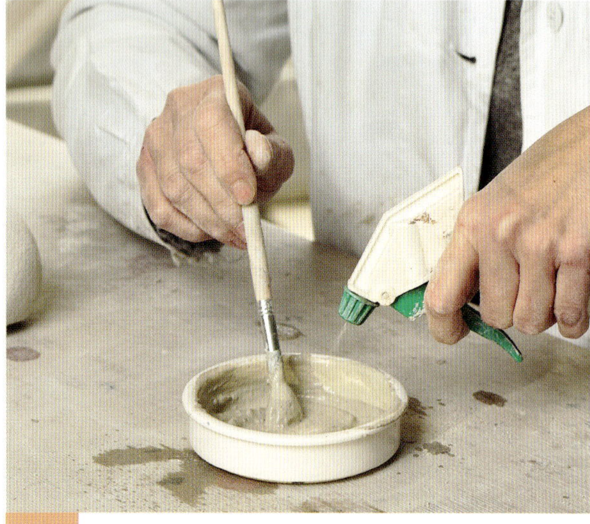

2 Mix the resulting powder with water until you get a consistency close to creamy yogurt, or a little thicker. The advantage of this technique is that the results are immediate.

Using Damp (or a Little Hard) Clay

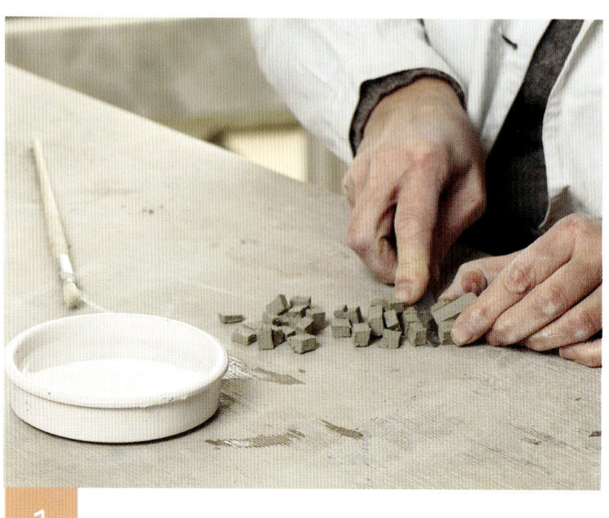

1 Dice the clay and put the pieces in water.

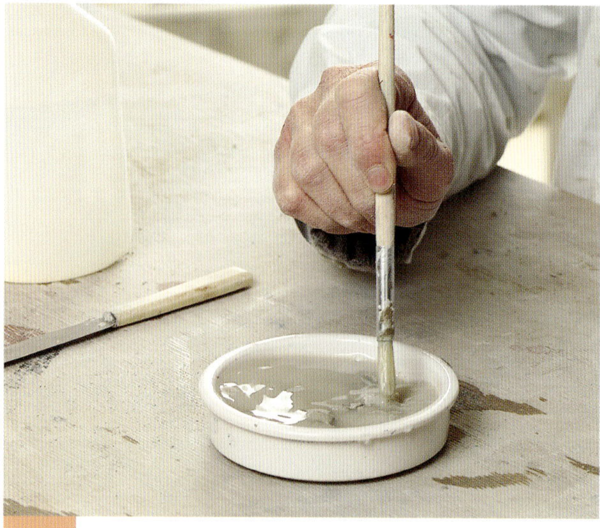

2 Mix with a paintbrush until you have the same consistency as creamy yogurt, which will take a little time.

Scoring

Scoring consists of making thin, crossed grooves on the surface of pieces that are going to be joined together after being coated with slip. Scoring is necessary when joining two pieces of clay, at least one of which has dried out and hardened. This practice is easy to understand, because when drying out the clay loses its water. Scoring opens the pores so that water can penetrate the surface easily. So that the pieces being joined soften up, the water in the slip must be able to sufficiently penetrate the clay's surface, and this is why they are scored. When the clay is really dry, scoring is even more important.

NOTE

In the example of a cube made by assembling slabs, another method could have been used, consisting of cutting six slabs of identical size, which would have then been beveled so that they adjust to the angle of each other. However, this method is somewhat more difficult.

Finishing Techniques

Hollowing Out

Before finishing a sculpture, any parts that are thicker than $^3/_4$" must be hollowed out or aerated, because while sculpting we have a tendency of creating air bubbles in the clay. Where the piece is thicker than $^3/_4$", it is possible that the air won't be able to escape, which is why hollowing out or aerating the clay is necessary. If the air can't escape, it will dilate during firing, and your sculpture will explode or crack. Hollowing out is difficult but essential because you will be able to fire your piece without risks. You'll also recuperate up to 50 percent of your clay—which is economical—and your piece will be lighter and easier to handle.

Before starting, you must wait until the first $^1/_3$" of clay has dried out enough. If your piece is still soft, leave it to dry out overnight or a bit longer, without covering it up. Hollowing out consists of lightening your volume, leaving a peripheral shell of between $^1/_3$" and $^3/_4$" thick. Hollowing out begins at the top of your piece, working down toward the bottom. If you do it the other way around, the base will be too fragile and the whole thing will collapse. When you join the hollowed out pieces, you start from the bottom, working toward the top for the same reasons.

Hollowing Out "A Child in a Chair" on Page 110

In the following example—the volume being large—the head was hollowed out first as usual, but it was fixed back together before the body was hollowed out. In this case we attach the top (here, the head), and the volume underneath is hollowed out later, once it is sufficiently dry. This shouldn't be a problem if the top part is hollowed out properly because it hardens a little once more, remains light, and won't make the rest collapse when it is being worked on. Clay progressively forms a sort of hard shell on the surface as it dries out, making hollowing out safe.

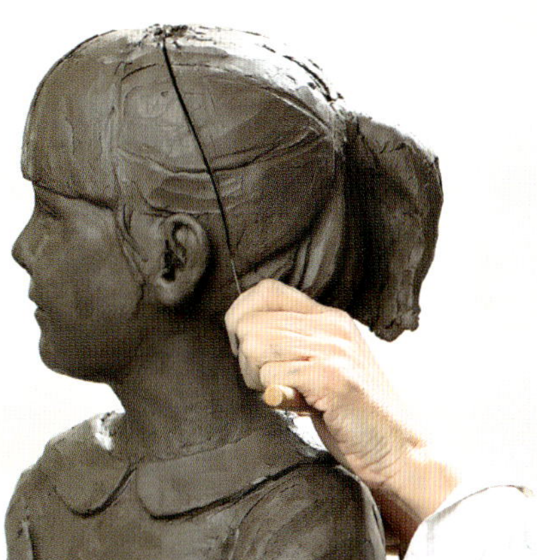

1 The child was hollowed out from the top, at the back of its head, to avoid touching the face. Cut the back of the head in a slanting direction with the cutting wire and place it on a piece of foam to avoid deforming it.

BE CAREFUL!

Avoid cutting through delicate parts such as the ears, unless you have no other choice. Never cut on the level of the neck. You will have a lot of trouble fixing the head back onto the shoulders, because the volume will be too heavy for the neck, which will either crack at the seams or collapse.

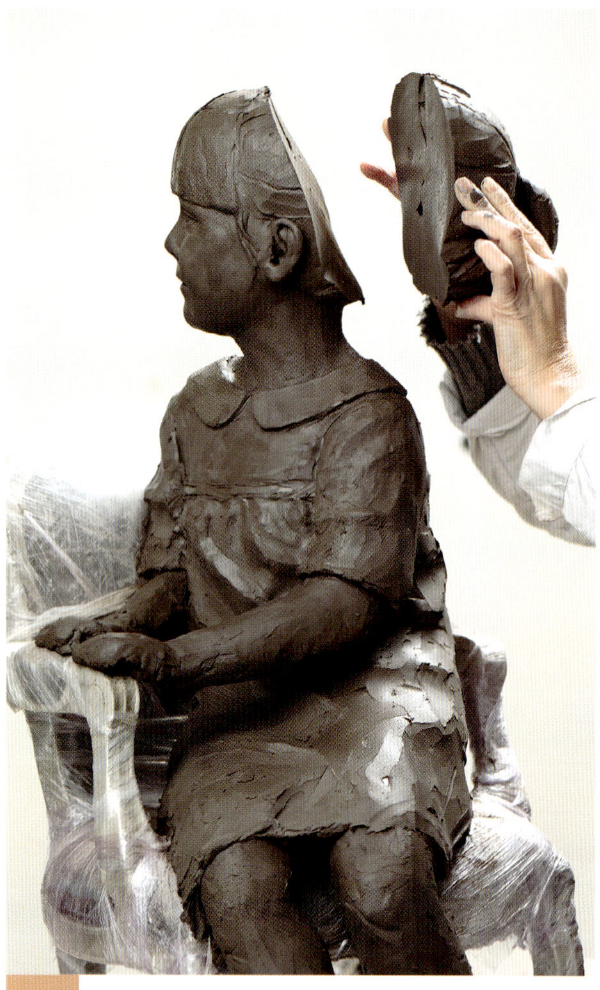

2 Dig out the clay in the two parts of the head with a loop tool, leaving a shell $^{1}/_{3}$" thick. While working, check that the thickness is even, and leave a little more in the places that support the piece you are working on: jaw, neck, and the back of the skull.

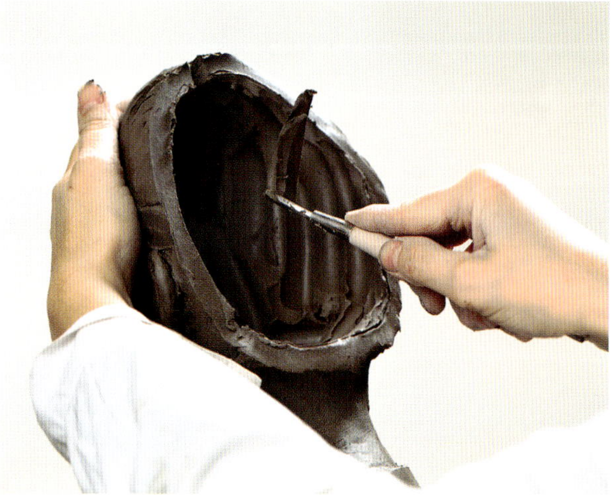

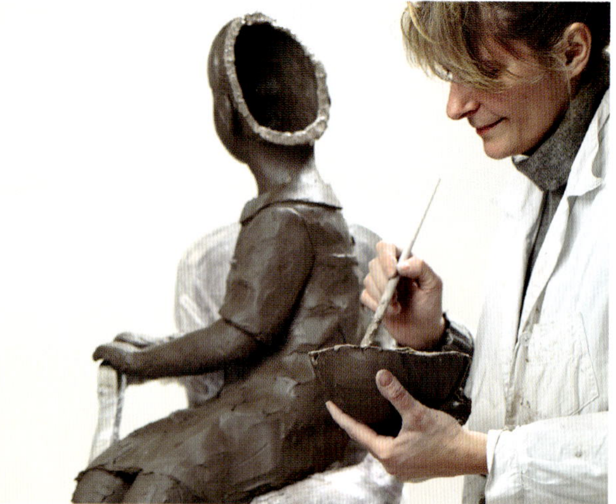

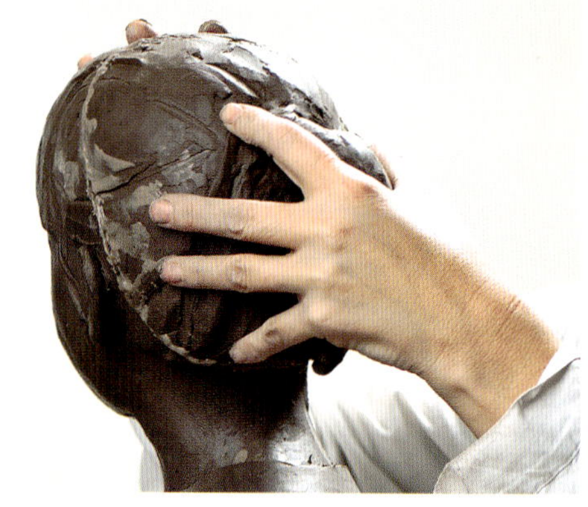

3 As I explained on page 27, the head is put back together before hollowing out the rest. Attach the two pieces together after scoring and applying slip (see "Slab Method—Assembly Techniques" on page 24).

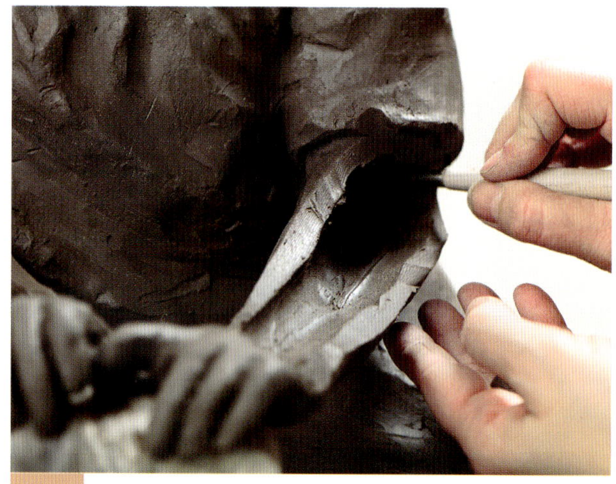

4 Following the same principle, hollow out the arms in two parts, as well as the insides of the hands. Get into the habit of placing each part that is cut away and hollowed out on pieces of foam.

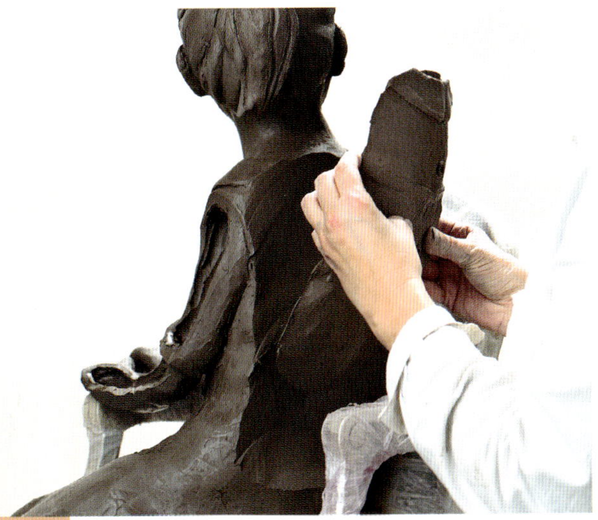

5 Now start on the torso.

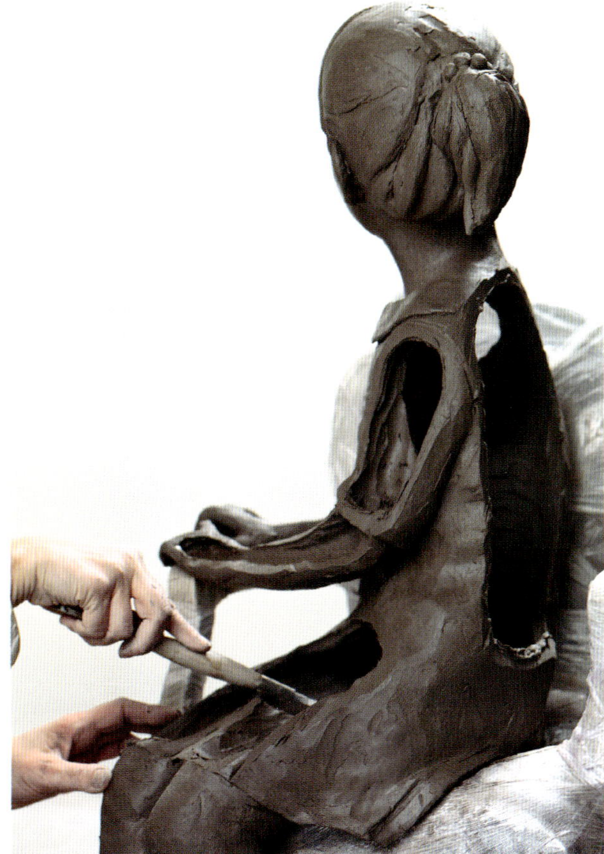

6 Because the child is sitting down, the pelvis and thighs are hollowed out in a single piece. Finish by hollowing out the calves and the feet.

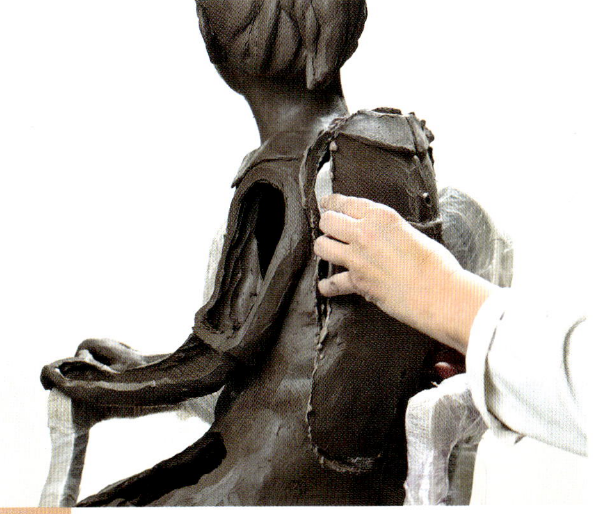

7 Normally, we fix the pieces back together from the bottom toward the top. Here, the head has already been hollowed out and replaced because it was much drier than the rest of the body, which dried out in turn before being worked on. Putting back the hollowed-out pieces is done in the following order: back, thighs, forearms, and arms. Since the child is sitting down, the legs are hollowed out afterward. Once fixed back in place, they will be cut off to be able to fit the pieces into the kiln. (See "Slab Method—Assembly Techniques" on page 24 and "A Child in a Chair" on page 110.)

ADVICE

You can choose whether to hollow out your piece from the front or the back, depending on the complexity of the piece. Sometimes it is necessary to cut the same part in several different places to hollow it out properly. Keep one hand on the outside of the part you are working on, to gauge the thickness and to avoid digging right through and making a hole. You can also control the thickness by using a pin, if you have doubts about it. It's best to leave a thickness of ⅓", and a little more at the last few inches toward the bottom of the sculpture, because clay is heavy and you don't want to weaken the base.

BE CAREFUL!

Any piece that has been hollowed out and rejoined must have an opening to the exterior (even one as small as a pin prick). If not, the volume of air contained inside will dilate during firing and break the sculpture into several pieces.

Scoring and Joining with Slip

See "Slab Method—Assembly Techniques" on page 24.

Treating the Clay before Drying

Once your piece has been hollowed out and rejoined, you should erase all signs of the seams. Scoring and smoothing the surface with your knife will eventually remove the seams. You'll have to be patient, because it might be necessary to repeat this operation several times in the same place before the seams don't show. If you can still see a slight trace of the seam, apply slip and a little fresh clay and smooth it out until the signs disappear. You can now add the finishing touches to your work: adding details of imprints, making sure to leave the surface of the places you have joined to dry out a little first, because certain parts will still be soft. Better to let them dry out first.

Imprints

Your hollowed-out clay has become "leather hard," but it can still be decorated with all sorts of ornaments and textures. Everything is good for decorating and giving life to your sculpture, such as the texture of clothing: imprints of lace (see the little girl's dress in the bas-relief below), cloth, netting, rope, or string, as well as the motives on wooden seals, notched scrapers, fork marks, etc. Give your imagination free rein!

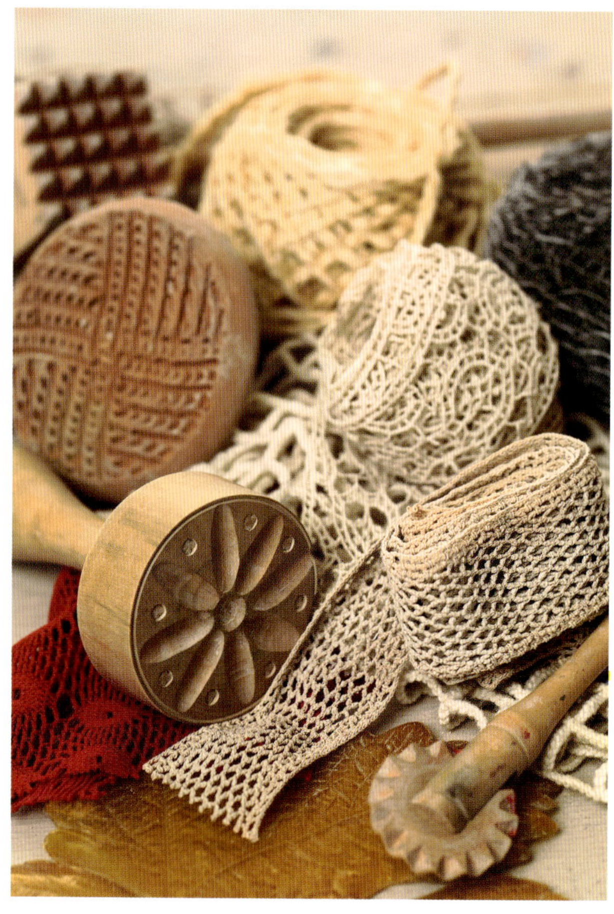

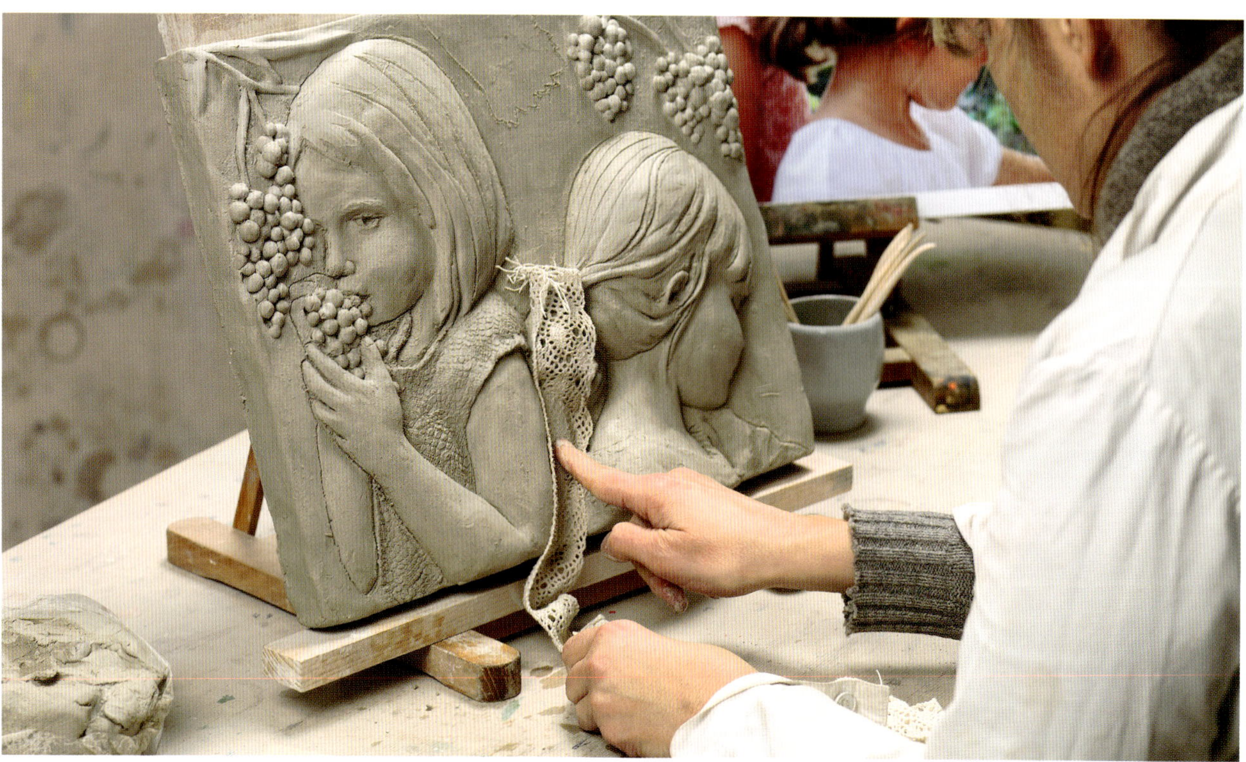

Sanding and Polishing

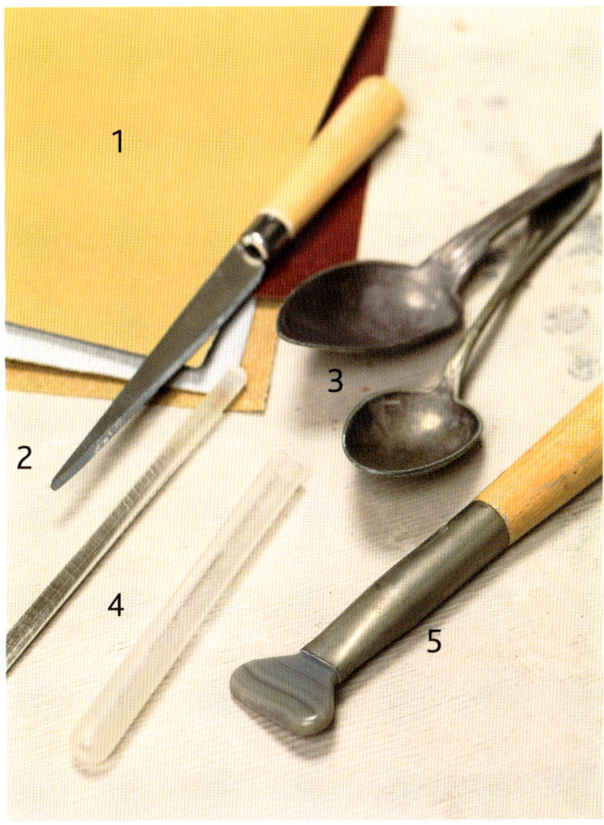

Sandpaper in different grains for sanding (1), a knife for scraping (2), metal spoons (3) and glass tubes (4), and agate (5) for polishing.

If you prefer to regularize a surface and leave it with a rough aspect, all you need to do is sand your piece with sandpaper before firing, to highlight its roughness and make it symmetrical at the same time.

If you prefer a smooth finish, you'll need to work on the surface with a metal spoon and then with a glass tube to close the clay's pores. It will become shiny before firing and satiny afterward. Polishing techniques need patience and care because the spoon, which is used in circular movements, can mark the clay and leave scratches. Proceed gently, slightly crushing the clay—which has dried out but is still damp—to progressively close the pores and glaze the surface, which will become satiny but eventually will become matte when drying out and become as soft as skin to the touch. For this reason, spend at least two days on polishing the entire piece to bring back the luster.

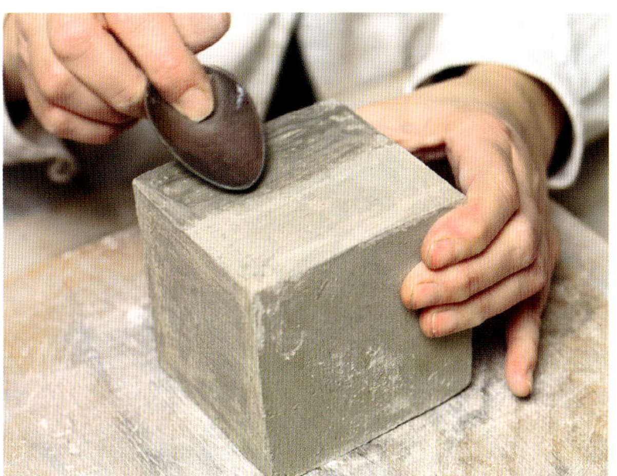

Eventually, when the clay is hard, you can start to polish with glass (a test tube is perfect for this). Fine particles of glass will be deposited on the surface during polishing. The glass will vitrify during firing, creating a satiny aspect, or even shiny if you have the patience to gently polish it every day and store it in a warm or hot place. The glaze obtained by polishing before and after firing looks like enamel. This means that the glass has entered into the surface of the clay.

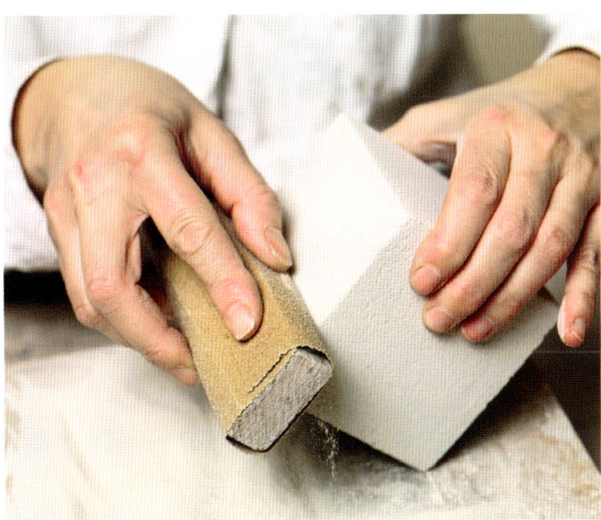

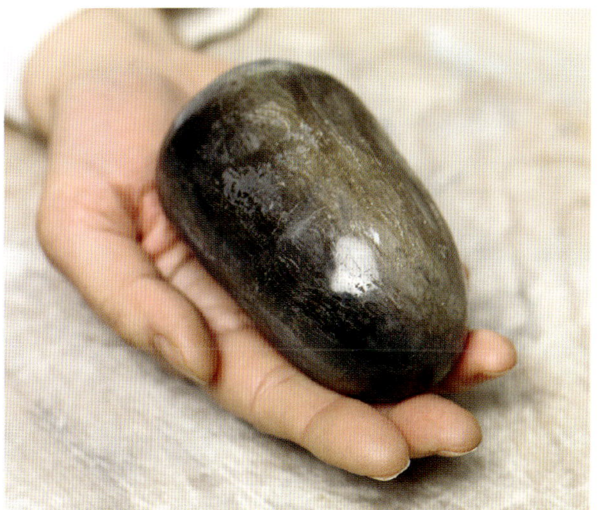

Engobe or Colors on Unfired Clay

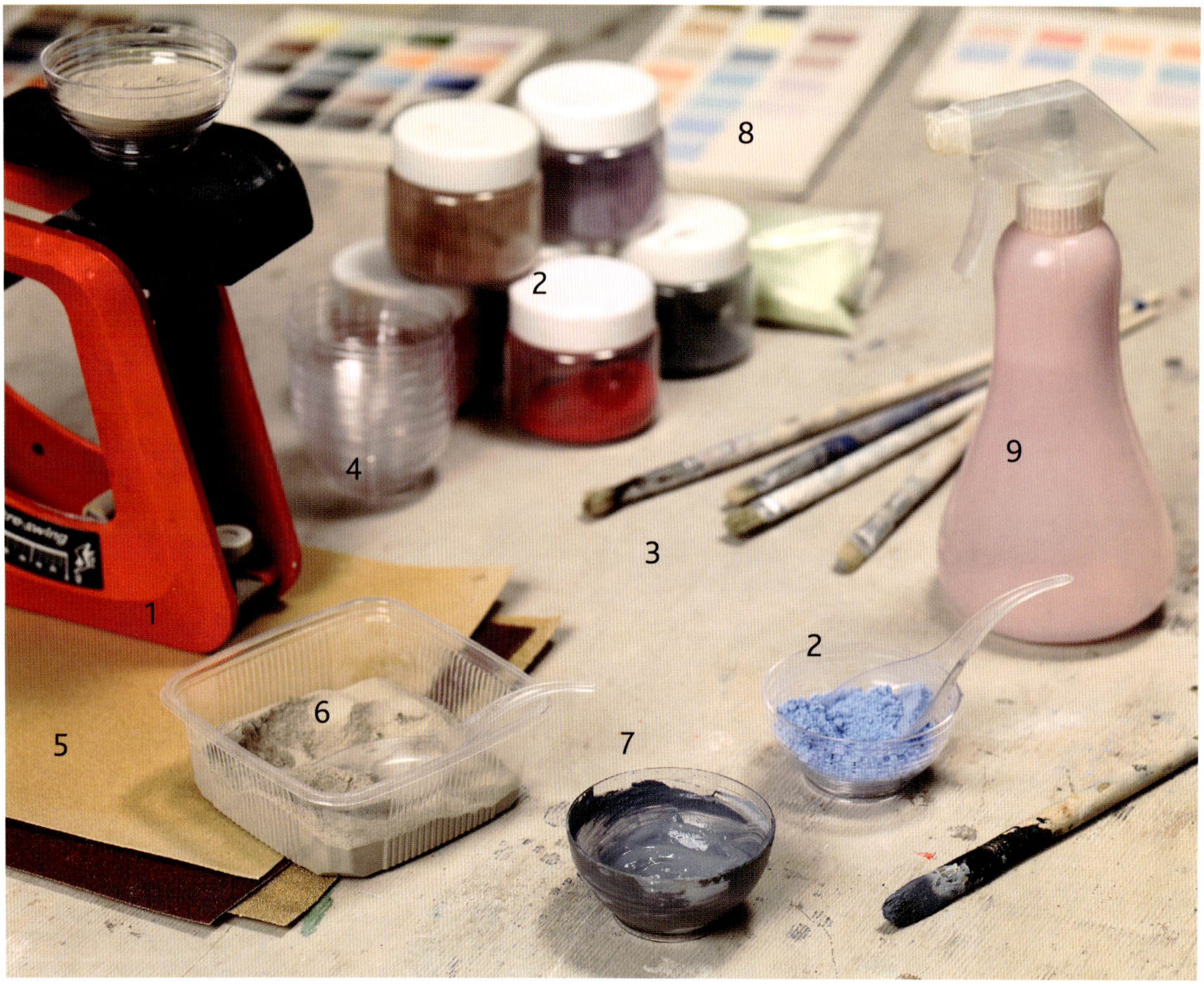

Precision weighing scales (1) for precisely measuring the powder; colored oxides (2); fine-haired brushes for applying the engobe (3); small recipients: plastic or glass yogurt pots (4); gross and fine-grain sandpaper for the engobe and finishing touches to the parts without engobe (5); dry powered clay (6); prepared engobe (7); slabs of color examples after firing (8); and a spray bottle (9).

Engobe is a coloring agent that is applied to unfired clay in a general manner. It is composed of heat-resistant colored oxides and unfired clay—preferably white. The clay, which serves as a medium and flux, settles the colored oxide. Its white color is neutral and therefore brings out the colored oxide. Engobe has a matte aspect after firing, except for porcelain, which becomes satiny at high temperatures.

Personally, I make my engobe from powdered white porcelain. Not only does its whiteness bring out the colors, but at high temperatures, porcelain vitrifies and gives a satiny aspect to the engobe.

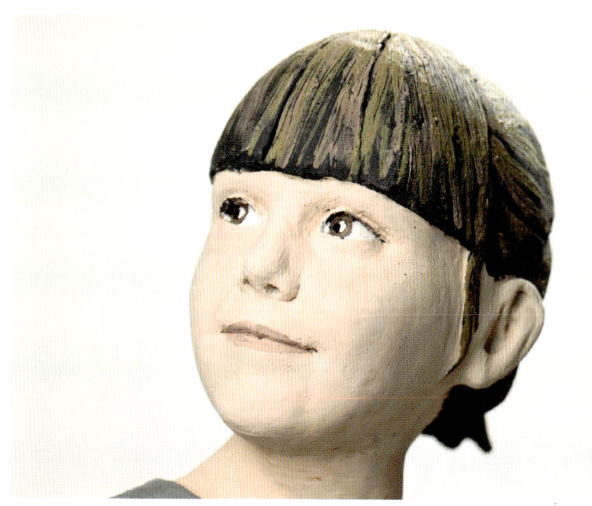

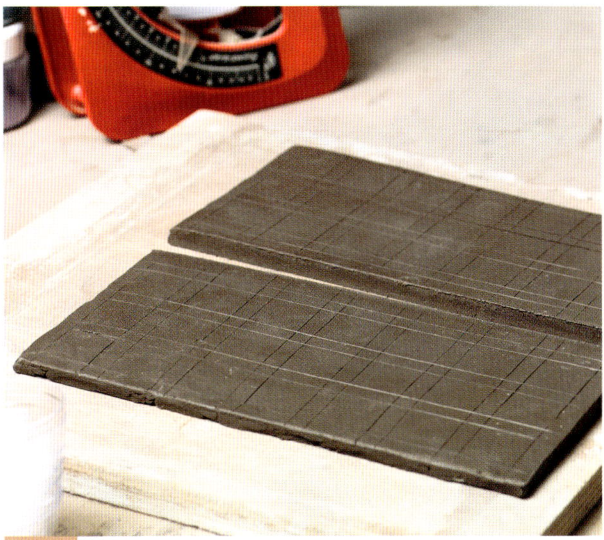

1 Make one or two identical slabs (see page 24). Using a slide rule and a potter's needle, trace out squares where you will paint on your examples of engobe.

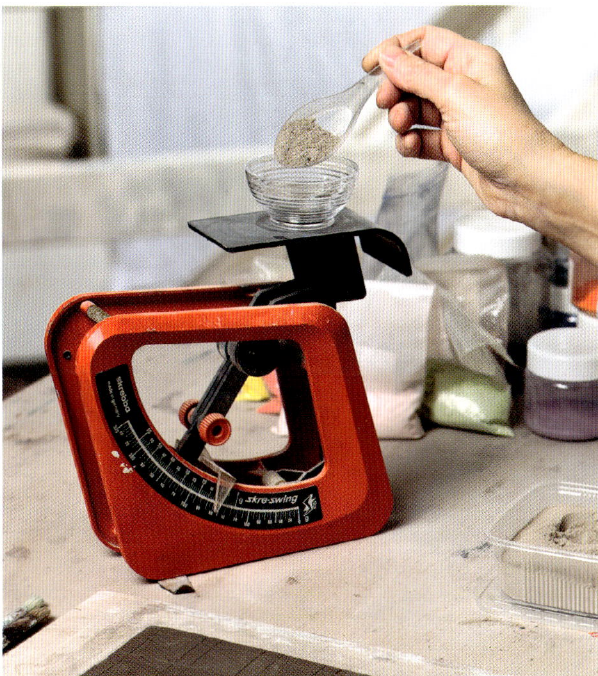

2 Weigh the powdered clay that you obtained by sanding down dry clay. Engobe can contain only 30 percent of its weight in colored oxide or the color won't settle and will clump. In fact, you need more flux than color and the clay is a flux. To make 10 grams (g) of engobe you would weigh out 7 g of powered clay, to which you'd add a maximum of 3 g of powdered color.

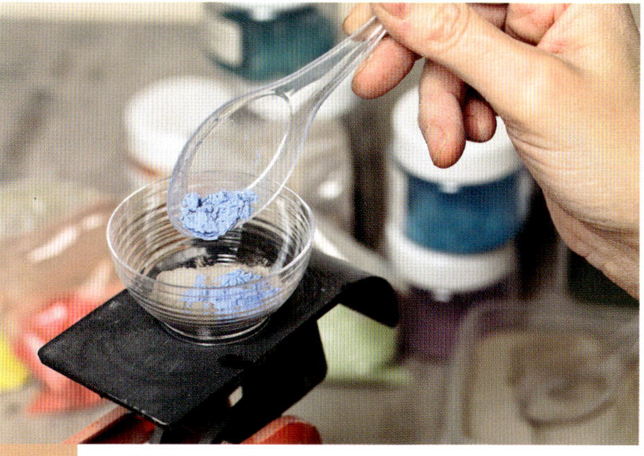

3 Add the color to the clay, respecting the proportions indicated in the preceding step.

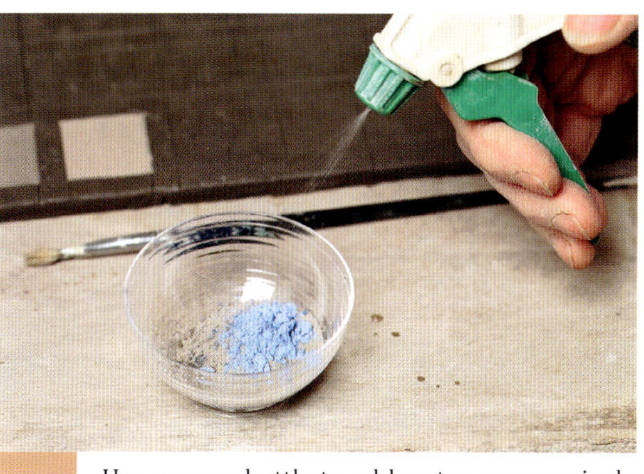

4 Use a spray bottle to add water progressively until you get the consistence of creamy yogurt.

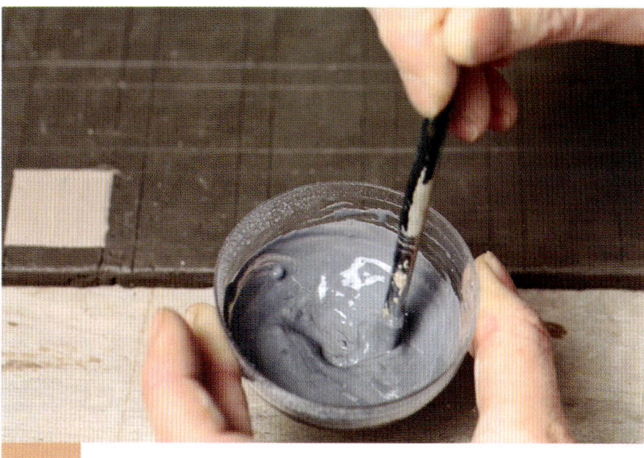

5 Mix the engobe with a brush to make sure there are no lumps.

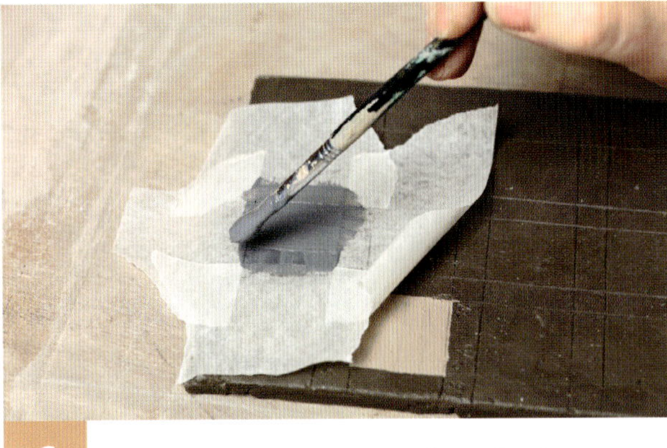

6 Paint one or two layers of engobe (maximum thickness: 1 mm). Put a band of repositionable adhesive around the squares on your slab.

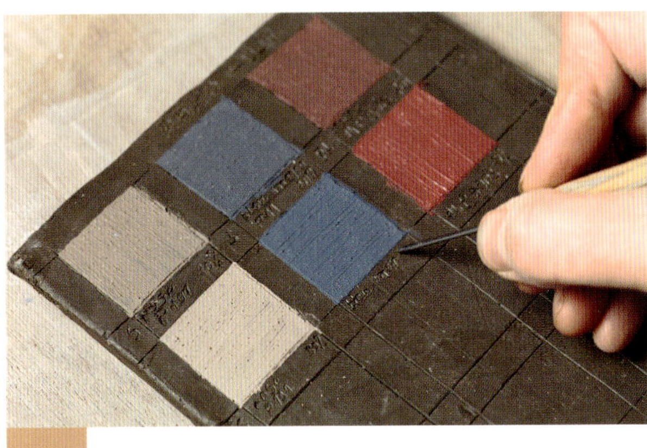

7 With a sharp point, write down the colors and percentage of colored oxide used.

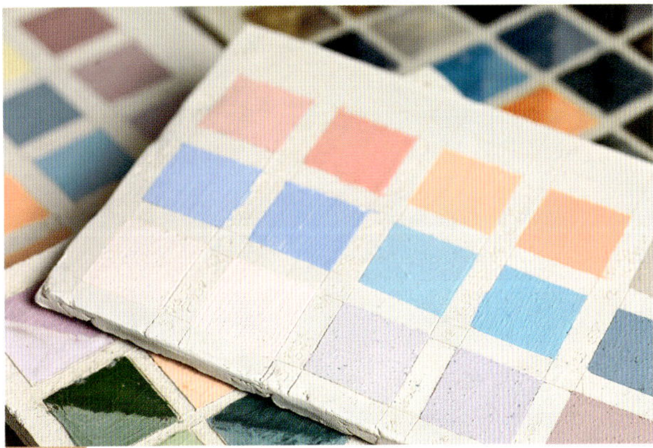

8 Here is the result after firing a slab of color tests. It's the slab I made for "A Child in a Chair" (page 110), made in dry white raku clay with fine grog (the grains are visible in the photo); the same clay I used to make the child.

Drying

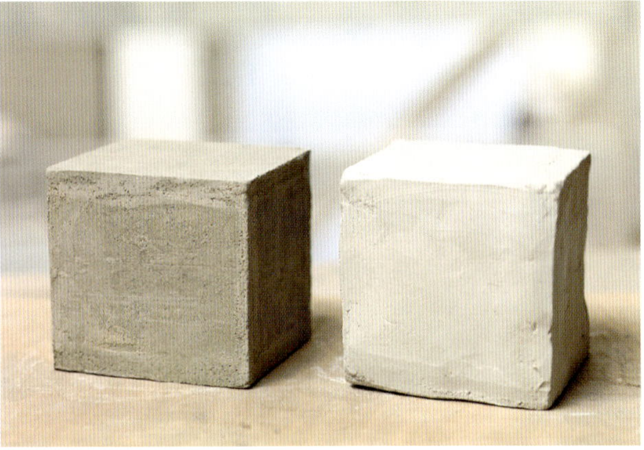

On the left is a cube made of white clay, now drying out; it is leather hard. The cube on the right has dried out, but hasn't been fired yet. (Unfired sculpture or pottery is called greenware).

Drying is an important phase that should be respected if the work is to be fired properly without breaking. A finished piece should be left to dry out and harden slowly. If the weather is particularly dry, you can put damp cloths around it so that the water, when evaporating, maintains ambient humidity that will disappear slowly. In truth, to avoid tensions and cracks on the surface between the parts of a sculpture that are thinner and more exposed to the air (meaning they will dry out faster) and the thicker parts, each must dry out slowly. To stop the finer parts from drying out faster than the rest, causing cracks on the surface, cover them in clear cling wrap for two or three days, until the rest of the clay has dried out. Drying will take longer under the plastic, and the entire piece will be homogenous. By retaining the water, the plastic will let it evaporate slowly, and the damper or thicker parts will let the finer, drier parts take advantage of this gently humid ambience. For the larger, more closed pieces, drying can be finished by placing them on top of a warm kiln. A dry piece ready for the kiln still retains water (6%), which will evaporate during the first 100 degrees of firing.

Firing

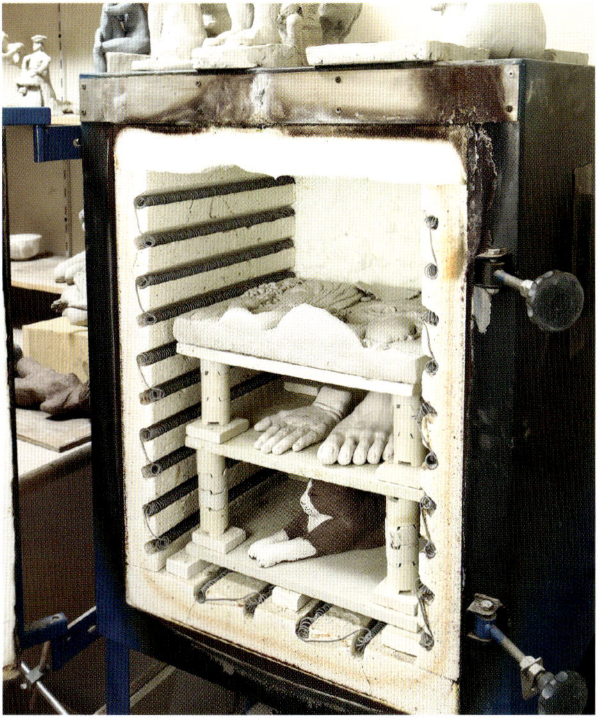

Electric Kiln

Filling the Kiln

The items are put on refractory shelves in the kiln. We use kiln posts of different sizes to separate the shelves; they can be placed three or four on each side of the shelf to give it more stability. These elements usually come with the kiln when you buy it. Start by putting the smaller items at the bottom of the kiln and the larger ones at the top.

Because sculptures are pieces that vary in shape and thickness according to their size, it is important to lengthen the firing time before the clay's fusion, which is at about 1,063°F. Electric kilns allow you to adjust temperature and to program the desired length of time.

> BE CAREFUL!
> Never fire your pieces in a half-full kiln, because this will damage the circuits and you run the risk of your pieces breaking during cooling. This is because when the kiln contains only a few items, the temperature descends too quickly for the clay, which needs time to fix as it continues to transform, even after firing. The temperature in your kiln should be allowed to descend at the same rate that it rises: 10 to 12 hours.
>
> Don't hesitate to put in hollow pieces, which can have small items put under them. You can even put in pieces that have already been fired, to make up the volume if you don't have enough. The fuller your kiln, the more slowly the temperature lowers, which takes into account the transformation procedure.

Earthenware Firing or Low Temperature (1,796°F)

So that earthenware and stoneware pieces finish shrinking and lose their water slowly, I program my kiln with a first stage of 4 hours at 392°F (which is very slow).

I set the second stage for another 4 hours at 1,063°F. At the end of 4 hours the 1,063°F temperature has been reached and the kiln becomes a glowing red: fusion is starting. So that it can "clean out," you should maintain this temperature for 15 minutes, so I program a stage of 15 minutes at 1,063°F, during which time the kiln will stagnate at this temperature.

Then I program the next stage at 1,796°F for 2 hours and the final stage at 1,805°F for 15 minutes. The temperature rises slowly during a firing time of 10 hours and 25 minutes to avoid "assaulting" the piece, which has various thicknesses.

Stoneware Firing (2,336°F)

The first two firing stages are the same as with earthenware, as well as the 15-minute stage at 1,063°F. Then we program at 1,832°F for 2 hours, 30 minutes, followed by 2,192°F for 1 hour, 30 minutes, and finally a last stage for 15 minutes at 2,345°F, or a rise of temperature over a period of 12 hours, 45 minutes.

Cooling

For the two types of firing, the thermostat stops rising and the temperature lowers slowly over a period of 12 hours, without turning the kiln off or touching the temperature dial.

No matter what, don't open the kiln until the temperature reaches 176°F, to avoid damaging the circuits. You can then open the kiln and check that everything has been properly fired, because the results can sometimes be somewhat dramatic if the basic principles haven't been followed (see "Accidents" on page 12). The result can be astonishing, because during firing the mix of colored oxides and the clay produces an alchemy between the different pieces that never produces an identical effect. This means that each firing is delicate and unique and entails risk that you should anticipate before starting.

Patina

Patina is a surface treatment that we give to the clay once it has been fired to give back the sheen it lost during drying out (evaporation) and during firing; the damp matter shows reflections of light, shine, and color that sometimes disappear in the kiln, and it takes on a matte aspect—dry, hard, and a different color. The result when it comes out of the kiln is therefore often disappointing, sometimes showing defects that weren't apparent before firing. Patina can also bring out certain details that firing didn't highlight, or modify the color if it isn't the desired result.

The Importance of Patina

Patina brings out and revives things that have been weakened or erased during firing, and restores reflections and the plasticity of the matter lost during the evaporation of water. Everything is a question of regard: patina should bring out the reliefs and soften the hollows. Just like makeup on a face, posing a lighter color around the eye adds light and hides the dark circles under the eye. Patina should act like the sun when it tans and magnifies the prominent parts of the face (cheekbones, forehead, nose, and chin), the rest being less tanned because they are less prominent. Light tones should be applied to the hollows and darker tones on the prominent parts to valorize your piece.

In spite of the multitude of patinas on sale, with experience you can be guided by your intuition and try out new ones, creating associations of colors or compatible materials that can be astonishing. Patina is the result of alchemy between chemical matters and the harmony of colors.

At first, it's a question of choosing the medium (or mediums) that will settle the pigments onto the fired piece. Personally, I work with two sorts of mediums:

- Thin water-based medium: Caparol binding medium (vinyl medium)
- Oily medium: shellac (natural resin)

For a long time now I have patinaed my pieces with shellac, and sometimes I add wax or polish after drying, but I have also started experimenting with Caparol—a vinyl medium—with very good results. You should know that a vinyl medium is chemically incompatible with an acrylic one, so choose one or the other but never mix them, or paint one on top of the other.

Shellac

Shellac is a medium obtained by dissolving a bronze resin (yellow/red/amber) secreted by the female *Kerria lacca* (Asian lac bug), which is collected in India and Southeast Asia. Imported in flakes, it is dissolved in ethanol to obtain a homogenous bronze-colored mixture with varying degrees of tone. This natural polymer can be compared to natural plastic and was used in the twentieth century to make the first vinyl records. These days it is used by cabinetmakers and violin makers to protect wood, but also in foodstuffs to protect fruit (wax) and in pharmaceuticals to shroud certain medications.

For patinas, it is best to use white shellac (to avoid influencing the color). More neutral, it won't influence (or will influence only a little) the color you want with the pigments. You can also use it neat to polish your sculpture. You can buy it ready-made or prepare your own in small quantities (see below) in small, airtight pots or bottles. Shellac becomes sticky or hard when drying, and it is sometimes difficult to open the top of the pot. In this case, soak it in ethanol, since the shellac softens up in contact with ethanol.

Using patina is a little like doing your own cooking recipes: it is difficult to give exact quantities. There should be enough shellac to settle the pigment and cover the clay with a sufficiently thick layer. So that the undercoat that entirely covers the sculpture lasts, it should be rich in shellac and have had dried out properly and hardened. When painting it on, use a thick, supple brush.

Making Your Mixture of White Shellac

Pour 200 milliliters (ml) of ethanol into a jar and add 50 g of white shellac flakes (you can find it in fine-arts stores).

Put the lid on the jar, turn it upside down, and shake it every two or three minutes—each time you see the shellac sinking to the bottom. Do this for about an hour to mix the flakes and the ethanol in a homogenous way, and to stop the shellac settling on the bottom in a lump that will be difficult to dissolve quickly. After about two hours the ethanol starts to dissolve the flakes, and the mixture darkens. Let it settle, shaking it from time to time. You'll have to wait until the next day for the ethanol to have finished dissolving the flakes and to have a homogeneous bronze-colored mixture that is very fluid and looks like honey. In stores, the mixture you'll find has different qualities and not quite the same tint.

Basic Patina Material

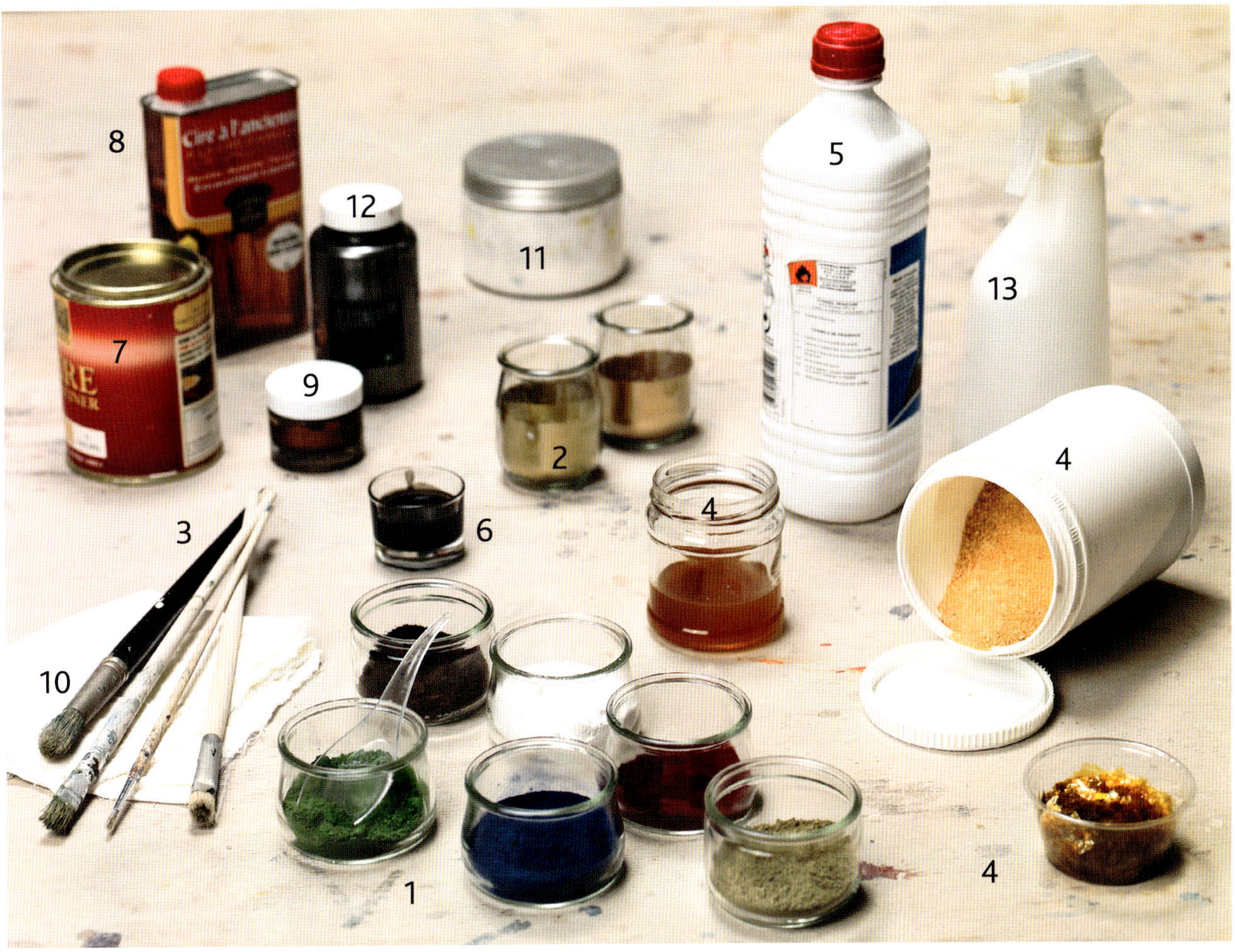

Natural colored pigments (1); gold-colored pigments (2); different-sized thick, supple brushes (3); white shellac in flakes or powder if you want to make your own, or ready-made (4); ethanol for diluting the shellac, cleaning the brushes, or patina (5); Indian ink for black color before using a patina with an oily or water base (6); colorless antique wax polish for shining after the patina (7); colorless liquid antique wax that can be used before the shellac or mixed with pigment (as a medium in this case) (8); gold-colored polishing wax or patina (9); cloths (10); Caparol (vinyl medium) (11); pencil lead for metalizing the patina (12); and a spray bottle for adding water to the Caparol (13). You'll also need glass recipients for mixing.

ADVICE

Some materials or mixtures are chemically incompatible. As in painting, we can pass an oily or solvent-based product onto a water-based undercoat, but not the reverse.

Shellac mixes nicely with antique wax, but you should never add water, because it doesn't dissolve in alcohol. You'll lose your shellac-covered brushes if you put them in water, which will harden the shellac and turn them into hard plastic. Oily or solvent-based products aren't compatible with thin, watery products.

You can use wax as a patina or acrylic, a vinyl medium, shellac, linseed oil, oil paints . . . You just need to have neutral mediums on hand and add them to the pigments that color them.

Patina Examples

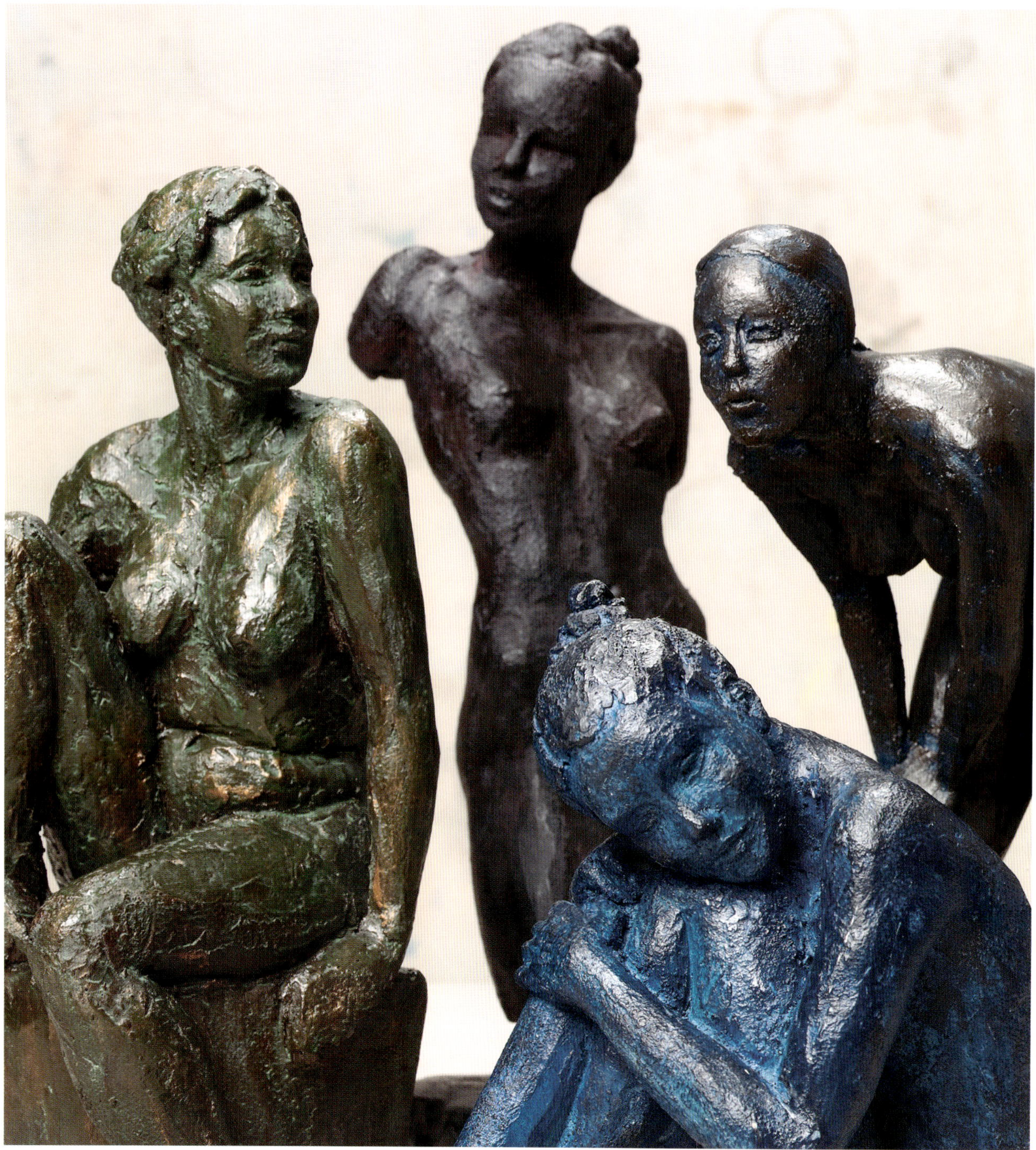

Center foreground: *blue patina: shellac base with thistle-blue pigment on white clay, then a superficial patina with shellac and thistle-blue and black pigments*
Left foreground: *bronze green patina: shellac base with burnt umber pigment, ethanol-based inlay with chrome-green pigment, superficial patina with burnt umber pigment, then polished with copper-colored wax polish*
Background center: *Bronze burgundy and black pigment: shellac and black pigment undercoat, ethanol-based inlay with magenta and burnt umber pigments, superficial patina with shellac and black and burnt umber pigments*
Background right: *blue-bronze patina with Caparol: Caparol undercoat with thistle-blue pigment on white clay, surface patina with Caparol, burnt umber and gold pigments, polished with pencil lead on a cloth*

Valorizing the Color of the Clay

If you are satisfied with the color of the clay and you just want to highlight and differentiate the reliefs and the hollows to valorize your work, you just need to rub the prominent parts with a tone slightly darker than the natural color of the clay. The medium can be shellac mixed with pigments and rubbed in almost dry (you need a dry cloth and little mixture). Or you can use an acrylic or vinyl medium (Caparol), or colorless wax polish mixed with pigments. Pass your patina in every direction, brushing with your brush almost dry. The color—very slightly darker—will bring out the matter and give it character.

Bronze-Green Patina and Caparol

Caparol is a vinyl medium that can be used instead of shellac. Its composition is thinner, and it can be diluted and cleaned with water. Some people use it highly diluted in a succession of colored touches, while others prefer it almost neat: it therefore gives a satiny aspect to the clay and works well with pencil lead if you want to add it when you have finished the patina.

Doing a patina on this foot was carried out in three successive operations: a first coat in Caparol and chrome-green pigment, a second dry coat on the prominent parts with Caparol and gold and burnt umber pigments, and finally, the last coat with pencil lead on a cloth on the prominent parts (see the steps showing the entire creation on page 54).

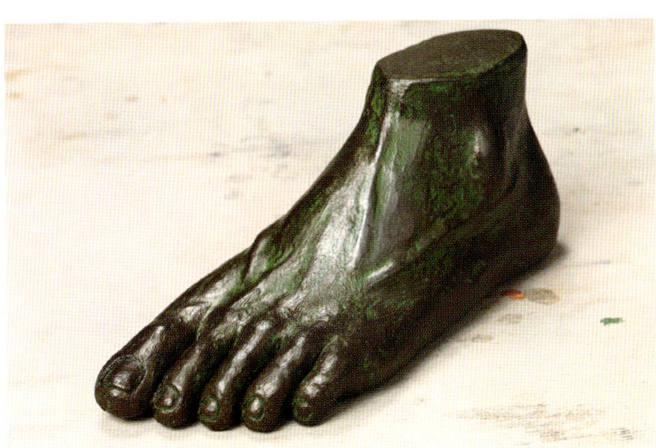

NOTE

You can also do a succession of acrylic or vinyl coats first and then finish with shellac, but never the other way round, since the thinner liquid won't adhere to the oily one. Do a patina in India ink and acrylic ink on the porous clay and finish with shellac or wax polish. Do a patina using linseed oil and wax polish under and over the shellac.

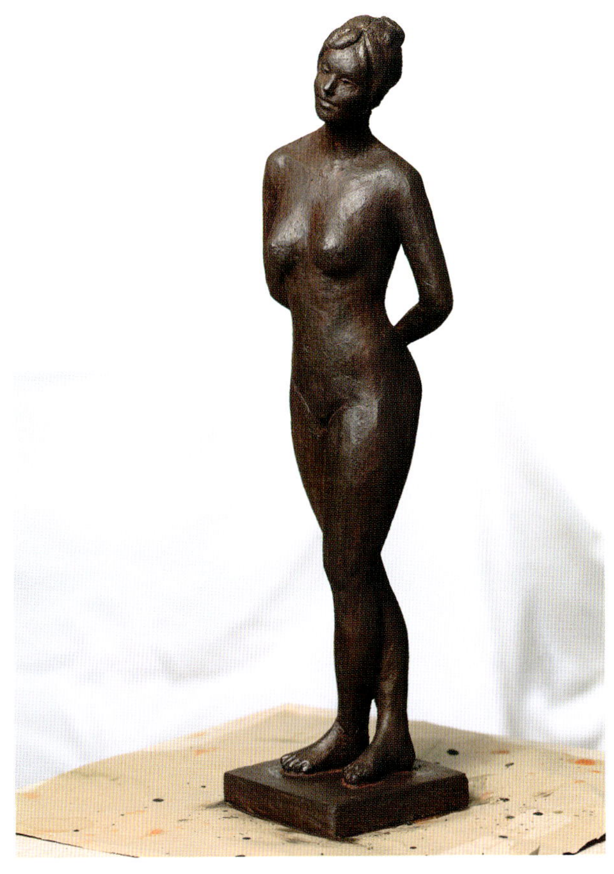

Rust and Shellac Patina

This patina is more complex. It was carried out in five successive operations: the first coat comprising shellac and gold pigment; the second coat with shellac and burnt umber; the third with ethanol and iron-red pigment; the fourth with shellac and burnt umber and gold pigments only on the prominent parts; and finally, the fifth coat with pencil lead on the prominent parts (see the steps showing the entire creation on page 82).

Cleaning Tools after Doing a Patina

- Shellac: Clean your brushes only in ethanol. Don't use water until the shellac has entirely dissolved in ethanol. Don't pour the residual shellac/ethanol down the drain—throw it in the trash, because ethanol will evaporate, leaving a residue of resin.
- Acrylic or vinyl: Clean with water, or if the mixture has dried, clean with ethanol and then rinse in water.
- Oil paint: Clean in turpentine and then soapy water.
- Ink: Start by rinsing in water and then clean in soapy water.
- Wax or polish: Clean in turpentine and then in hot, soapy water.

The Human Body

The Skull

Before starting on the face, it is necessary to observe and represent the skull. This exercise and the one following it are very important because they will help you learn and spot the underlying structure better. Naturally, when you do a portrait you represent only the exterior aspect of the face.

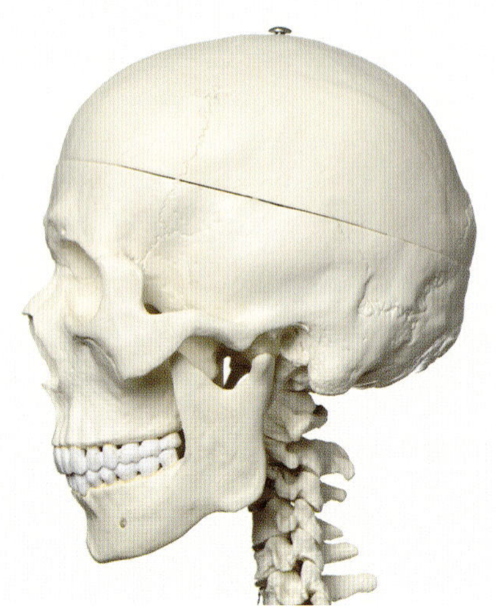

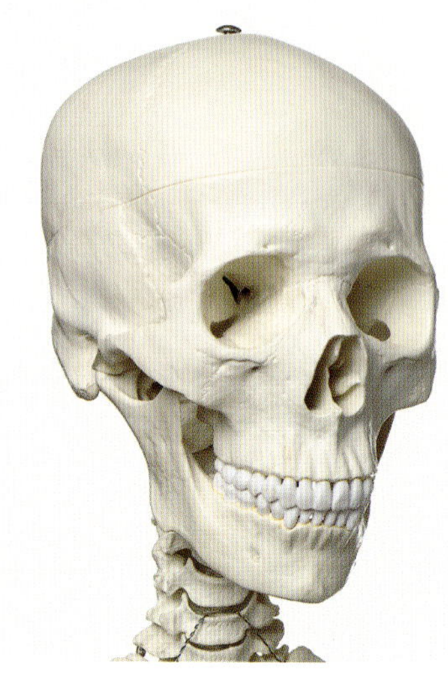

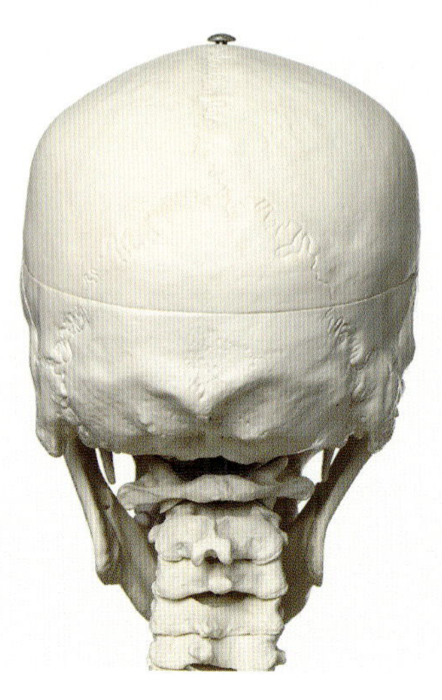

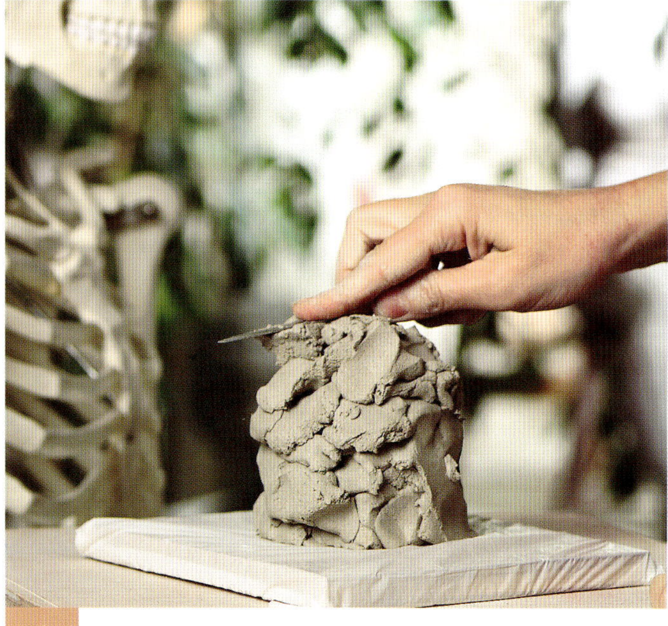

1 Place a skull in profile or a photo nearby. Start working on the contours of the profile, imagining the neck that supports the skull upright; build a solid cylindrical base.

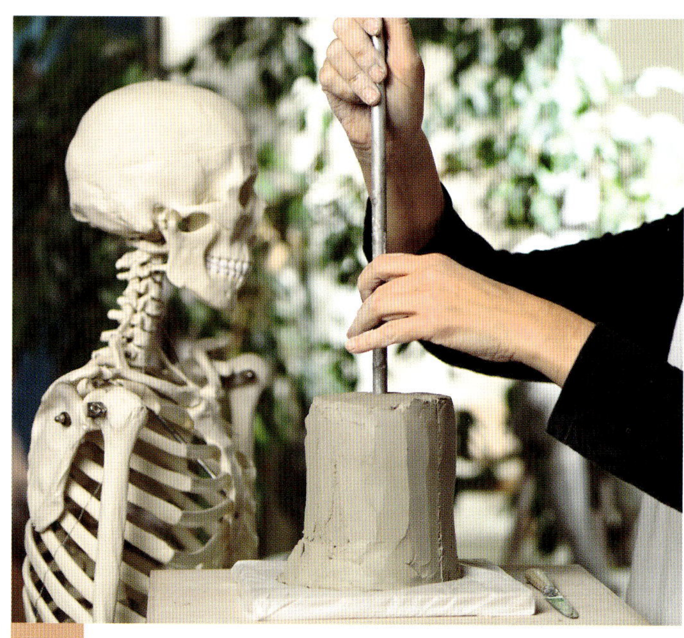

2 Place a rod in the center, where the backbone would be. This rod will also give the clay something to adhere to while you build the base.

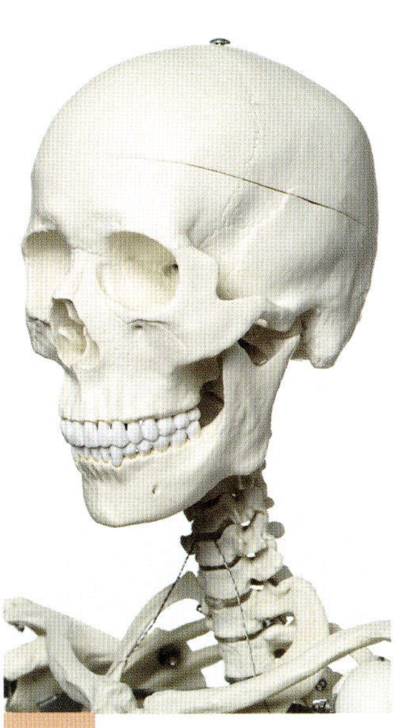

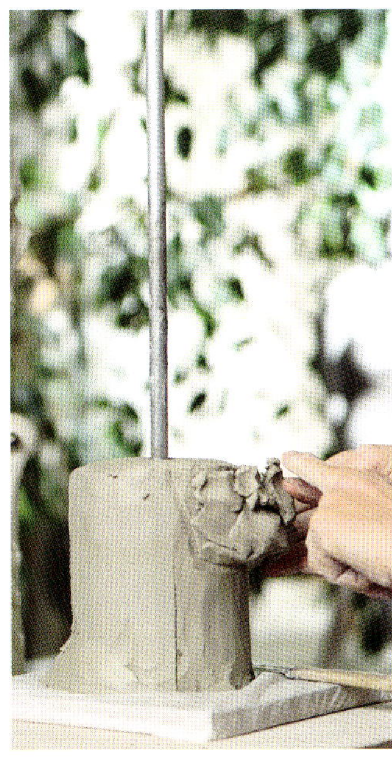

3

Trace a vertical line to divide the neck's profile in two. The jaw is the basis of the skull. Seen in profile, it forms an "L" (or an elbow) of equal sections. Seen from below it is triangular and rounded. Seen from the front it seems both triangular and rounded at the base. From a three-quarter point of view we can see that its projection has a rounded point. On the basis of your model, place the base of the jaw, noting that it extends out from the neck by about half its width.

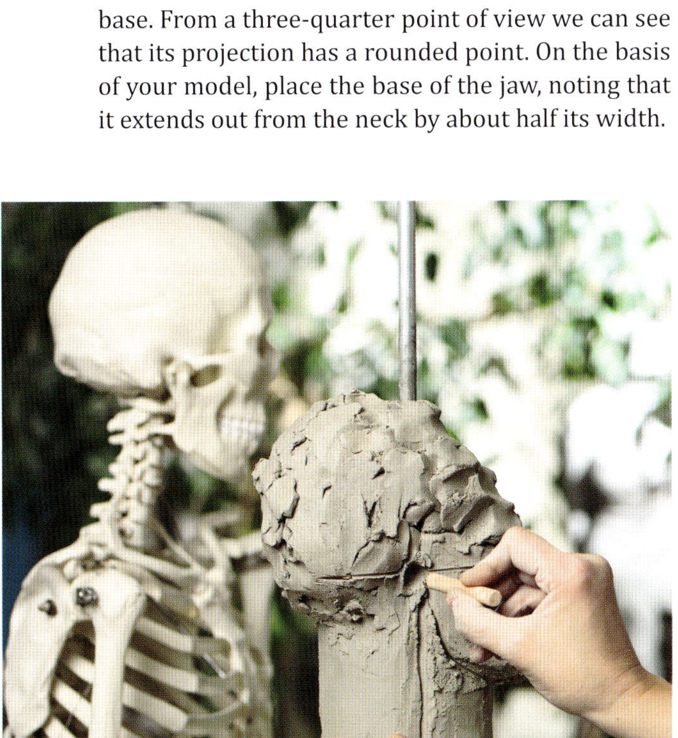

4

Start shaping the back of the skull. The earhole is at the extremity of the jawbone. It is at this point that the back of the skull begins and extends out from the neck by about half of the neck's width.

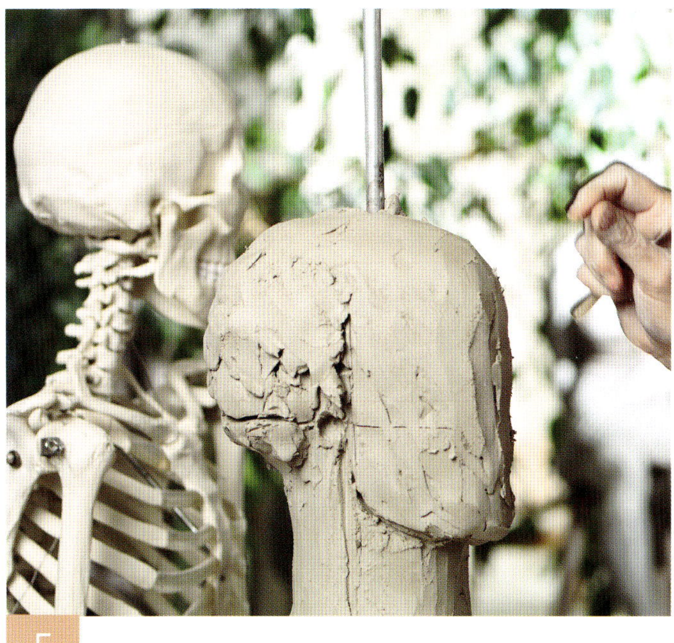

5

Increase the neck to this point and continue to work on the profile, using the central rod to adhere the clay. Build the face's profile vertically from the chin to just over the forehead, the arch of the eyebrows aligning with the chin. Round out the top of the skull slightly.

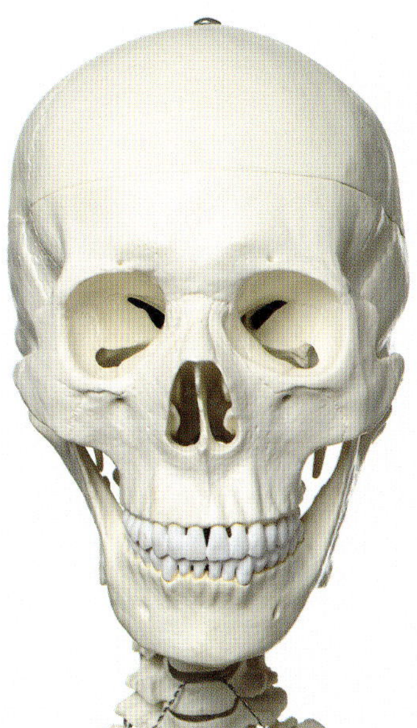

6

Continuing from the contours of the skull's volume, start working face on to build the general oval shape. Fill your volume face on, starting from the general contour. Seen from above, the forehead is narrower than the back, seat of our brain, and is slightly hollow in a slanting direction on a level with the temples. These are the temporal fenestrae.

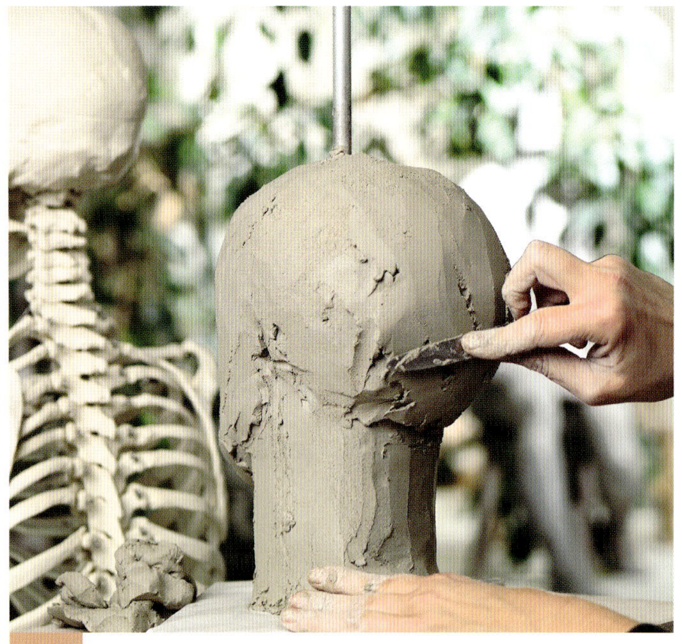

7 Finish the back of the skull; it has a rounded shape. Compare it to your model and correct missing places or surplus where necessary.

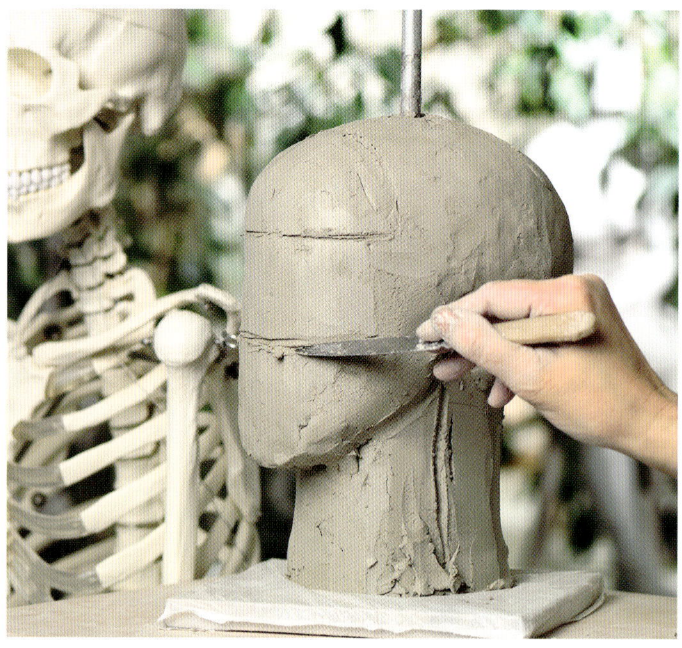

BE CAREFUL!

When you do a portrait, check that the face is "three part" or not (see step 8), because some people have different proportions. In addition, the proportions of the parts that make up the face of a child are different to those of an adolescent and those of an adult, because they develop with time: the top part of the skull decreases and the others increase.

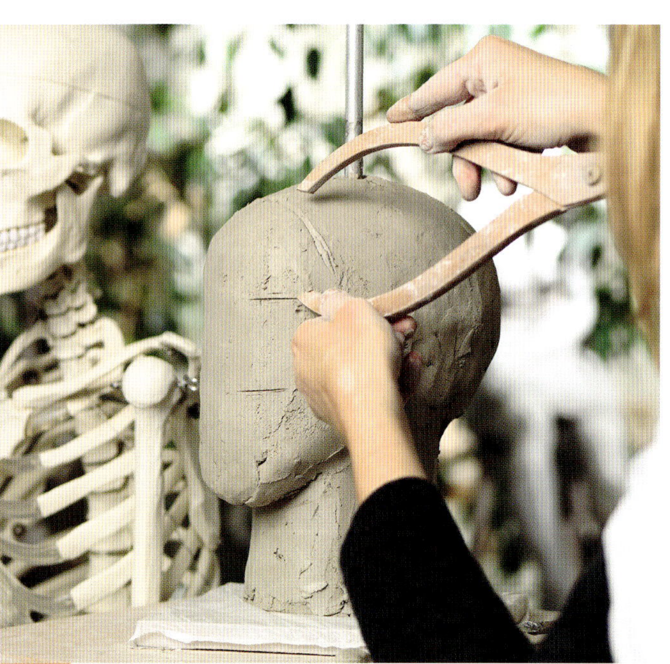

8 Trace the main lines of the face's structure in profile. The top part (the forehead) starts at the hairline and ends at the eyebrows' arches. The central part (eye sockets, nose, and cheekbones) ends at the roots of the teeth. Finally, the bottom part corresponds to the jaw (teeth and chin). Each of these three parts has the same height; it is a "three-part" structure. The eyebrows' arches are on the same vertical plane as the chin. The volumes that stand out are the cartilage of the nose and the teeth.

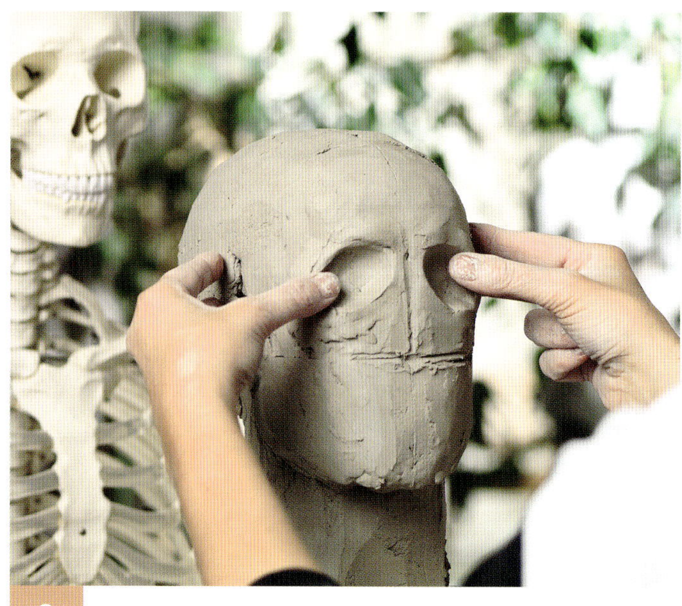

9 Draw a vertical line for the nose. The eyebrow's arches surmount the eye sockets. Draw in the cavities and hollow them out on a slanting direction toward the temples.

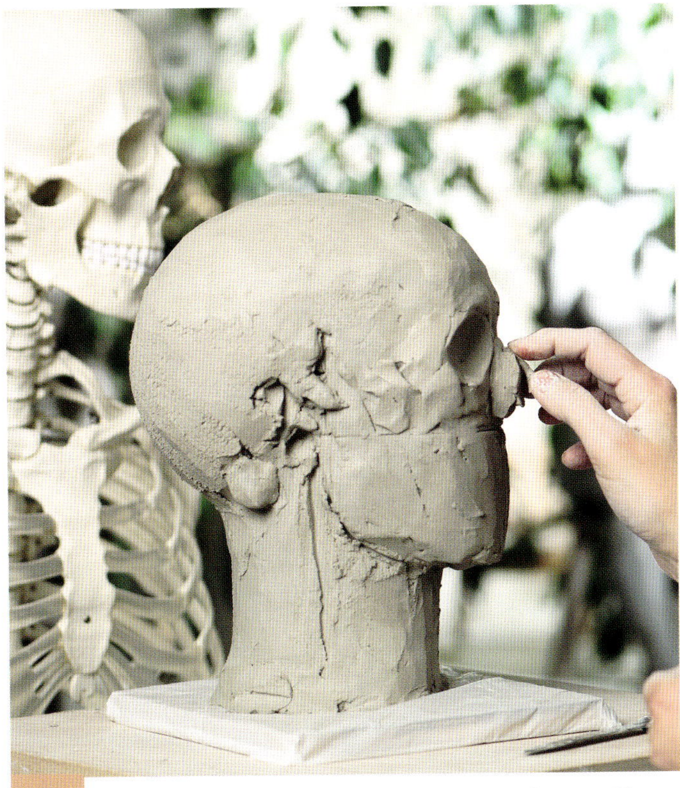

10 In profile, two volumes will stand out: the nasal bone and the upper maxilla (the roots of the teeth), and also the teeth. Do these from a profile view.

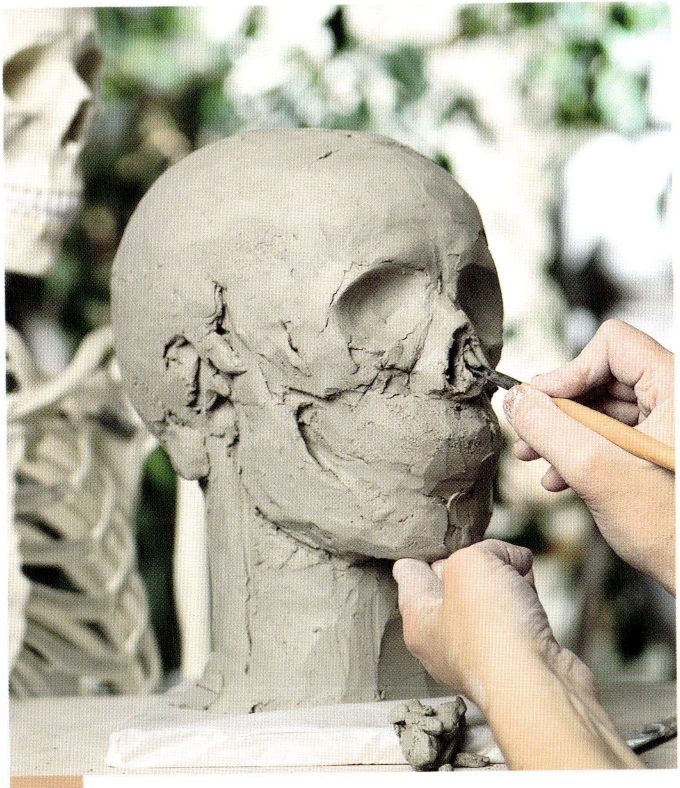

11 Turn the head toward you and open the nasal fossae.

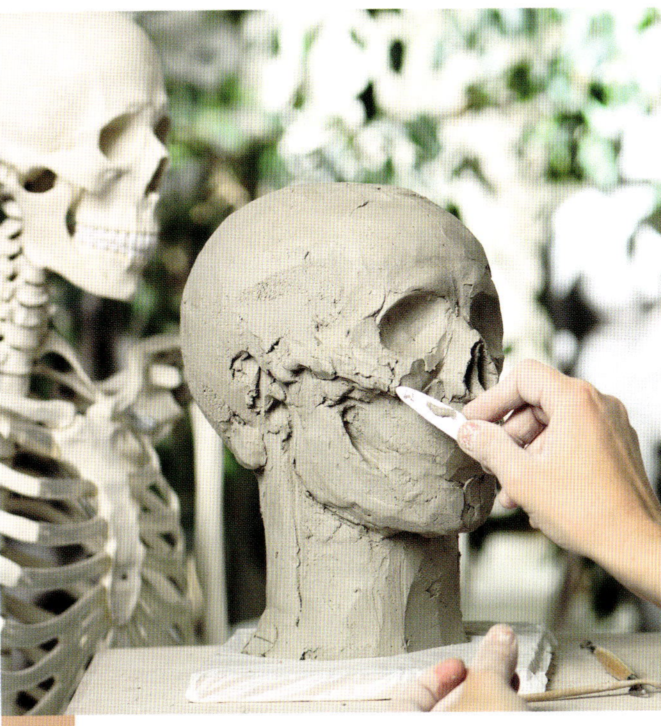

12 The jugal bone, which forms the cheeks, is found under the eye sockets. It is rather slim and slightly set back from the eyebrow arch, and it extends toward the extremity of the jaw to the meatus (opening of the ear canal) by a long, thin bone: the zygoma.

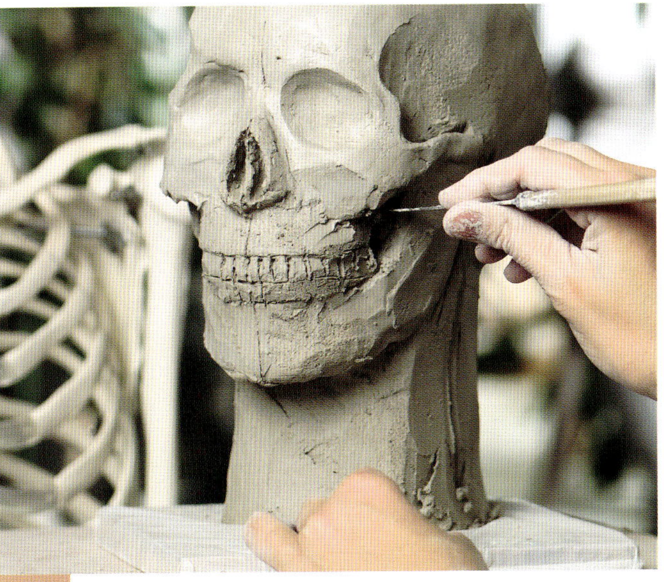

13 To finish the skull, do the teeth on the domed part that you made, below the base of the nose and descending toward the chin. There is an empty space between the teeth and the mandible.

The Face

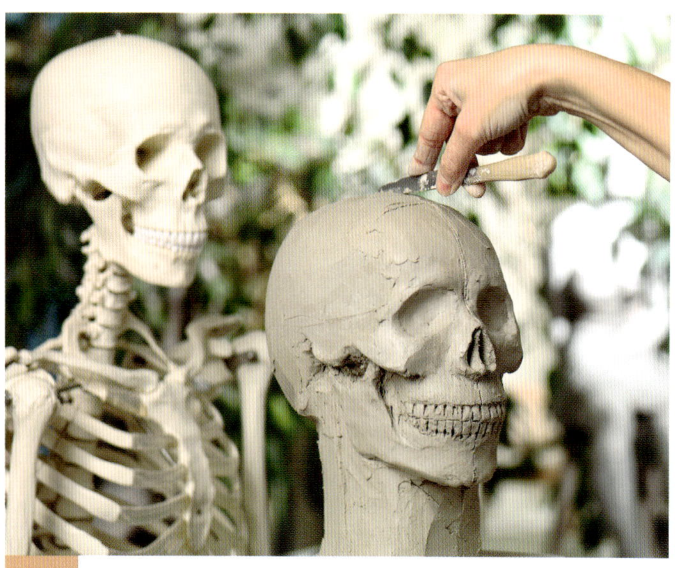

1 We are now going to reconstitute half of the face onto the skull by adding the facial muscles and elements of cartilage that structure the volume. Start by tracing a vertical line to separate the skull in half.

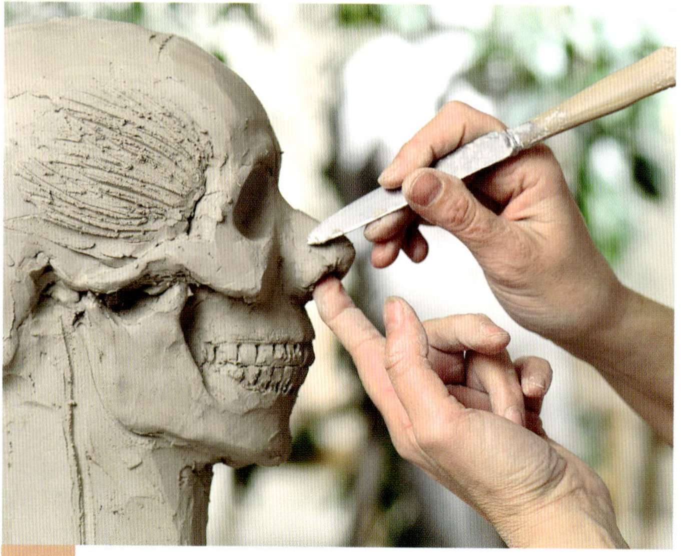

2 By adding on clay, place the temporal muscle over the temporal fenestrae and score it. Now shape the nose. If your skull's structure is correct, the volume of the nose should descend, slanting on each side toward the cheekbones and the cheeks.

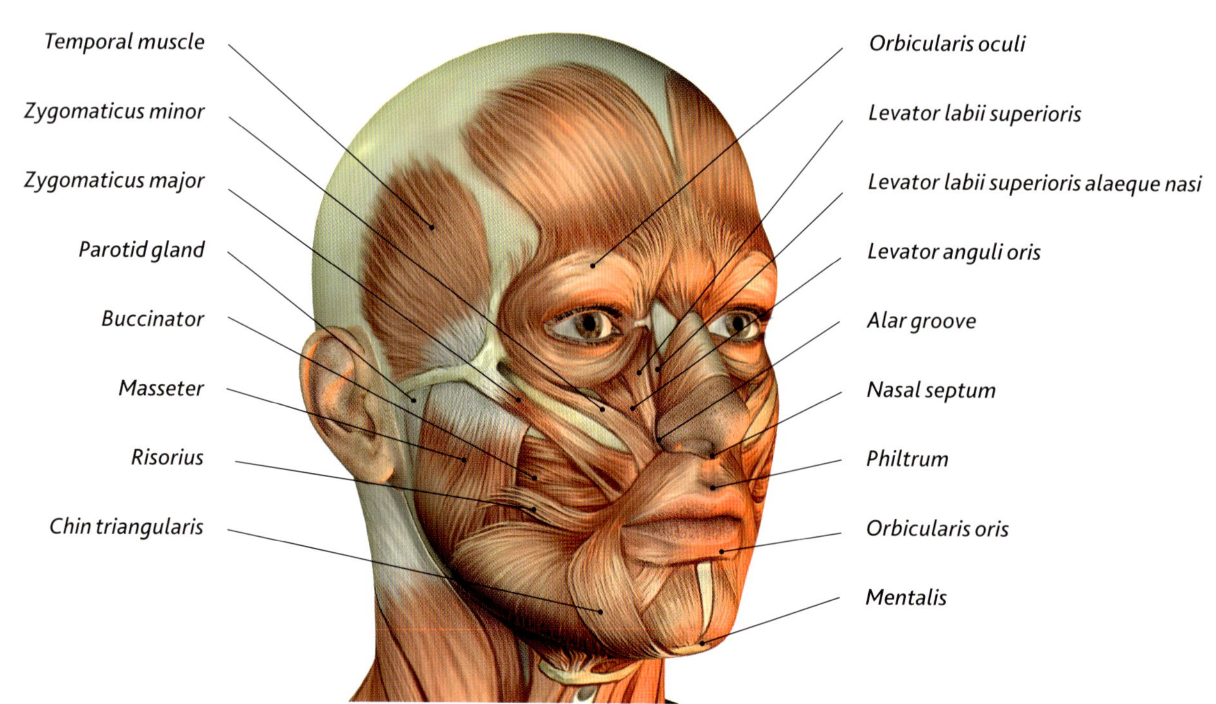

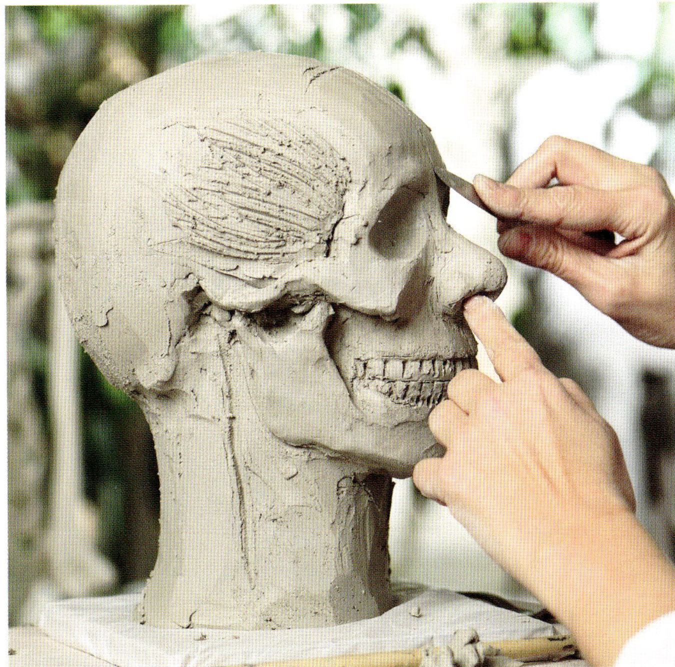

3 Form the nose's wing and the alar groove. For the cartilage at the tip of the nose, which is rounder, place a ball of clay at the end of the nose and join it by pressing on it gently. Shape the nasal septum with a small sausage of clay between the two nostrils. Hollow out the nostrils and make sure the wings don't overlap the septum, since they are slightly behind it, leaving a glimpse of the nostril hole.

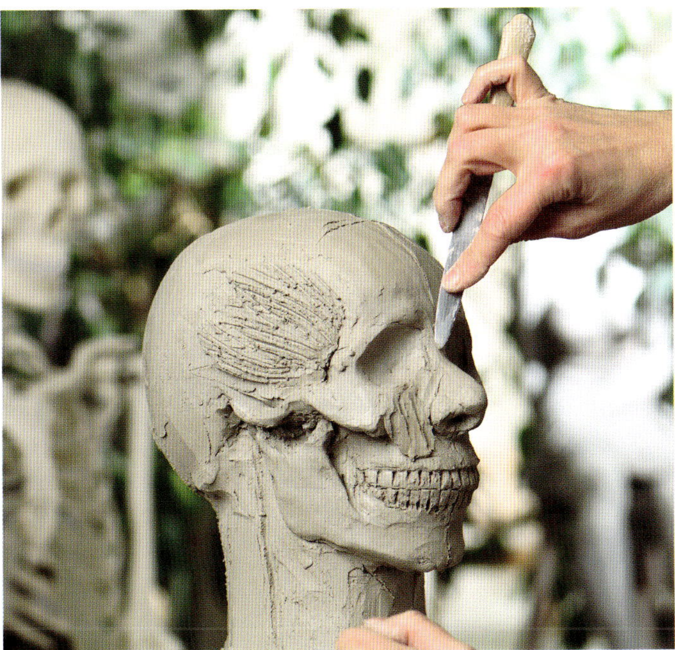

4 Place three long, slim muscles (the levator labii superioris alaeque nasi, the levator labii superioris, and the levator anguli oris) onto the jugal bone, along the nose and down toward the maxilla bone.

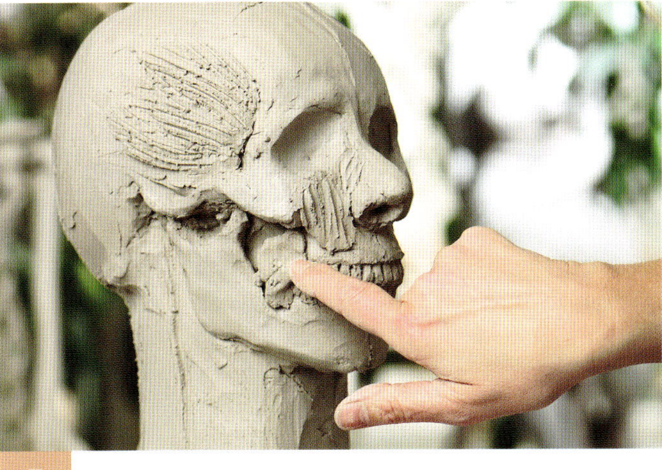

5 Fill in the hole between the mandible and the teeth with the buccinator (a deep horizontal muscle).

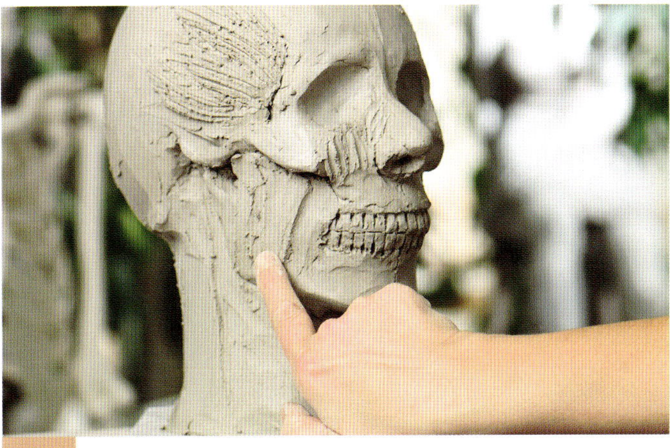

6 Now place the masseter (the vertical muscle that goes from the zygomaticus bone toward the mandible). The buccinator and the masseter superimpose in an orthogonal manner.

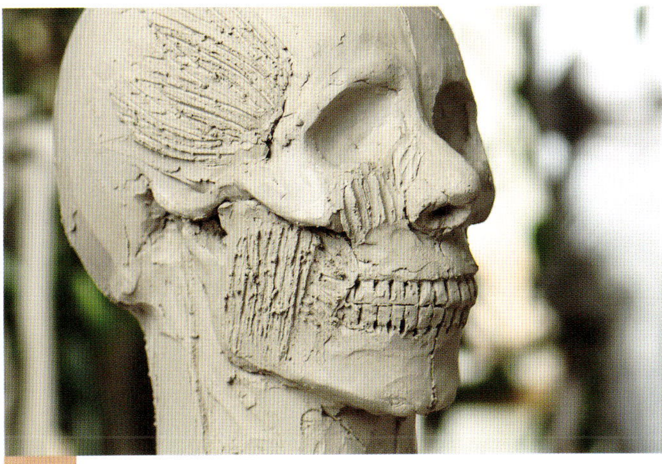

7 Score the different muscles to see them more clearly.

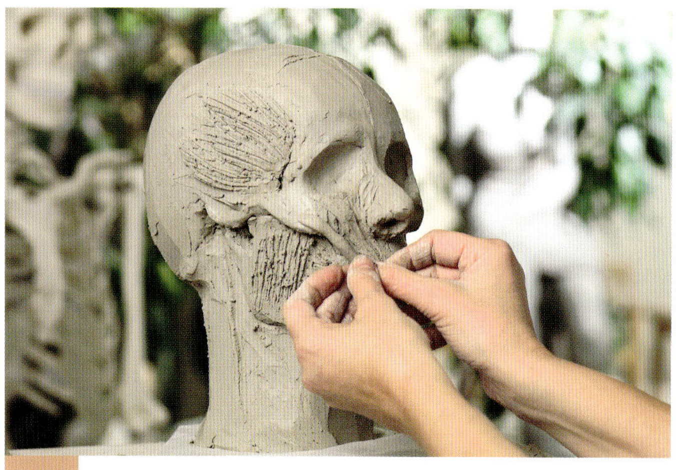

8 Place the two zygomatica (the smaller is closer to the nose).

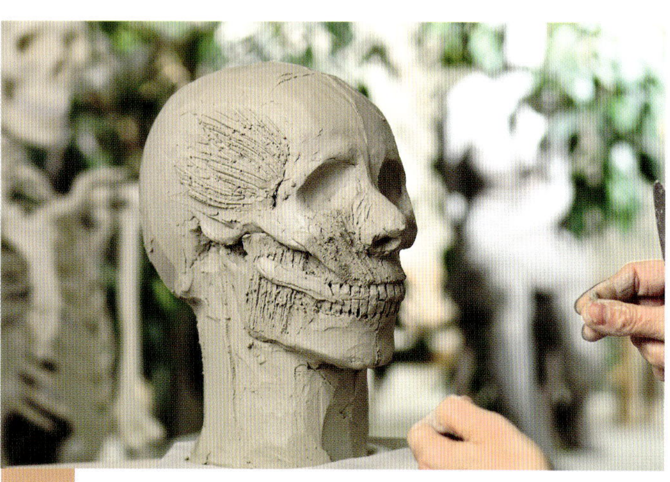

9 Add the risorius (a long, thin muscle).

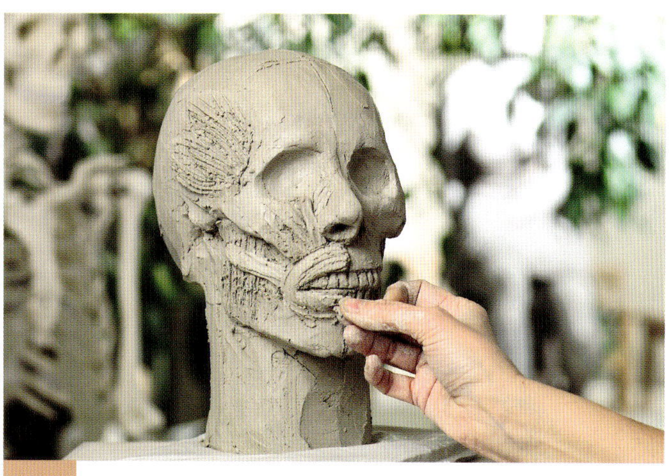

10 Slightly cover the maxilla and the mandible with the orbicularis oris muscle.

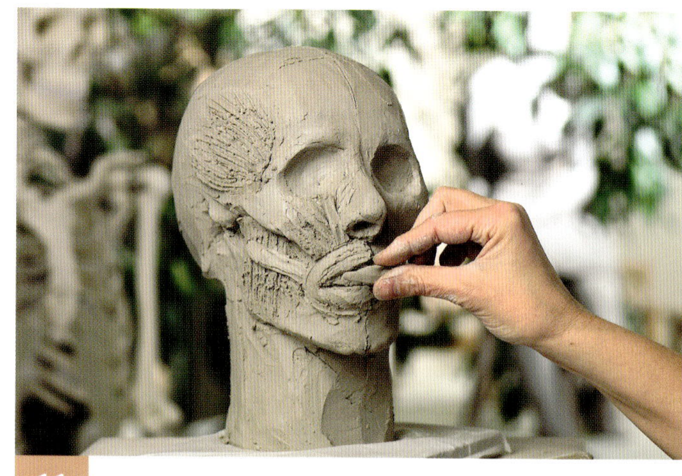

11 Place the upper lip at the edge of the orbicularis over the upper teeth, and the bottom lip over the bottom teeth.

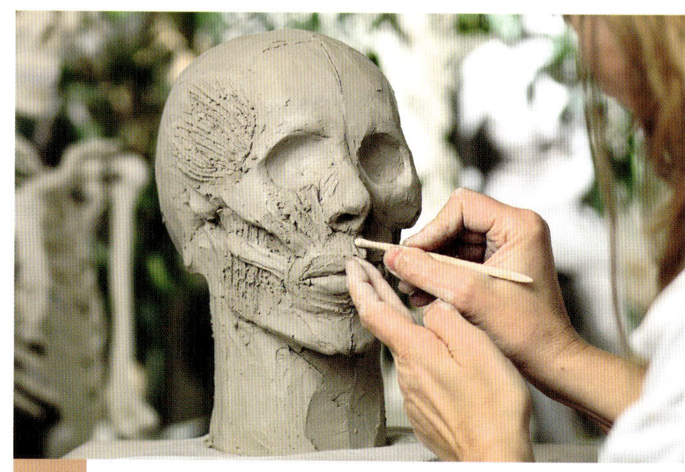

12 Shape the philitrum (the dimple in the center of the upper lip) under the nasal septum by scraping slightly with a small, roundheaded clay knife.

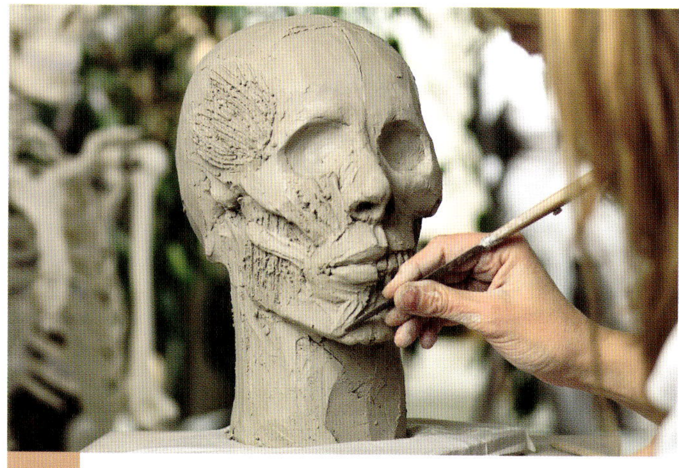

13 Place the chin triangularis and the mentalis under the curved part that will be the mouth. Join each added on part with a spatula or with your finger.

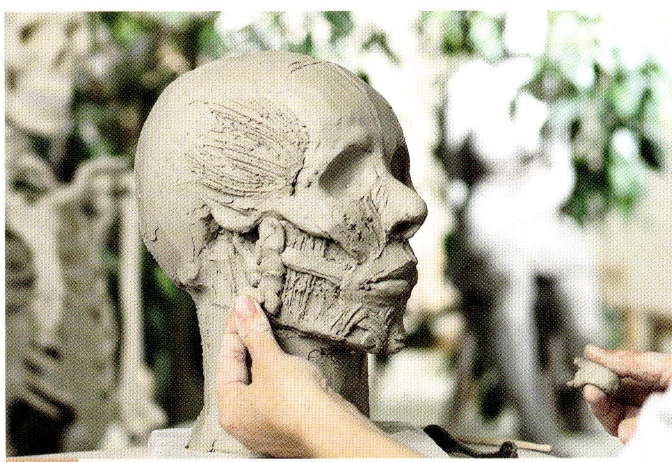

14 Next, place the parotid gland at the extremity of the mandible.

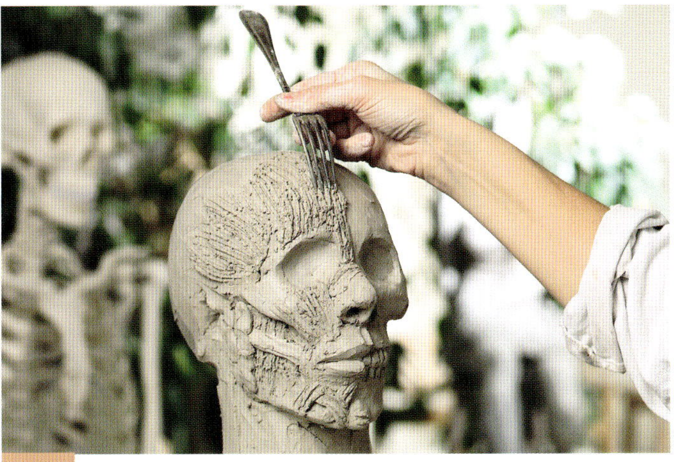

15 Add the fine top nasal and forehead muscles.

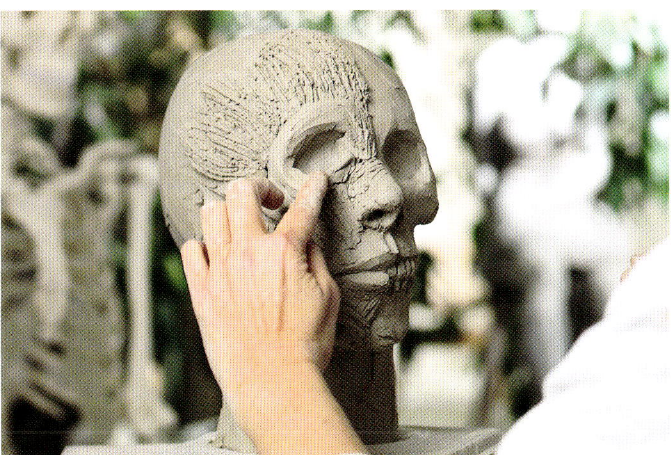

16 Now we are going to work on the arch of the eyebrow and shape the eye. Place the peripheral muscles around the eye and puff out the arch above; this is the orbicularis oculus.

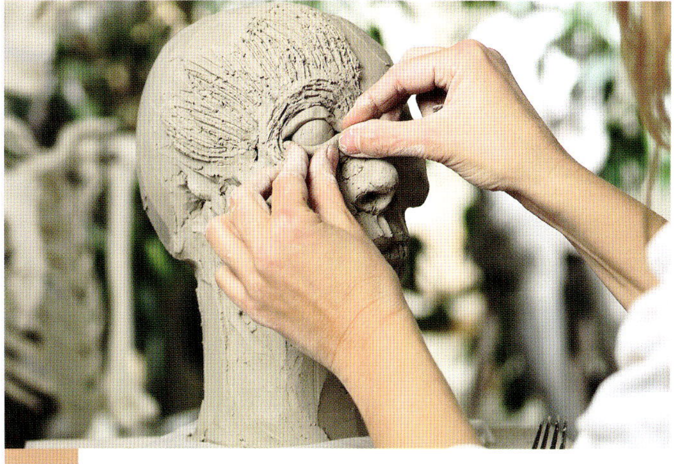

17 Place a ball of clay (for the eyeball) in the hollow of the eye socket and then shape the upper and bottom eyelids with clay sausages that you will add around the eyeball.

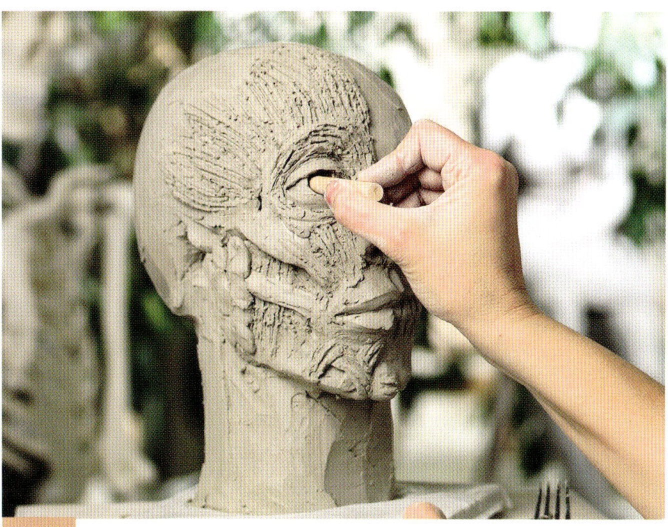

18 The almond-shaped globe you have placed must be properly rounded off, because the eye is a sphere embedded in the socket and can't be flat. Dig out each extremity to accentuate the spherical aspect. Now shape the regard by creating a hole vertically aligned with the corner of the mouth.

NOTE

Light-colored eyes are represented by a circle that we trace, and then we dig out several small holes very lightly to simulate the light and the depth of the regard. Dark-colored eyes are dug out and also have several small, deeper holes that simulate the regard and the light it reflects.

19 Using a clay knife, slightly smooth out the white of the eye around the pupil and delimit the corner of the eye (tear duct). Smooth out the eyelid, and if you want, you can add eyelashes with a small, thin, lightly grooved clay sausage.

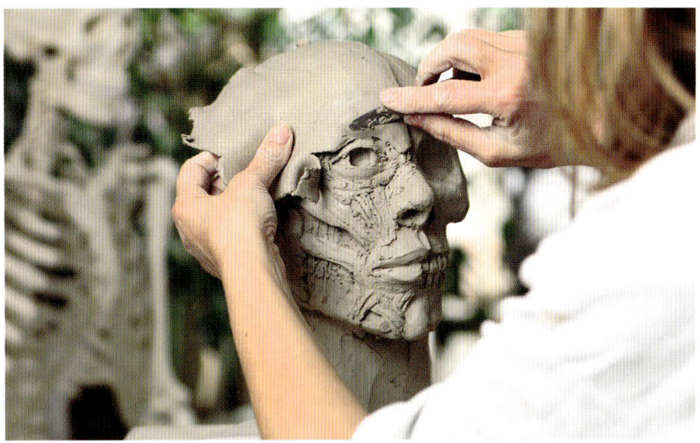

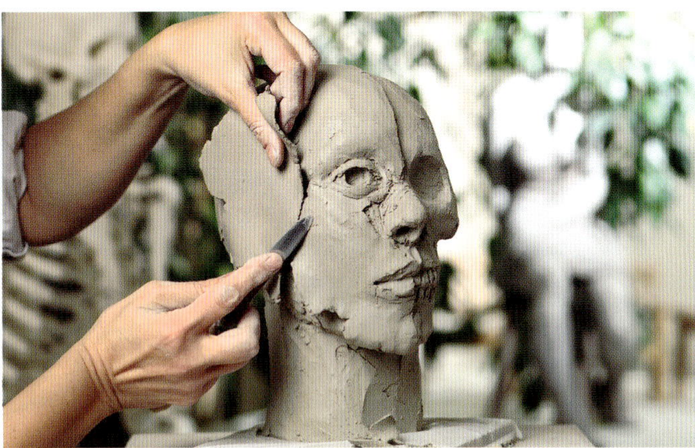

20 Make a small, thin slab that will act as skin to hide the muscles.

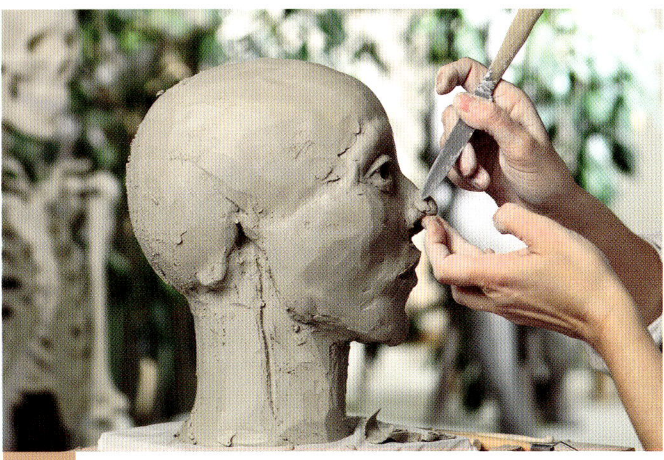

21 Place the slabs over the muscles with slip and smooth out the seams with a knife.

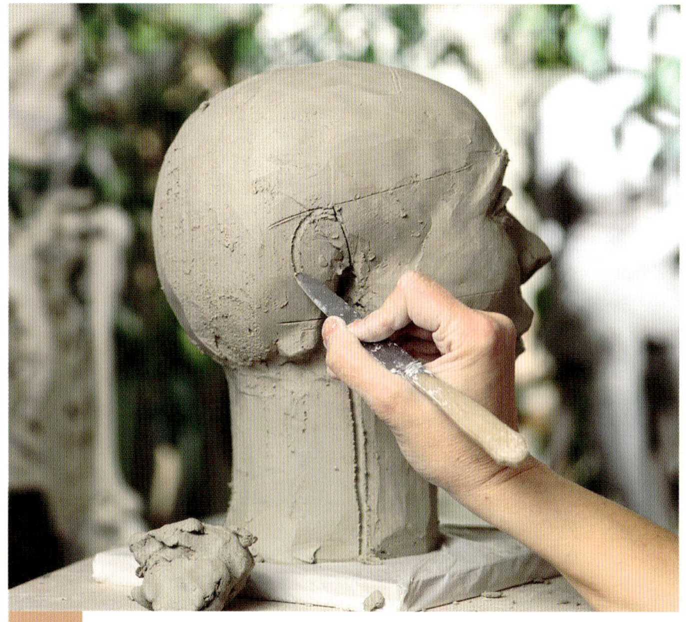

22 The ear looks like a corolla—a complicated piece of jewelry—and adds the finishing touch to the face. Determine its location in profile: it is situated level with the earhole (the meatus) at the extremity of the maxilla and can be placed on a straight or slightly slanting line toward the back of the skull.

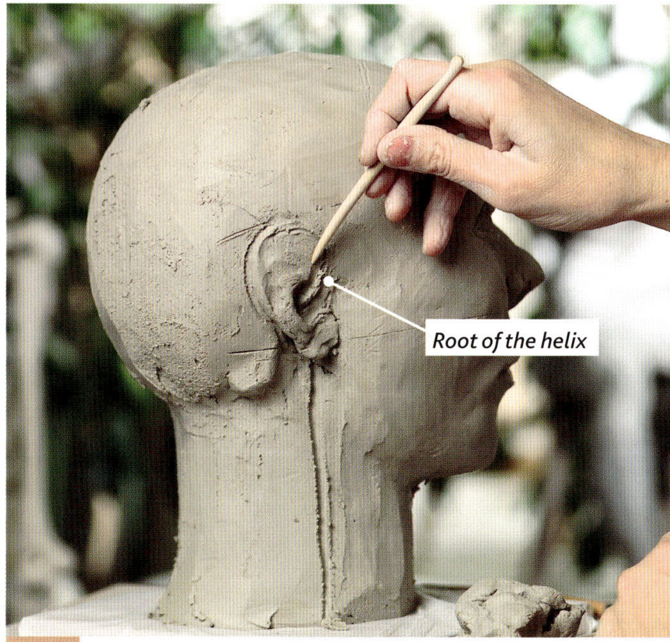

23 To place the flat shape of the auricle, trace a slightly descending line from the eyebrow and a straight line from under the nose. The ear will be placed at this spot. Its flat shape sticks out from the skull. Behind, its shape is puffed out. To shape the circumvolutions, which seem complex, you just draw and form the root of the helix (snail) that enters into the ear on a level with the cavity called the "concha" and divides it into two parts.

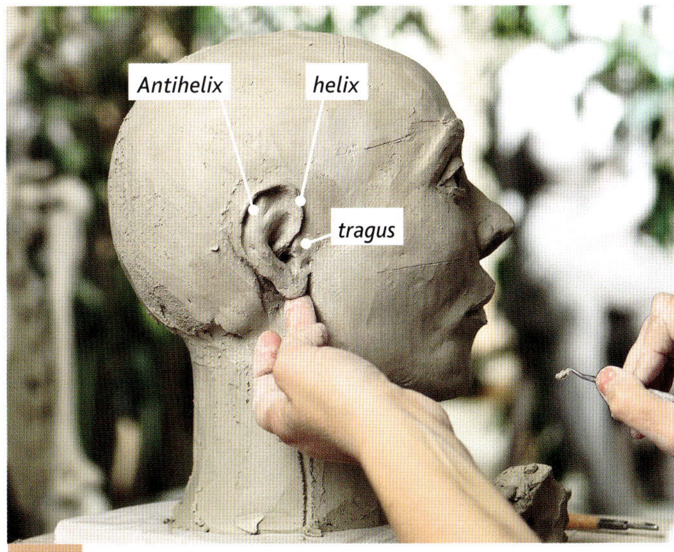

24 Continue by placing the folded part of the helix all around the auricle. It looks like a question mark. Add the tragus toward the front like a small tongue. Then mark out the two branches of cartilage, between which is a triangular hollow. Now add the central part of the ear (the antihelix) at the top. Add a ball of clay to the lobe to make it rounder.

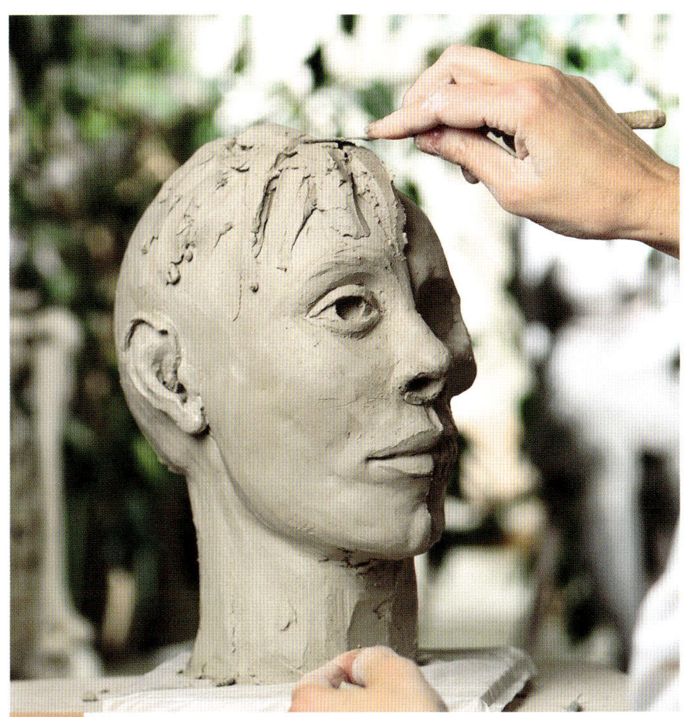

25 Start to place the hair, which should be treated as a volume organized around the skull. Even when hair is messy, we can see the mass, groups of locks, and more-voluminous parts. However, each lock seeming to detach itself from the rest should be attached (even discreetly) to the skull by a volume that supports it.

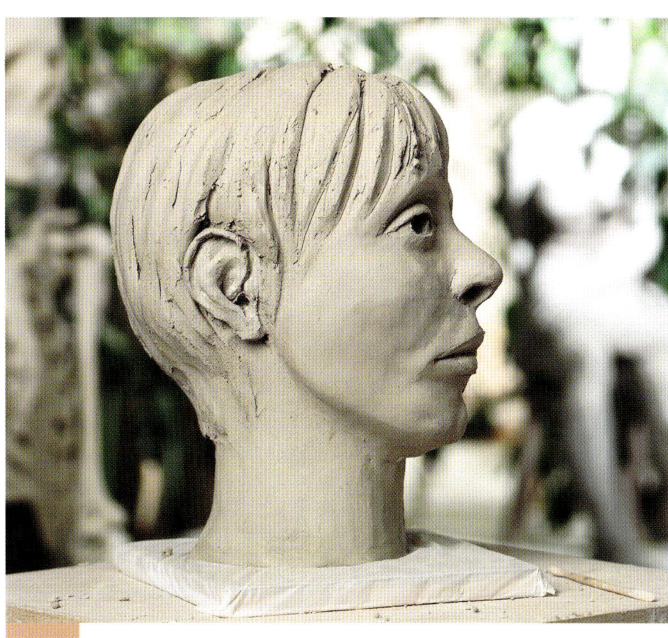

26 It isn't necessary to do a lot of lines, but it is important to organize the different masses around the skull. Start at the bottom and finish with the upper locks that you can give movement to. Separate a lock from time to time.

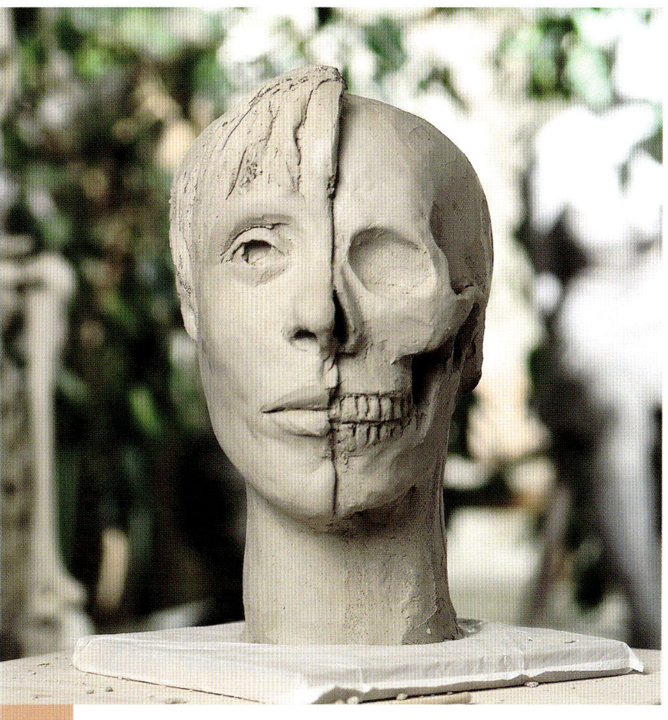

27 This exercise is very instructive, and I advise you to keep it and fire it to give you inspiration each time you have a doubt when creating a face. It will act as a guide, helping you create the proper structure and learn from your errors. Take photos of each different step so you remember how you made this item.

The Hand

1 At first a hand seems very complex. In fact, it is the element of the human body that is the most articulated, the most elaborate, and the supplest. Therefore, the hand needs to be schematized and its representation synthesized. It is made up of three large parts:

- the palm, which regroups the eight carpal bones constituting the wrist and four metacarpal bones
- the fingers, comprising three phalanges as a continuation of the palm's metacarpi
- the thumb, which articulates sideways with a fifth metacarpus followed by two phalanges

The carpal bones (wrist) are directly articulated by the radius of the arm.

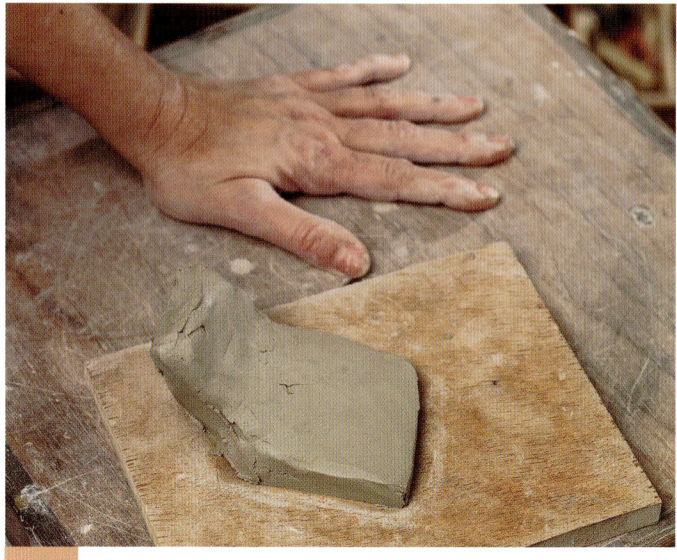

3 Debutants often don't position the hand properly in relation to the forearm because they forget the articulation of the wrist and the forearm, which guide and accompany the movements of the hand.

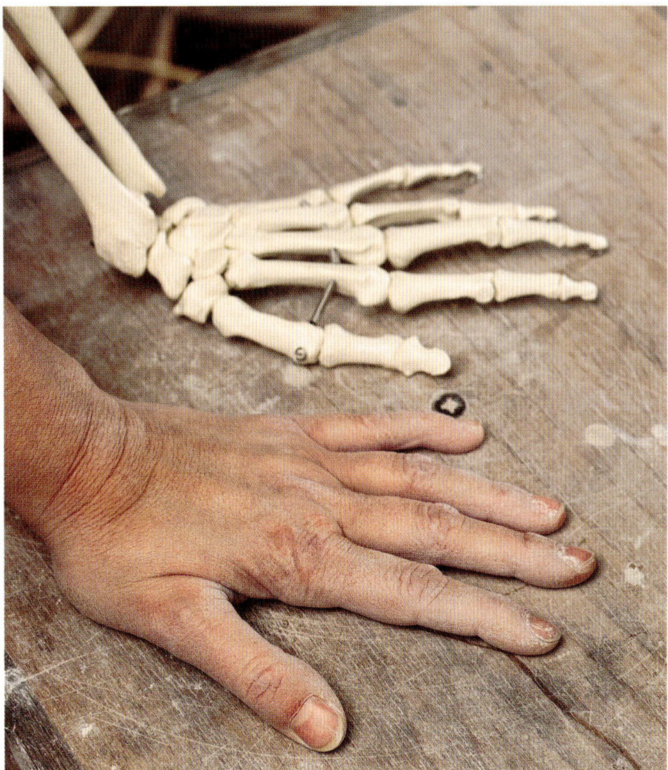

2 The palm—larger than the extremity of the forearm—has an almost square shape that ends slightly slantwise on a level with the first finger phalanges. Therefore, we can represent it by a square, horizontal, beveled plane.

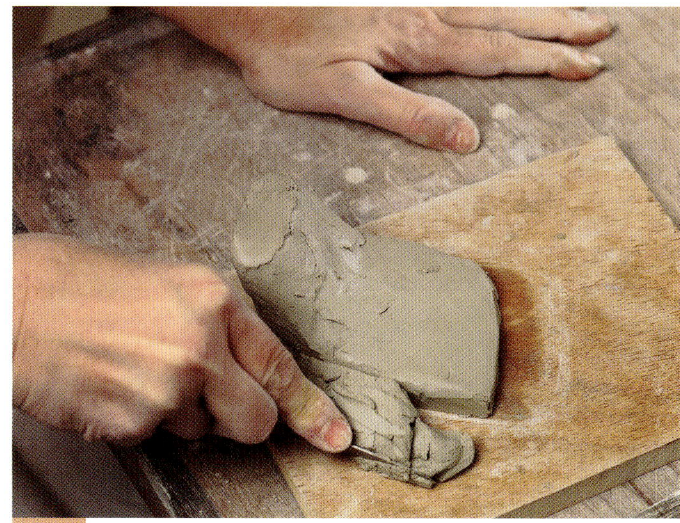

4 Place the thumb, which can be simplified by a triangular plane that slopes toward the base. It has only two phalanges. Placed flat, it reaches the first phalange of the forefinger. The other fingers have three phalanges.

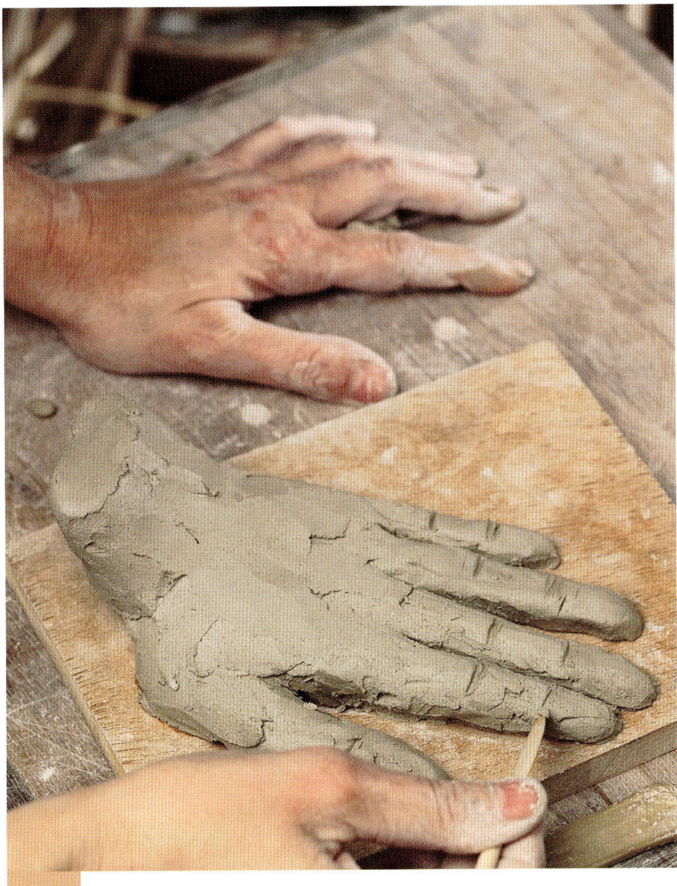

5 Place the middle finger, which is the same length as the palm. The ring finger is a little shorter than the middle finger, while the forefinger is very slightly shorter than the ring finger. Finally, the little finger is level with the second phalange of the ring finger.

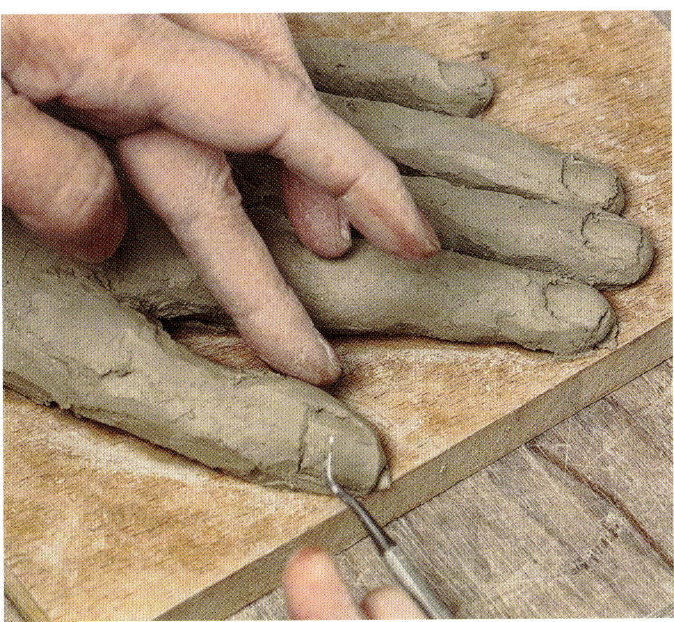

6 Form the nails by using a fine, flat tool to scrape out the clay on each side of the nail and plump out the surface. Smooth the surface with the blade of your knife.

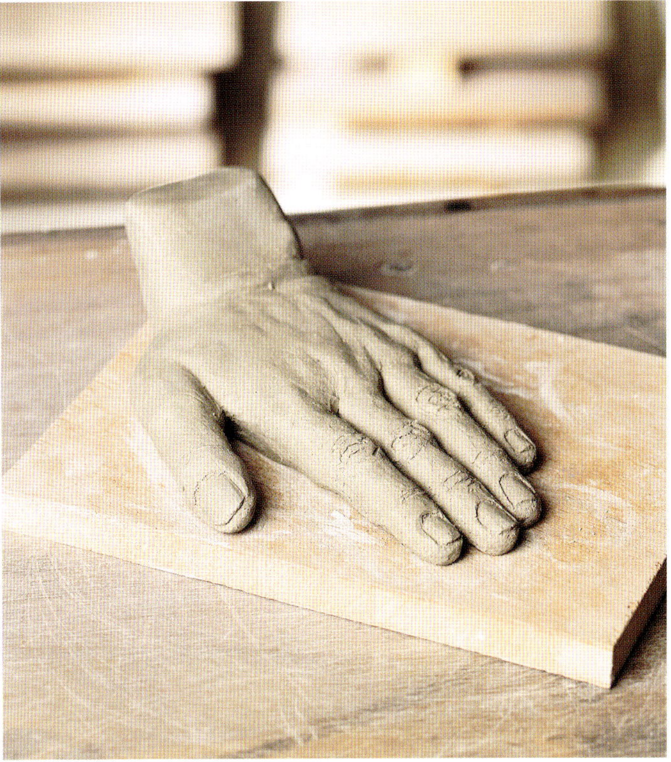

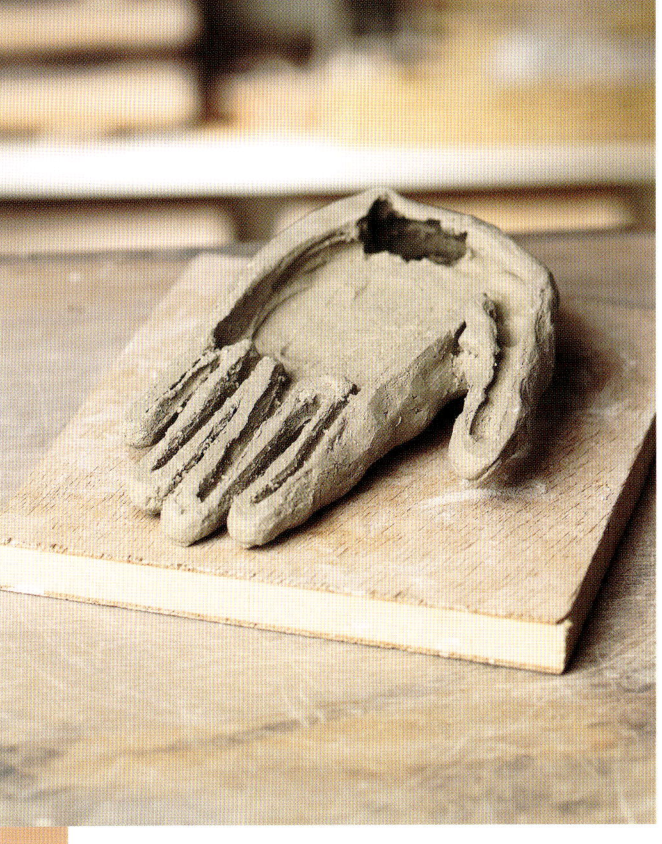

7 To terminate, add the finishing touches. Use little clay sausages to add the folds between the forearm and the wrist. In profile the hand isn't very thick, and it descends slightly toward the fingers. Leave it to dry out for a day before hollowing it out and firing it (see the introduction on pages 27 and 35).

The Foot

The foot's structure—triangular and pyramidal—is as complex as the hand. Start by taking photos from all sides: face on, in profile, from above, from behind, and a three-quarter-view shot. Then look carefully at the print you have chosen to spot its proportions and its shape, because there are several types of feet: Roman, Greek, and Egyptian.

In the following example the foot is Egyptian: the first two toes are the same length and the others are in decreasing length.

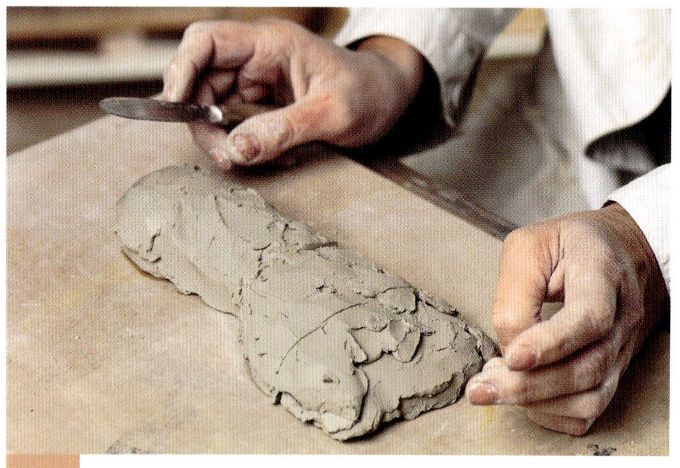

1 Start the foot by shaping the contour, which looks like a sole. The heel, narrower than the rest, is aligned to the exterior of the foot. If you divide the length by two and then by two again, you will find the beginning of the toes, placed at a quarter of the total length of the foot as seen from the inner side (great toe), starting from the heel.

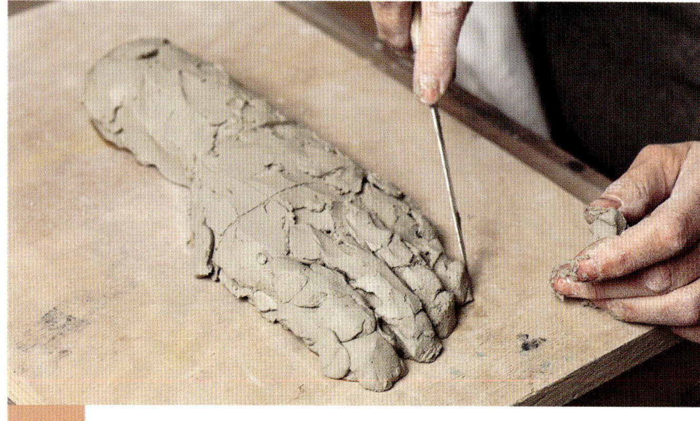

2 Create the five toes by using a clay knife and adding on pieces of clay.

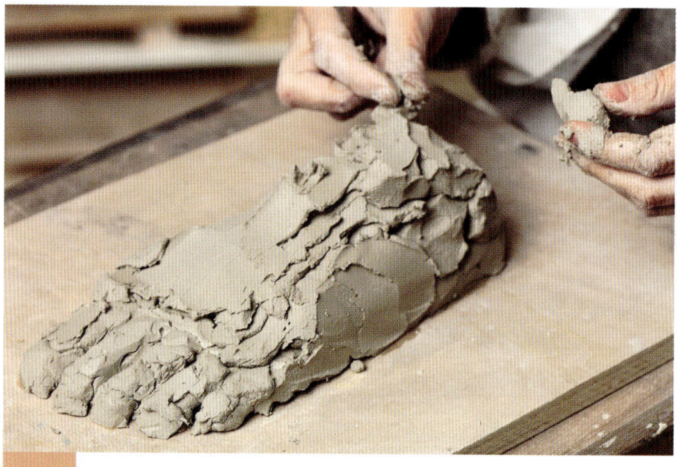

3 Increase the volume progressively: the foot takes on a somewhat pyramidal shape face on and in profile at the instep.

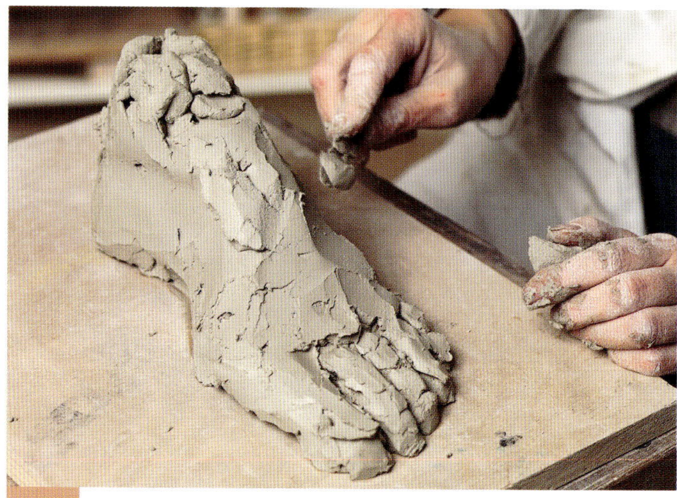

4 Accentuate the bump of the instep and hollow the arch toward the interior.

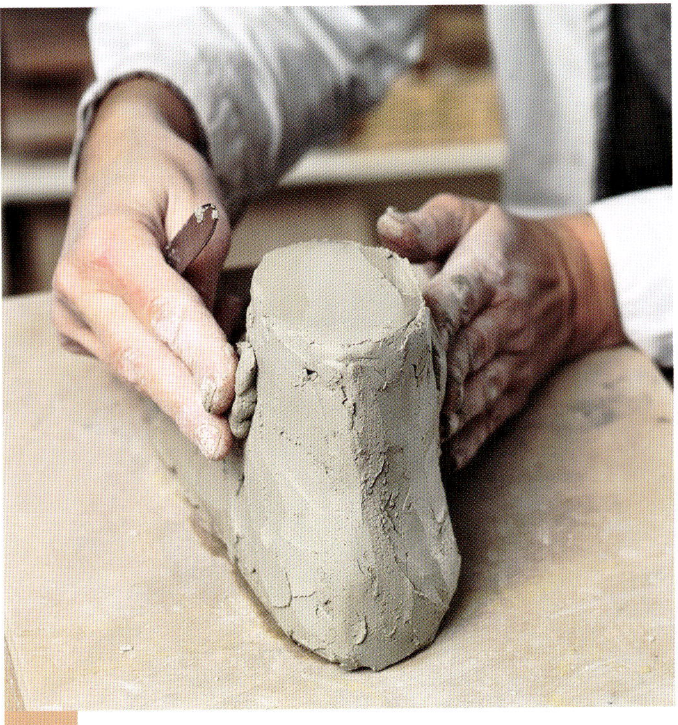

5 Add bumps on each side of the ankle (the ankle bones) to highlight the articulation between the leg and foot bones. The inner ankle bone corresponds to the inferior extremity of the tibia, and the outer ankle bone—more pronounced—corresponds to that of the fibula.

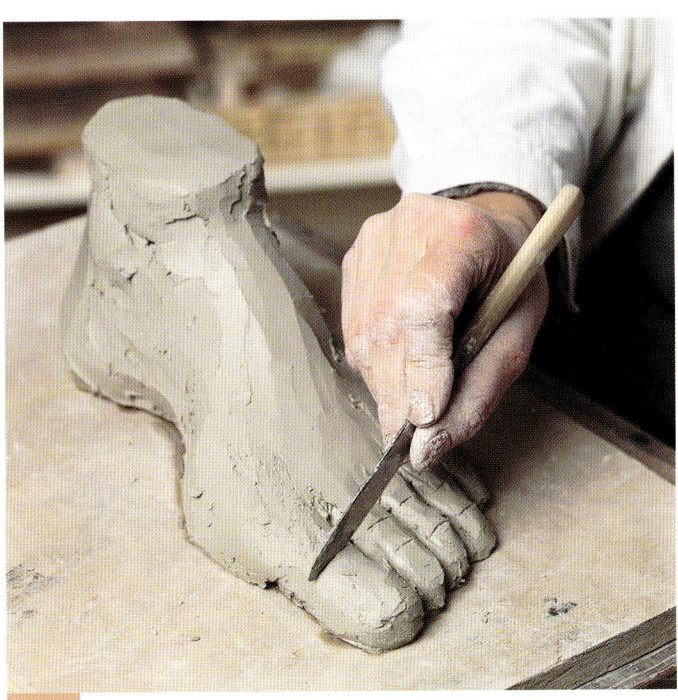

6 Delimit the toes' phalanges. The great toe and the little toe have only two phalanges; the others have three. Pass your knife between each toe to round them out and round them toward the right. Then do the same rounding them out toward the left.

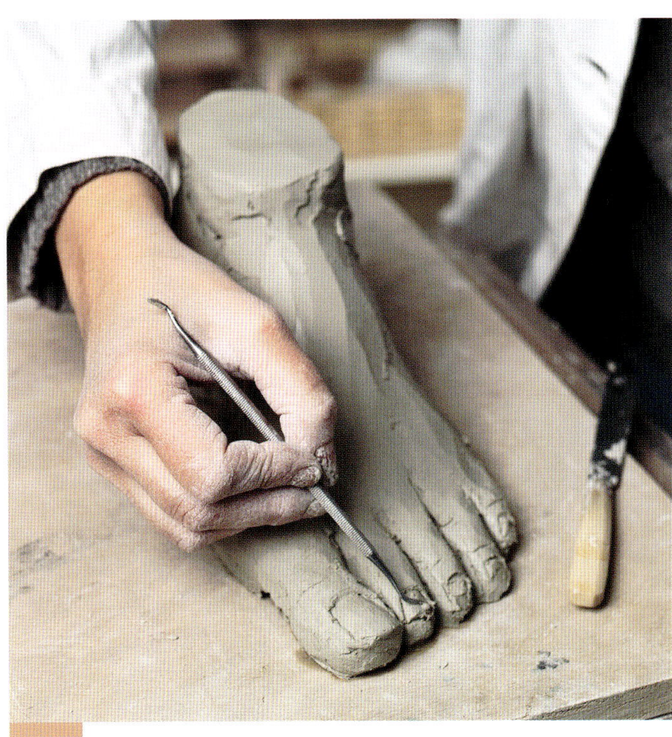

7 Shape the nails by using a fine, flat tool to scrape out the clay on each side of the nail, and round out the part that corresponds to the cuticle. Plump out the nails by adding clay, and round them out and smooth them with the knife blade.

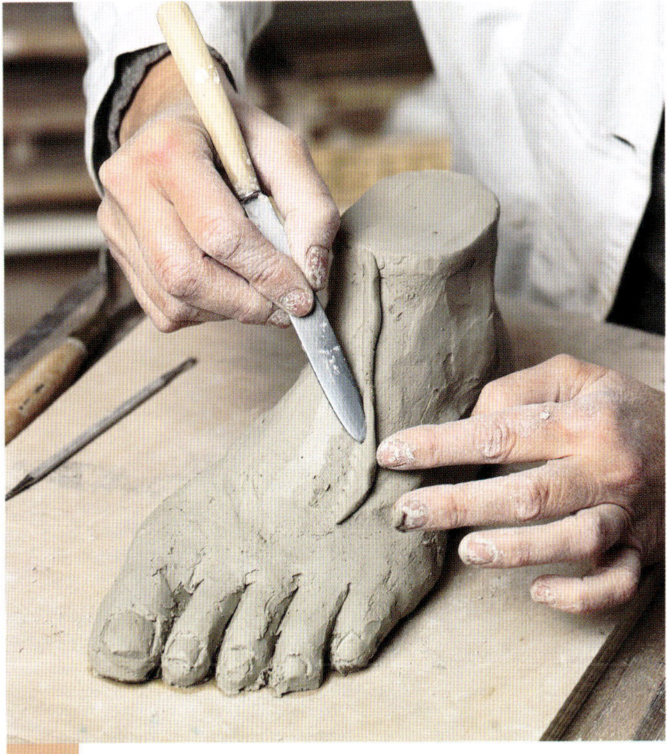

8 Roll out very thin clay sausages. Place them so that they represent the more visible veins by flattening them lightly with your knife and then with your finger.

9 Place the Achilles tendon at the back, using a thick clay sausage. Your foot is finished. Leave it to dry out overnight and then hollow it out. Let it dry out for a week before firing at earthenware or stoneware temperatures if your clay fires at a high temperature (see the introduction on pages 27 and 35).

Bronze-Green Caparol Patina

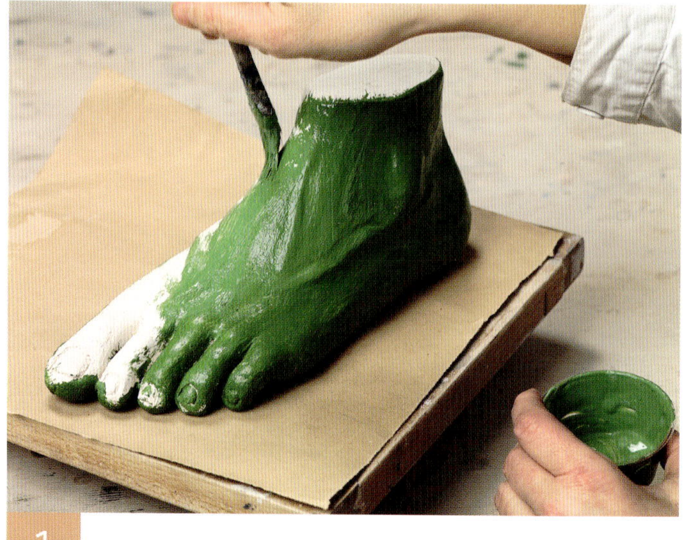

1 Once the foot has been fired, you can add a patina to it. Mix Caparol medium and chrome-green pigment in a bowl, adding a little water to obtain a thick mixture. Paint this onto the foot, using a soft-haired brush, and let it dry.

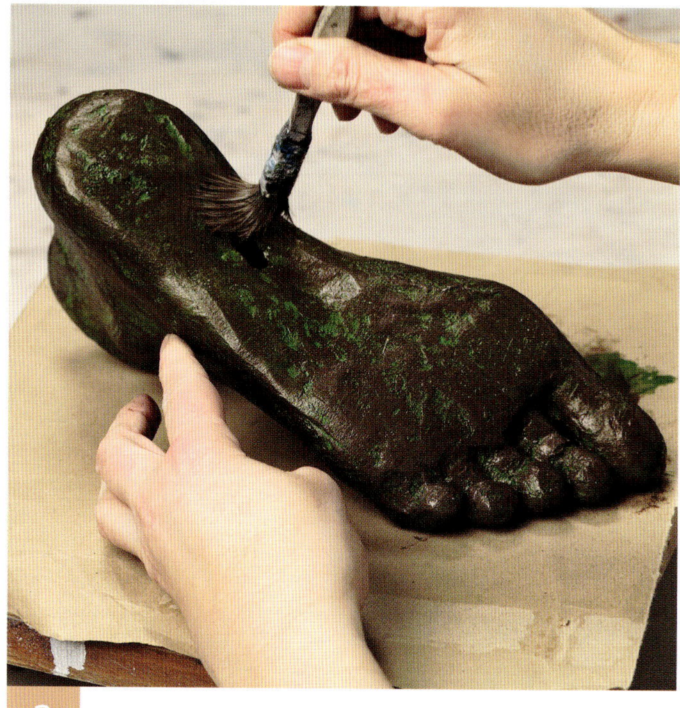

2 Mix Caparol and burnt umber and gold pigments in another bowl. Use only a little Caparol, because you are only going to brush lightly over the prominent areas. Just dip the tip of your brush into the gold pigment so that the brown doesn't become too golden. Paint this brown-gold mixture over the surface by using a large brush, leaving the hollows green. Let it dry.

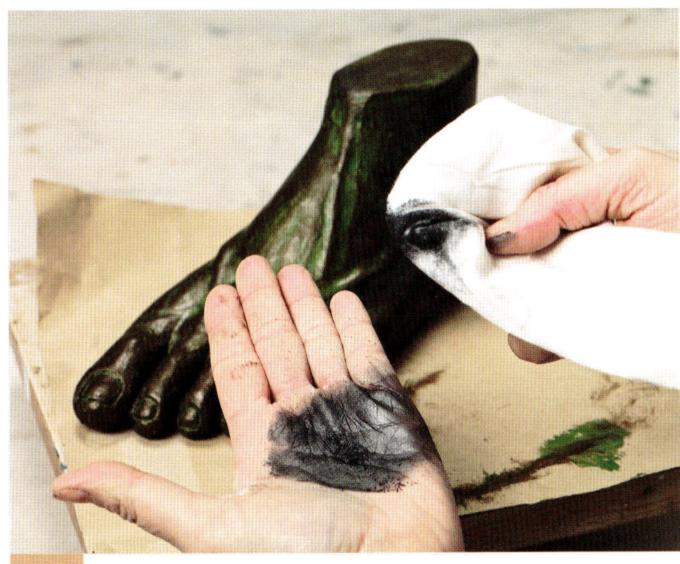

3 Since the Caparol was very nearly pure, the result is very satiny. Now you are going to metalize the results. Use a cloth to take powdered pencil lead directly from the pot. Rub it into the palm of your hand to spread it out before applying it.

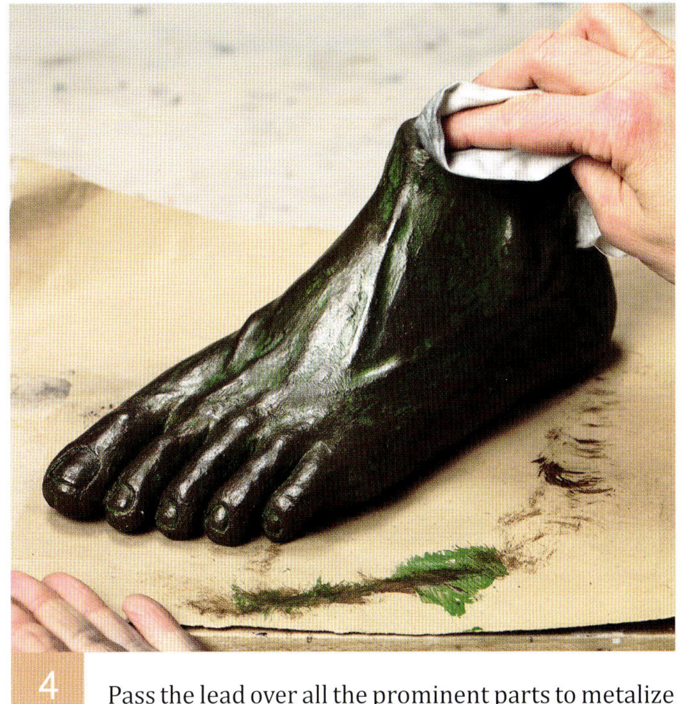

4 Pass the lead over all the prominent parts to metalize your patina.

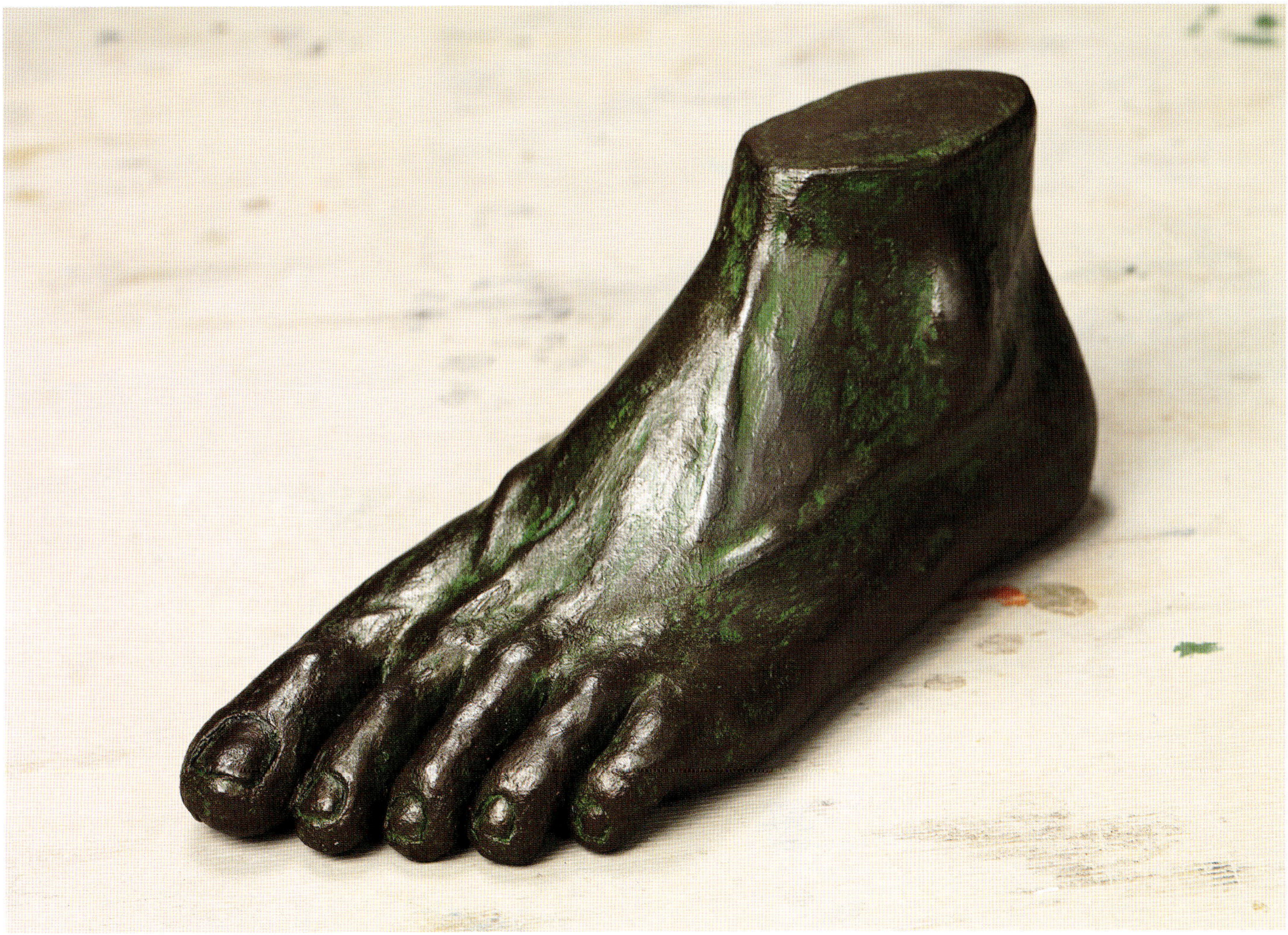

The Body

To be able to see and understand the structure and proportions of the human body, this exercise will allow you to schematically construct a body with little blocks of articulated clay.

The body comprises rigid blocks joined to each other by articulations that animate and give suppleness to the whole, with everything being covered by muscles and soft masses. In this exercise we will dispense with the muscles and soft tissues, which will be approached with a model; see "Standing Nude" on page 82.

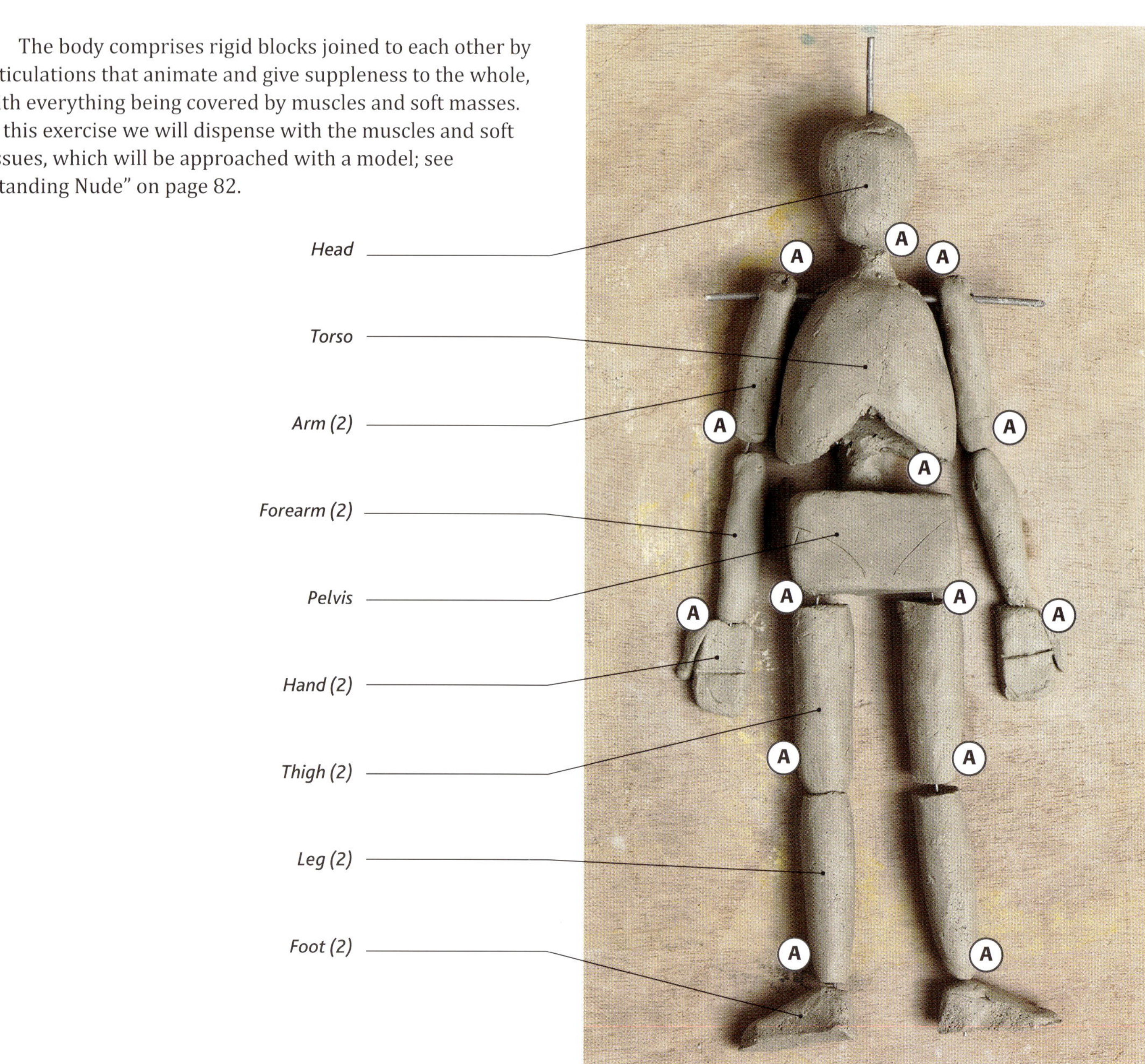

Our body is made up of 15 blocks and 14 articulation zones (A).

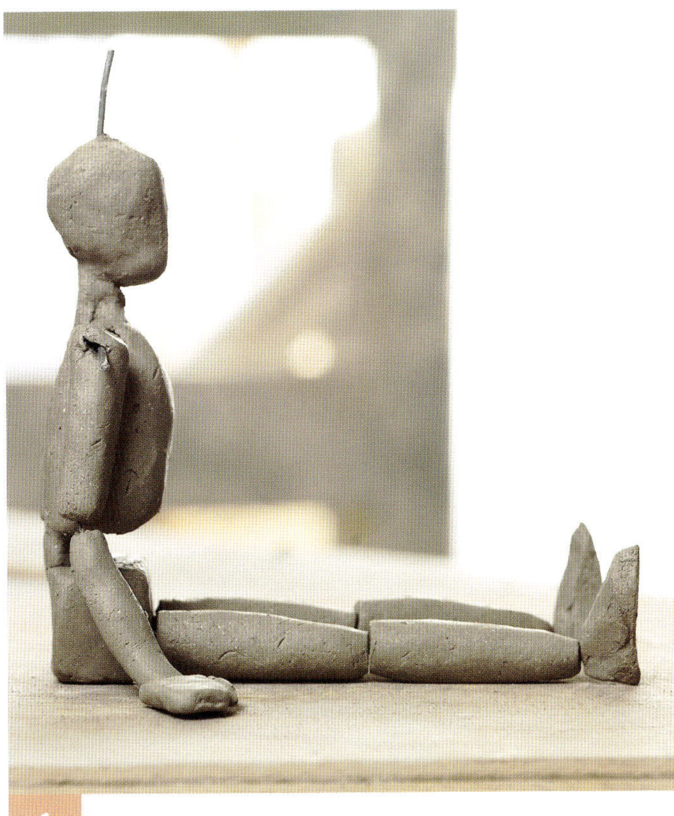

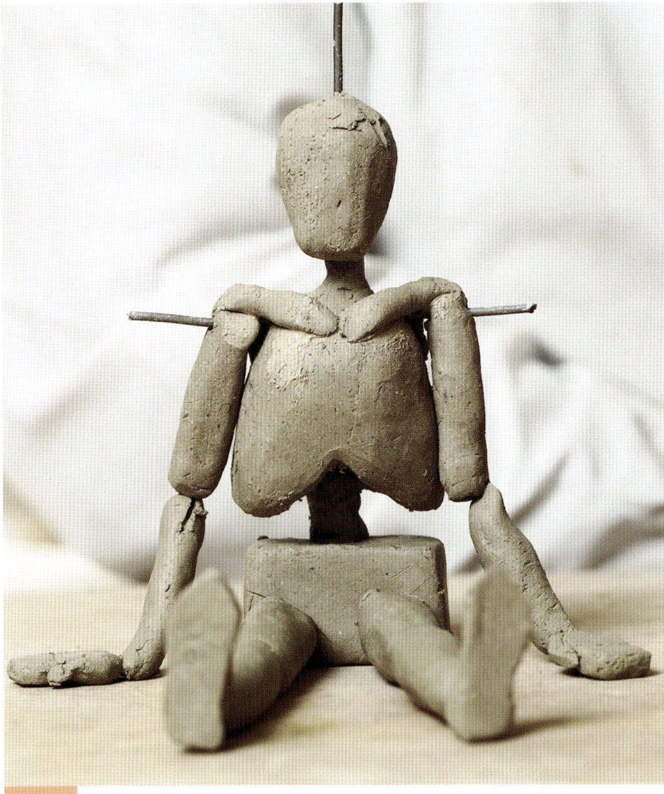

1 Start by shaping the pelvis: it's the first thing we look at when starting to sculpt a model, because it is from there that the architecture of the body spreads out. It is joined to the torso by the backbone, with a structural void (the waist) between them. The pelvis can be schematized by a parallelepiped—longer in women. Its upper part corresponds to the hips, and the inferior part to the pubis in the center of the body.

2 Continue with the torso, which is an egg-shaped box, slightly plumped out and the same depth as the pelvis. Their ratio of proportion in height is 1 to 1.5: that is to say, the trunk is one and a half times larger in height than the pelvis.

3 The backbone passes between the pelvis and the torso: the waist. This represents a quarter of the height of the pelvis. Don't hesitate to reinforce the void corresponding to the waist, to stop the torso from collapsing under the weight of the clay.

4 Shape the thighs. Made up of the thighbone, they correspond to the length of the torso from the shoulder. When the body is sitting down, we can see an "L" with equal sections on both sides: the vertical line, going from the shoulder to the base of the pelvis, and the other, horizontal, going from the back of the pelvis to the knee.

5 Now make the legs, made up of the tibia (the finest bone) and the fibula. They are the same length as the thighs from the knee to the ankle.

6 Thread a thin metal rod where the shoulders are to accentuate them. The arms, which join them, are made up of the humerus, which ends at the elbow, on a level with the waist. The forearms are made up of the radius and the ulna (closest to the torso) and are the same length as the arm from the elbow to the wrist.

7 The torso is joined to the head by the neck and the top of the shoulders. The height of the head represents an eighth of the total height of the body (or a seventh if you count from the neck to the feet).

8 A hand covers the surface of the face from the chin to the hairline. A foot is as long, if not a little longer, than the height of the head.

9 Once you have finished making your different blocks, join them at the articulation zones (see the photo on page 58) by planting metal wire in the fresh, firm clay.

10 Add thin clay sausages to represent the clavicles, which start from the shoulders, and fix to the torso at the base of the neck.

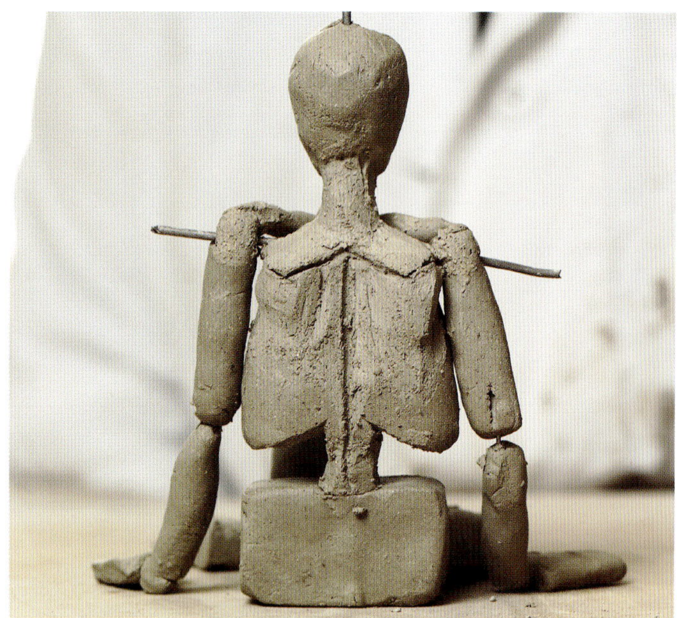

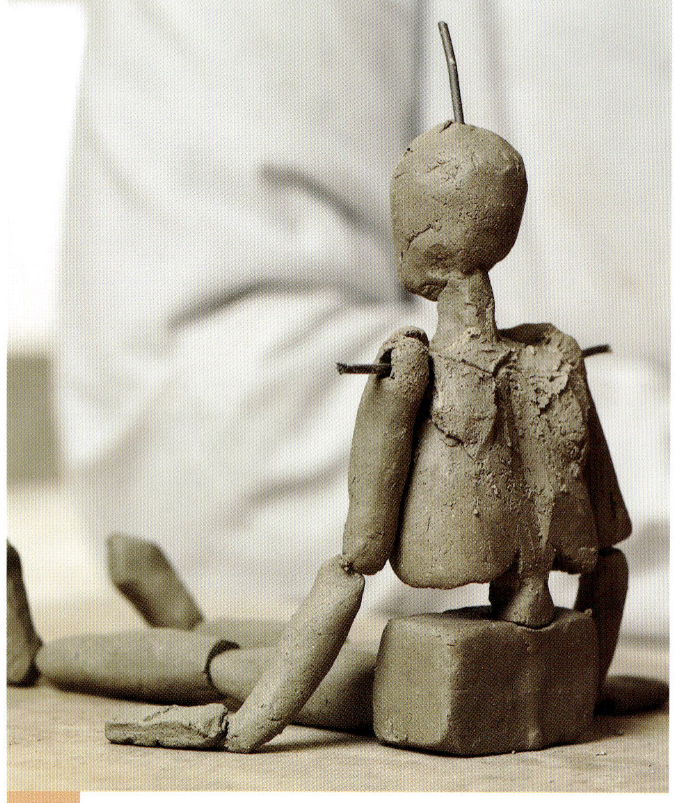

11

When the back is static, we can clearly see an underlying "W"-shaped structure: the shoulder blades, which accompany the movements of the arms. Seen in profile they show a slight separation behind the torso, then a slightly sloping plane toward the neck. To show them, trace in the W and add a little flat piece of clay under each point of it. Add clay to the shoulders to shape a gently sloping plane above the shoulder blades toward the neck. Then slightly bevel the hollow formed by the clay added to the shoulder blades, so that it follows the groove of the backbone to the pelvis.

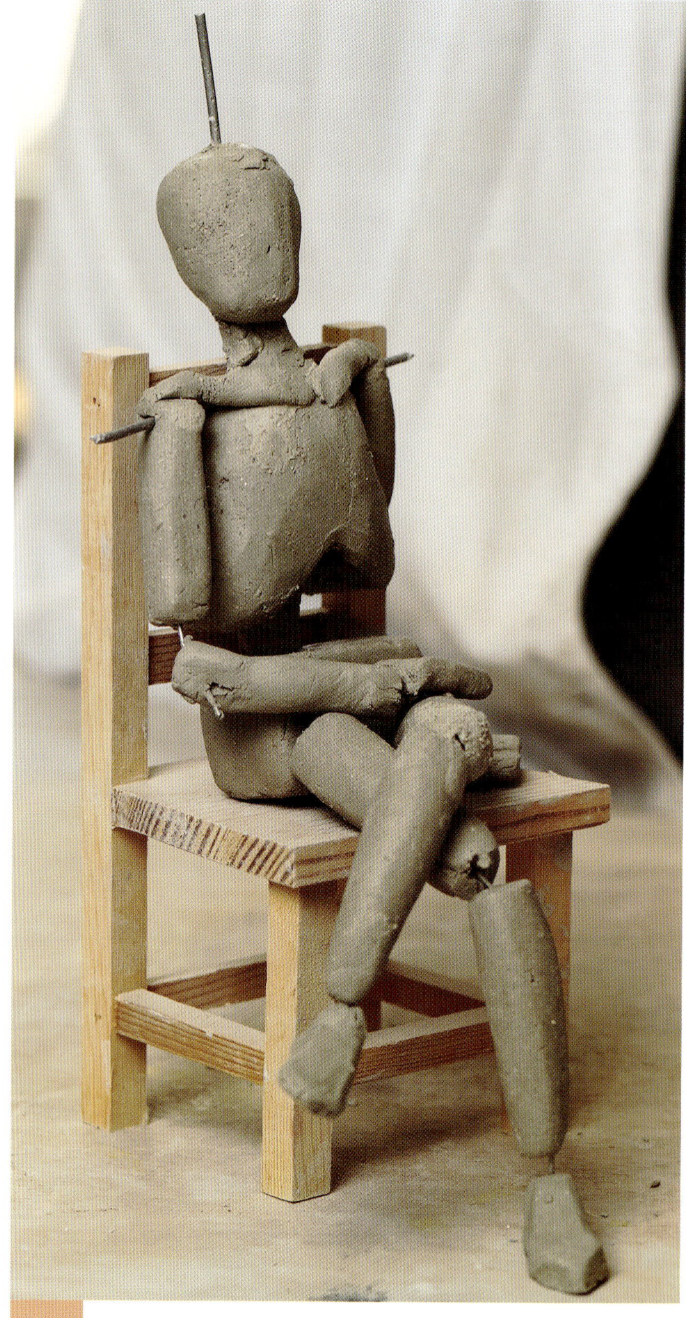

12

When you are working from a model, you will start by the position of the pelvis, then the backbone, the torso, the limbs, and the head. The hands and feet are added on at the end. The muscles, tendons, and soft tissue come next. These latter parts can't be sculpted before the structure because they cover it.

ADVICE

Don't work too quickly; schematize—look for the structure, the shape, and the proportions of the large blocks. Your technique will quickly improve.

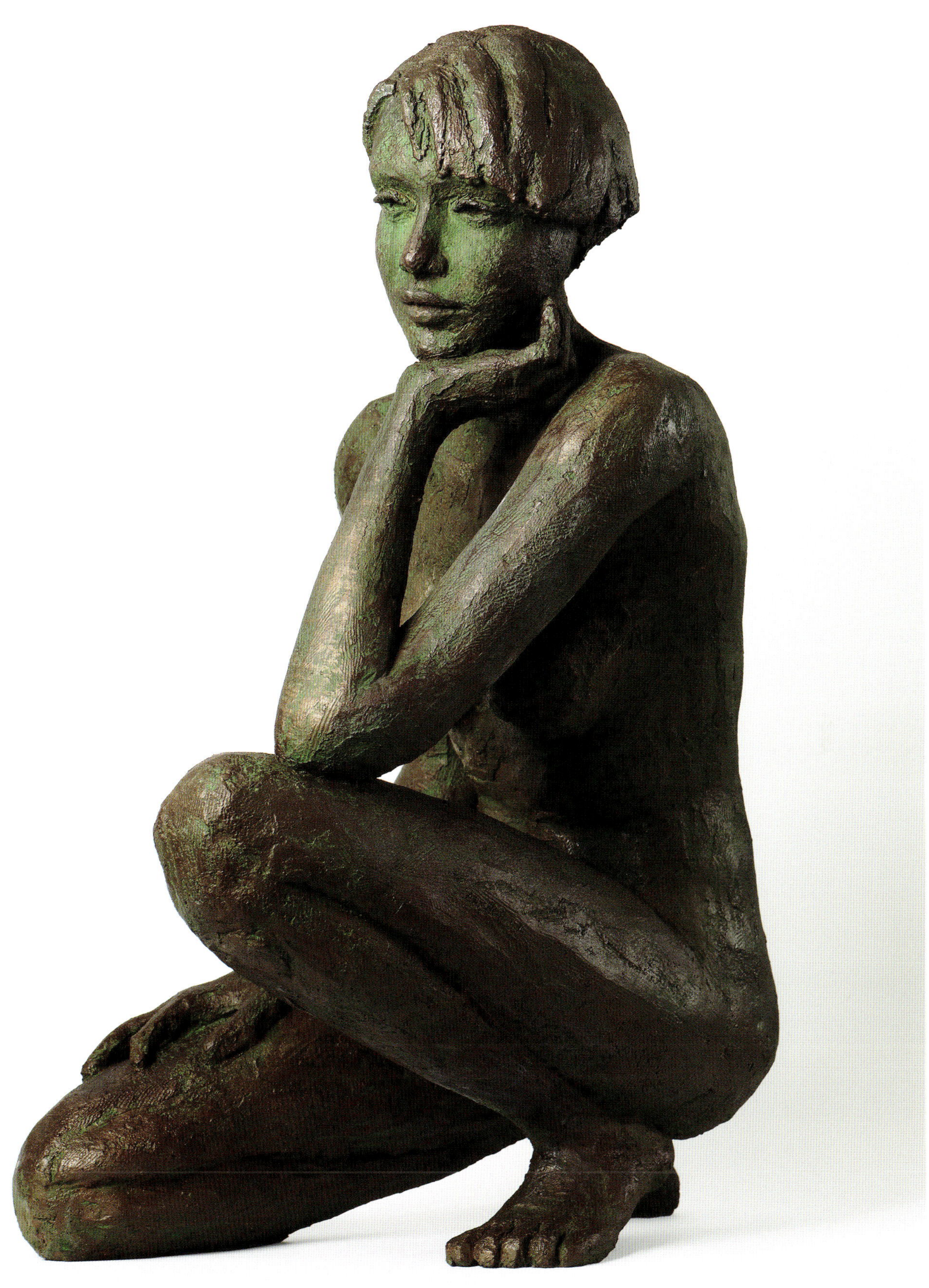

Sérénité, *earthenware with patina. Height: 3 ft.*

Creations

Girls with Grapes

A bas-relief is a representation of a slight thickness on a slab of clay that can be more or less thick. It can be made up of parts that meld into the slab and others that stand out, and can even be detached (this is called sculpture in the round, or high relief). To give an illusion of depth, we can organize the place and the thickness of the elements into a hierarchy within the space of the representation.

Bas-relief is the combination of a drawing that gives the illusion of depth on a plane and a sculpture that creates a real depth. One must therefore cheat to restitute the illusion of a complete volume on a flat volume and create an illusion of perspective. Certain volumes are prominent and others are less noticeable—or just a suggestion—with their outlines traced out to give an illusion of distance. The clay used here is raku clay with 0.05 percent of grog.

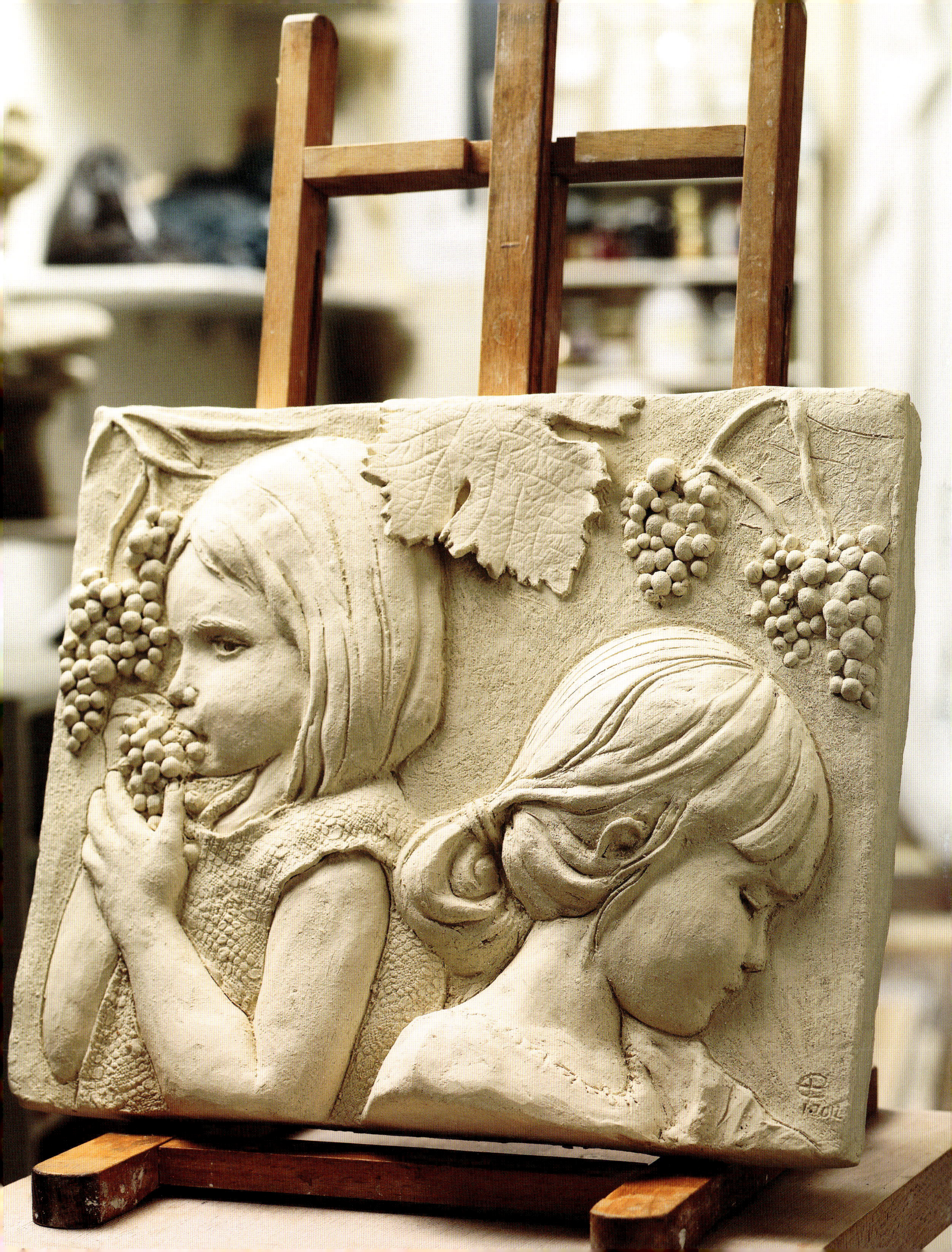

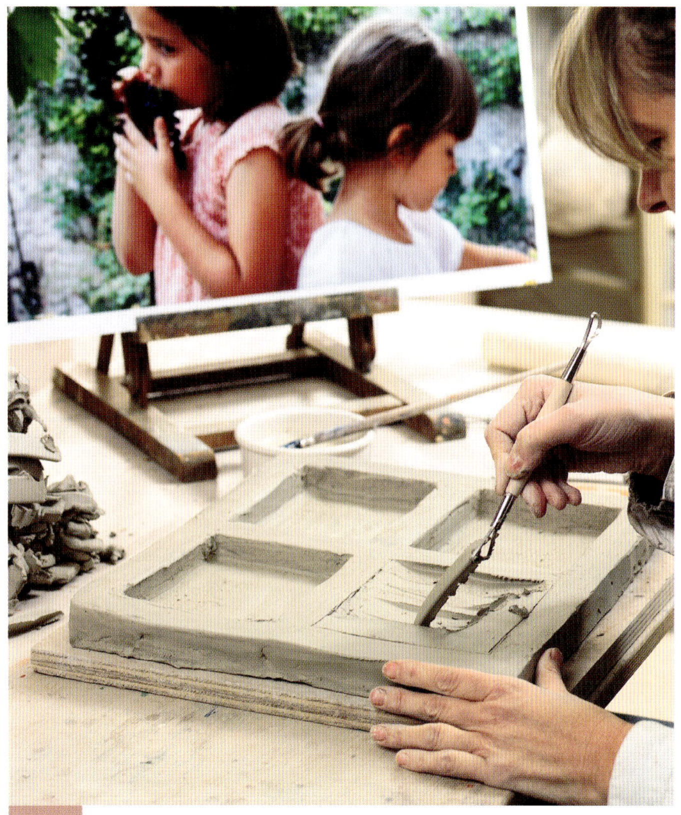

1 Make a background slab (18" × 13$^3/_4$" and 1$^1/_3$" thick), using a piece of wood 1$^1/_3$" thick as a guide (see page 24). Let it harden overnight and then cut out four identical squares on the back. This will make a reinforcing cross that will stop the slab from deforming during your work and when being fired. Leave $^1/_3$" thickness at the bottom of the squares and $^3/_4$" width around the edges and the structure of the cross.

NOTE

To make sure your slab remains flat and stiffens properly, be sure to place it directly on unpolished plywood. Cover it with a piece of plastic and another weighed-down board and leave it to dry out overnight.

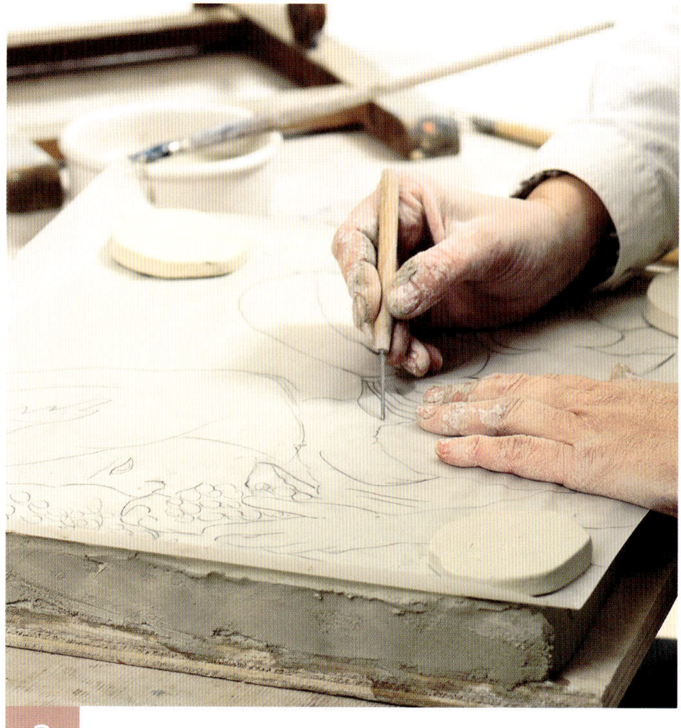

2 Trace your image onto the slab. Do the main lines with a pencil or potter's needle. Don't press down too hard, since the clay is still soft and only $^1/_3$" thick in most places, in spite of the cross underneath, which gives the surface stability.

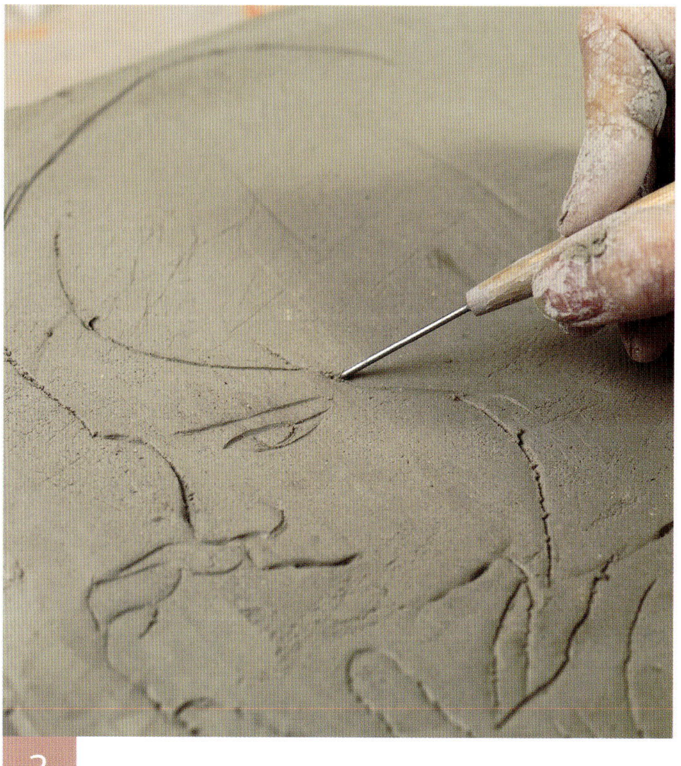

3 Remove the tracing paper and go over the lines that aren't very clear with a potter's needle.

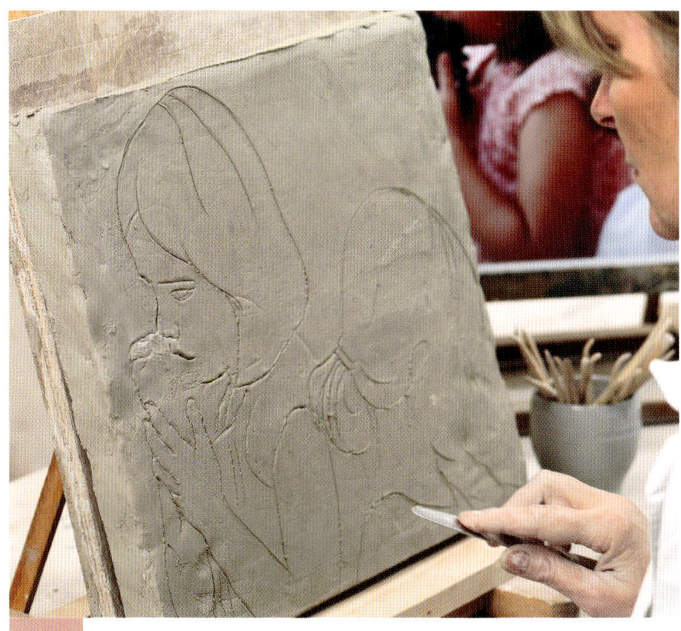

4 Analyze what you see in the picture to be able to restitute it and create the illusion of volume. Here, the picture has a perspective that presents the girl on the right in front of the girl on the left. Since they are back to back, the most-prominent volumes (the shoulders in the foreground) will be the center of the picture.

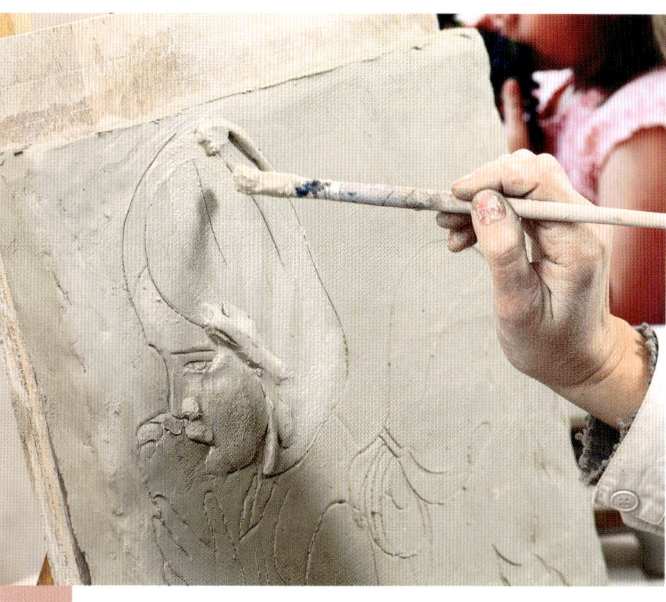

5 The volumes of the girls have perspectives that go in opposite directions, and, at the same time, there is a general perspective that puts the girl on the right in front of the girl on the left. The culminating point is therefore almost in the center and descends on each side. Before adding the first pieces of clay, paint on your slip, starting with the cheek, forehead, and hair of the girl on the left.

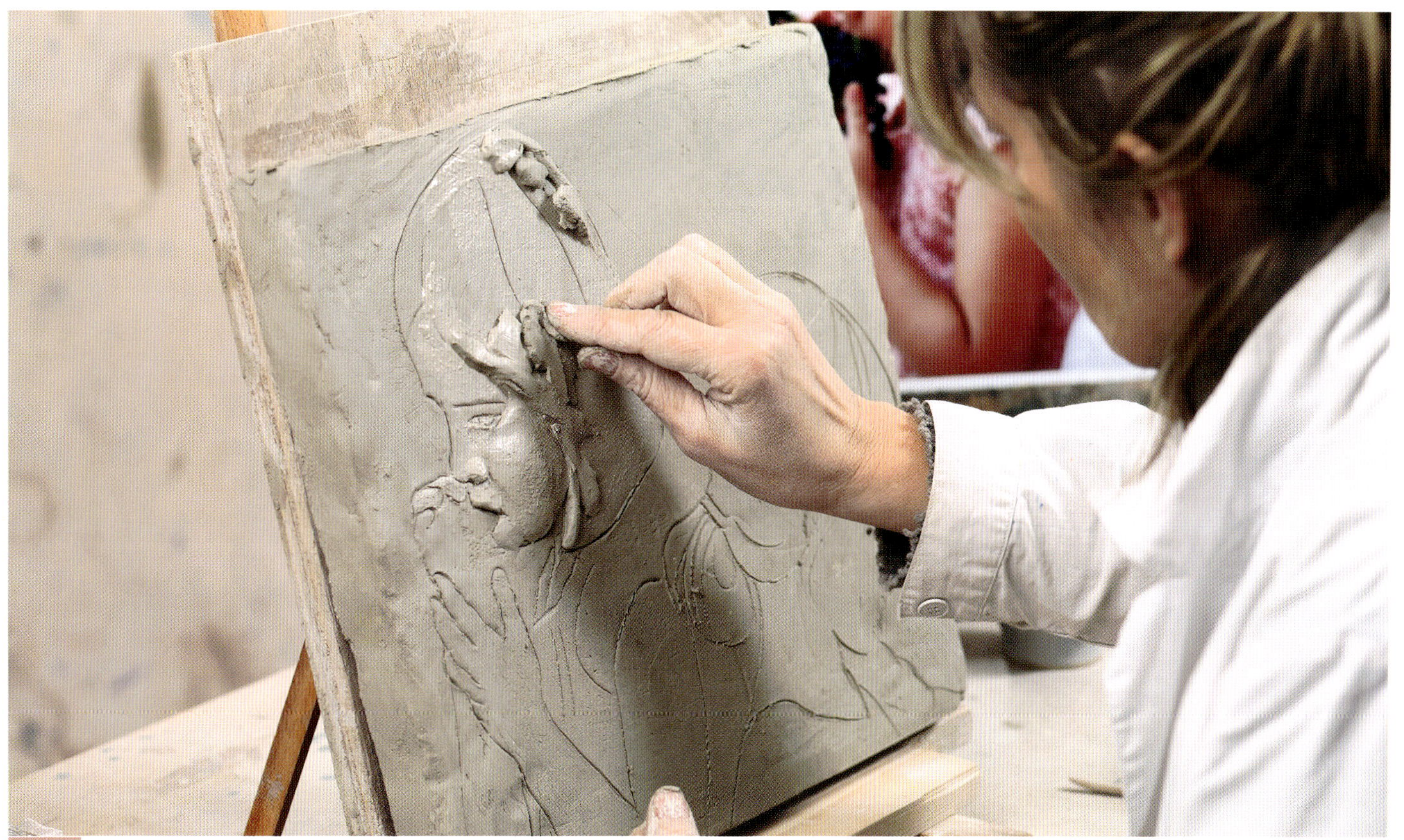

6 Add clay little by little. The cheek, forehead, and hair of the girl on the left stand out only a little from the background, getting thicker toward the right part of the frame. Stand back from time to time to check on your work.

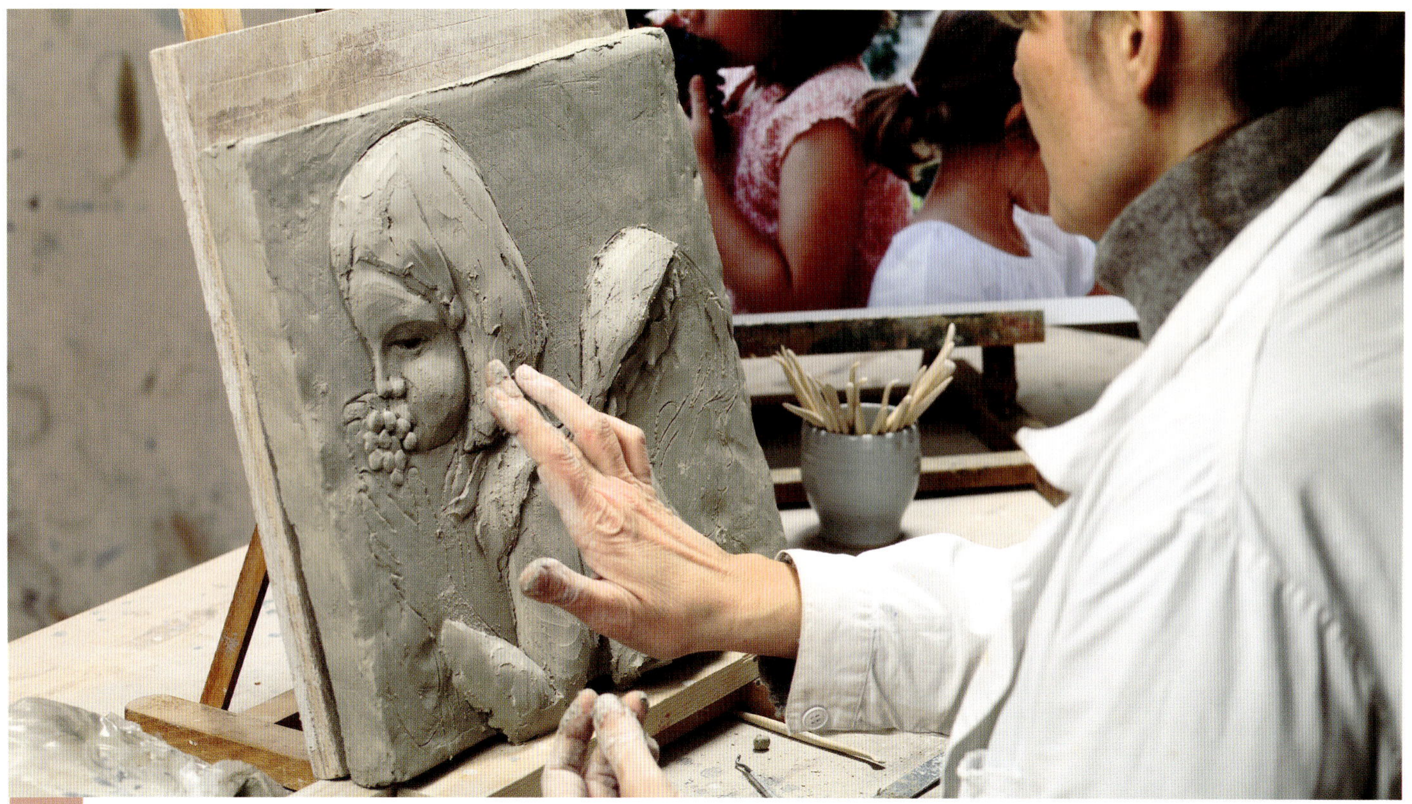

7 Continue with the volume of the shoulder and the arm of the girl on the left. Proceed in the same way for the girl on the right, starting with the volumes of the hair and the shoulder—the most-prominent parts of the bas-relief.

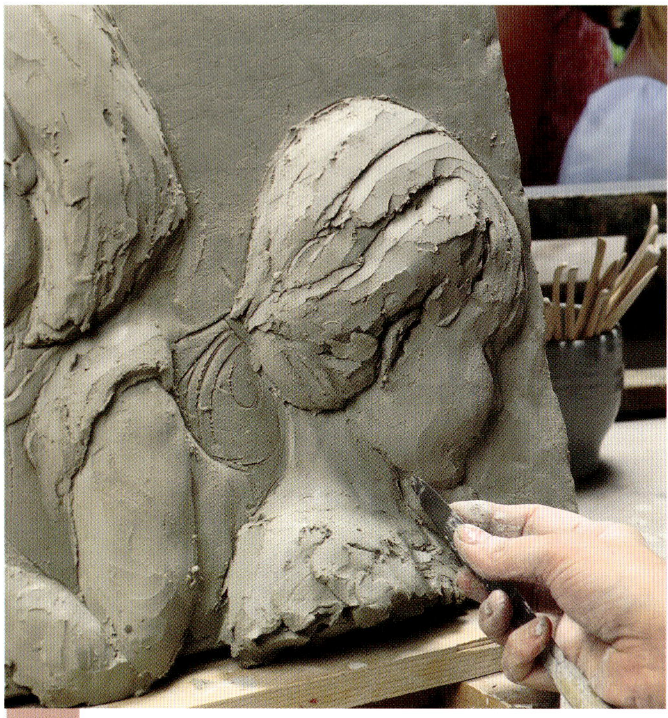

8 Now work on the neck and the cheek of the girl on the right. Once the thickest parts are done, you can smooth them in a gentle slope to the background of the picture.

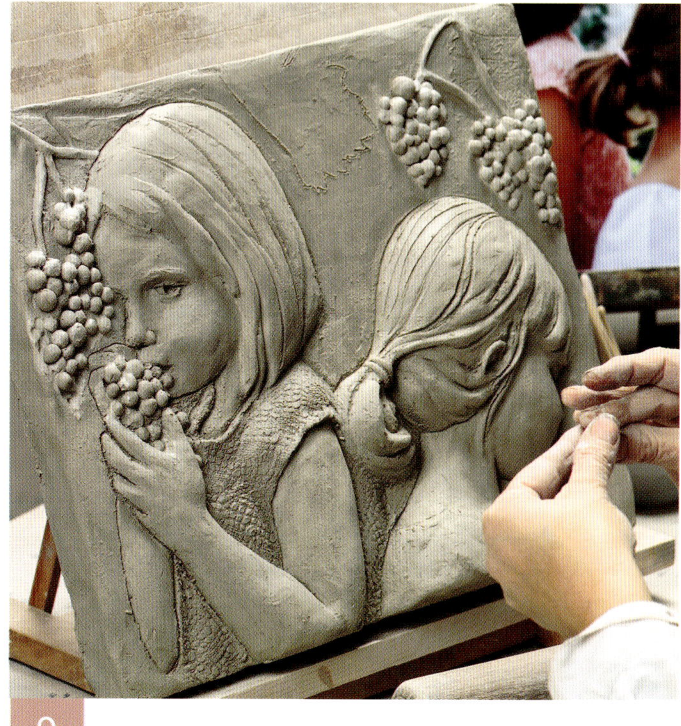

9 Do the lace imprint on the dress on the left (see "Imprints" on page 30). Continue to increase the volumes and refine the details. Shape bunches of grapes, with clay sausages for the branches and small balls of clay for the grapes. Glue them on with slip.

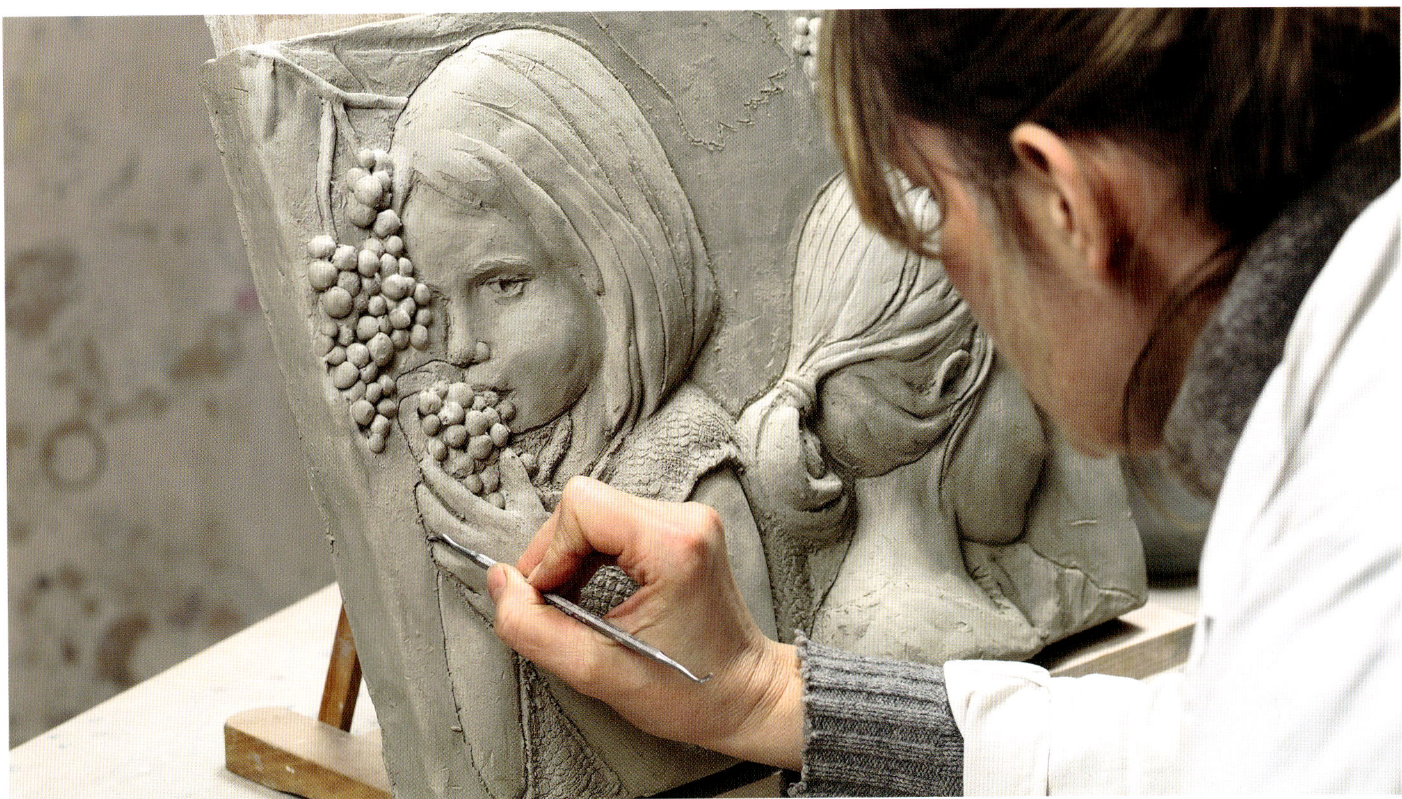

10 Touch up the outline of the arms and faces with a thin metal tool to make the girls stand out more.

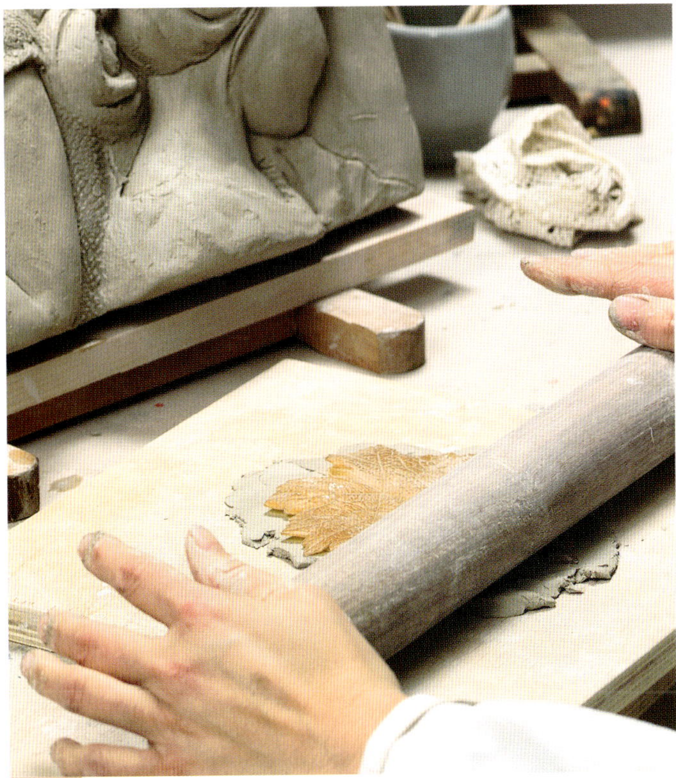

11 Roll out a slab of clay about 3 mm thick and place a vine leaf on it to mark its imprint on the clay.

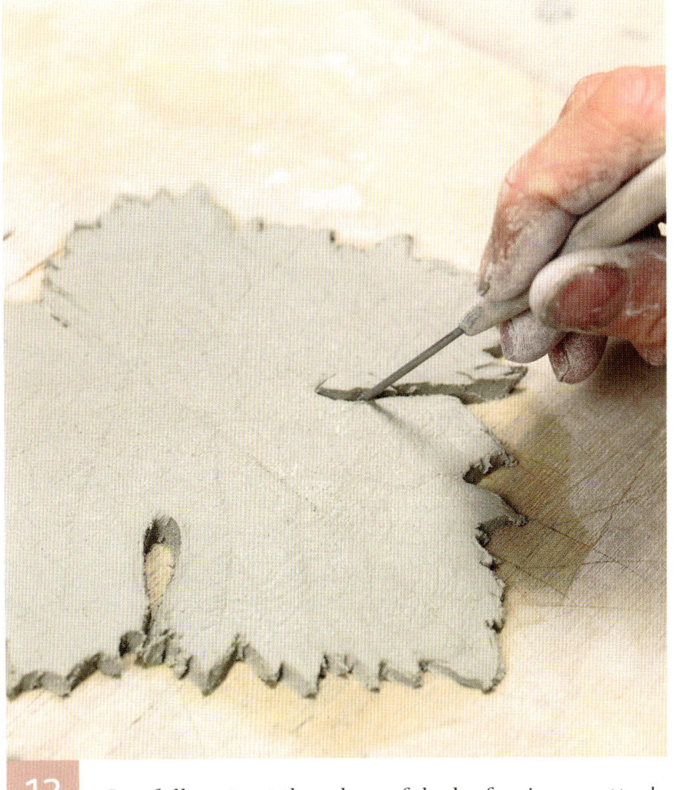

12 Carefully cut out the edges of the leaf, using a potter's needle.

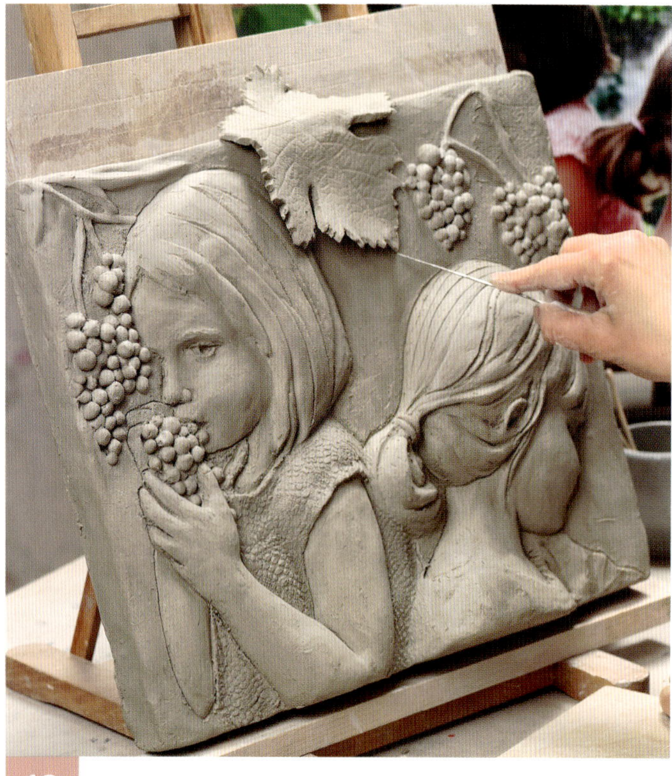

13 Turn your leaf over so that the imprint of the veins is uppermost. Paint on slip at the top of the frame and over the edge, and place the leaf.

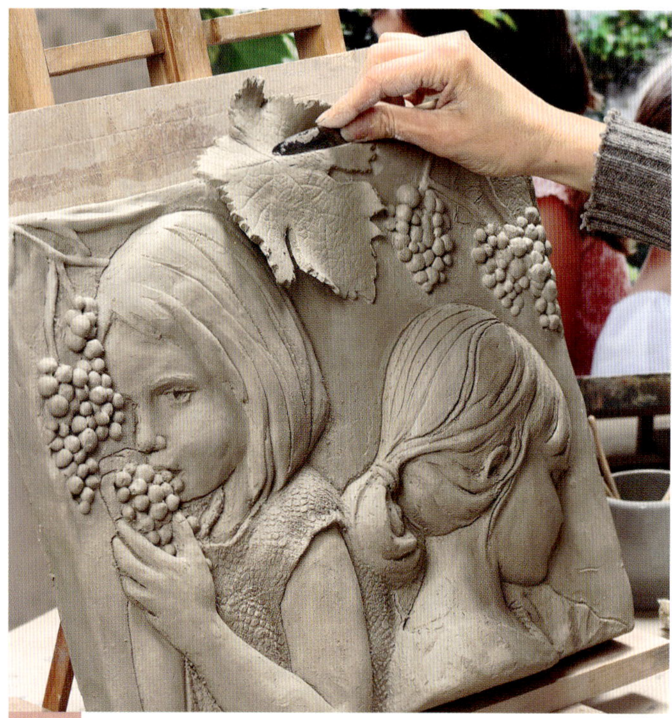

14 Placed in a slantwise direction, the leaf reinforces the perspective of the image; it is raised on the left and flattens into the background on the right.

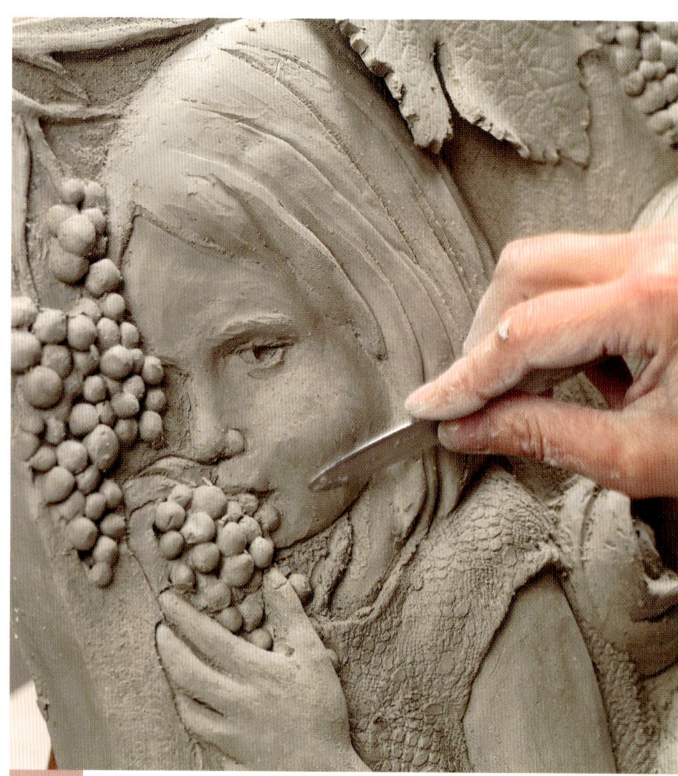

15 Take time to improve the overall appearance of the surfaces, and touch up and smooth the faces with a knife blade. Accentuate the contours with a potter's needle.

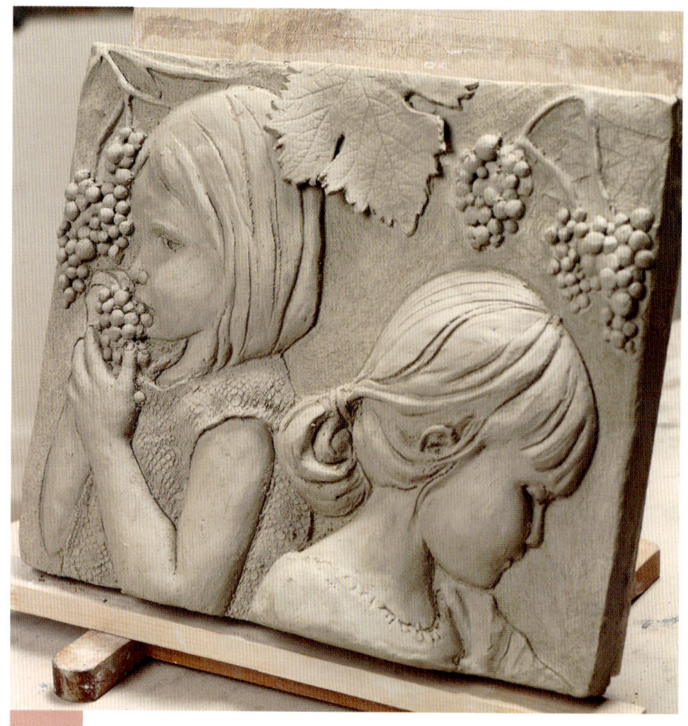

16 Let your bas-relief dry out overnight and then hollow it out from behind (see "Hollowing Out" on page 27) by going through the squares already hollowed out, without touching the frame. Remember to make a hole in the central cross that will allow you to hang up your bas-relief.

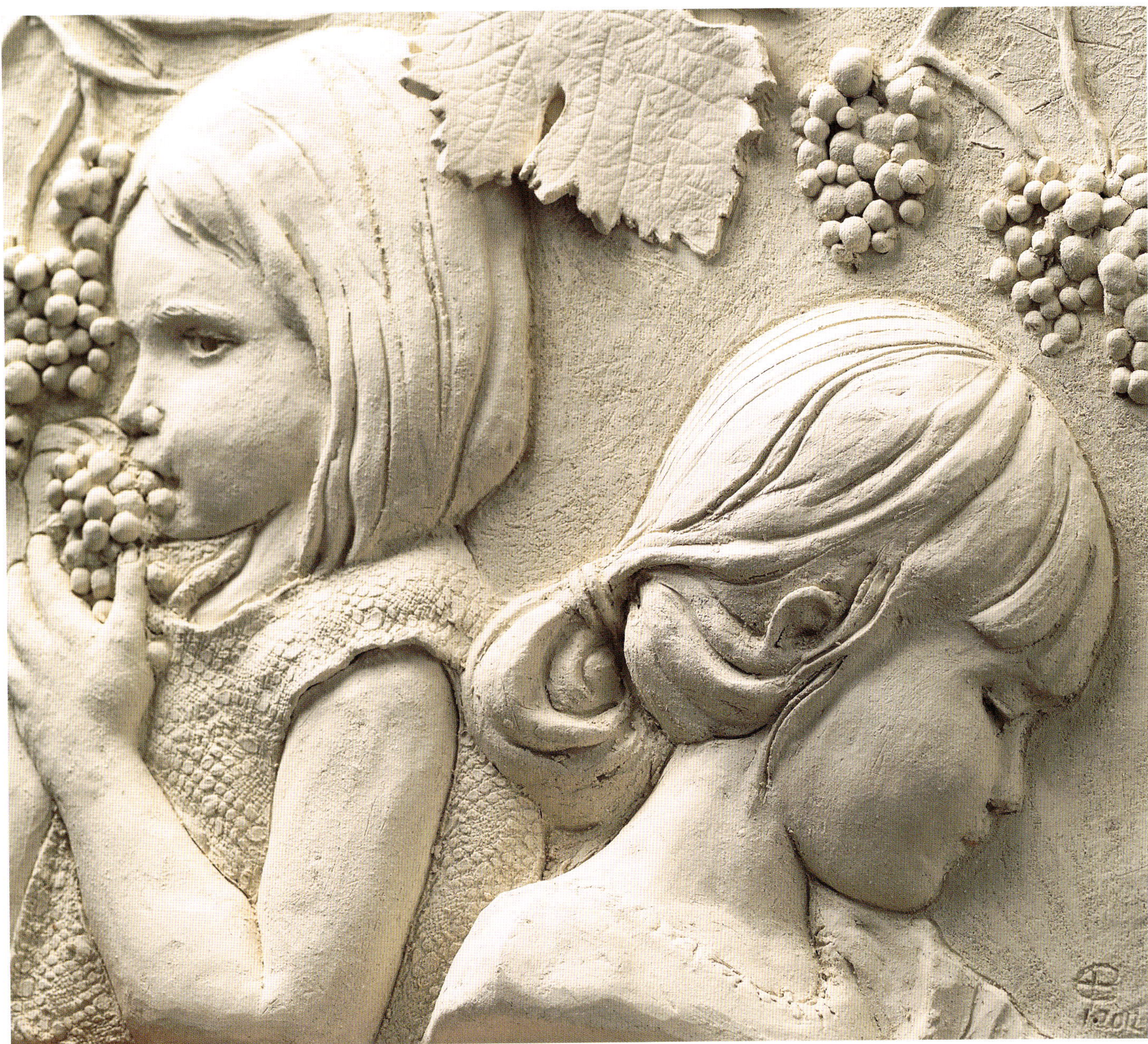

17 Let the bas-relief dry out for 10 days and then fire it at stoneware temperature (2,336°F). The result is close to porous stone, containing grains in relief in an off-white tone tending toward yellow.

Séraphin the Cat

Representing an animal seems pretty easy at first. The underlying structure that animates it is as complex as the human body, but the thickness of the skin and the fur hides this. This is why we find that representing an animal seems easy. If you want to re-create an animal in clay, you should know its skeleton to be able to give your piece strength. For this exercise I chose my cat Séraphin as a model; he was lying down, his paws outstretched and his eyes closed. I used red stoneware clay with grog, and I added white porcelain engobe here and there.

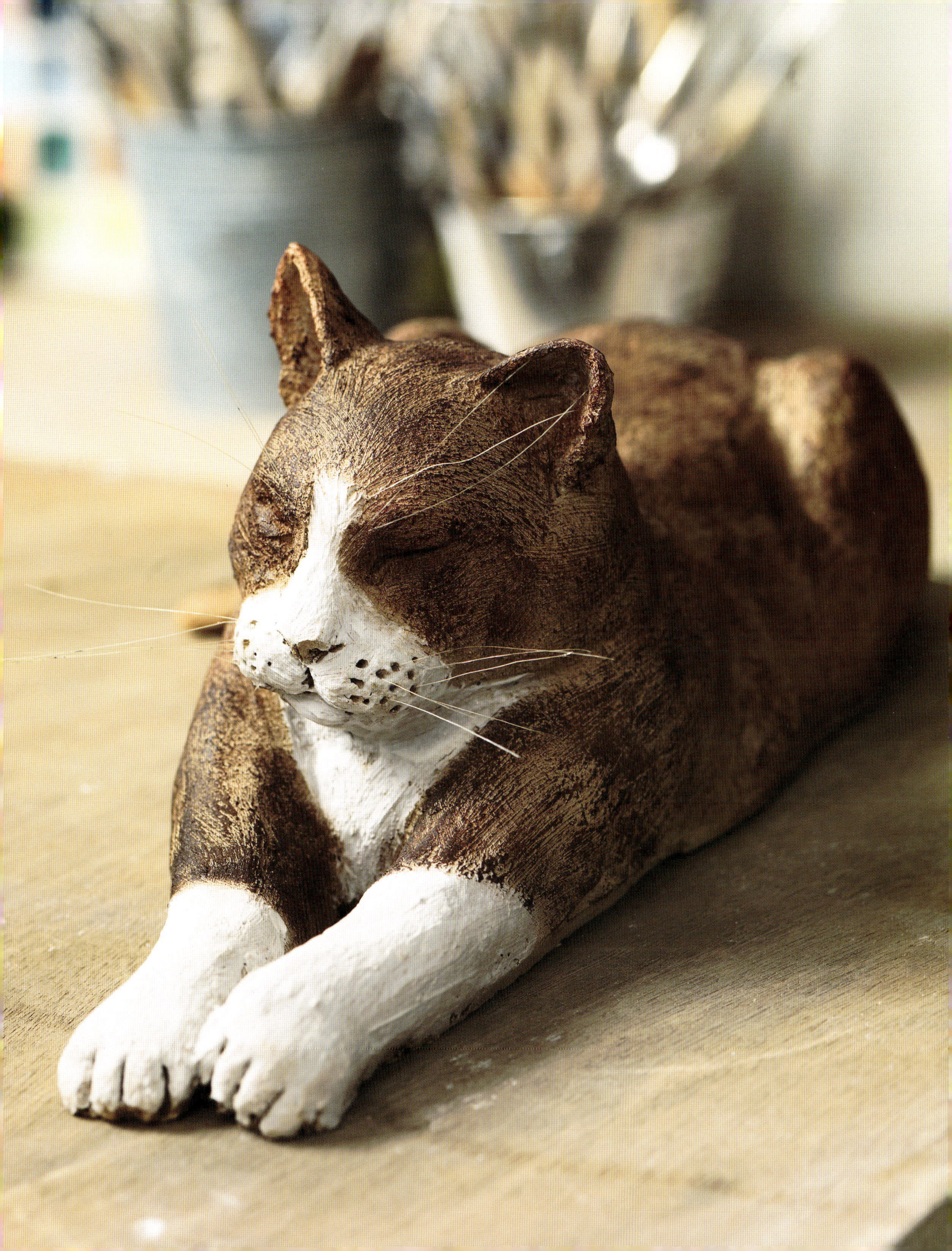

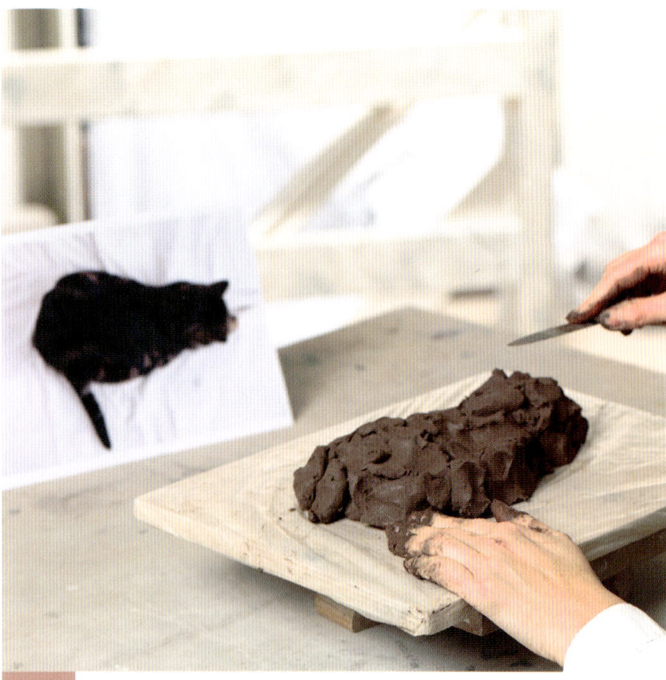

1 Take photos from different angles of a cat lying down, starting with the view from above, which will give you the contours of the volume. Place the base of the body, respecting its proportions: the body's length is equal to two and one half times the length of the head (from the base of the neck to the muzzle).

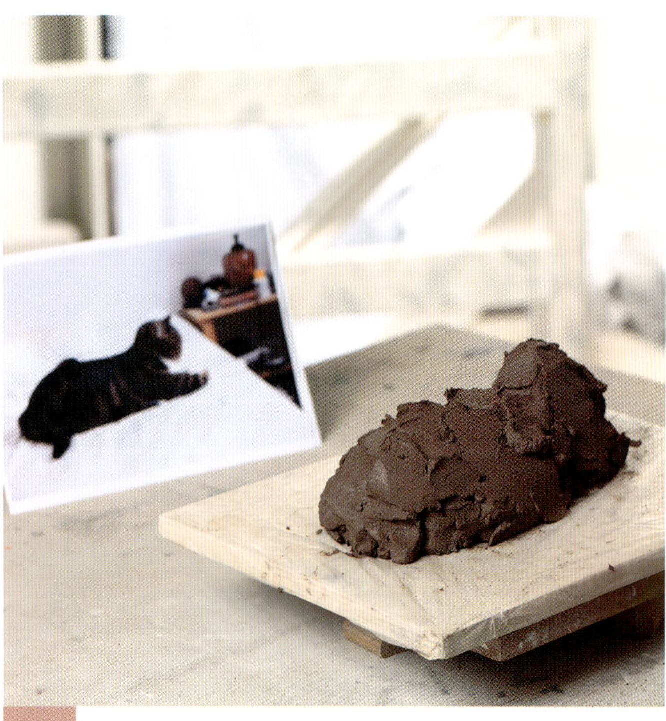

2 Change your point of view regularly to follow the cat's contours from its profile, from head on, from three-quarter view, and from behind. Build the volume progressively by adding pieces of clay and following the contours from different viewpoints.

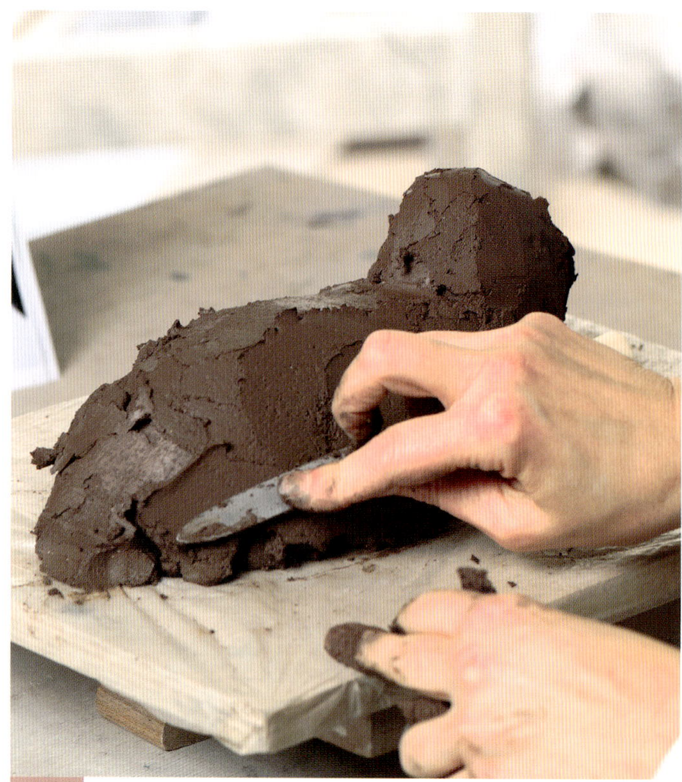

3 Settle the clay as you increase the volume. You don't need a support in this type of piece, which is somewhat flat with a large basis.

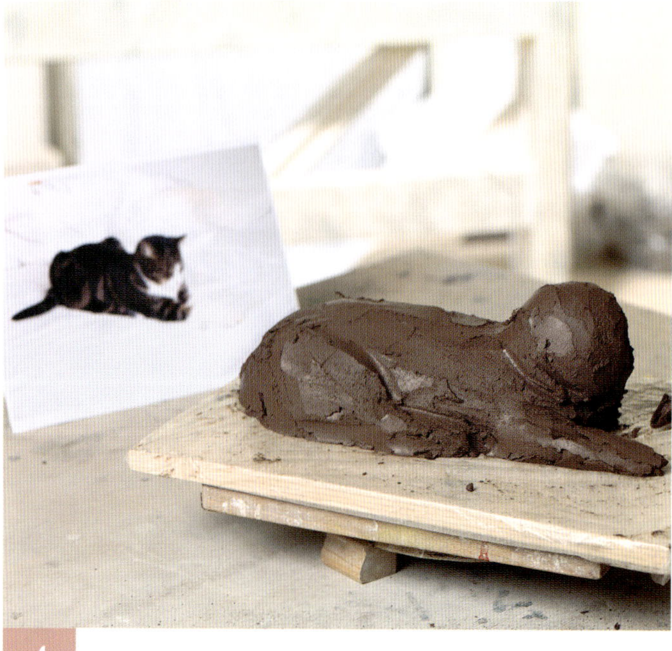

4 The piece quickly takes shape: the back, the thighs, the shoulders, the neck, and the head (rather round from a head-on view and rather egg shaped in profile). The forepaws are stretched out and touch each other. The back legs aren't visible because they are folded under the pelvis; all that appears is a band of skin on each side. The haunches stand out at an angle.

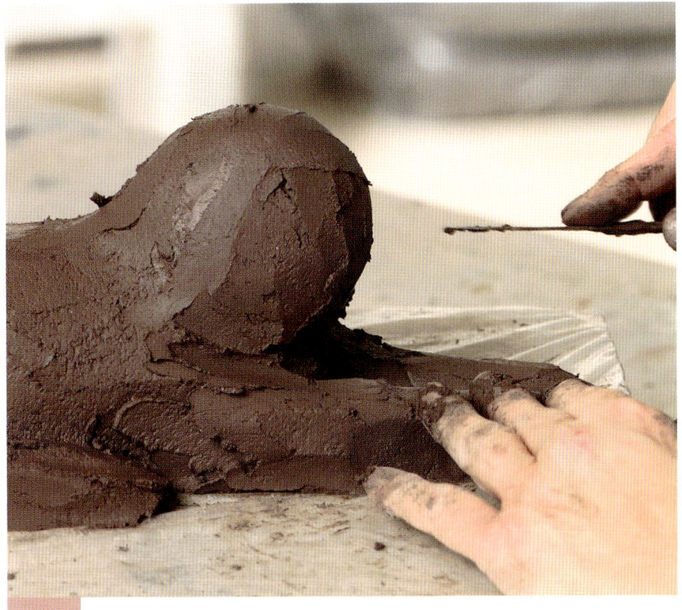

5 You should pay particular attention to the skull: the top part is round and flat in profile—almost squashed like an egg. In profile there is almost no demarcation between the rounded forehead and the tip of the nose. Face on, the top of the head is rounded (forehead and eyebrow arch).

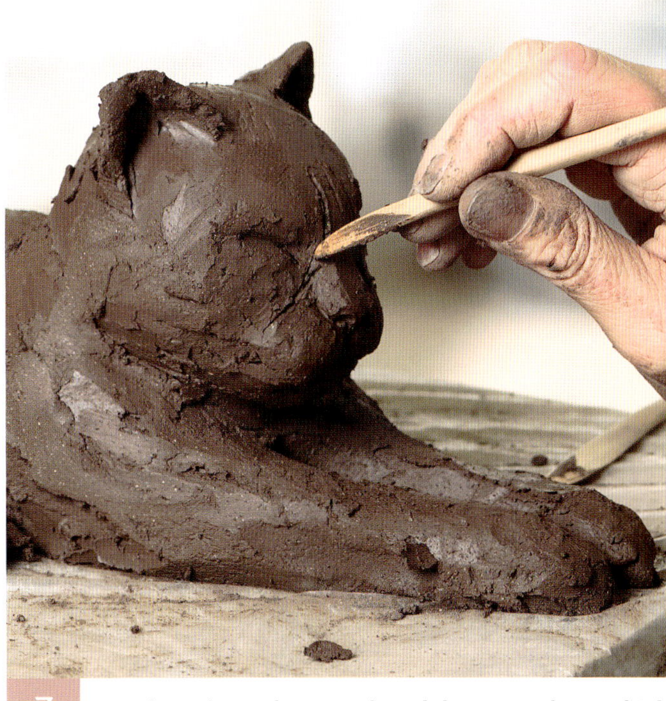

7 Work on the eyebrow arch and the eye sockets, which are slightly hollow, and then shape the tip of the nose and the muzzle.

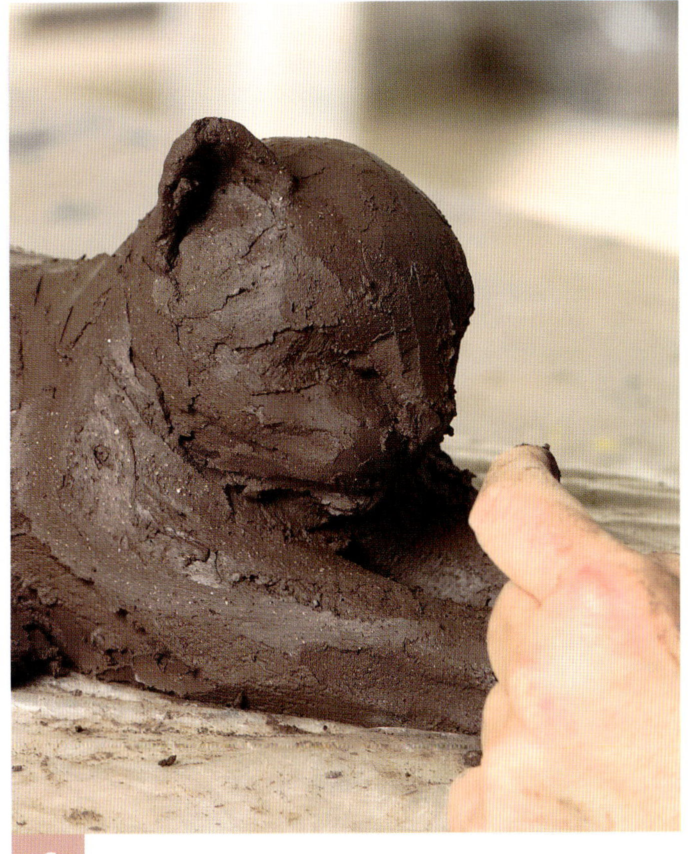

6 Add the ears to the back of the head.

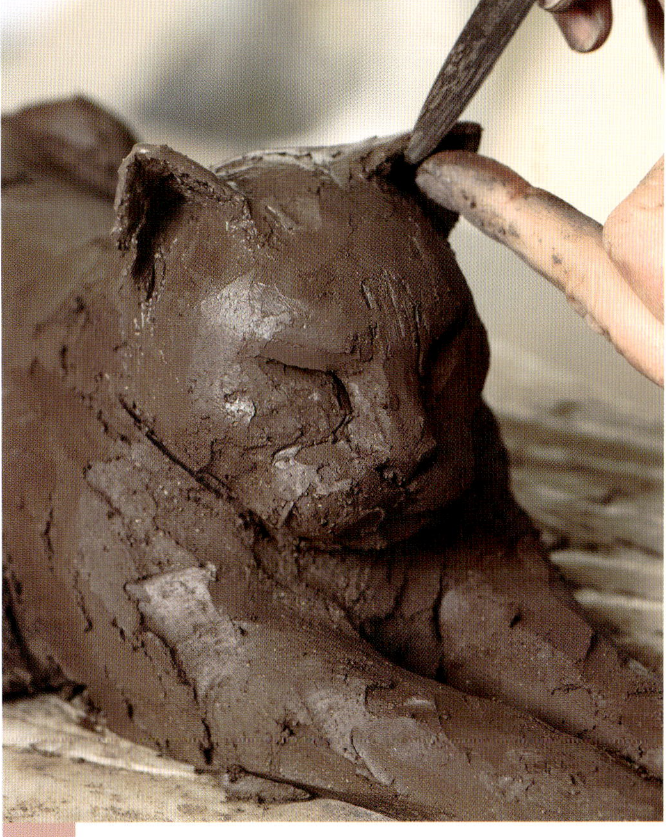

8 Improve the shape of the ears. They aren't completely symmetrical because a cat uses them like antennae when it listens to sounds around it.

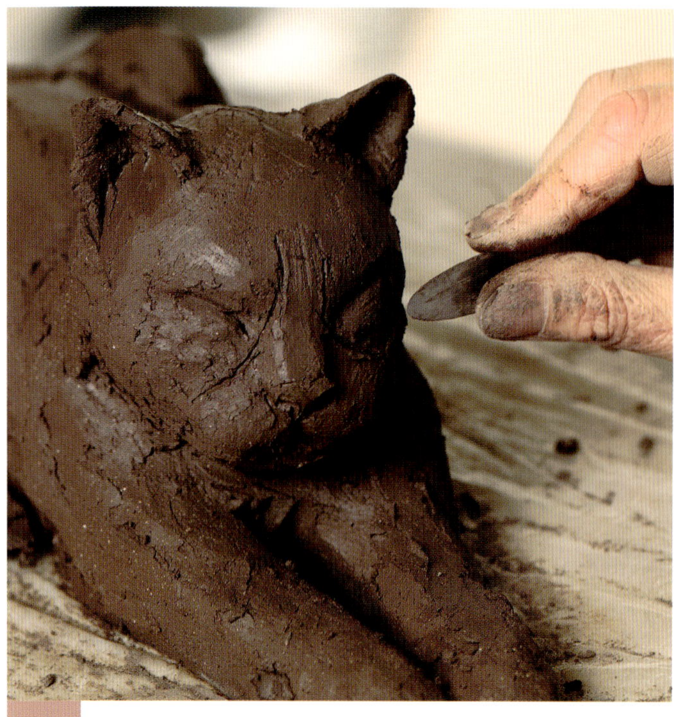

9 Underneath its closed eyes (which have the shape of a grain of rice), accentuate the jugal bone (cheekbone). Seen from above, the cheekbones form a triangle with the muzzle. You should also delimit the areas of the head that have different tonalities by tracing their contours with a potter's needle.

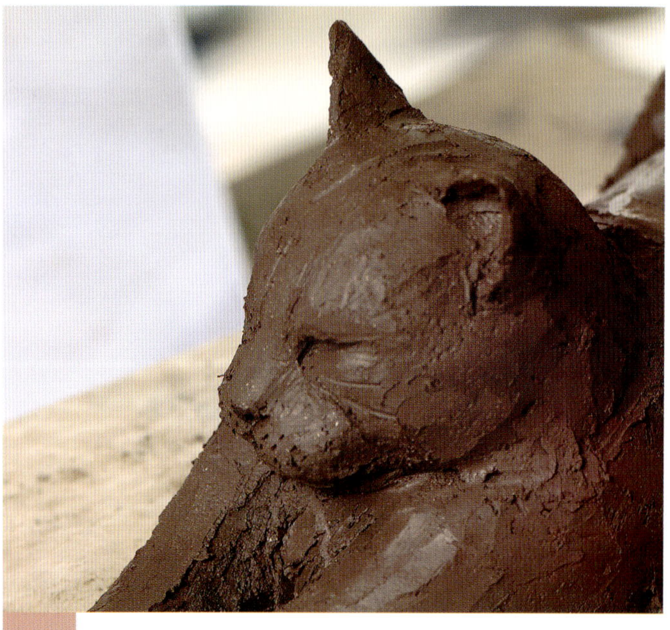

10 The cat's face is complicated to reproduce because the eye sockets and the jugal bones are very large. The two rounded parts that form the muzzle and protect the canines are narrower and detached from the jugal bone, while in profile the forehead and nose are smooth. Make the holes for the whiskers on the eyebrows and the muzzle with a potter's needle.

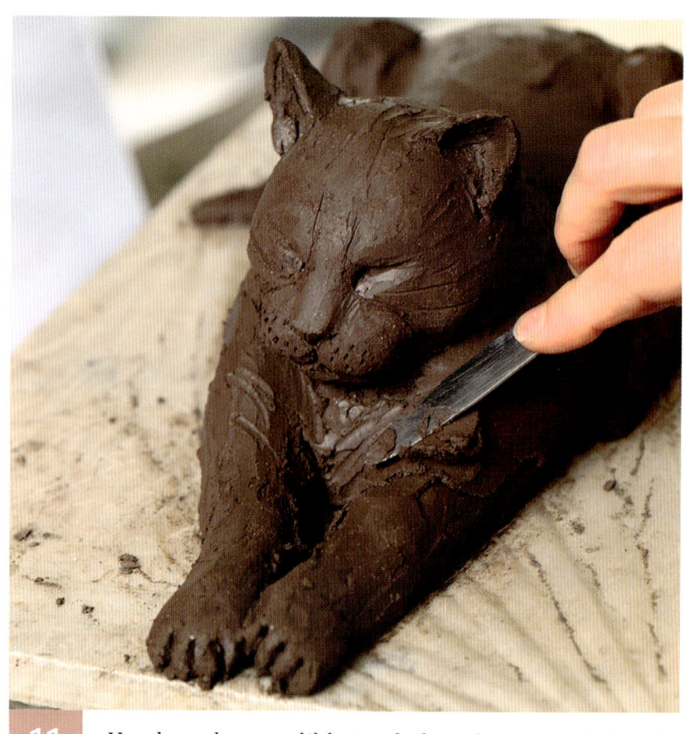

11 Head on, the mandible just below the muzzle is hardly visible. In profile, we can see that it is farther back than the muzzle. Add a little volume to the front part of the rib cage. At this spot the skin is creased, so work on it with a knife.

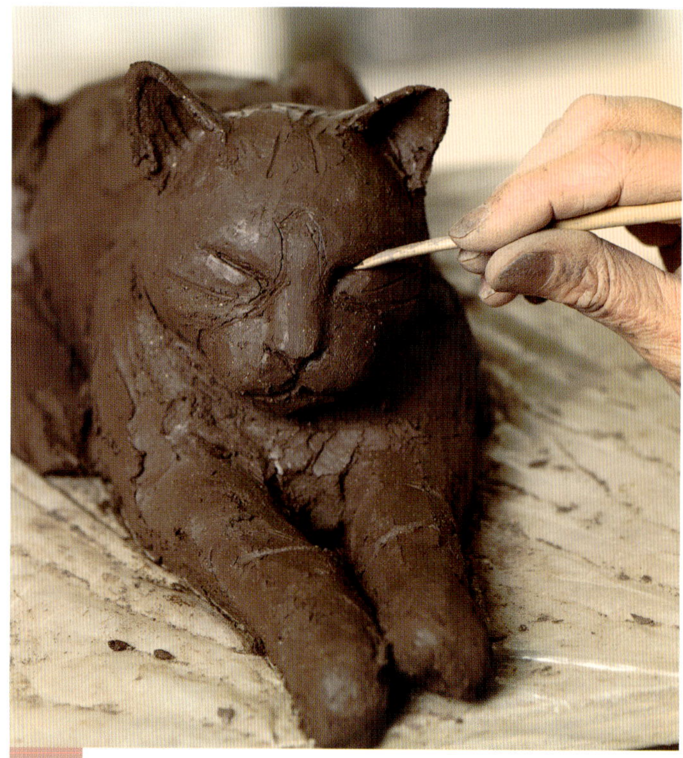

12 The piece is almost finished, so go back over the details. Here, the line of the closed eyelids is improved by using a boxwood modeling tool.

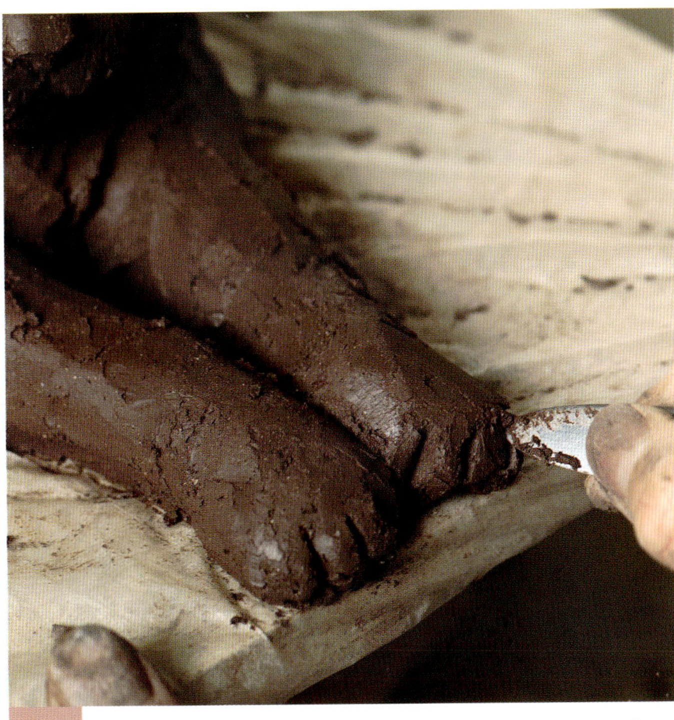

13 Detail the paws and claws with a knife and polish them with a wooden sculpting tool.

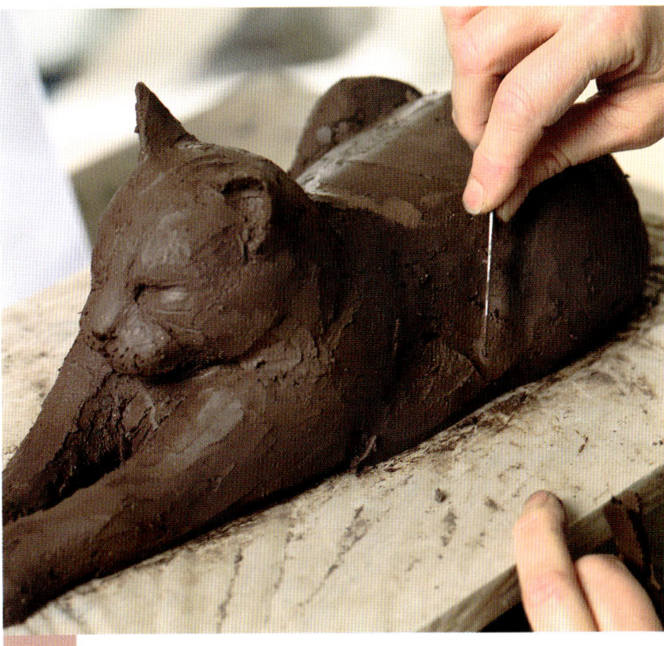

15 Retouch the cat's flanks. On each side, a band of skin forms a tongue-like shape. This is not the back feet, which are folded under the body, but the cat's ample and supple coat. Finish the last retouches and then leave it to dry out overnight.

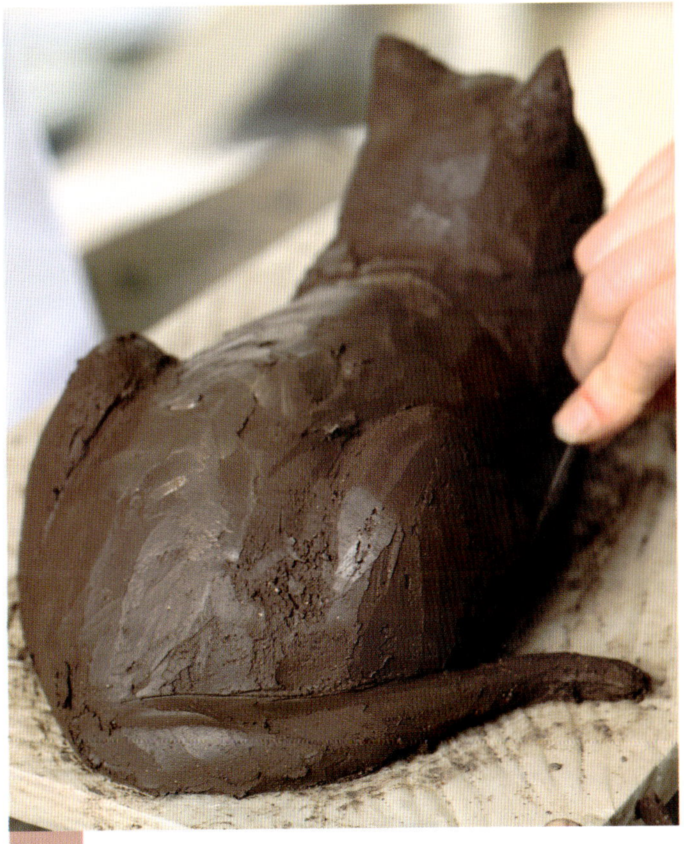

14 Do the cat's tail with a knife. It lies along the right side of the haunch and is mostly attached to the body.

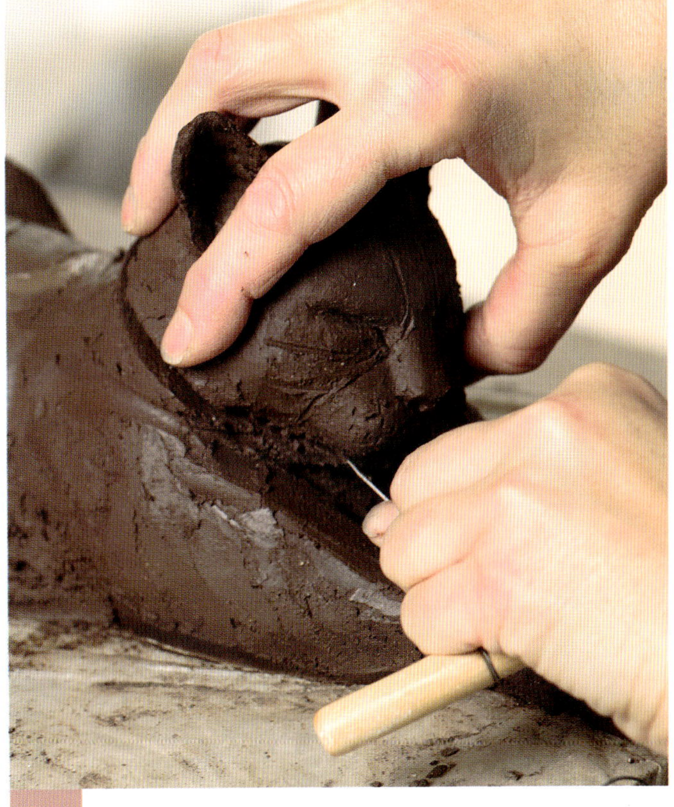

16 Now it's time to hollow out your sculpture, starting by the head, which surpasses the body. Cut it off at the base with a wire clay cutter. It will be easy to stick it back on because the neck is large.

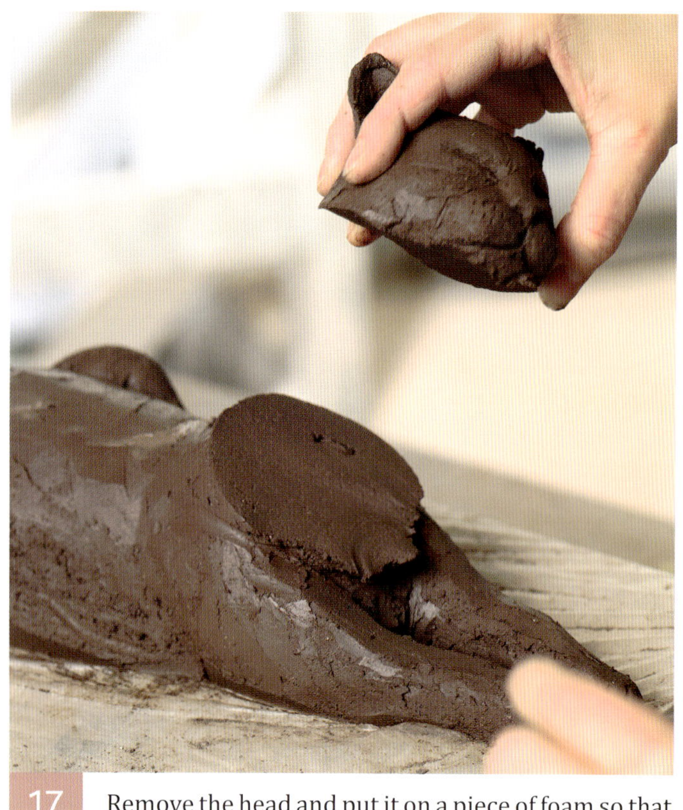

17 Remove the head and put it on a piece of foam so that it doesn't get deformed.

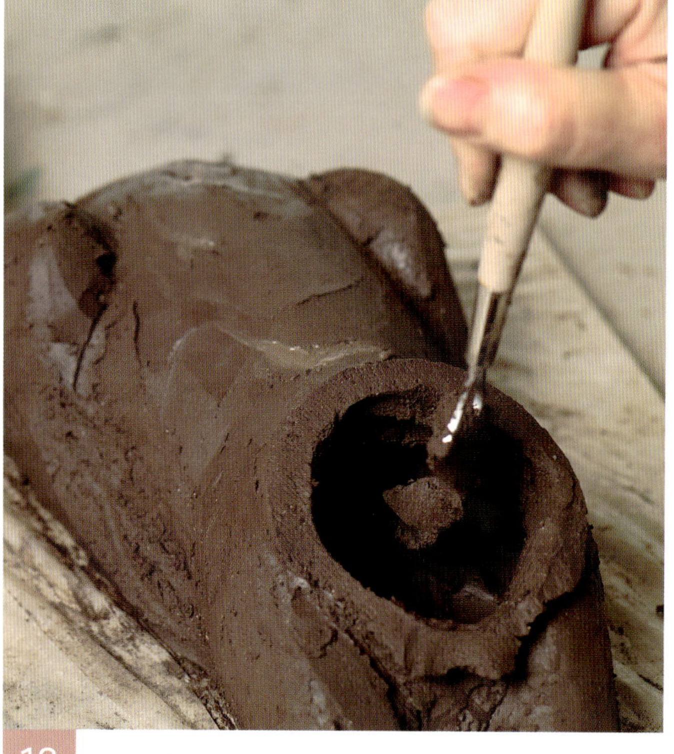

18 Use a large loop tool to dig out as much of the neck and shoulders as possible, leaving a shell of around $^{1}/_{3}$" thick.

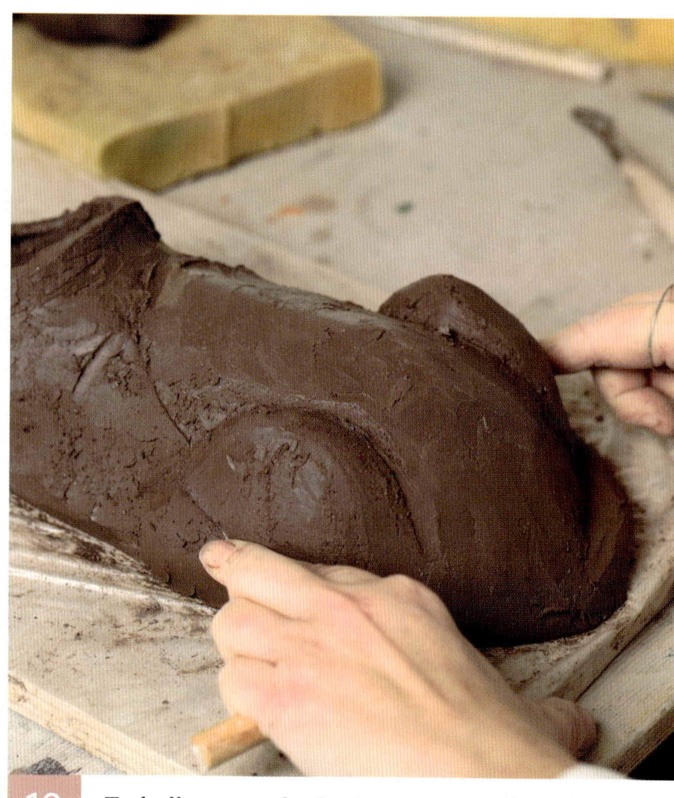

19 To hollow out the body, use your clay wire cutter, starting from the base of the neck and cutting backward, removing as much clay as possible.

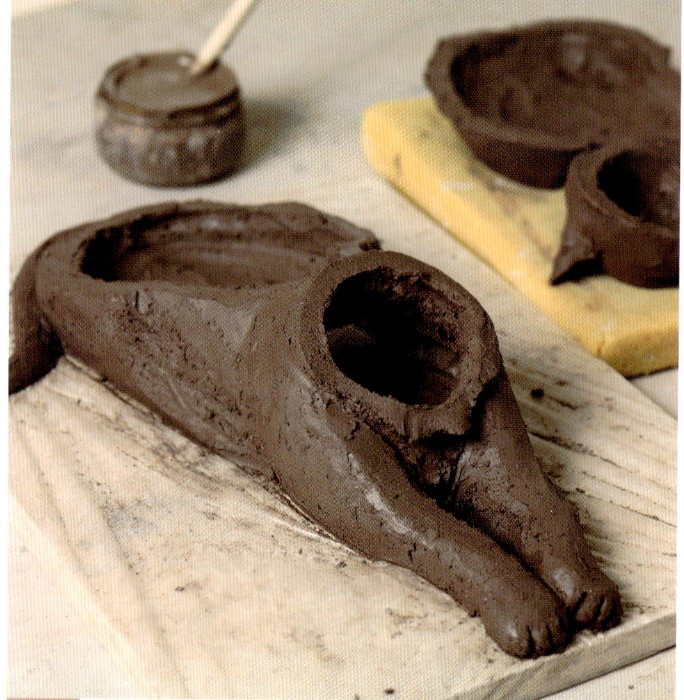

20 Remove the back and put it on a piece of foam. Then hollow out the pieces put aside (head and back) with a rounded loop tool, leaving a shell of $^{1}/_{3}$" thick.

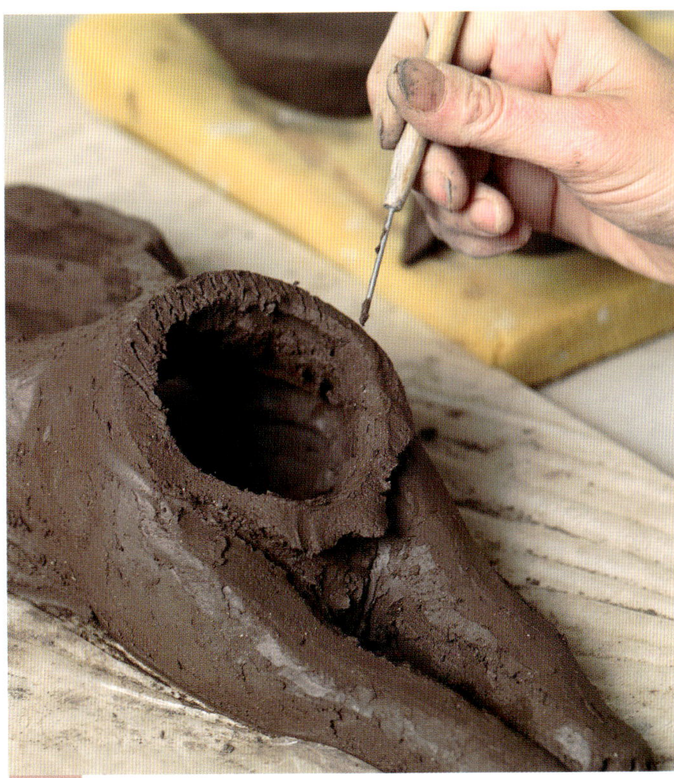

21 Score the edges of the seams (see "Scoring" on page 27).

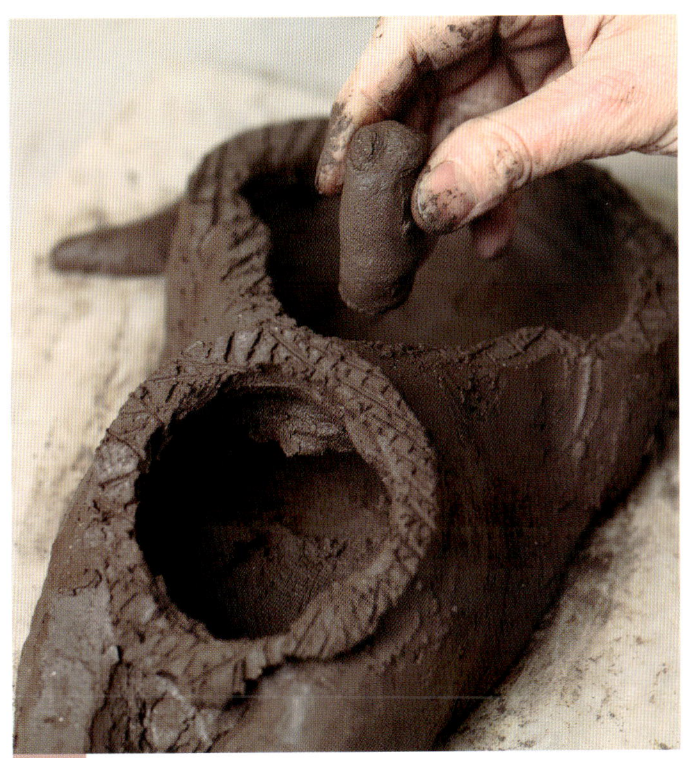

22 Make a small clay column, which will support the neck when you put your piece back together. The volume is almost empty, and the neck might subside a little at the bottom when you put the back in place.

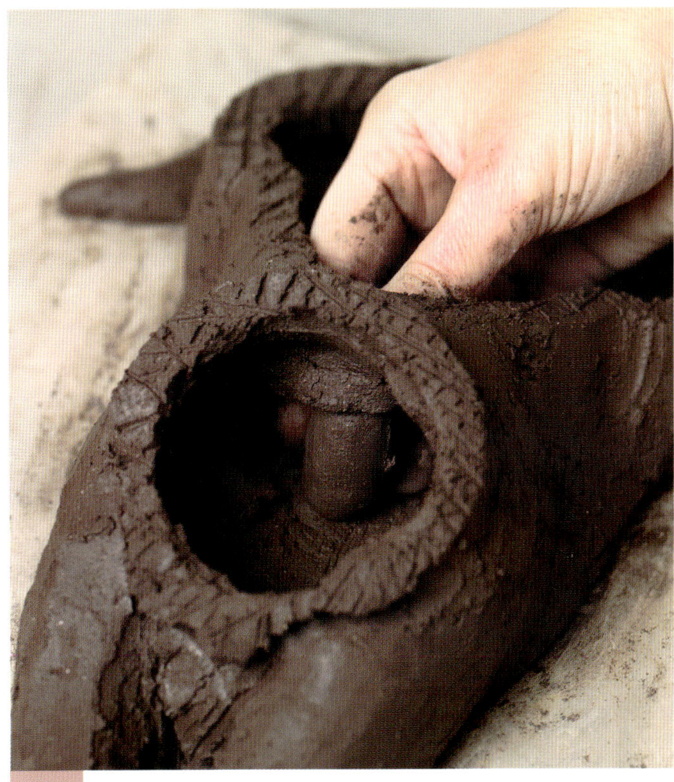

23 Place the column under the band of the neck. It will support this fragile part while you put the back in place and work on the seams.

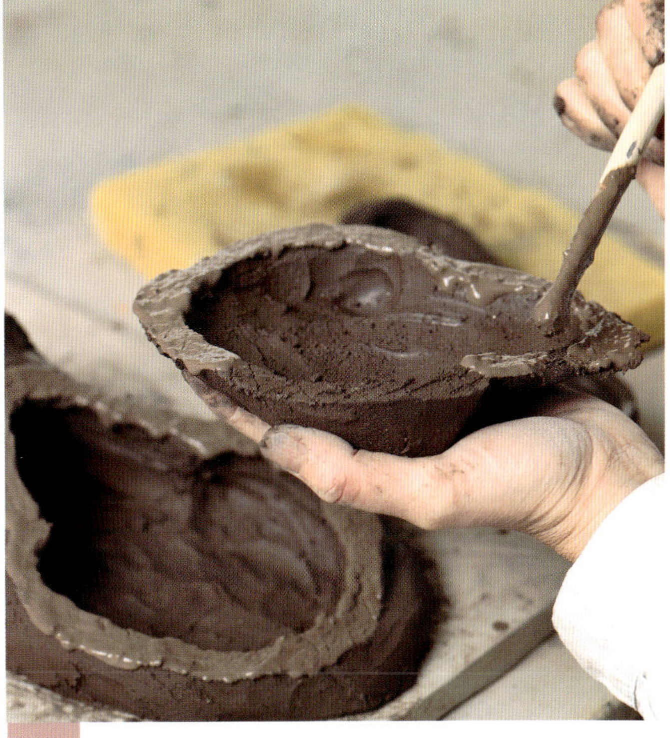

24 Paint slip in the edges to be glued together, and put the cat's back in place.

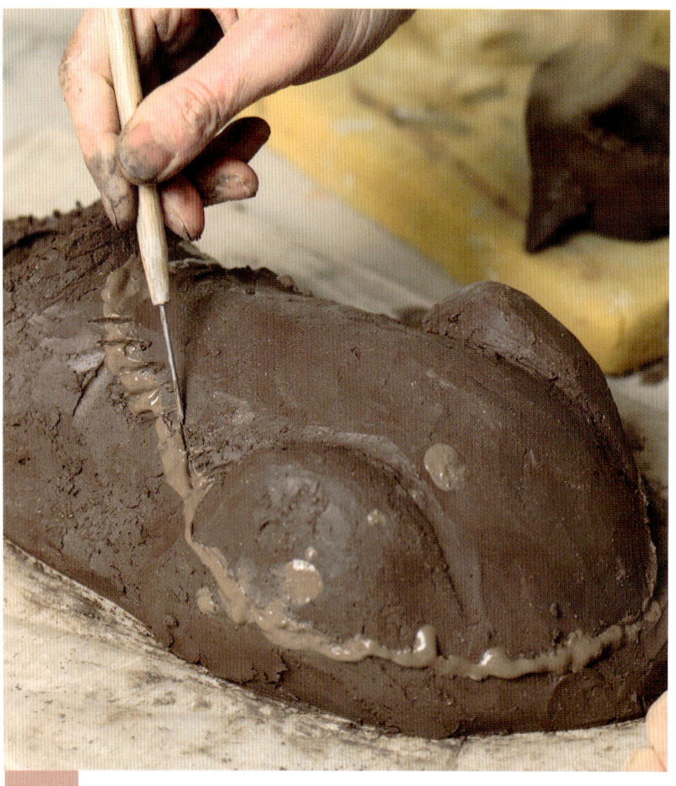

25 Score along the seams to mix the clay.

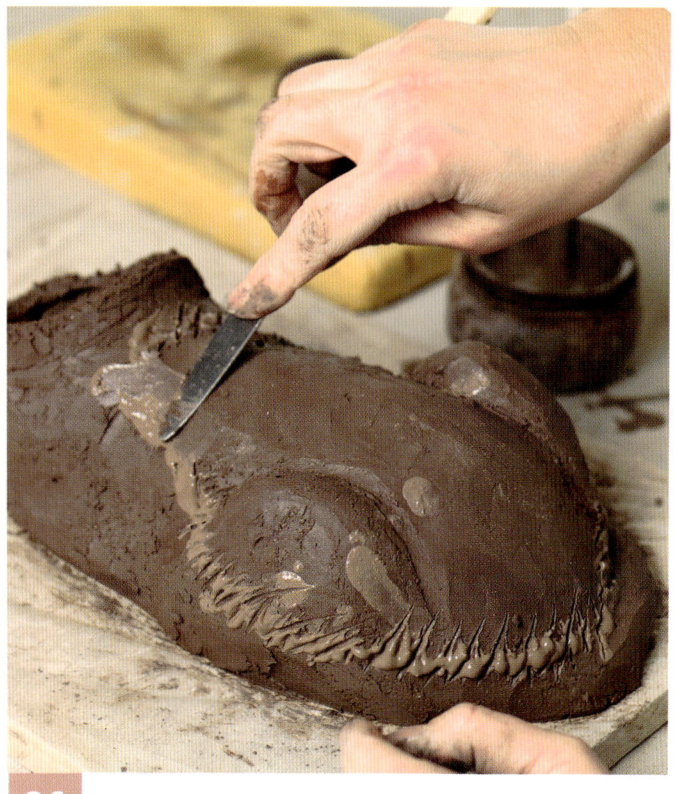

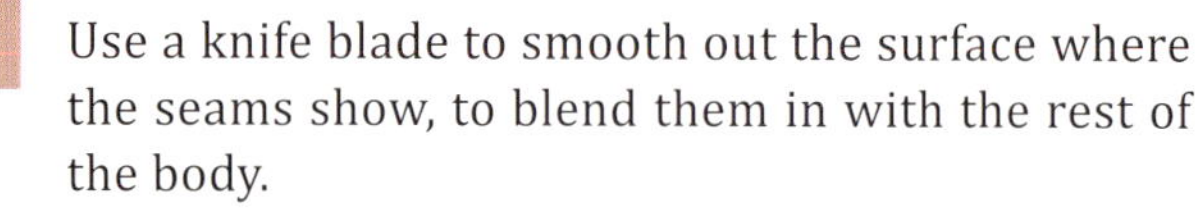

26 Use a knife blade to smooth out the surface where the seams show, to blend them in with the rest of the body.

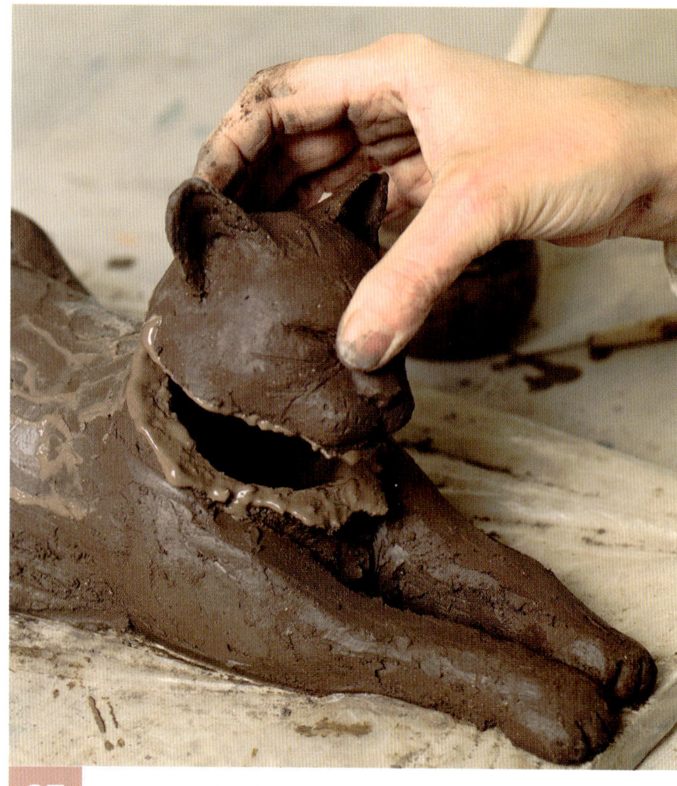

27 Once the back is in place and the seams no longer show, remove the small column of clay and replace the head in the same way as the back.

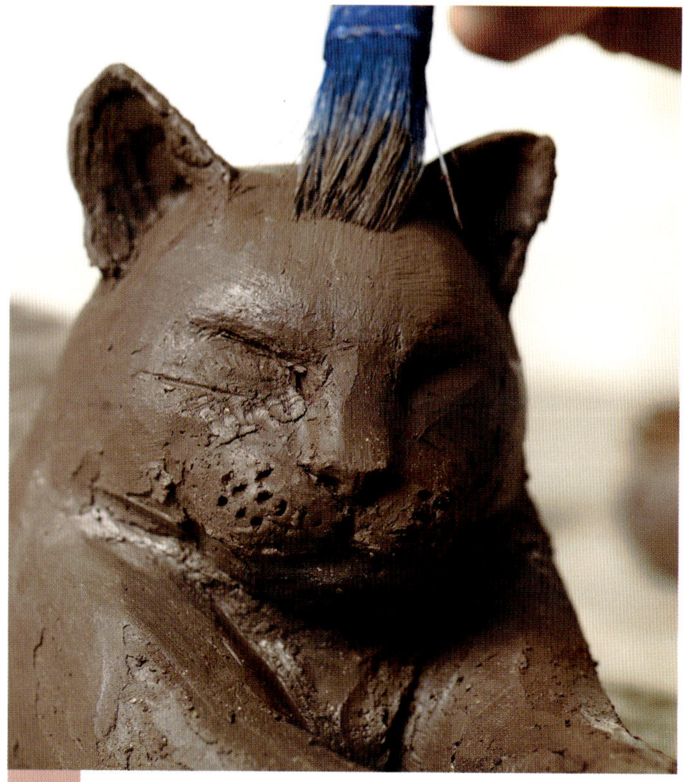

28 To create an impression of fur, use a stiff-haired brush all over the surface of the damp clay.

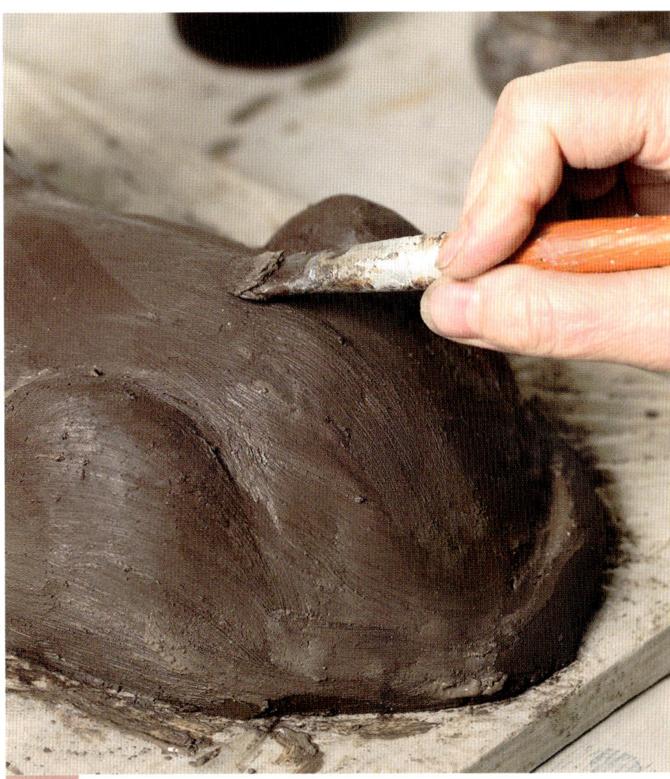

29 Follow the direction the fur lies with your brush.

30 Before leaving your sculpture to dry out, add an engobe in another color (porcelain white) to represent the white patches of fur. In a week's time, your cat will be dry enough to fire.

31 Don't forget to pierce a hole under the body so that the air trapped in the hollowed-out body can escape and fire your cat at 2,336°F (stoneware temperature).

Patina

1 Once your cat has been fired and cooled, you can put a patina on its fur (see "Patina" on page 36) with Caparol (or shellac) mixed with red ocher and burnt umber. The tint should be a little darker than the color of the clay to bring out the imprint of the fur made by the stiff-haired brush.

2 For the whiskers, use plastic thread glued into the holes you made around the eyebrows and muzzle (use heavy-duty glue such as Araldite).

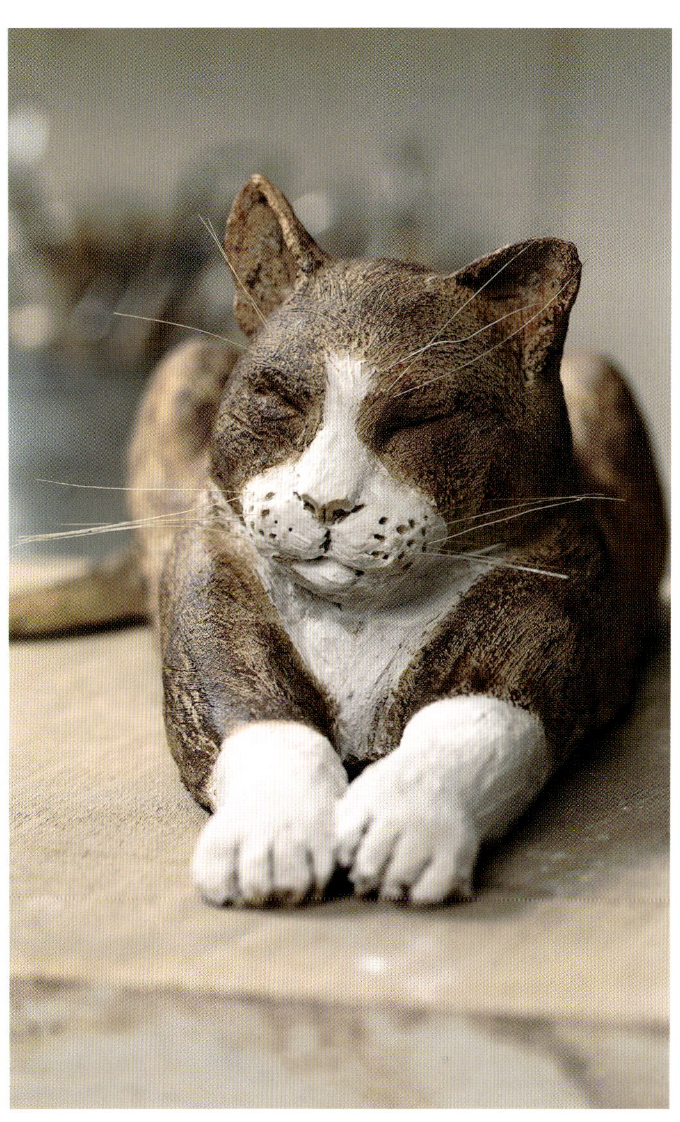

Standing Nude

The naked body is difficult for beginners because it is often overwhelming to find oneself faced with a living model with all its complexities. Working from a photo allows you to take your time and go back over details, while a living model means you have to work faster. Take your time at the outset, because you really need to observe your model to understand its proportions and the articulations of the different blocks of its structure. In addition, due to the height of the structure and the softness of the clay, the representation will never remain upright without the help of supports (armatures), which are removed as you go along, or a back iron.

In the case of a standing model, one rule is important: the lower half of the person (the legs) must be a solid block of unfired clay as long as the top half (hips, belly, torso, head, and arms) isn't finished. When the latter is finished (and hollowed out if possible), the matter will have stiffened and it will be possible to work on the legs and define the ankles and the feet. Without a support (back iron), working on the lower half of the body is difficult and dangerous. With a back iron, the piece is stable and you can reduce the volume to the desired shape and finesse without weakening the entire structure (if the upper half has been hollowed out). This sculpture was done in raku clay with 0.05 percent grog and with a rust-colored shellac patina.

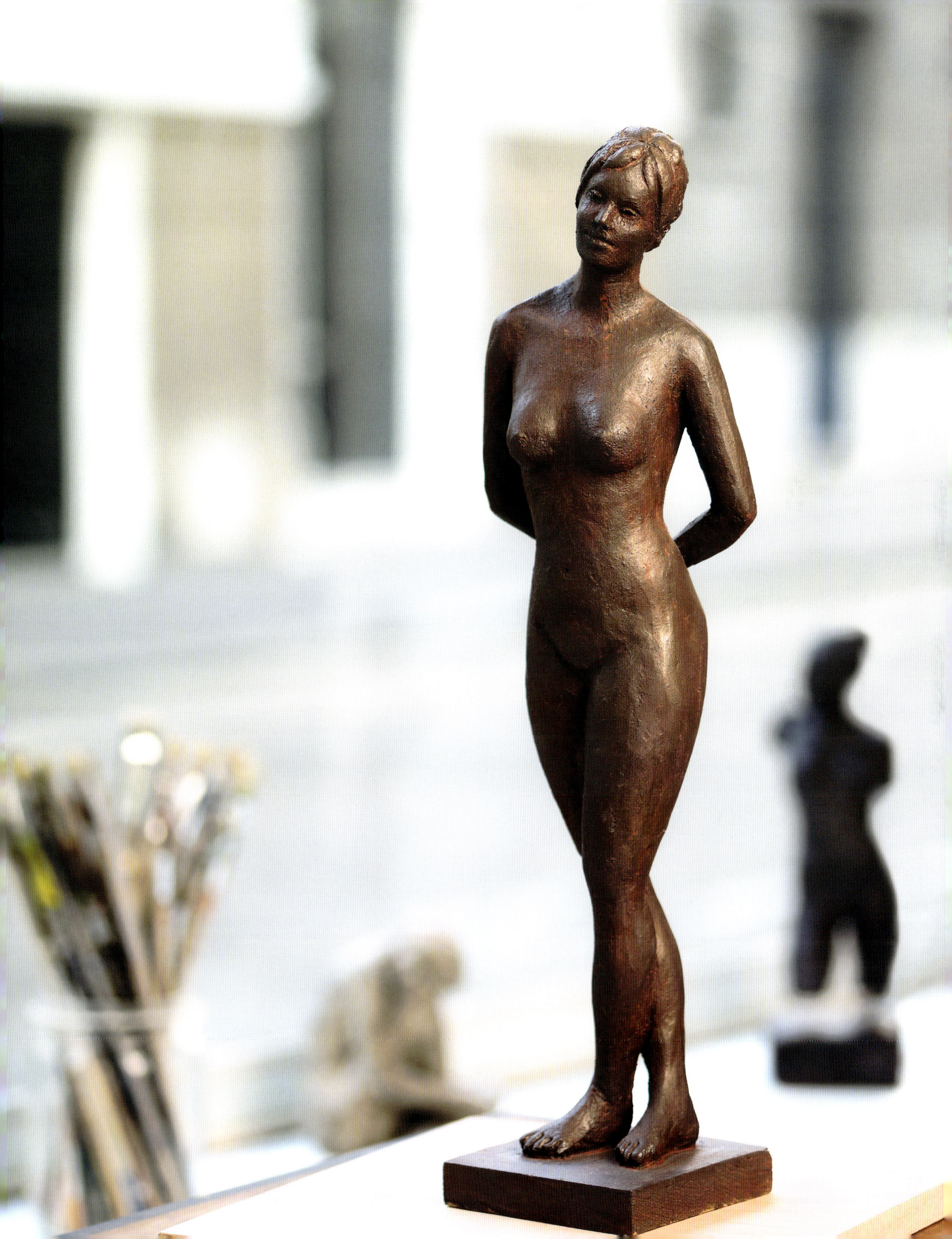

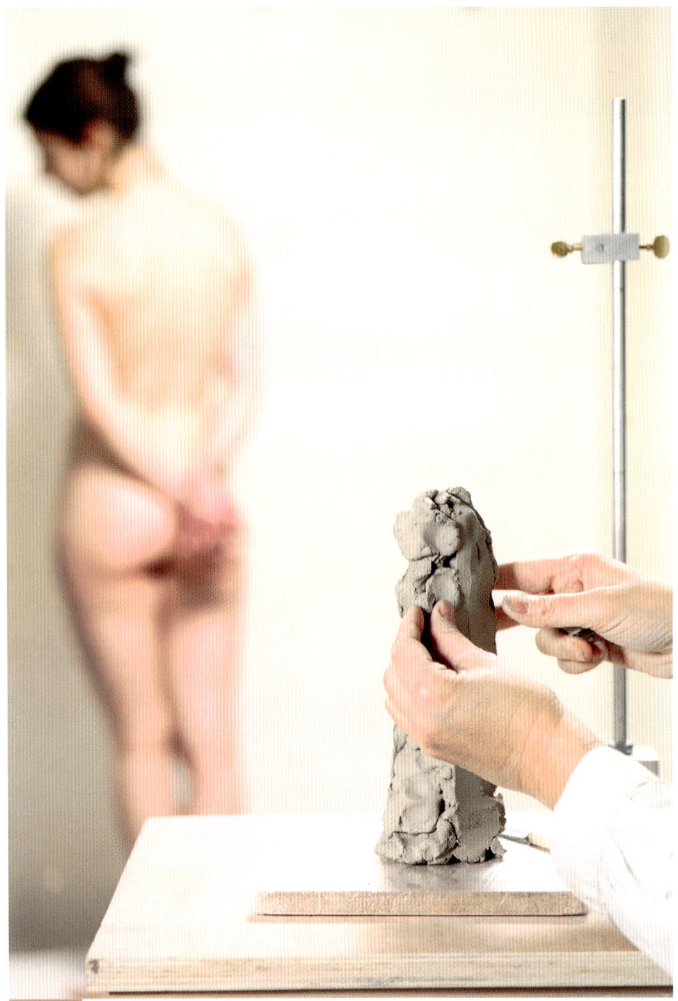

1 Here, the model's torso is very long, and the middle of the body is situated above the pubis. The hips are horizontal, and the crossed feet (where they touch the floor) are situated directly below the navel and the base of the neck. The torso is twisted to the left, the left shoulder is lower, and the head is turned toward the left. Imagine the simplification and the construction of the model before starting. Place a small board protected by plastic wrap alongside your back iron. Build, by means of small added pieces, a parallelepiped in height that schematizes the volume of the legs and pelvis. Pack the clay so that it doesn't settle on its own with the weight you will be adding to it.

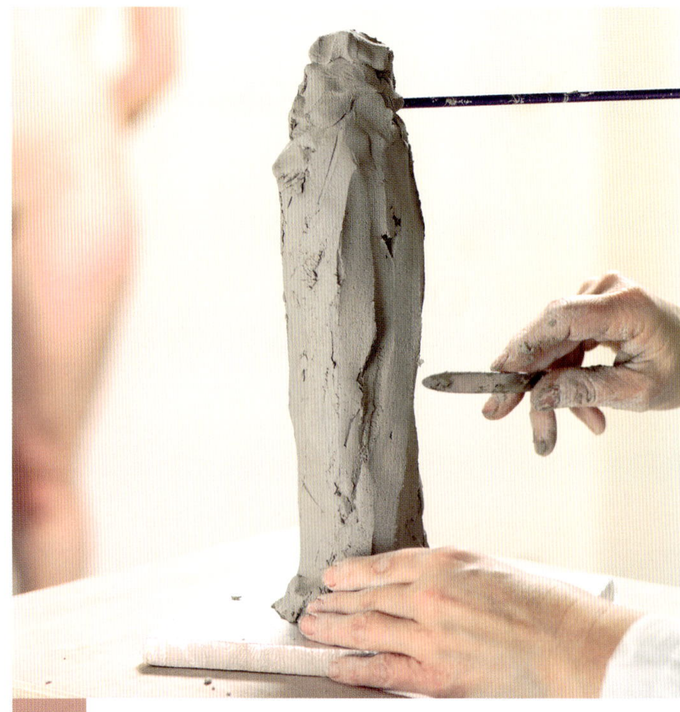

2 Support the volume with the back iron by pushing the bar through the clay's thickness. This bar will stay in place until you have hollowed out the upper part of the body and finalized the legs and feet. A single horizontal bar is sufficient for a volume of this dimension and form.

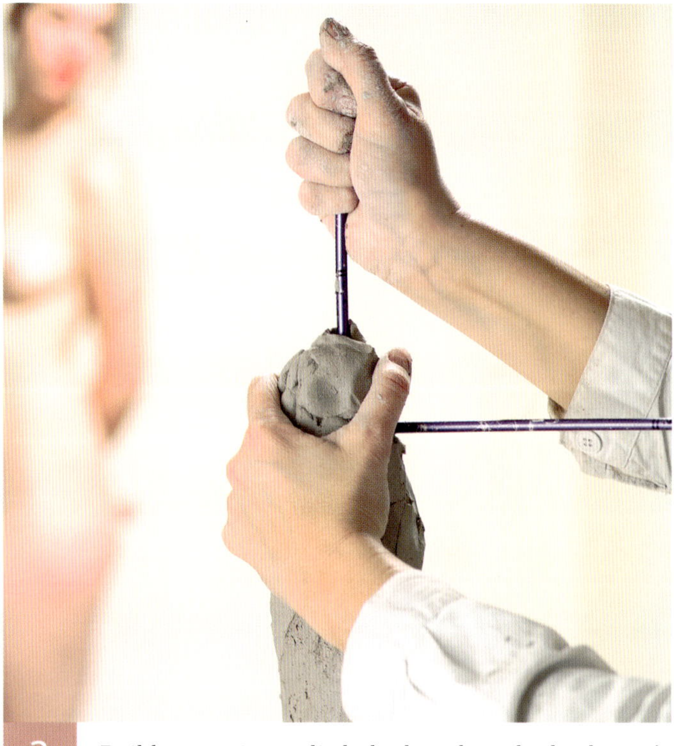

3 Build your piece a little higher than the back iron's horizontal bar and then plant an aluminum rod vertically through the center. This reinforcement will help the clay adhere at the top and will strengthen the lower part.

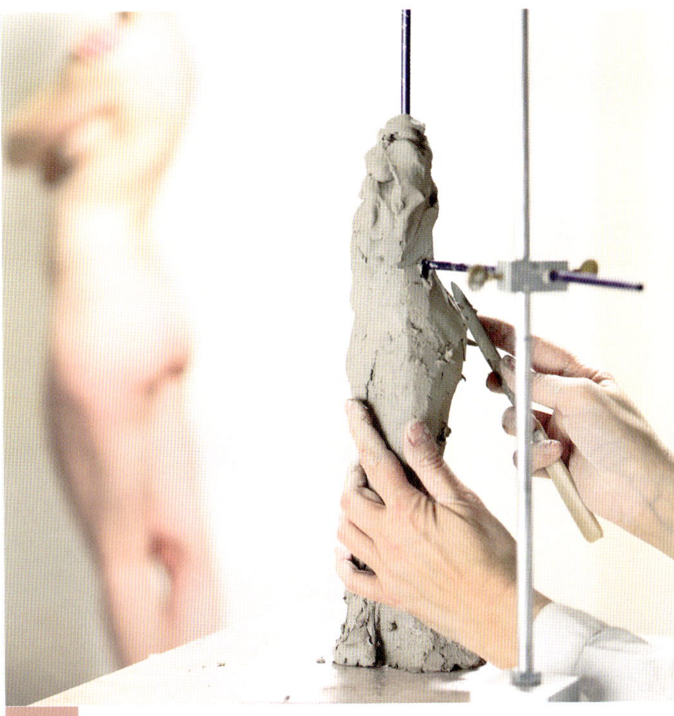

4 Shape the pelvis, which has a horizontal parallelepiped shape. At the back, shape the roundness of the buttocks in profile.

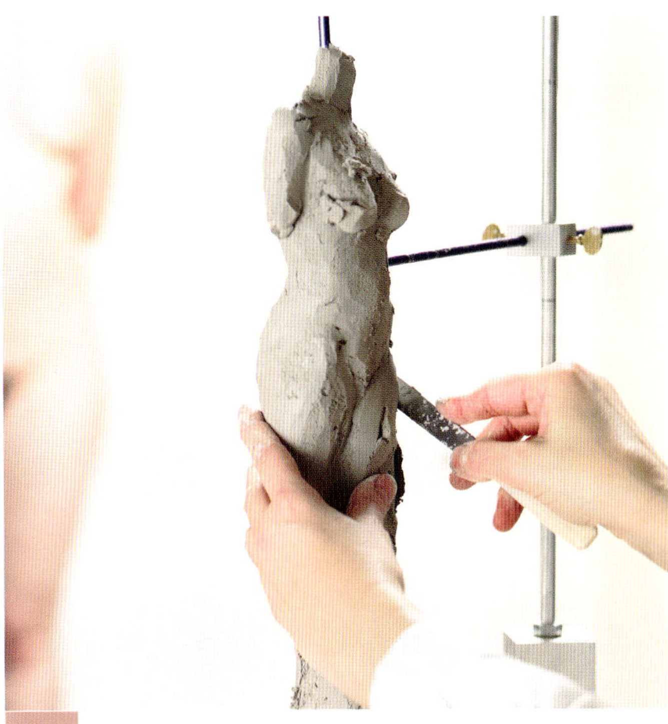

6 The torso's block is slightly twisted to the left in relation to the pelvic block. Add on the breasts.

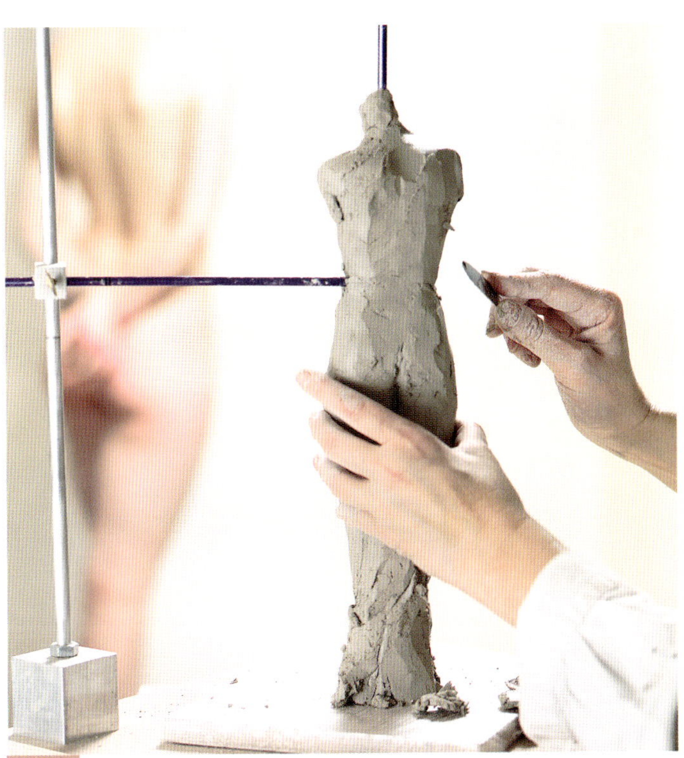

5 Then form the rib cage, which is slightly slanting, and in which you can create the appropriate egg-shaped form. Add on the shoulders on each side, the neck in the center, the trapezius on each side of the neck, and the "W"-shaped shoulder blades (see "The Body" on page 60). The model's left shoulder is lower than the right one.

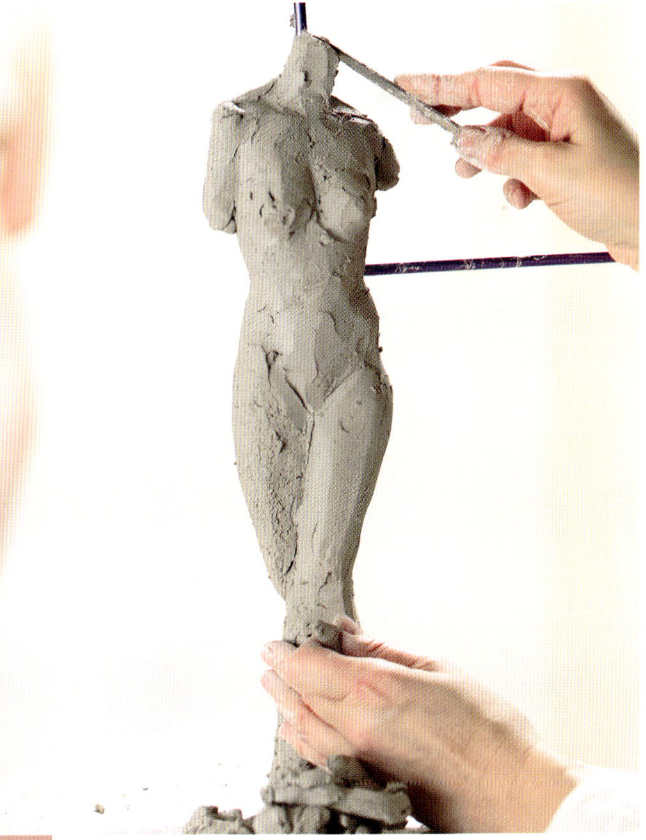

7 At this stage you have built three blocks: the legs (vertical parallelepiped shape), the pelvis (horizontal parallelepiped shape), and the rib cage (vertical parallelepiped shape).

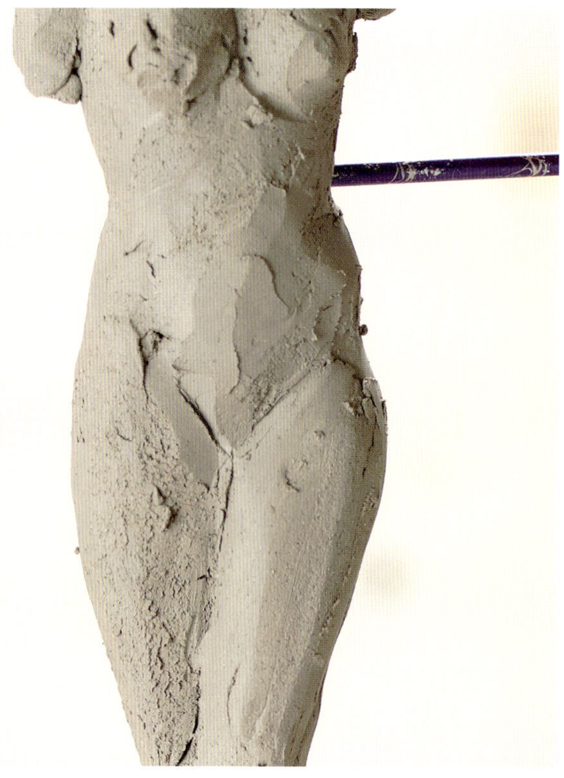

8 Shape the stomach and round out the hips. Smooth out the thighs, making sure not to refine the ankles, because the bottom block is supporting the volume for the moment and ensures its equilibrium.

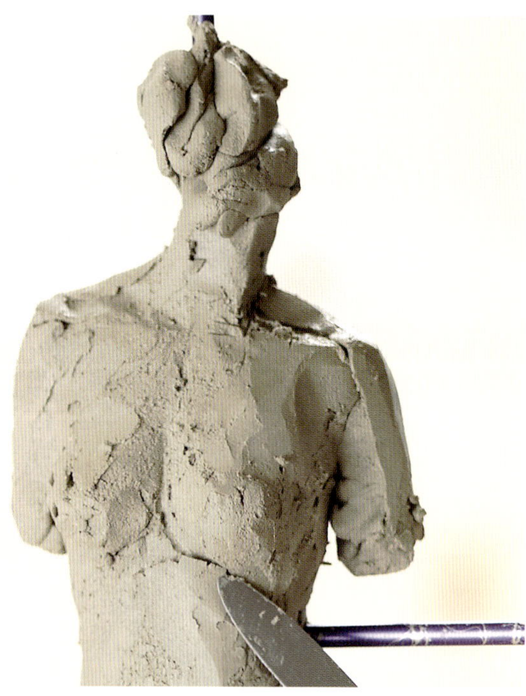

9 Add on the head, working in profile to base the structure of the jaw and the way it juts out in front of the neck (see "The Skull" section, on page 43). Check your proportions, remembering that the head represents $^1/_8$ of the total height of the body.

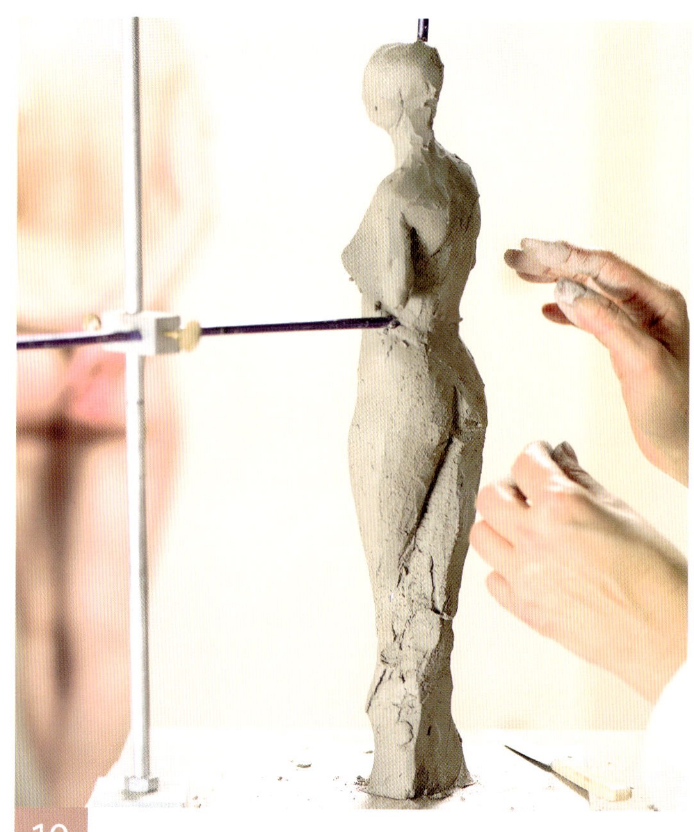

10 Control your work by comparing it to your model. At this stage it doesn't have its upper arms or forearms.

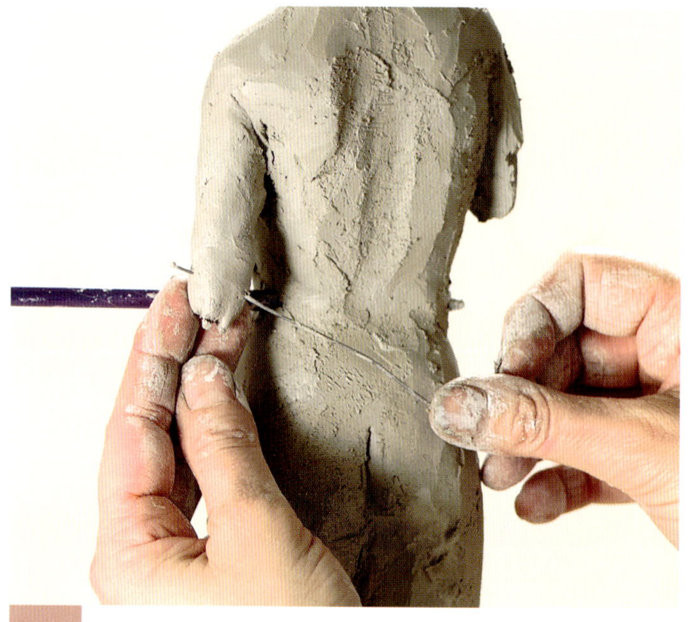

11 To create the arms, which are crossed behind the back, use special nickel-chrome wire, which will guide the clay and can be fired at high temperatures. It will be removed before the clay dries out. It will help you build in a straight line easily from one point to another, reinforcing the constructed portion. Plant it at the elbow and place the other end where the wrist will be.

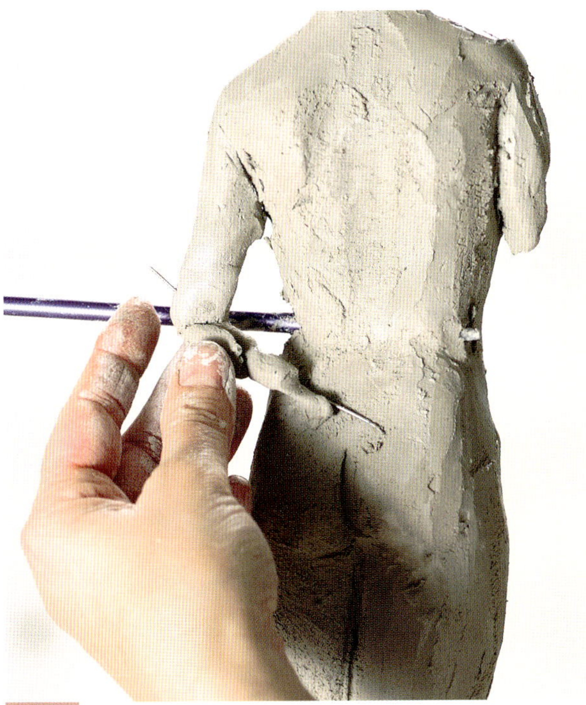

12 Form the arm by pinching the clay around the wire, and then increase the volume with slip to regularize the surface and glue the pieces of clay together.

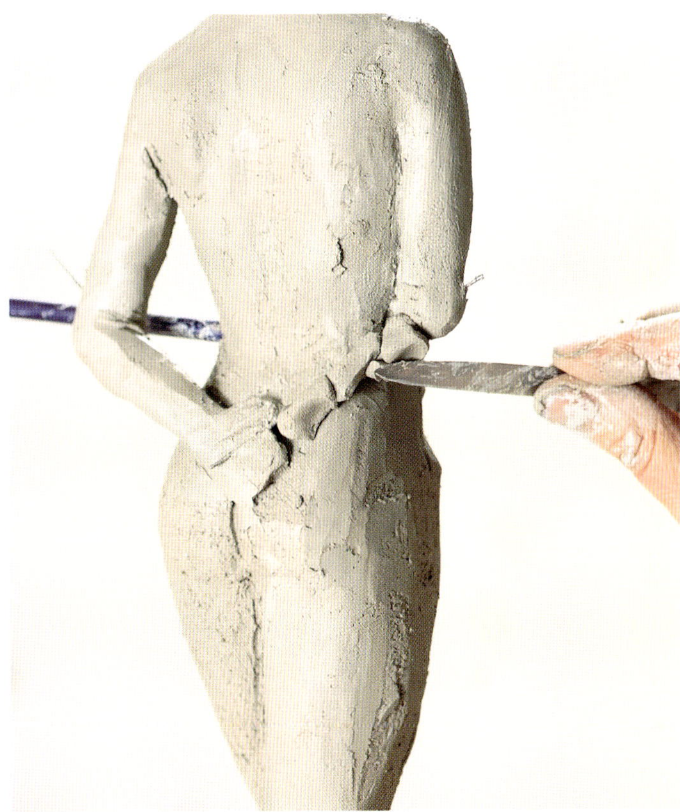

13 Work on the arm with a knife and then do the same for the other arm.

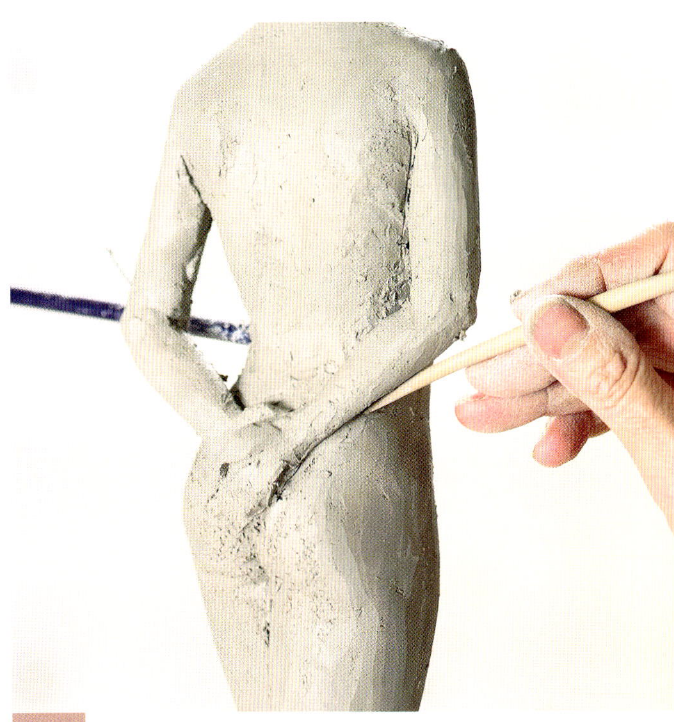

14 With a twisting gesture, retouch the contours of the arms by using a small, wooden clay tool to accentuate the rounded planes of the volume.

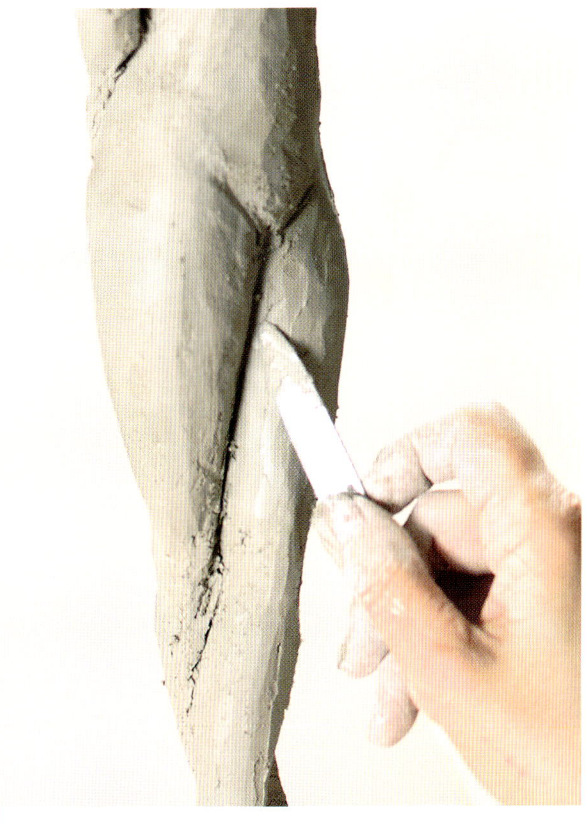

15 Little by little the clay hardens, and you can thin out the legs. Continue to work slowly without separating or completely refining their contours.

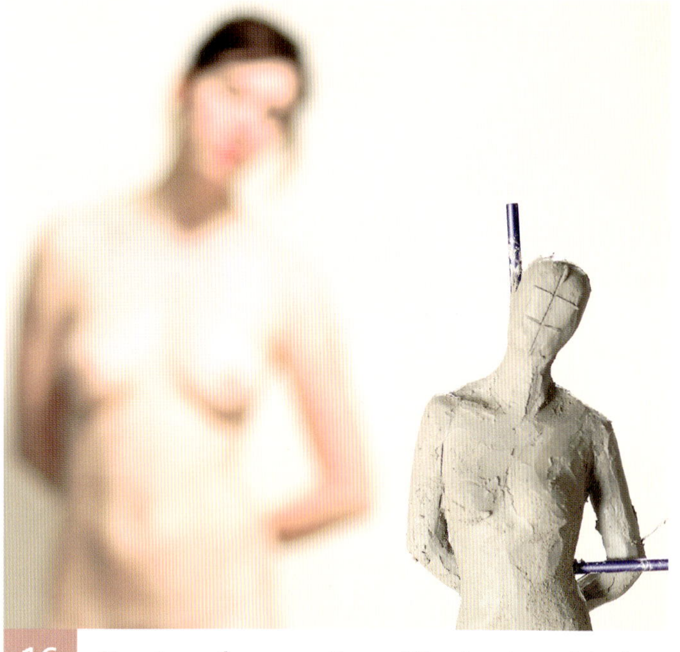

16 Now trace the proportions of the structure of the face. You can now remove the vertical rod that is sticking out of the neck.

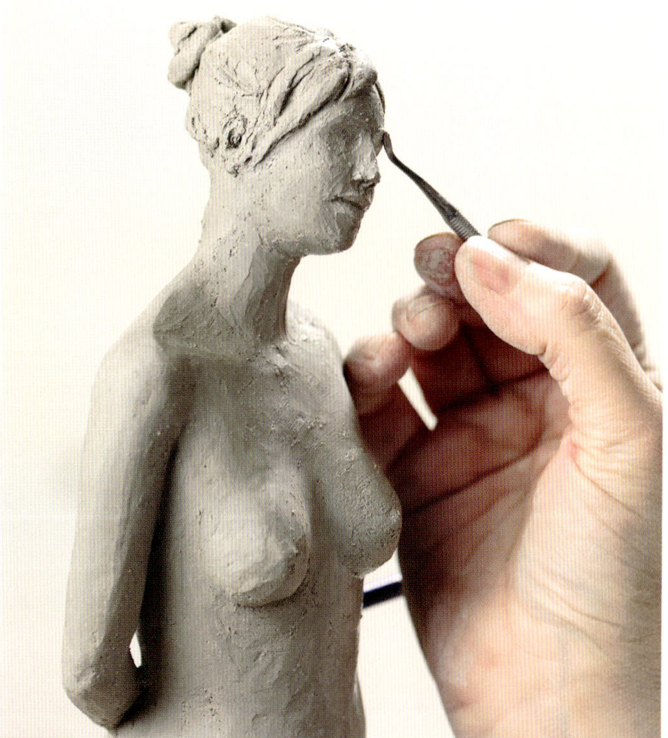

17 After clearing the elbow-shaped form of the jaw in profile, starting from a line that goes from the center of the neck and the skull, create the eye sockets. The arch of the eyebrows is situated on the same plane as the chin. Indent the temples slightly, plump out the jugal bone to create the cheekbones, and shape the nose.

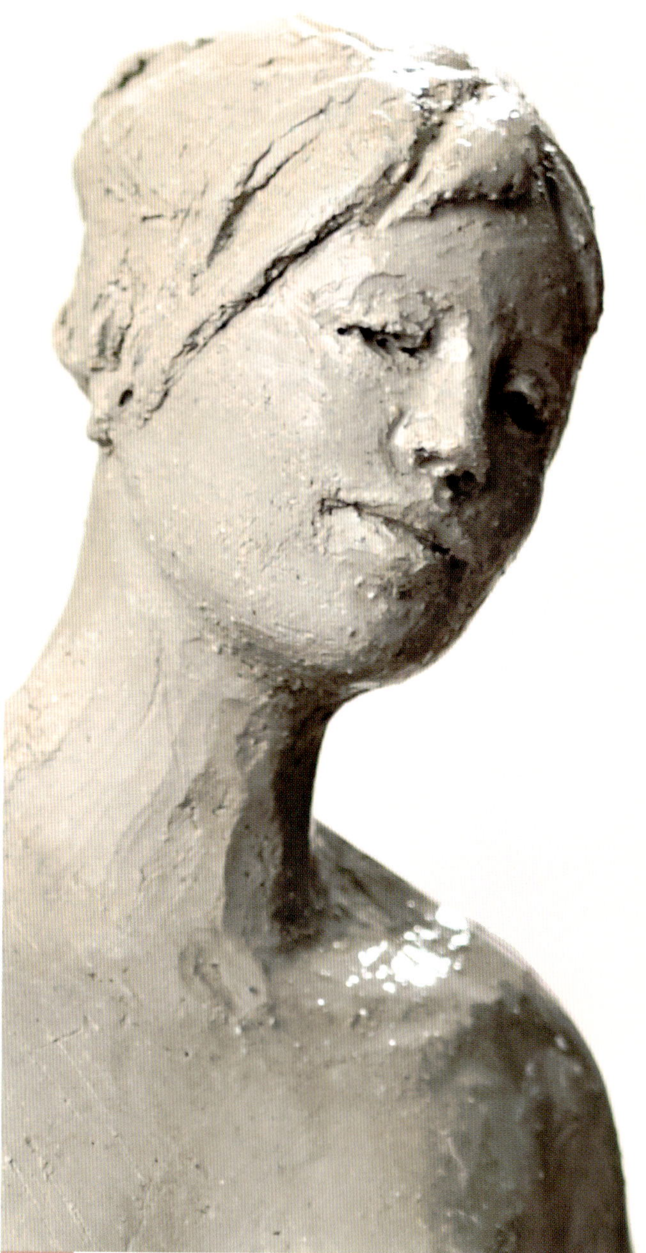

18 Place the teeth. Trace the mouth's opening, and open the lips by driving your flat clay tool into the opening and pushing the clay upward to form the upper lip and downward to form the bottom lip. Add tiny clay sausages to puff out the lips and work on the shape of their outline.

19 Make each eye with an elongated piece of clay placed inside the eye socket. Split this into an almond shape and open it to form the pupil. Carefully dig out the inner corner (lachrymal caruncle) and the outer corner of the eyes to give them a rounder aspect. Shape the pupil by using a pointed clay tool (see "The Face" section, pages 49–50).

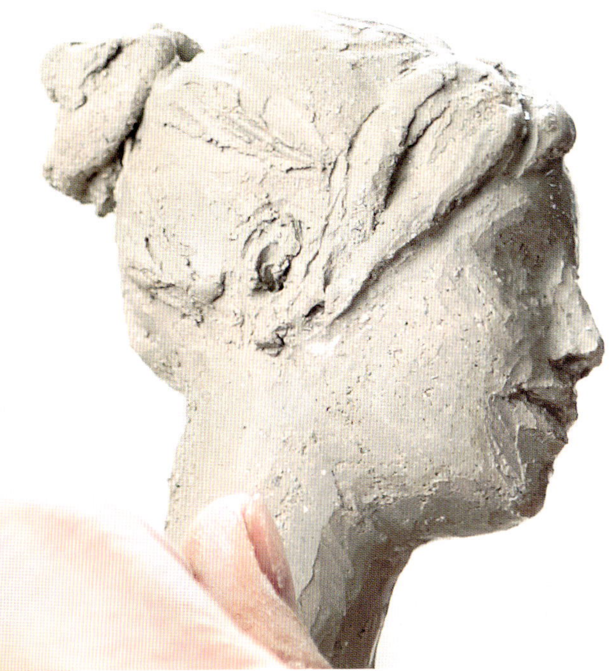

20 Make the ears at the junction between the mandible and the back of the head (see "The Face" section, on page 50).

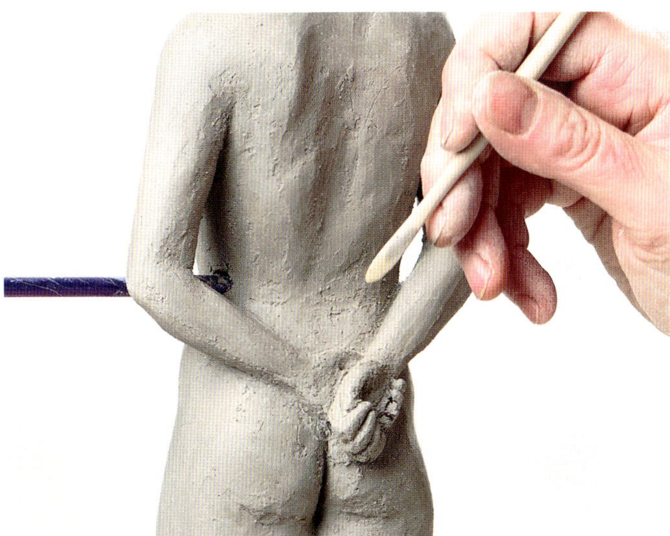

22 Take time to retouch the features with tools adapted to the size of the piece and to your gestures.

ADVICE

Remember to hydrate the clay from time to time with your spray bottle, because the piece is small and will dry out quickly. The clay should be firm and malleable for your tools.

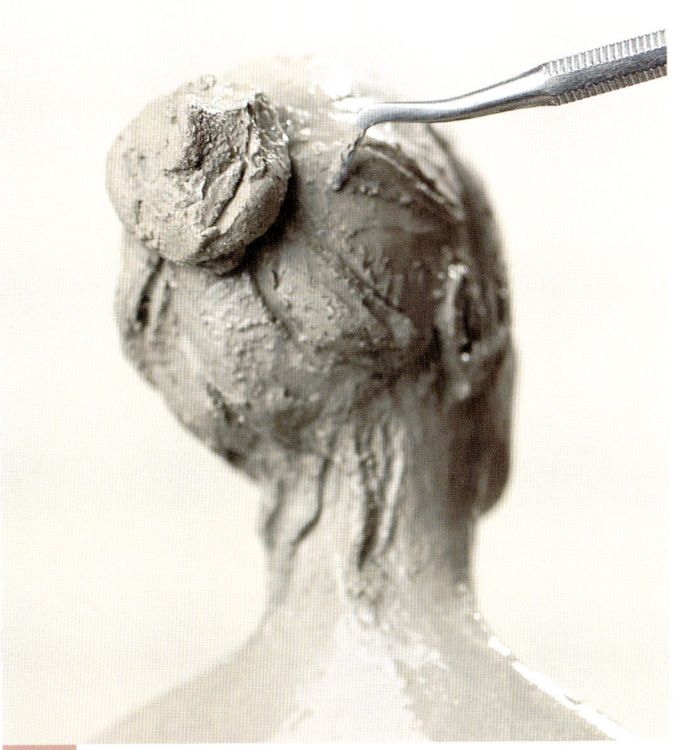

21 Place the clay that represents the hair around the face, after being sure to mark the principal axis (the implantation of the hair on the head and the direction of the different volumes from the starting point, which can be a side parting, for example).

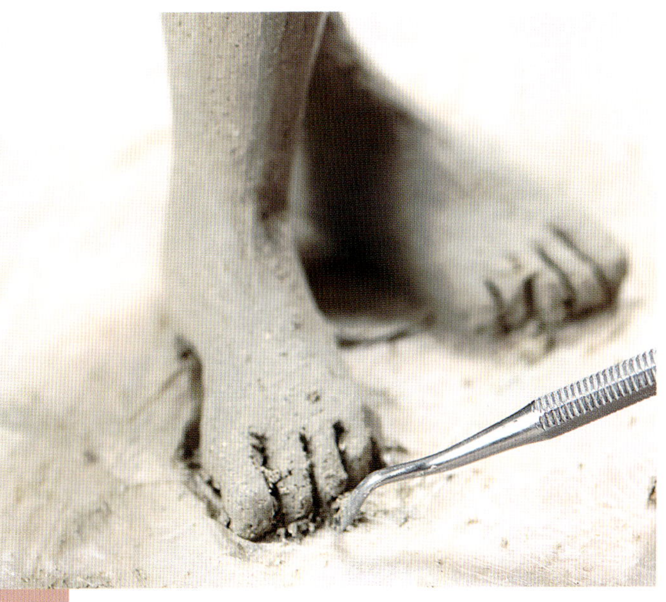

23 At this stage, hollow out your piece, starting by the back of the head. Continue with the front of the torso, the pelvis, and then the top of the thighs, without touching the legs. Close the hollowed-out shape with slip, starting by the last hollowed-out part and going up toward the head. Work on the seams to erase the marks (see "Hollowing Out" on page 27). Finish the feet's details.

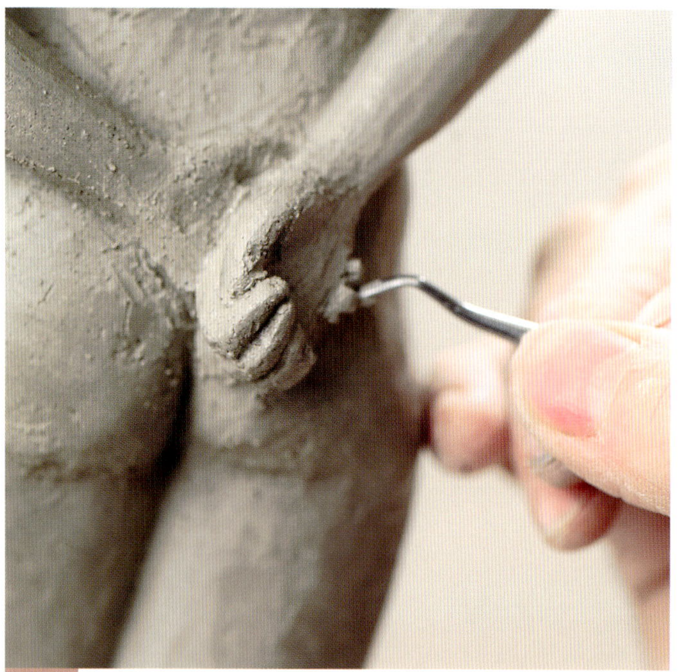

24 Retouch the hands and gently round out the fingers, using a tiny metal tool.

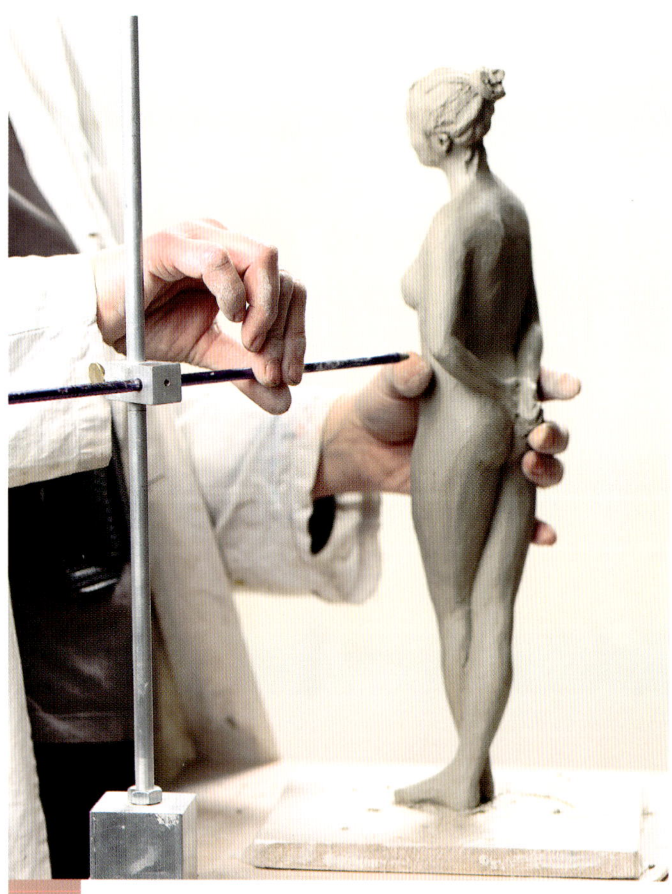

25 You can now remove your statue from the back iron. Don't forget to leave a small hole so that the air can escape before drying out.

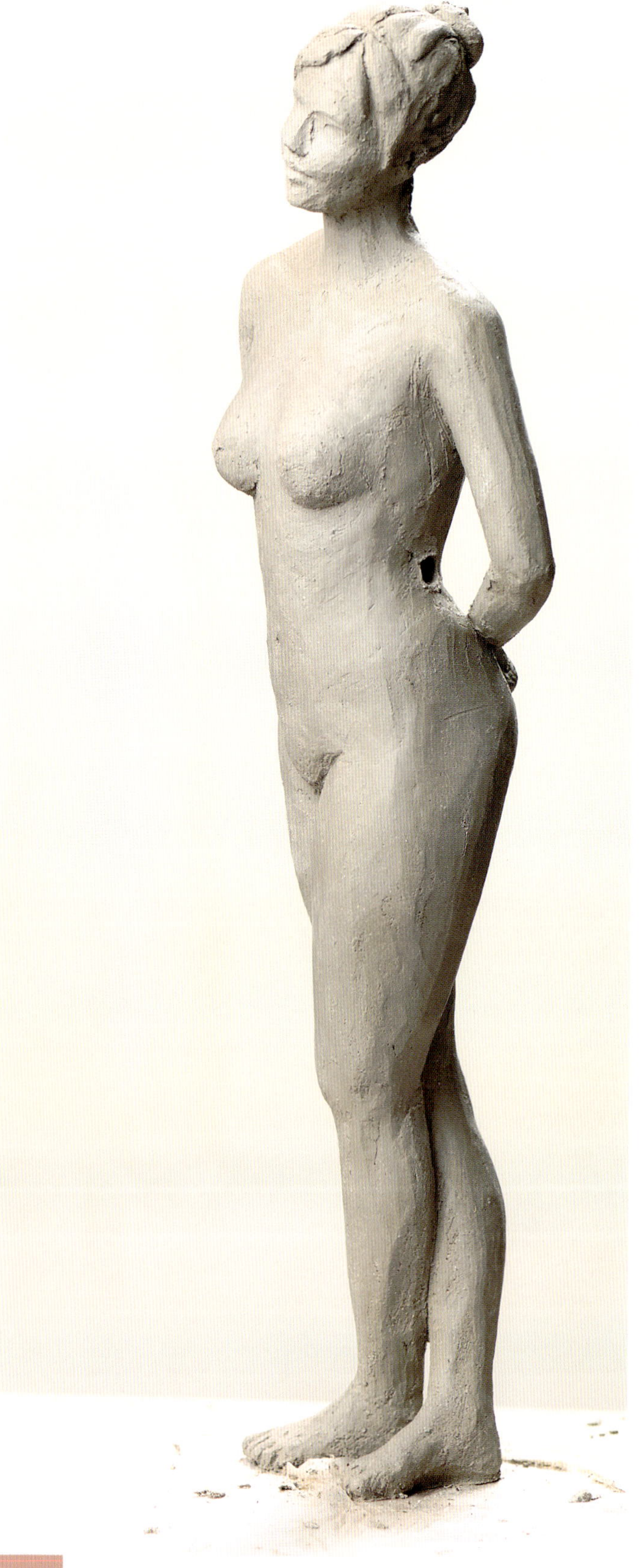

26 Your statue is well balanced; it stands upright without the help of the back iron.

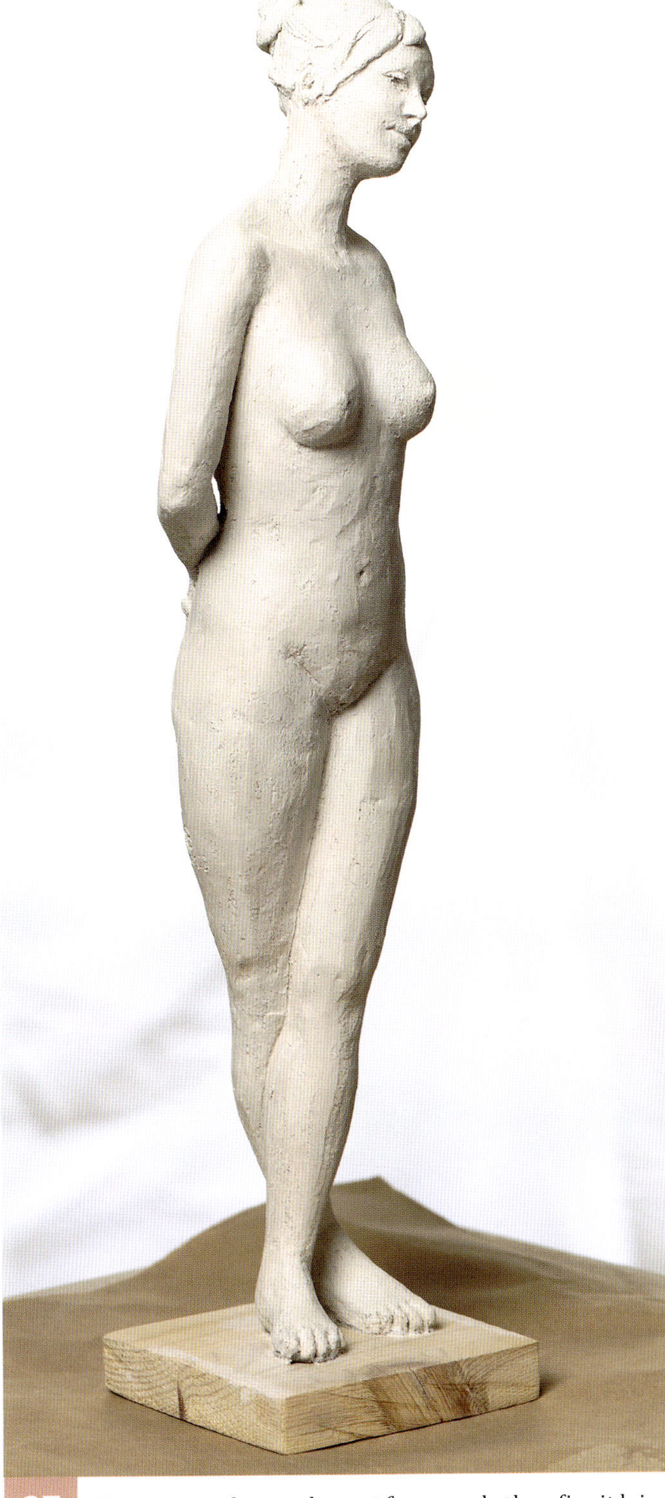

27 Let your sculpture dry out for a week, then fire it lying down, because the legs are slim and risk getting deformed by the weight. In this case we are firing at earthenware temperature (1,796°F) because the clay will be more porous at a lower temperature and the patina will stick to it better. To help your statue remain upright and not fall over once it has been fired, glue the feet to a small clay or wooden base, using strong glue (Araldite).

Rust-Colored Shellac Patina

1 Once your statue has been fired, leave it to cool down completely and fix it onto a small base before doing your patina (step 27). Pour a little white shellac into a bowl and add gold pigment. Paint this all over your statue, using a paintbrush, and let it dry.

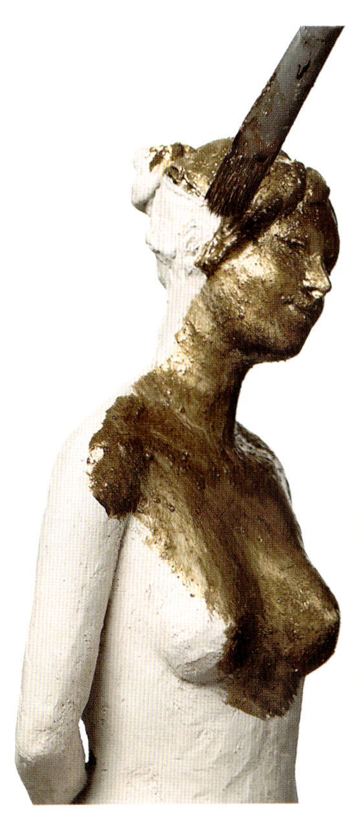

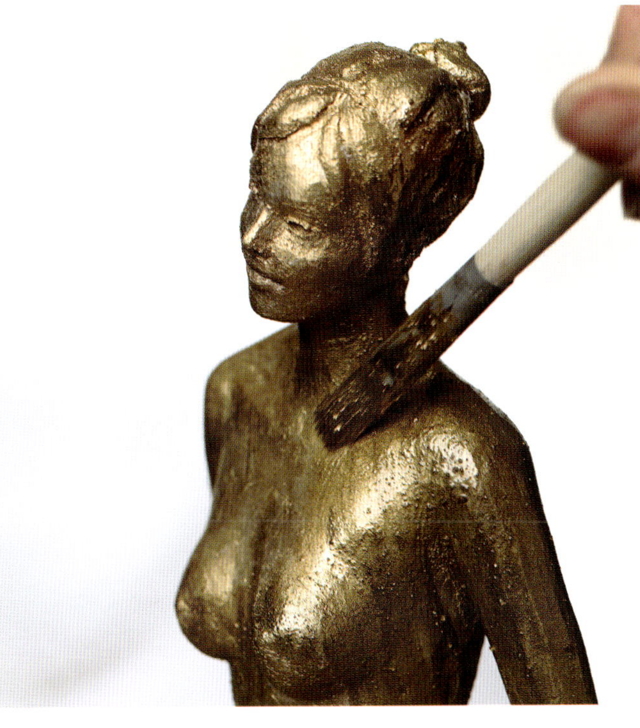

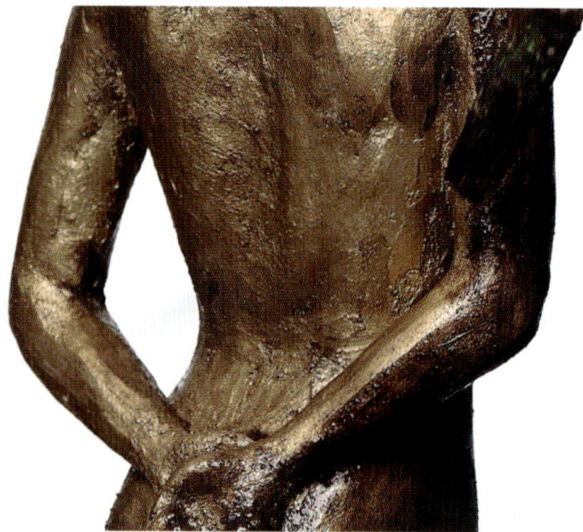

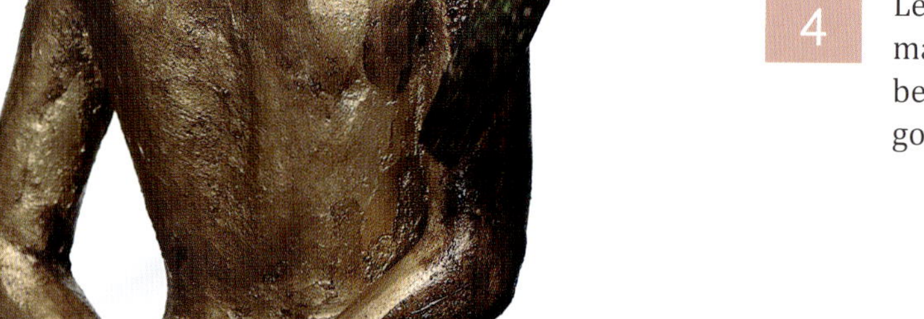

2 Pour more white shellac into your mixture and add burnt umber pigment. Paint this all over your statue. Make sure that no part has been missed, by turning the figure in every direction after it has dried. Leave it to dry for a couple of hours or even for a day, so that the shellac can harden properly.

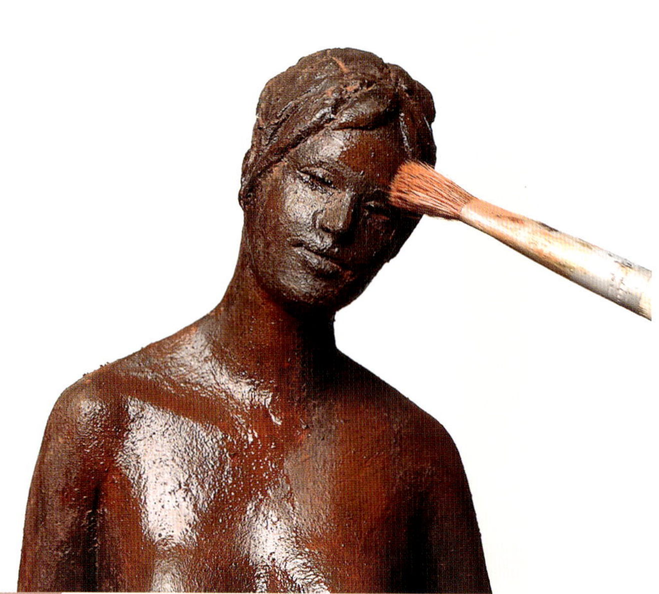

3 Now that the base tint has been done, you are going to paint on a surface stain. Pour a little ethanol into a bowl and add a little ocher-red or iron-red pigment. Apply the stain by lightly brushing it over the entire sculpture without going over the same place twice, to avoid dissolving the shellac. Ethanol, being a solvent, will soften up the two earlier layers (gold and burnt umber). Then, when it evaporates, it will allow the pigment it has carried to fix into and onto the inferior layers.

4 Let the sculpture dry for at least 30 minutes before manipulating it. The hollows start out very red and become matte, while the prominent parts reflect the golden-brown undertone.

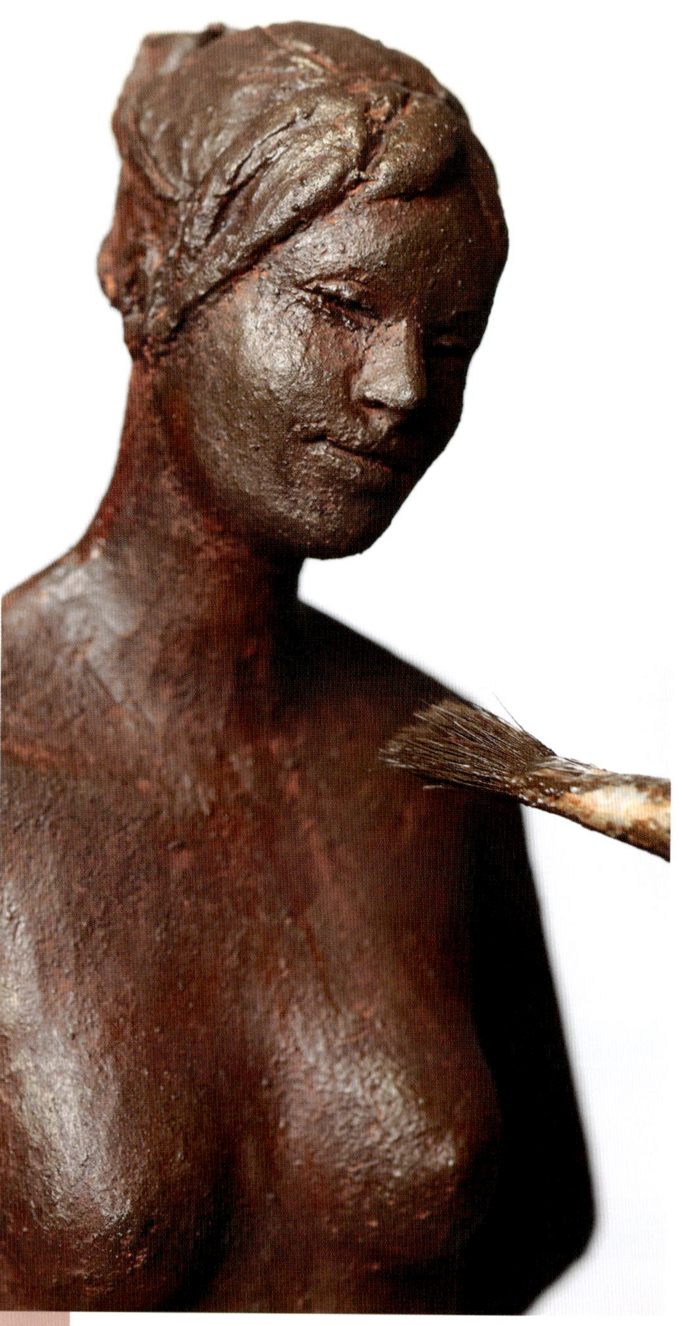

5 You are now going to lightly brush over the prominent parts with a paintbrush loaded with shellac and gold and burnt umber pigments. Pour a few drops of shellac into a dish and mix the pigment with the tip of your brush. Paint over the prominent parts, avoiding leaving clumps, since the hollows should remain red. Let it dry for 30 minutes.

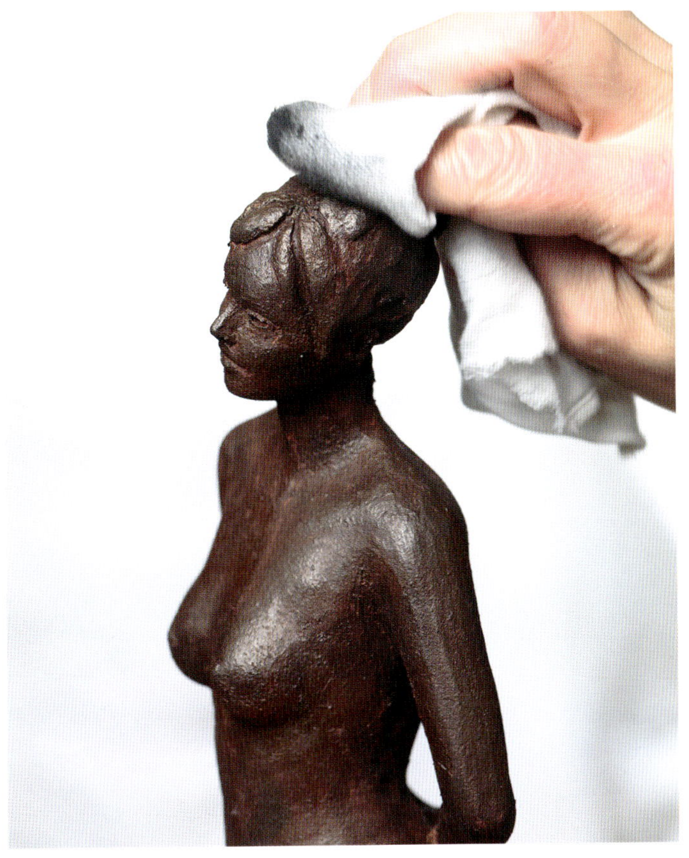

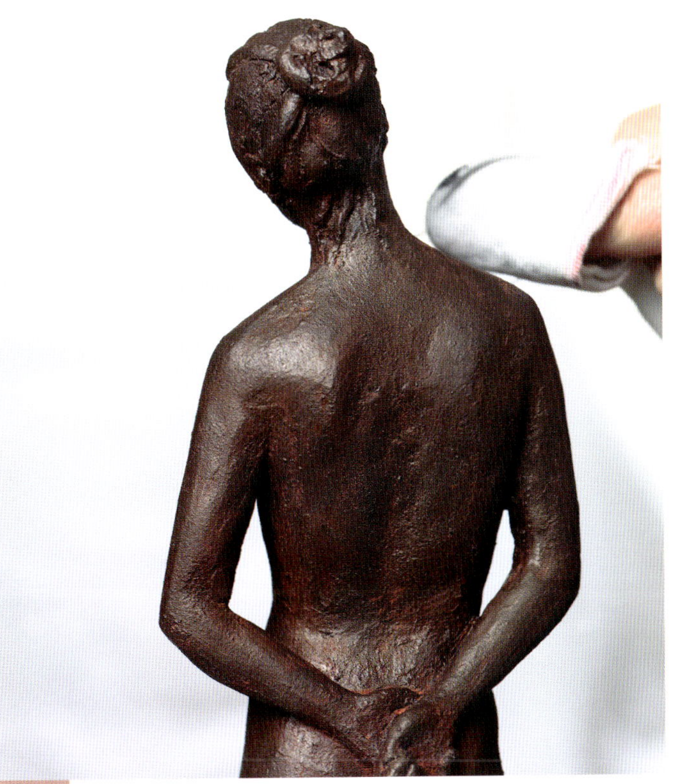

6 Now put a little powdered pencil lead onto a cloth. Rub it into the palm of your hand and then apply it to the prominent parts of the sculpture to polish them (see patina for the foot on page 56).

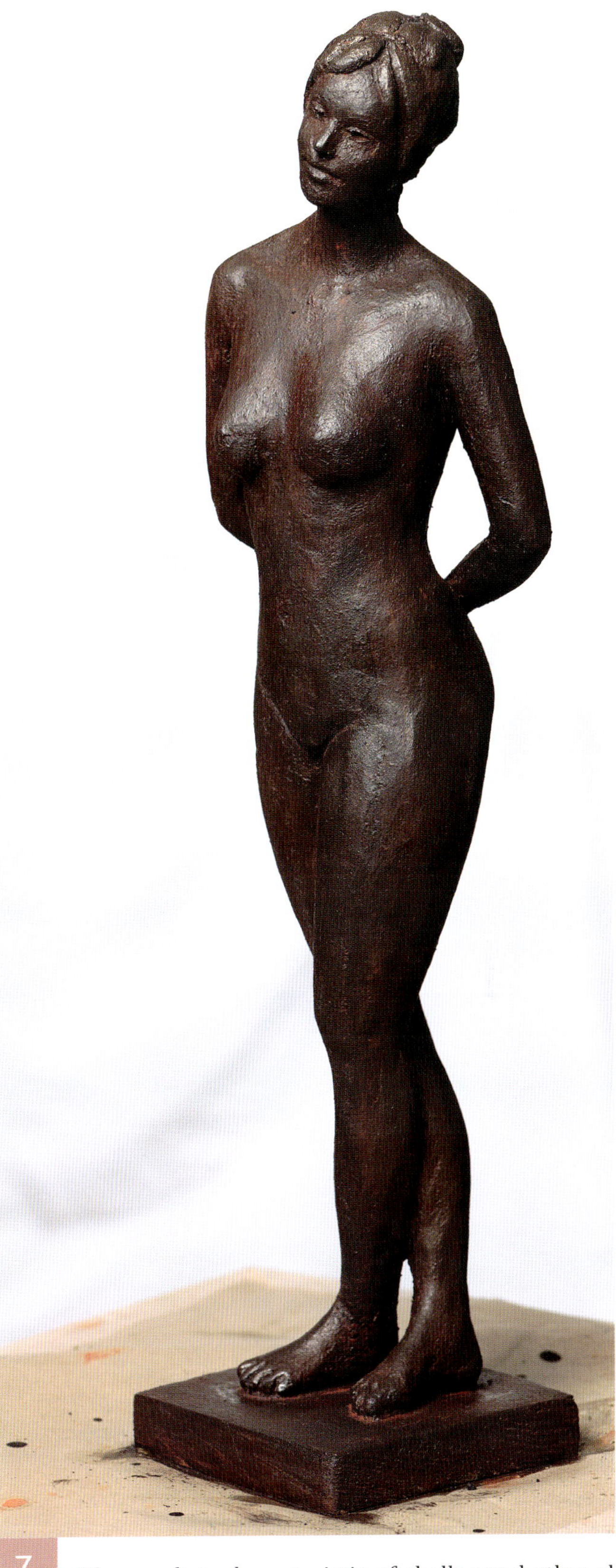

7 The result is characteristic of shellac and ethanol patina: the hollows are completely matte and slightly pearly, while the prominent parts are satiny, almost shiny (it depends on the amount of resin in the shellac you have used).

A Bust

Before approaching the technique of a bust, it is important to have first made a skull and have worked on facial reconstruction. The exercise on pages 42–51 will have familiarized you with the structure of the face.

A bust is one of the more difficult realizations because the stakes are high. Not only is the immediate recognition of the represented person desired, but you also have to restitute what it puts out—its personality, its particularities. You are no longer in the world of making a simple face that can be imaginary, but in the understanding and deciphering of proportions, planes, and the features that will identify and characterize this person and him alone. You must therefore find the expression that characterizes him the best.

When we sculpt a face for the first time, we have a tendency to represent ourselves without realizing it, by unconsciously projecting our proportions onto the model. This is understandable because these physiognomic proportions are the ones we know best, since we see our reflection every day in the mirror. To create a bust, you must carefully observe your model to understand his proportions and his structure, and to avoid projecting your own characteristics. This bust was made from finely grogged raku clay and a Caparol patina.

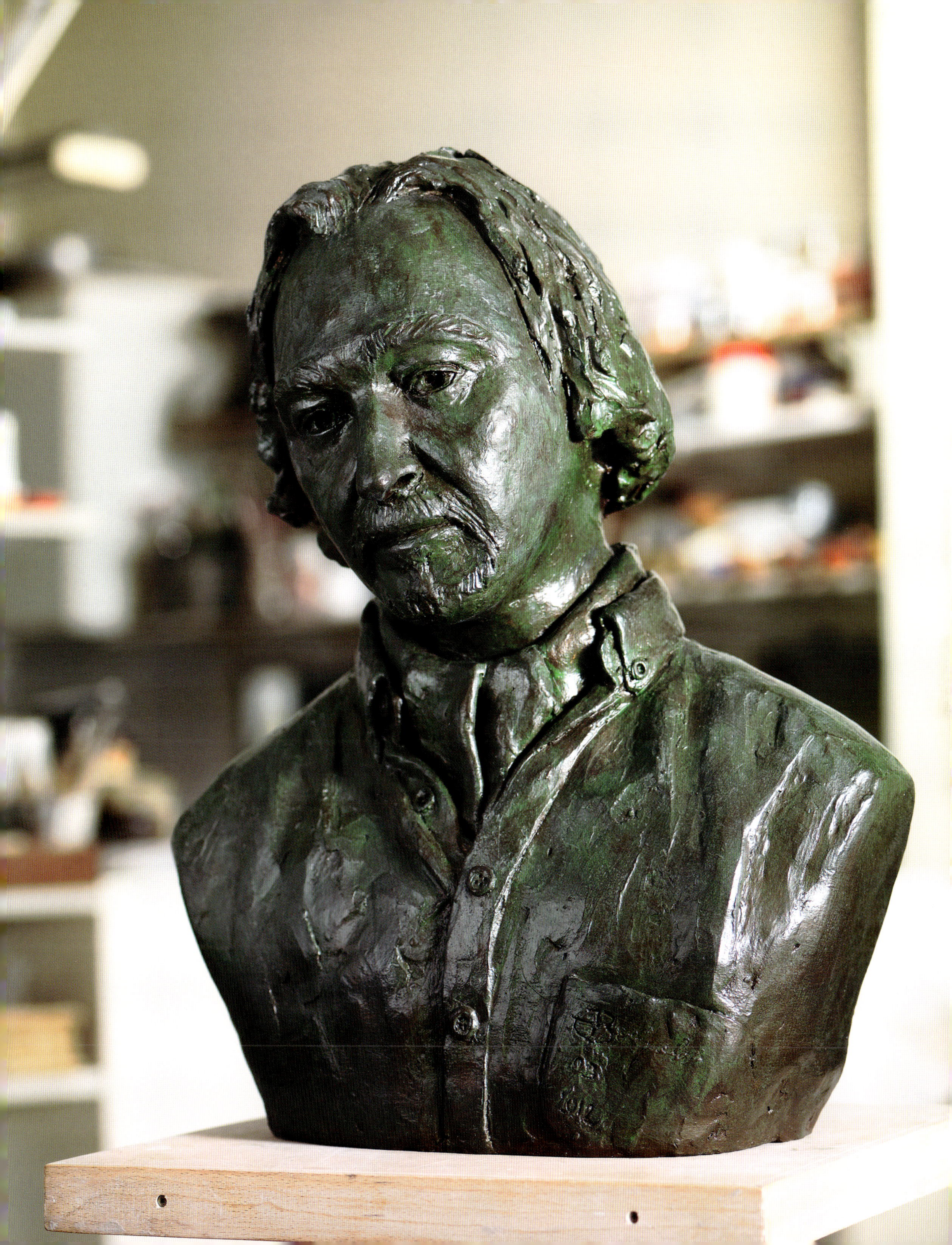

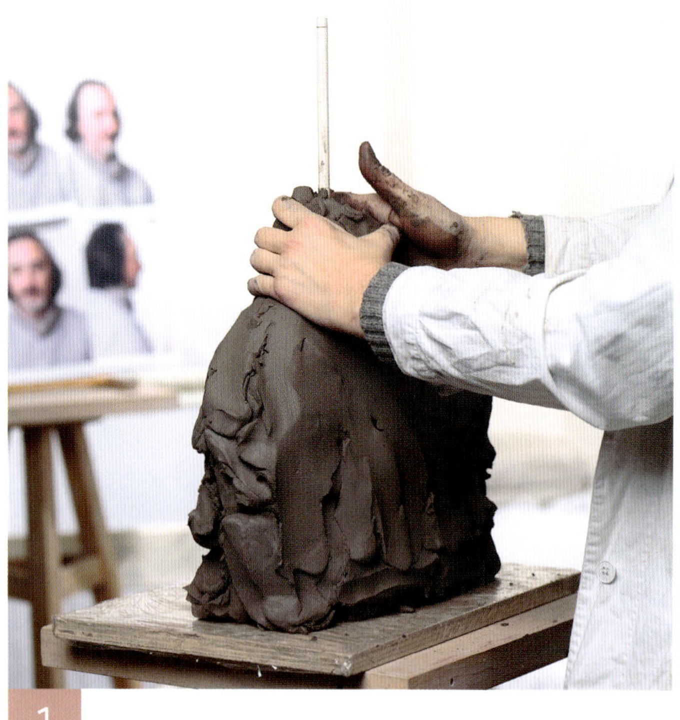

1 Start by taking photos of your model from all angles: front, back, profile, three-quarter view, from above, and even from below. Pin them onto a support in front of you. For the bust, mount a parallelepiped 11¾" high and about 15¾" wide by adding on pieces of clay. Add the shoulders by widening the volume toward the top. Plant a metal rod vertically through the center.

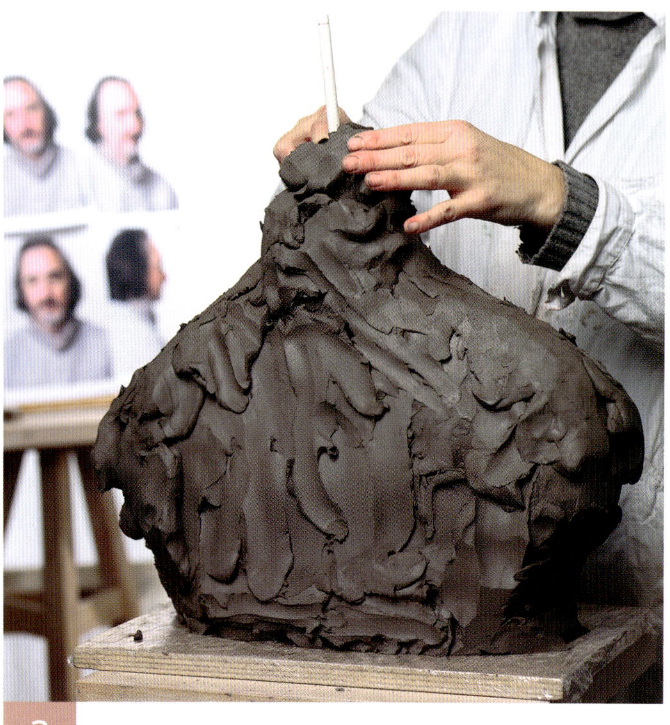

2 Build a cylinder for the neck around the metal rod. Start to shape the shoulder blades and the trapezius.

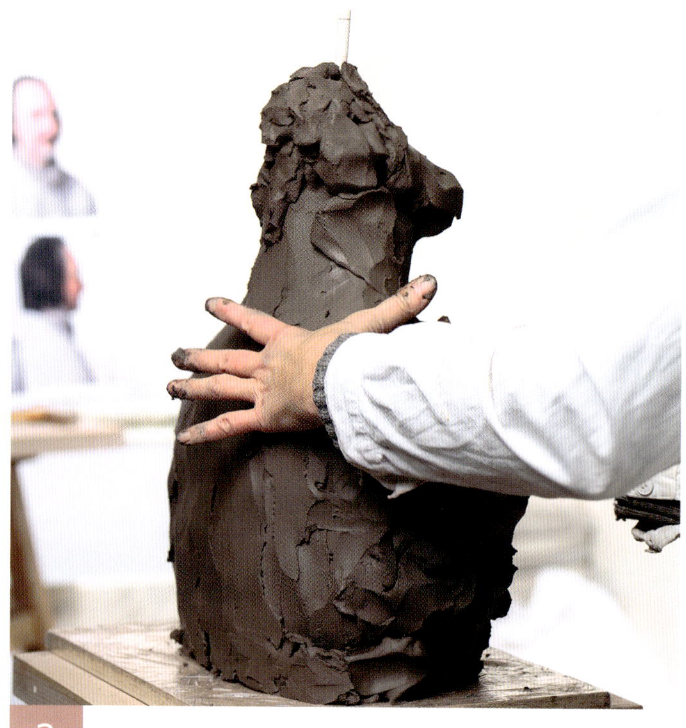

3 Carefully observe which plane the face is in compared to the bust. It is directed in the same plane as the bust in front of you, but the model's head is tilted slightly to the right. Start the construction of the head in profile, taking this slight tilt into account.

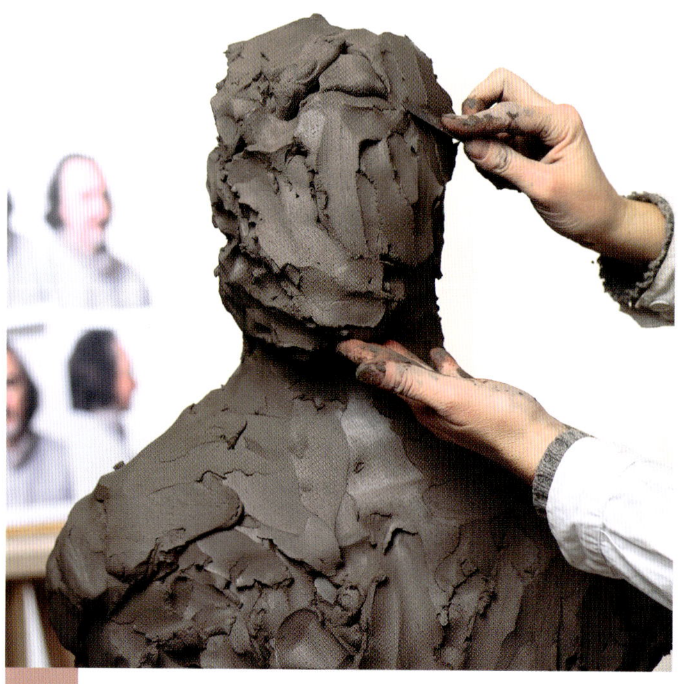

4 Continue to form the face, turning it toward you.

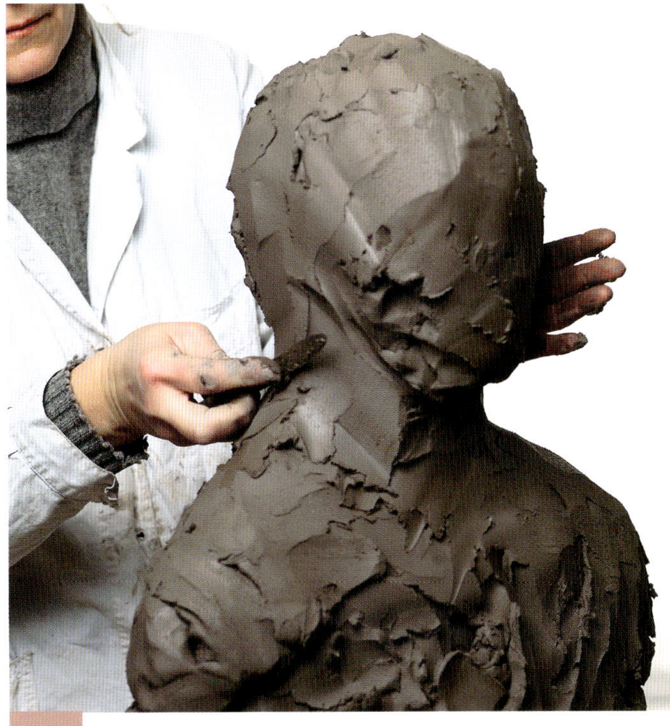

5 The face will be slightly tilted to the right, and its initial surface should be smooth. It is now a question of schematizing the entire face onto a single plane to be able to trace the proportions of the different parts.

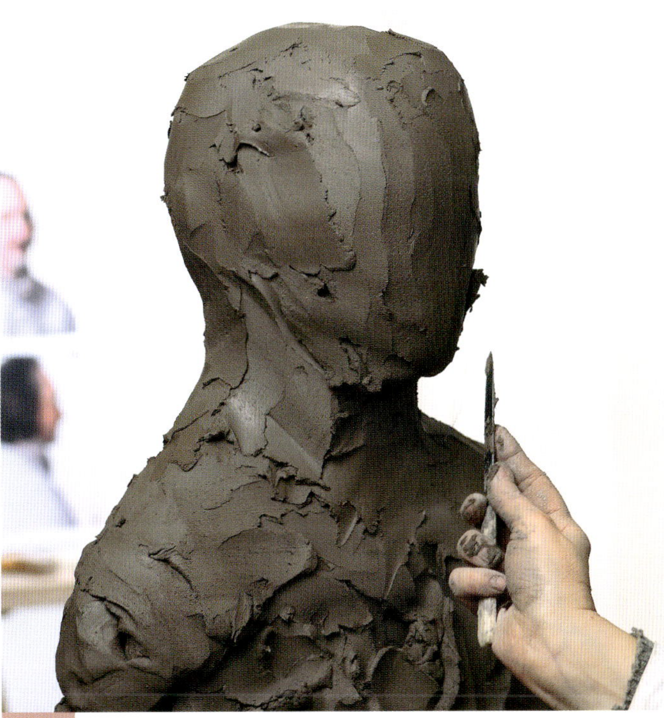

6 Refer to the contours of the skull's volume that you can see in the photos of your subject, to model the global volume of the head. You should form the contours of the shape you are creating in relation to the contours of the photos from all sides (front, profile, back, etc.)

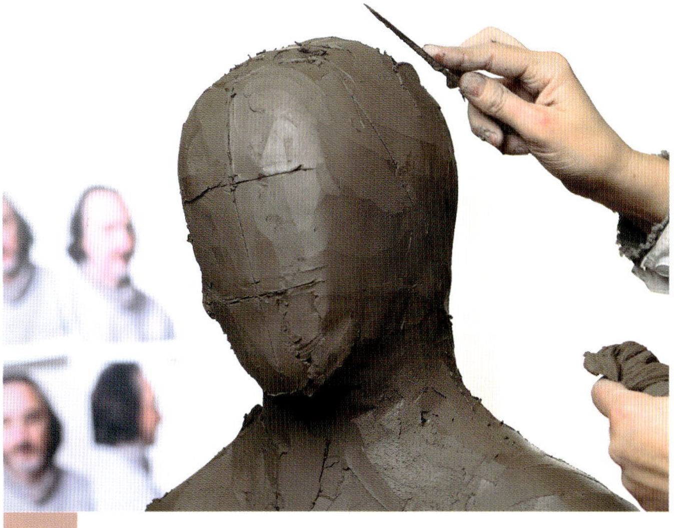

7 Draw a vertical line on the smooth plane of the face to mark its center, and the two horizontal lines to locate the proportions that are going to construct it (see "The Skull" section, on page 44).

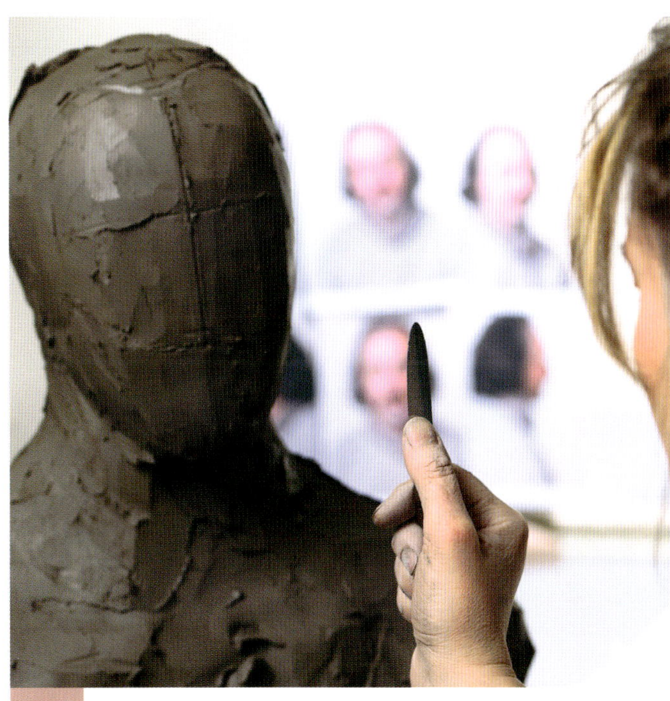

8 After checking the proportions, you will find that the three zones of the face are the same height.

IMPORTANT!

For more details, remember to go back over the chapters about the construction of a skull and a face (pages 42–51), as well as the schema of the facial muscles on page 46.

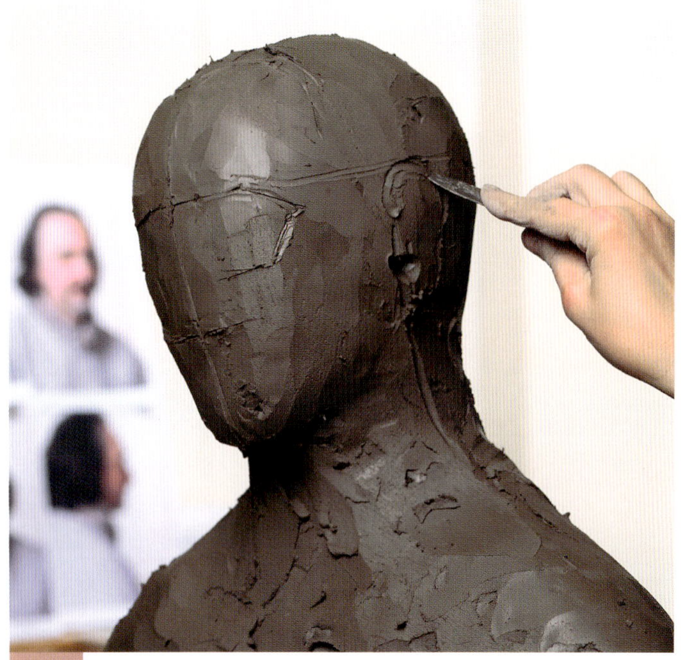

9 Below the line of the arch of the eyebrows, draw in the eye socket, which widens toward the temple, like a brace. In the middle of the side of the neck, draw a line, which will indicate the extremity of the maxillary and the center of the crane in profile. Place the earhole and the form of the ear between the line of the eyebrow's arch and the line of the tip of the nose.

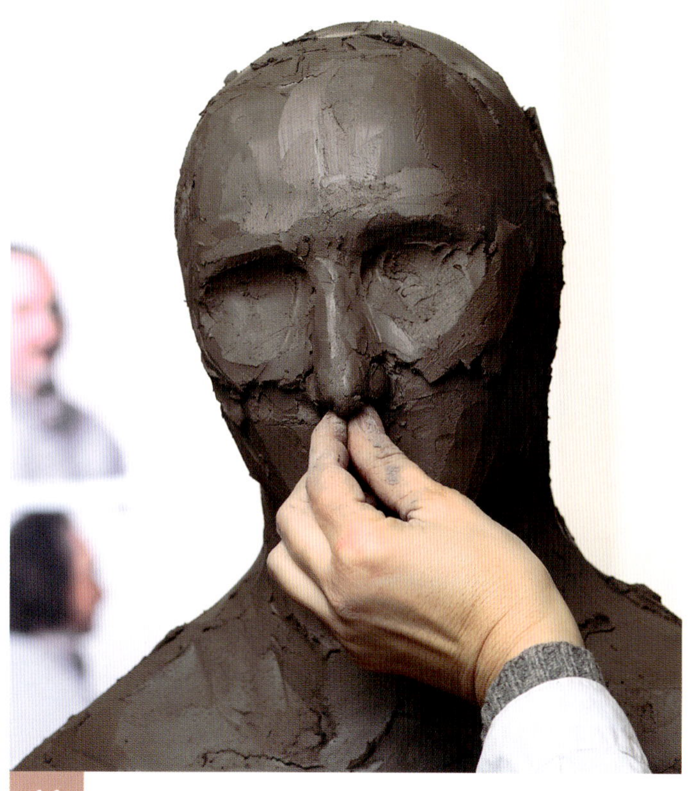

11 Adjust the volume of the nose, the septum, and the tip of the nose, which is rounder.

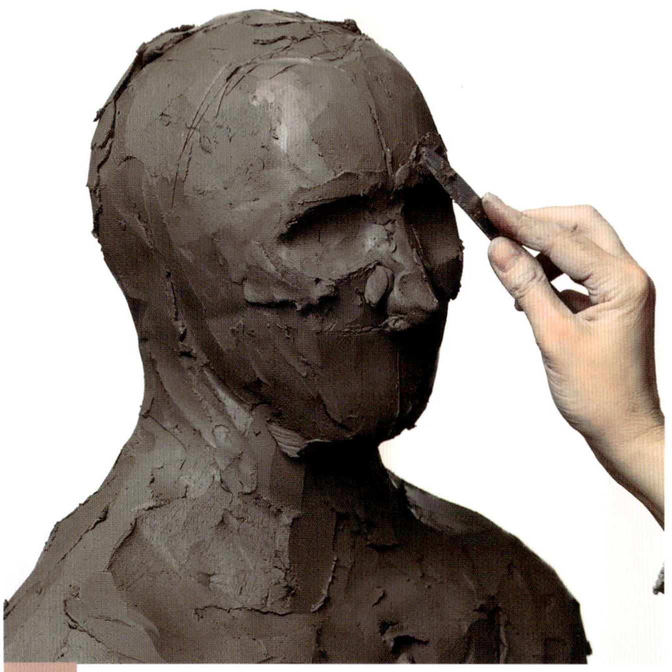

10 Dig out the eye sockets a little, following the shape of them you made earlier. Place the nose's cartilage and plump out the jugal bones to form the cheekbones. Reinforce the arch of the eyebrows.

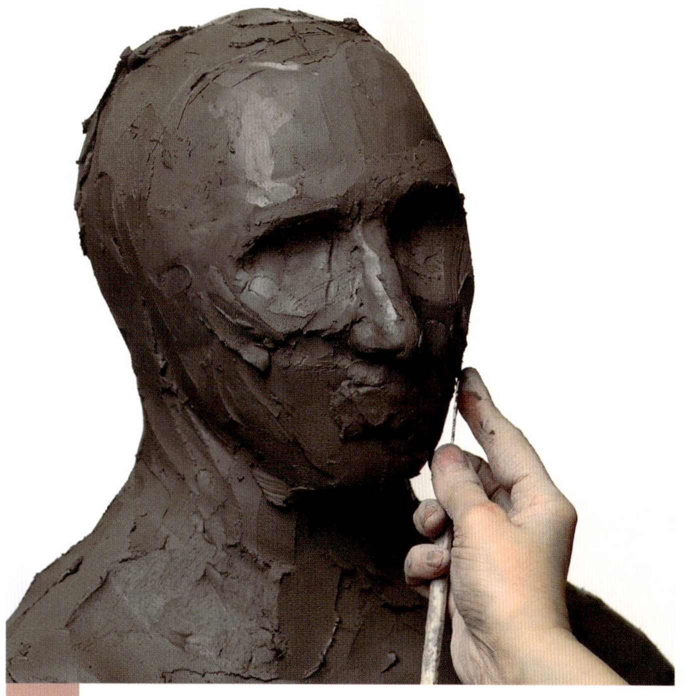

12 Place the volume of the teeth and increase that of the cheeks.

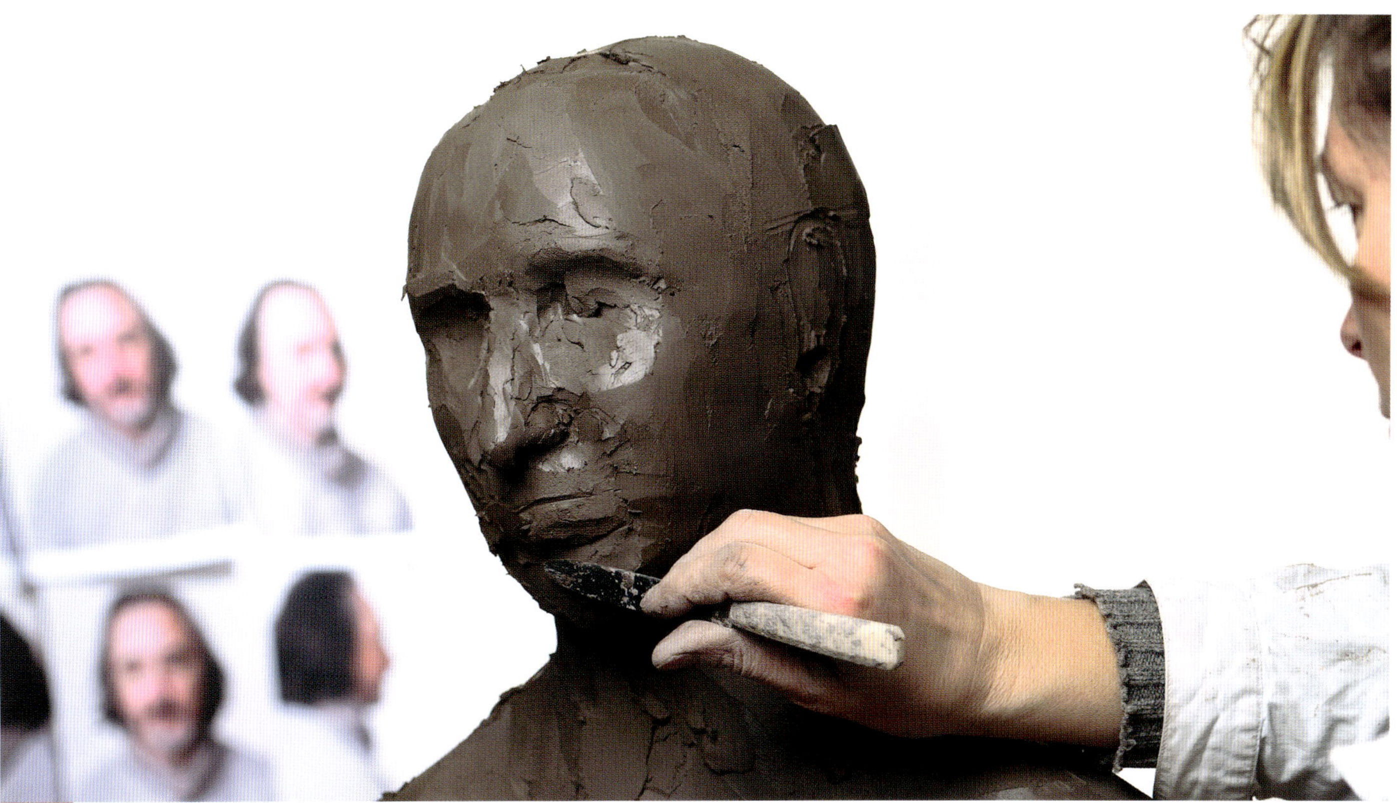

13 Dig under the volume of the teeth to bring out the volume of the chin.

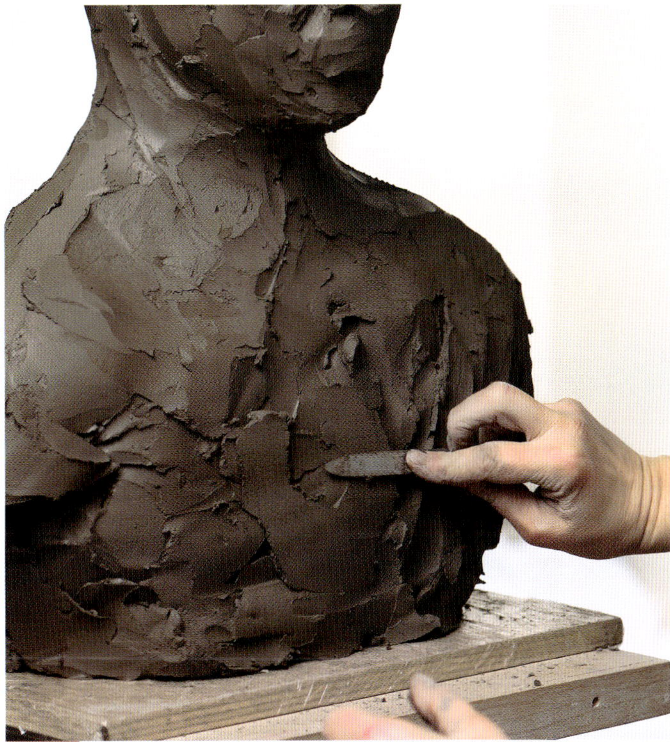

14 From time to time, complete the volume of the bust, which is just roughed out for the moment.

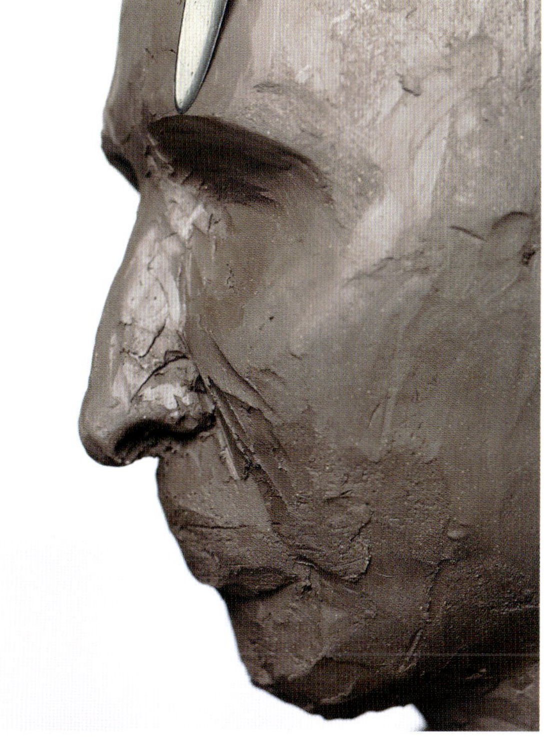

15 Take the time to compare your piece in profile with the photo of your model, and do any necessary retouches. Work on the details of the nose.

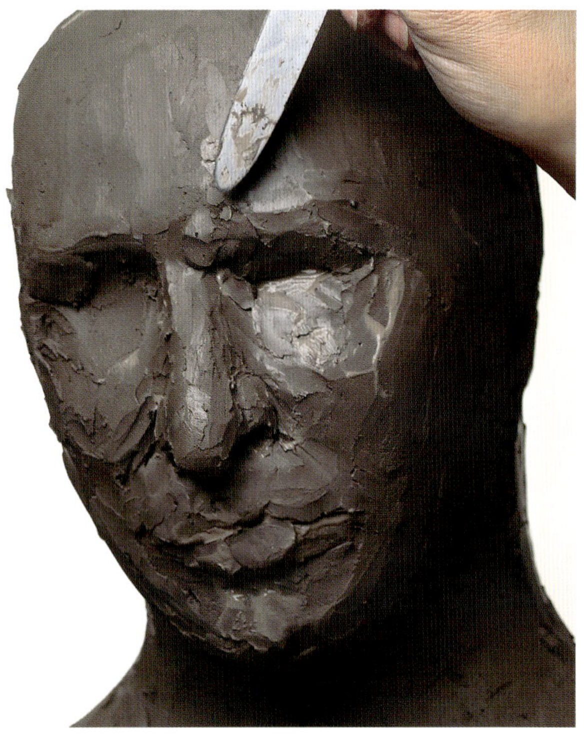

16 Shape the orbicular muscle of the eyes, which droop onto the eyelids.

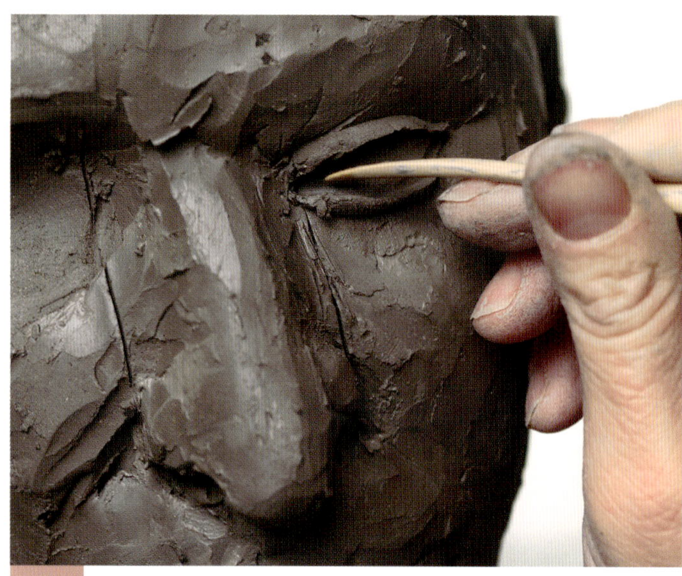

18 On each side of the nose, draw two vertical lines to mark the beginning of the eyes (aligned with the nostrils in this case). To represent the eye, place a small, olive-shaped piece of clay in the middle of the eye socket, starting from the vertical line and ending before the brace shape of the socket (see step 9). Open the olive with a wooden clay tool, pushing the clay toward the top and bottom to form the eyelids.

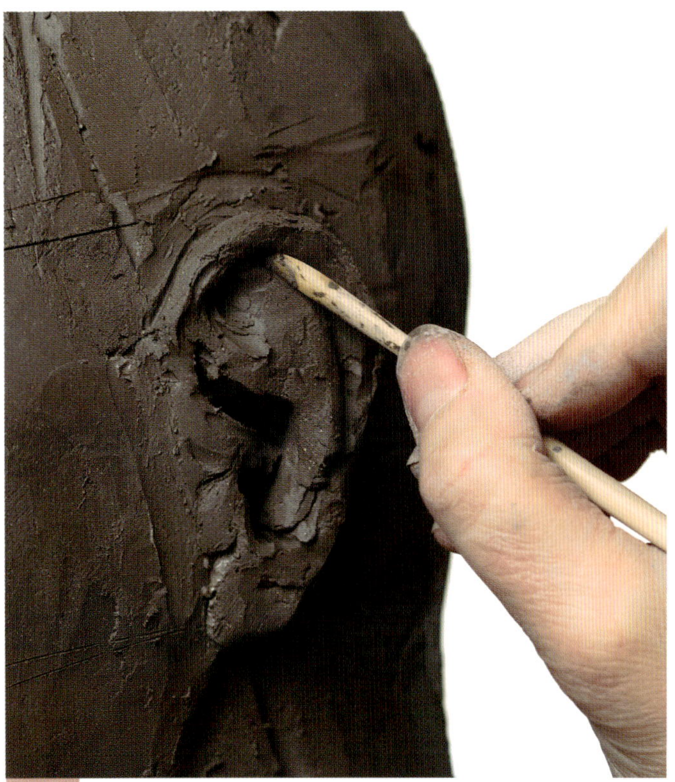

17 Do the ears, starting by the root of the helix.

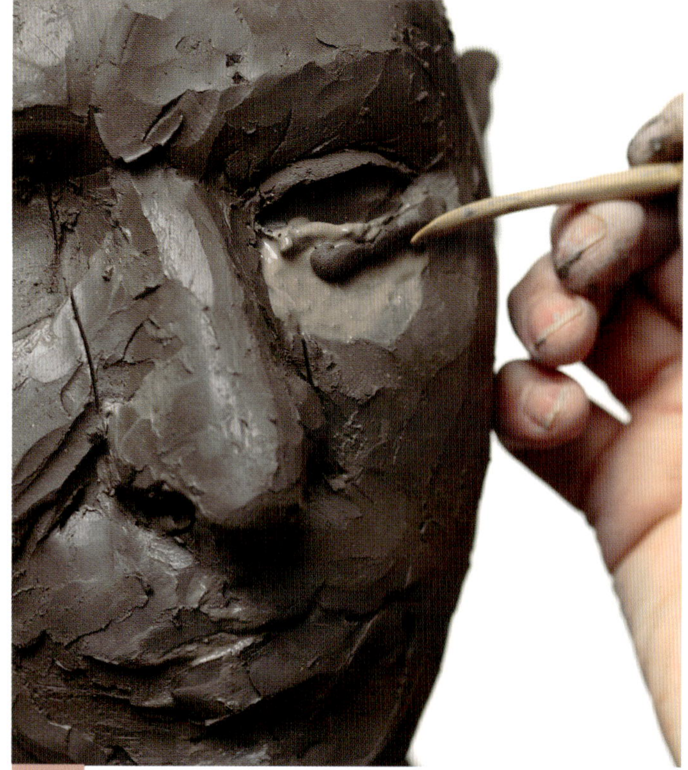

19 Add a thin clay sausage to plump out the lower eyelid.

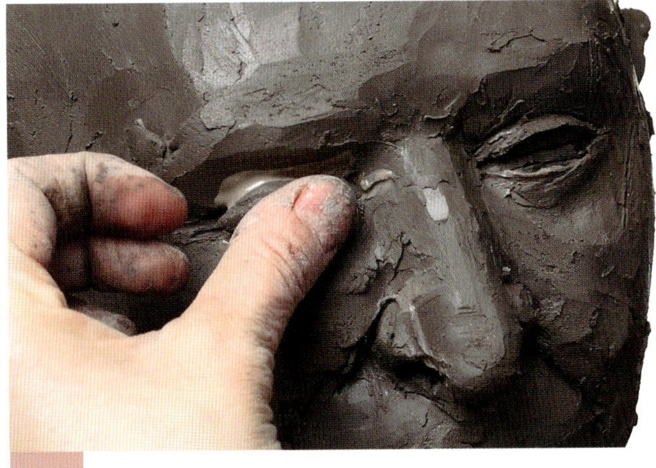

20 Do the same for the other eye.

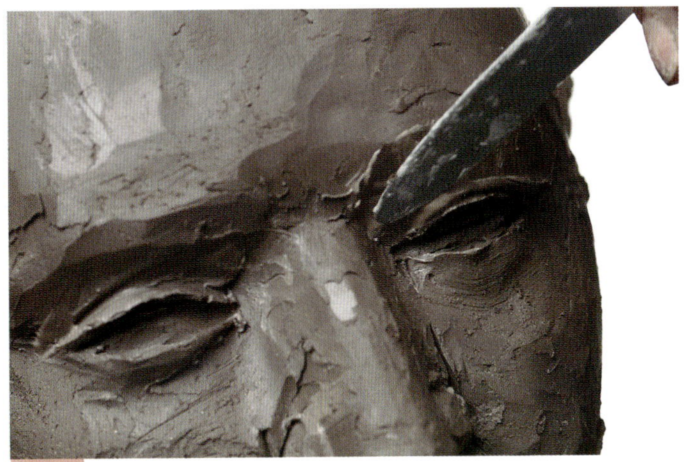

21 Increase the volume of the lower eyelid.

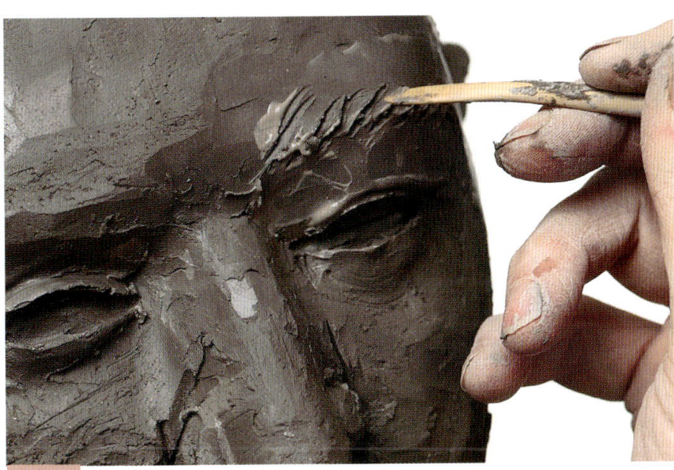

22 Draw in the eyebrows with a wooden clay tool. They will be touched up later.

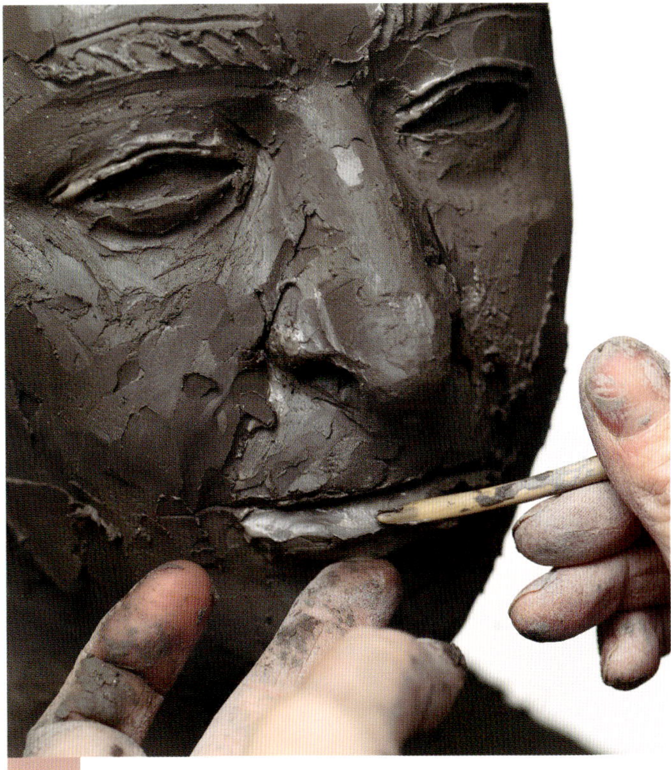

23 To shape the lips, open the volume of the teeth you placed earlier.

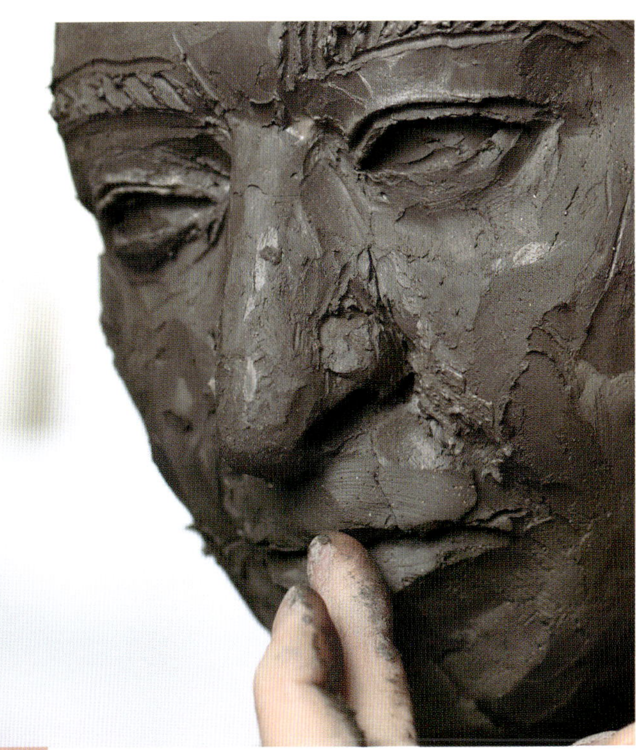

24 Retouch them with your finger and control the proportions with those of the model, face on and in profile.

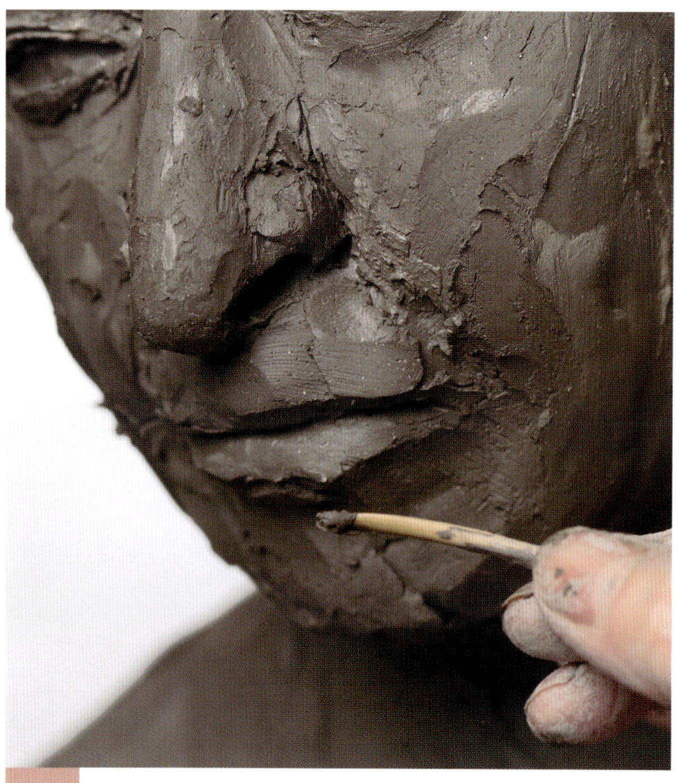

25 Retouch the chin, because at this stage it's lacking in height. Observe the model closely or refer to your photos.

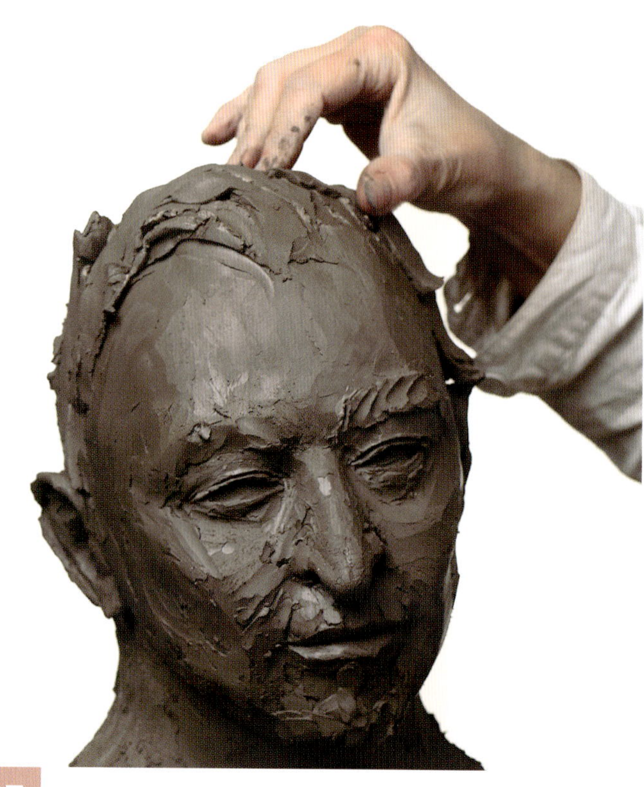

27 Now that the lower part of the face has been lengthened, you will start to construct the volume that represents the hair, starting with the implantation of the roots.

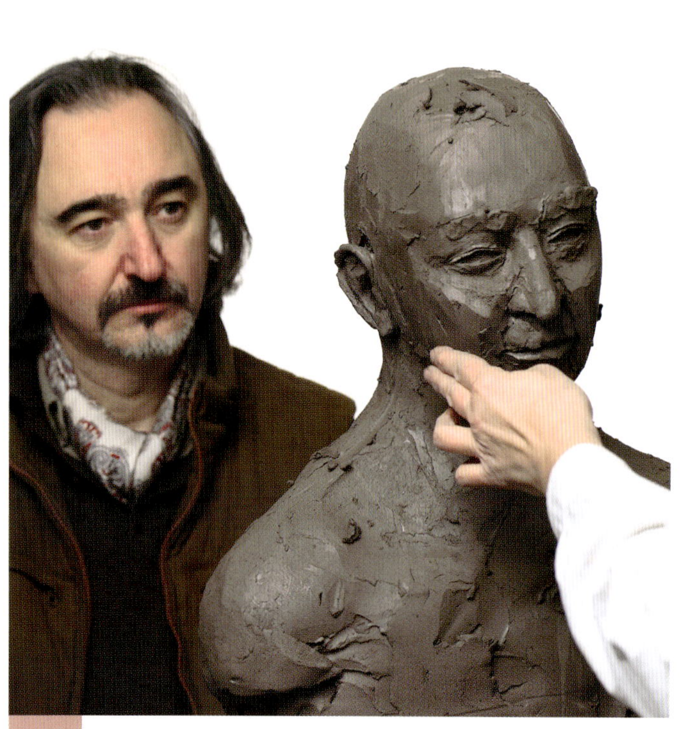

26 Referring to your model, continue the retouches to adjust the lower part of the face. Add the volumes for the beard and the mustache.

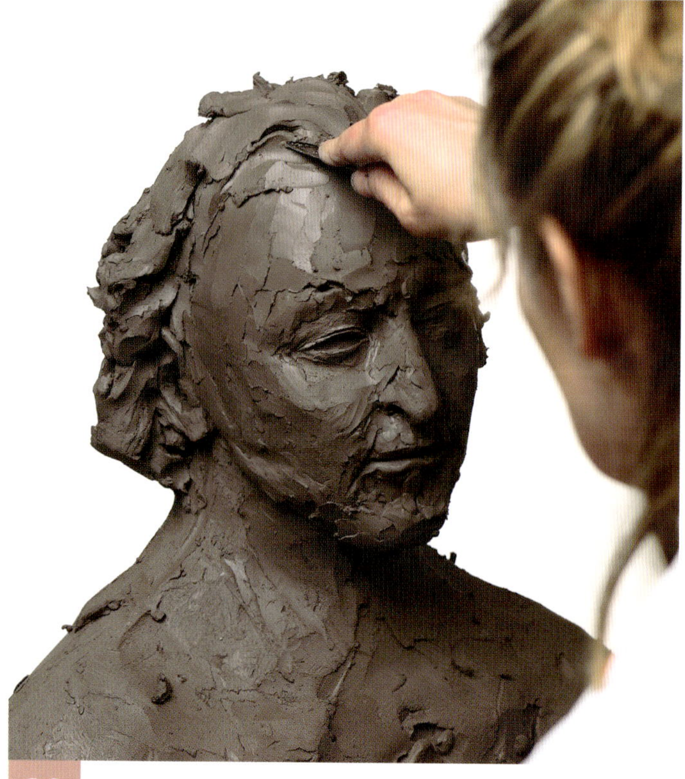

28 Build up the mass of hair around the volume of the head. Start by the volumes underneath and finish with the locks on top.

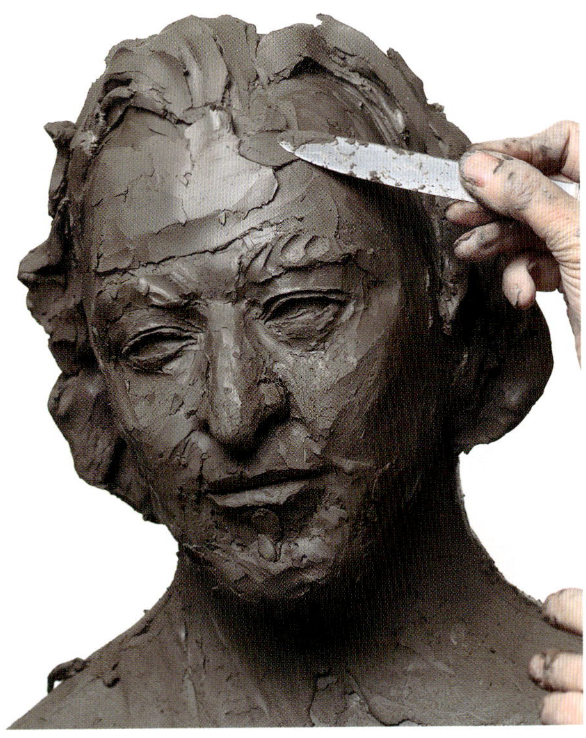

29 Adjust the volumes of the different parts of the face as your work progresses, and compare it with your photos.

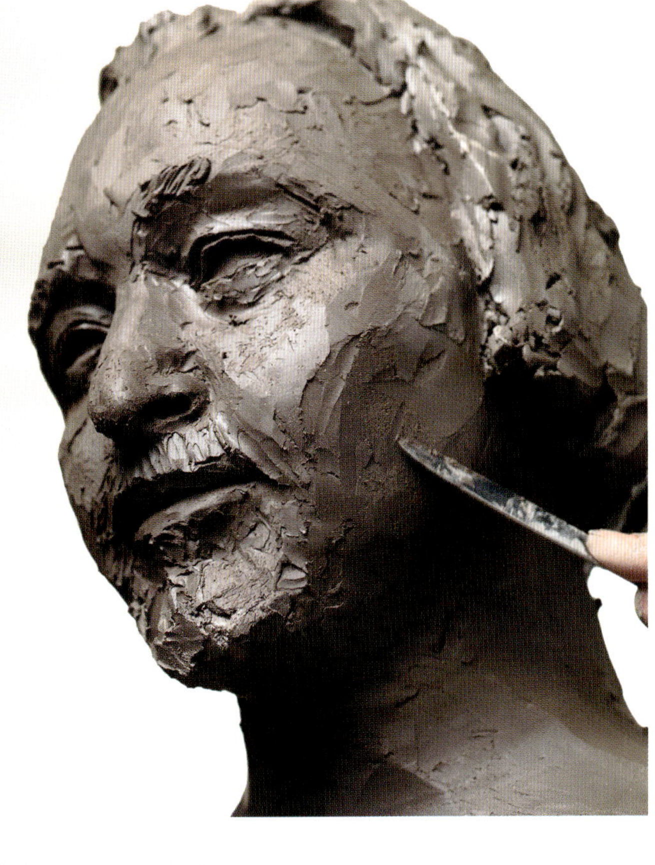

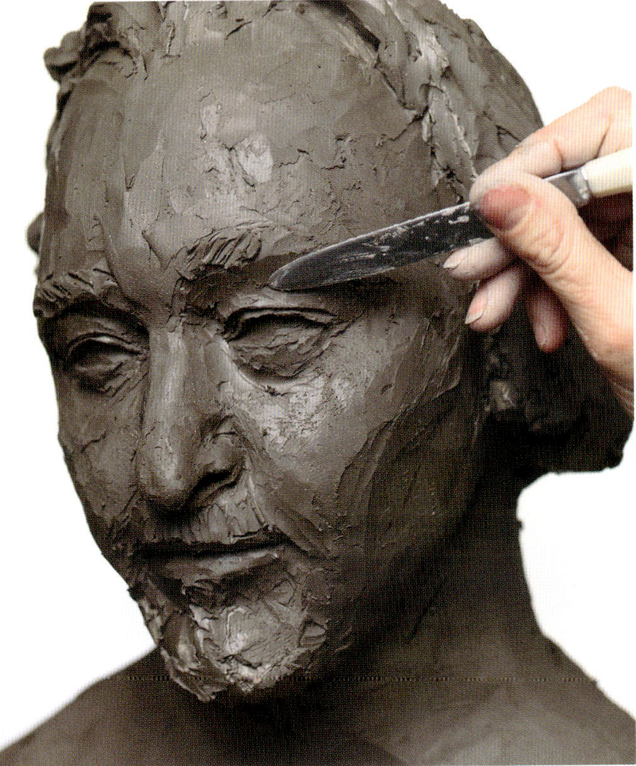

30 Refine the shape of the eyelid, which droops and hollows out under the eyebrow arch.

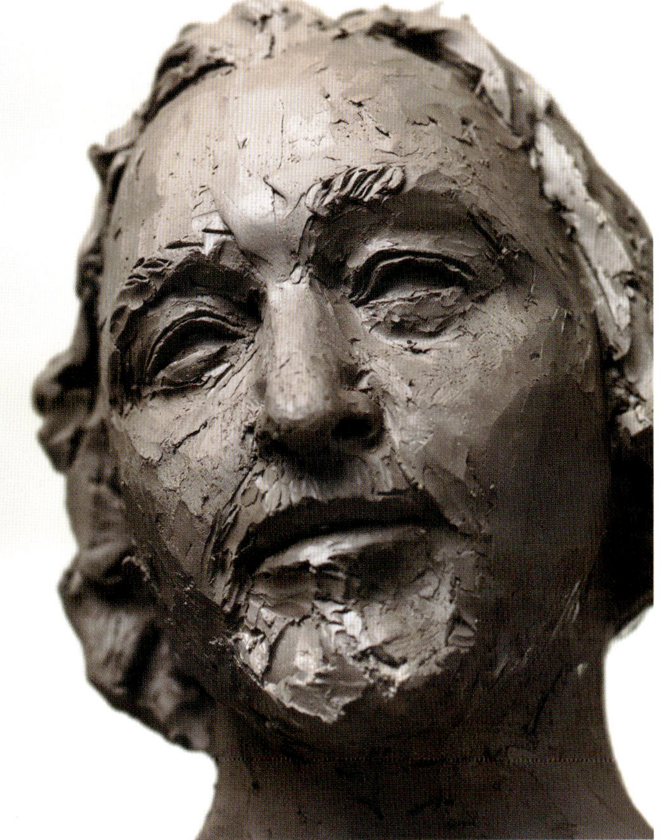

31 Stand back and observe the face from below to correct any eventual disproportions.

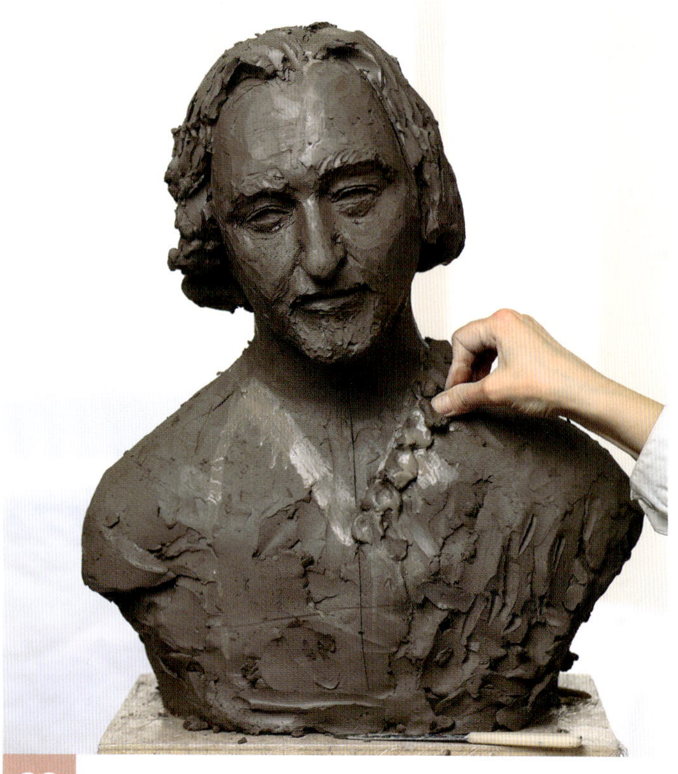

32 Draw a vertical line in the center of the bust and start making the edges of the shirt by adding on clay with slip.

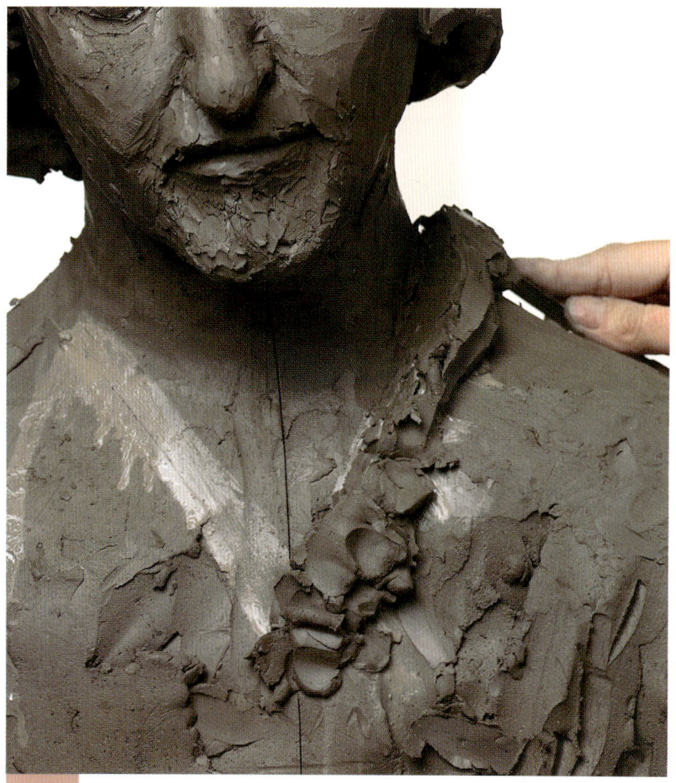

33 Construct the shirt's collar, leaving an empty space around the neck for the scarf.

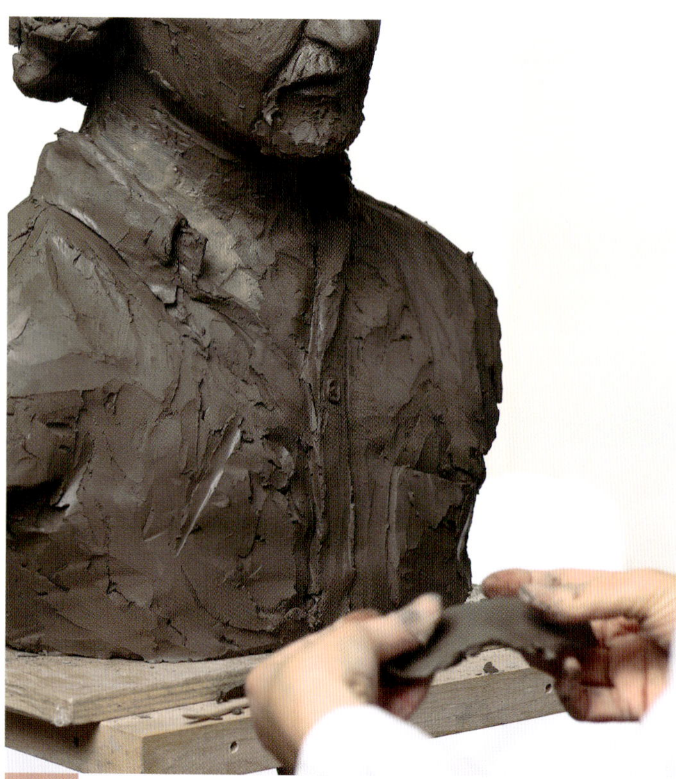

34 Detail and regularize the edge of the shirt and the collar with a knife. Make small, elongated slabs for the scarf.

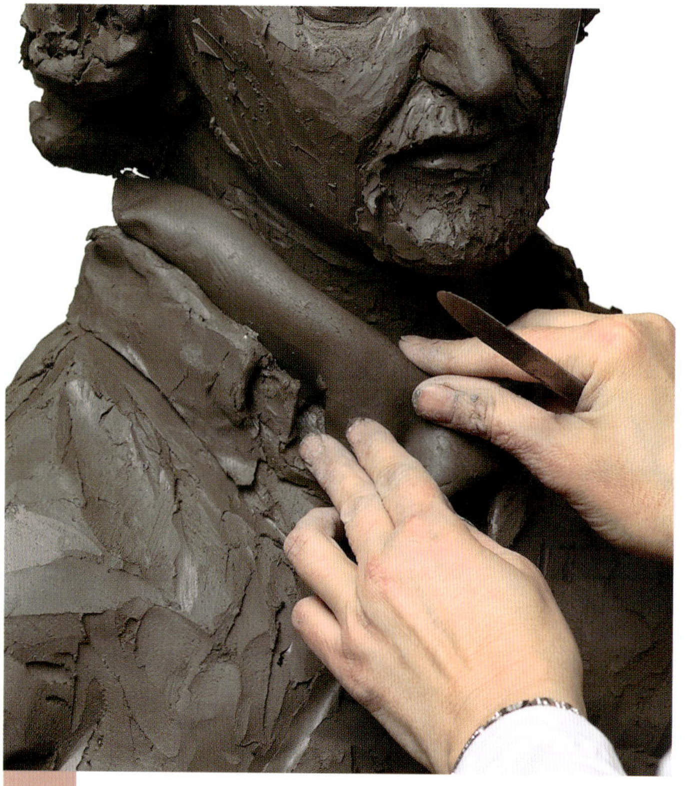

35 Plumb out a first slab and place it to suggest the volume of cloth on one side of the scarf. Fix the slab in place with slip. Do the same on the other side.

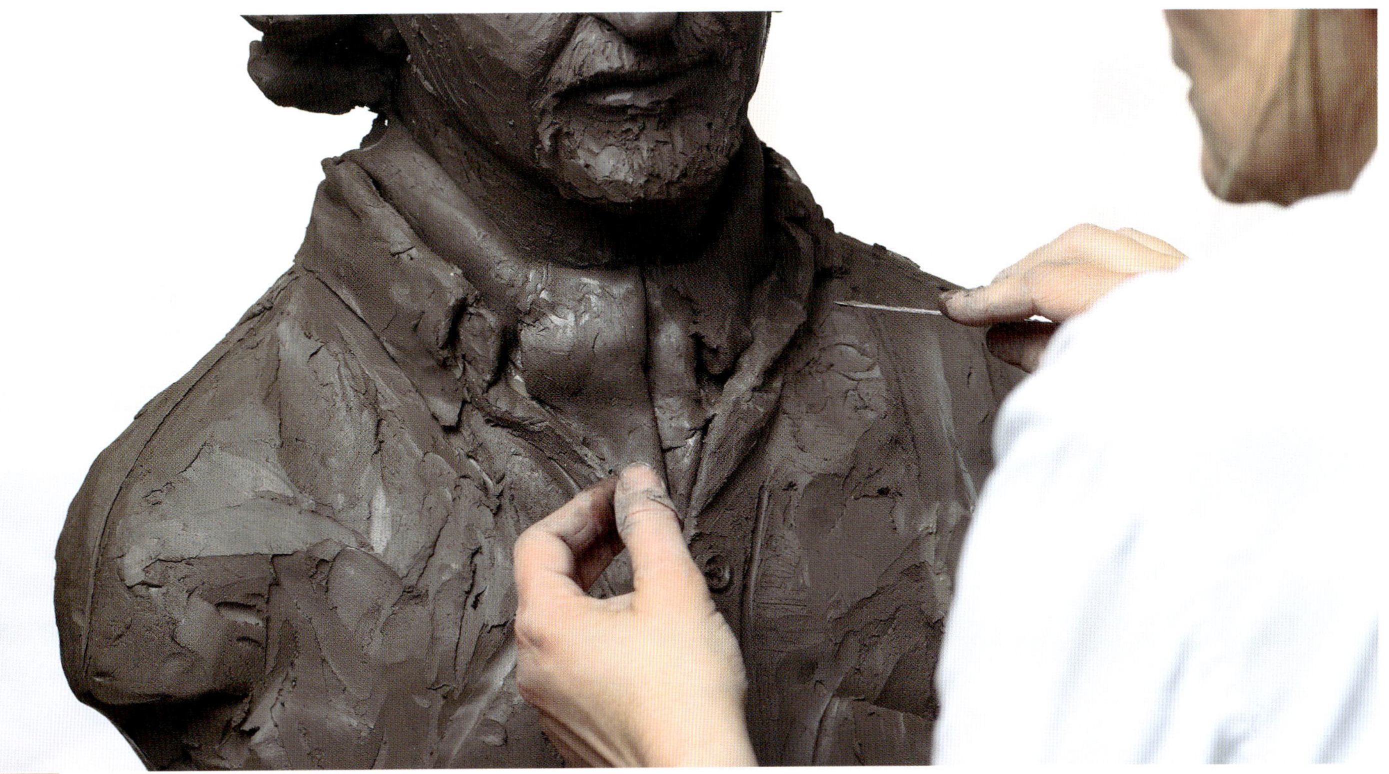

36 Make more slabs and superimpose their edges to form the knot in the scarf.

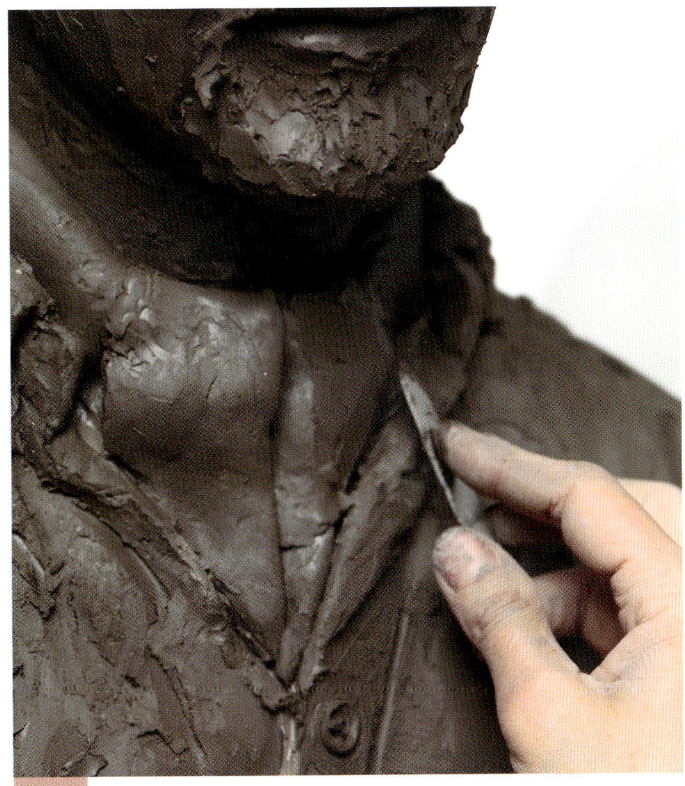

37 Retouch the pieces with your knife.

38 Go back over the contour of the eyes to refine the details. Mark the flat plane under the eye, where the jugal bone begins.

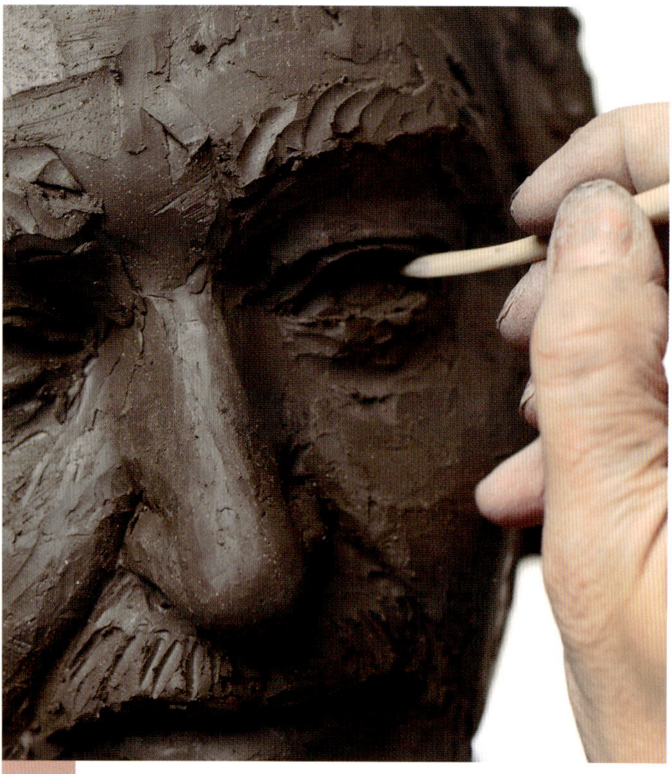

39 Work on the interior of the eyes with a small, wooden clay tool and compare their shape with the photos.

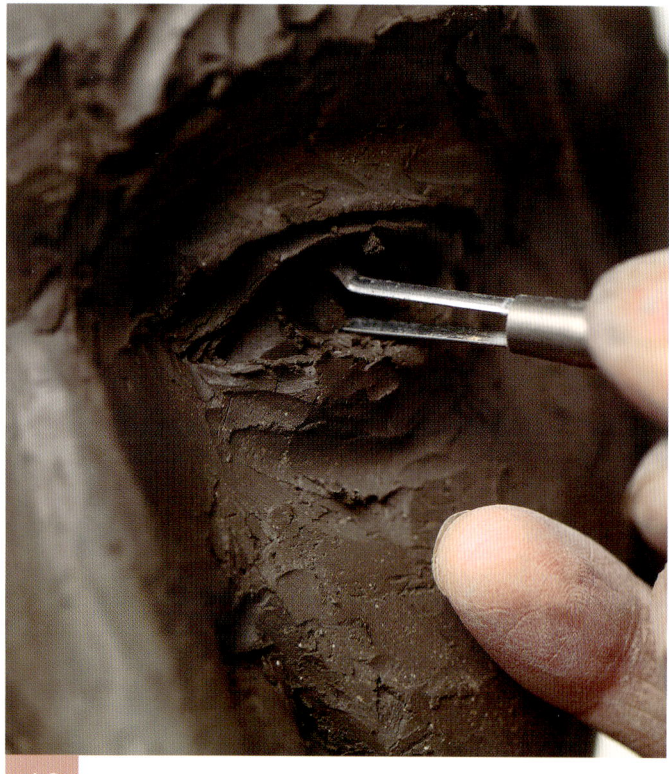

40 Form the regard (see "The Face" section, on page 49) by emptying out the eyes with a trimming tool.

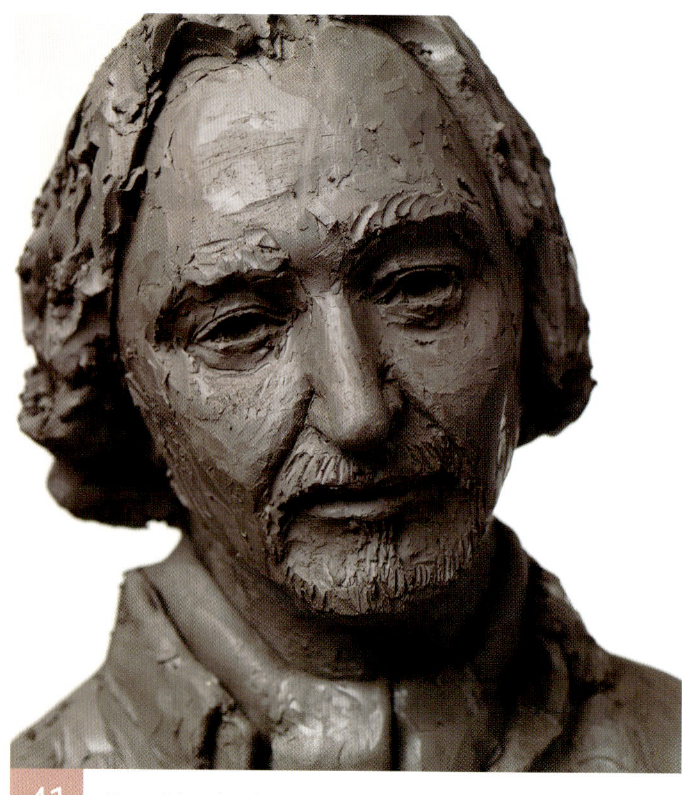

41 Stand back; the face is still rough, so you'll have to refine it more and go back over each part from different views.

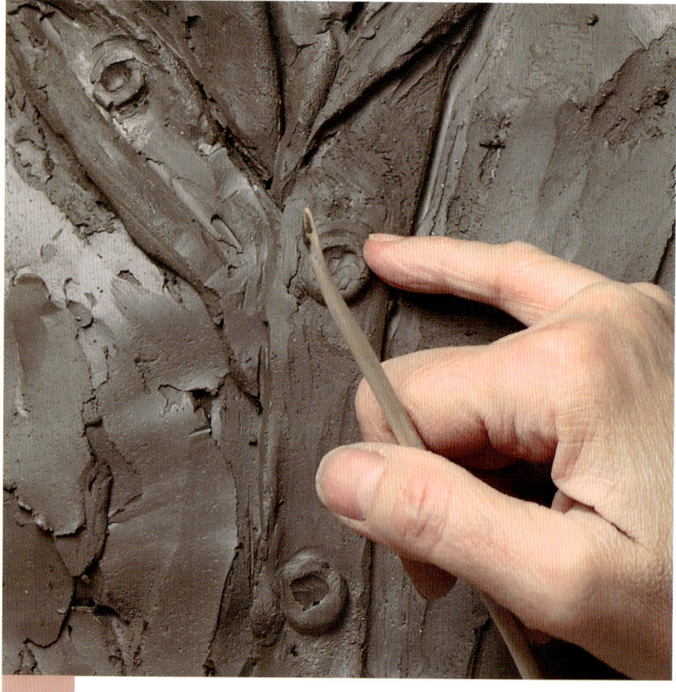

42 Place the buttons on the front of the clothes, making sure that they are at an equal distance. Make them from small balls of the same size, attached with slip and then squashed with the rounded end of a clay tool—small enough to create a hollow in the center and a rim around the edge.

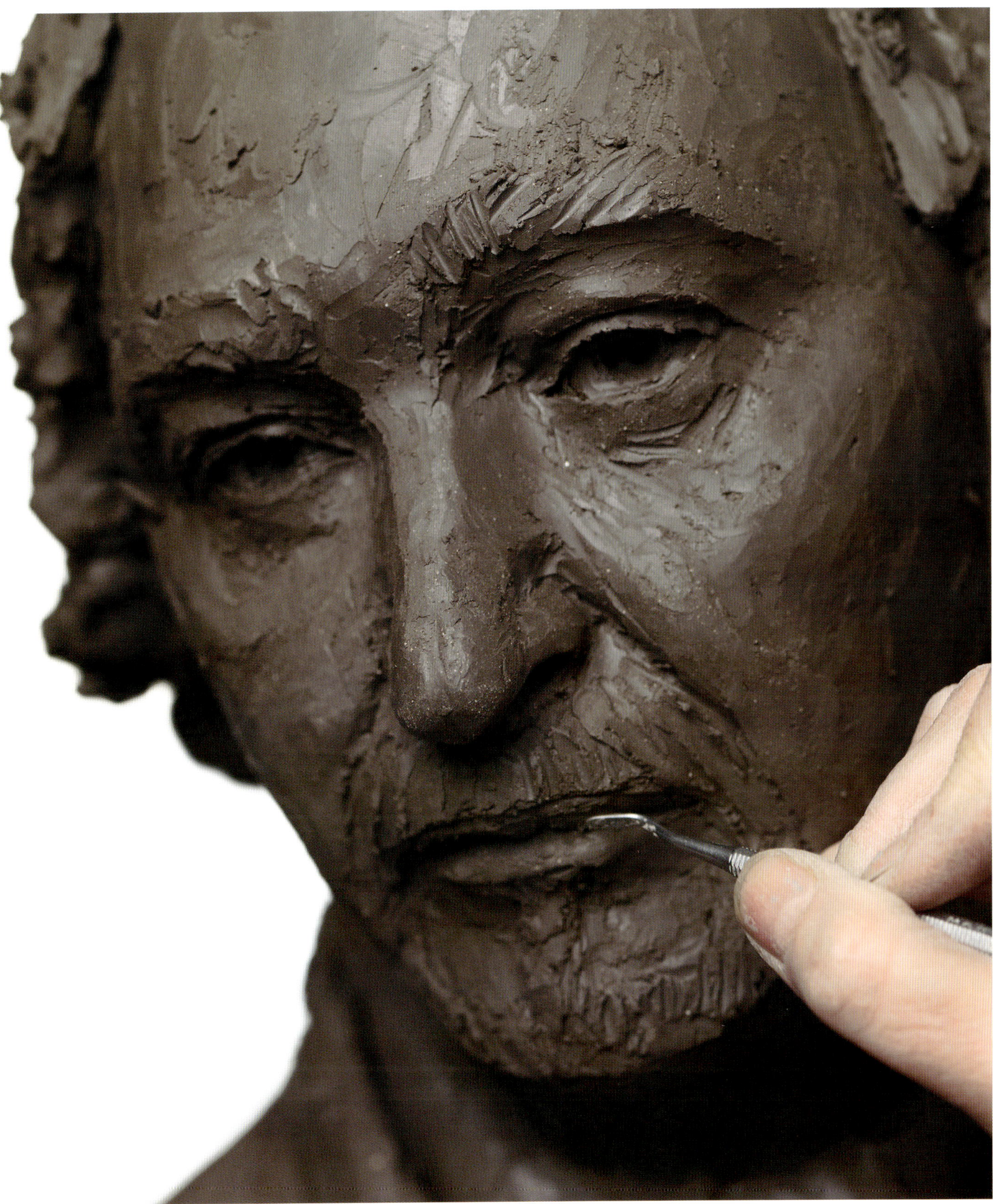

43 Using a slim metal or wooden clay tool, smooth the skin and work on the traits to soften them and to make them more lifelike (the nose, the eyebrows, the mouth . . .) Your bust is finished.

44 Compare the bust with the model for the last time, and do the last retouches if necessary.

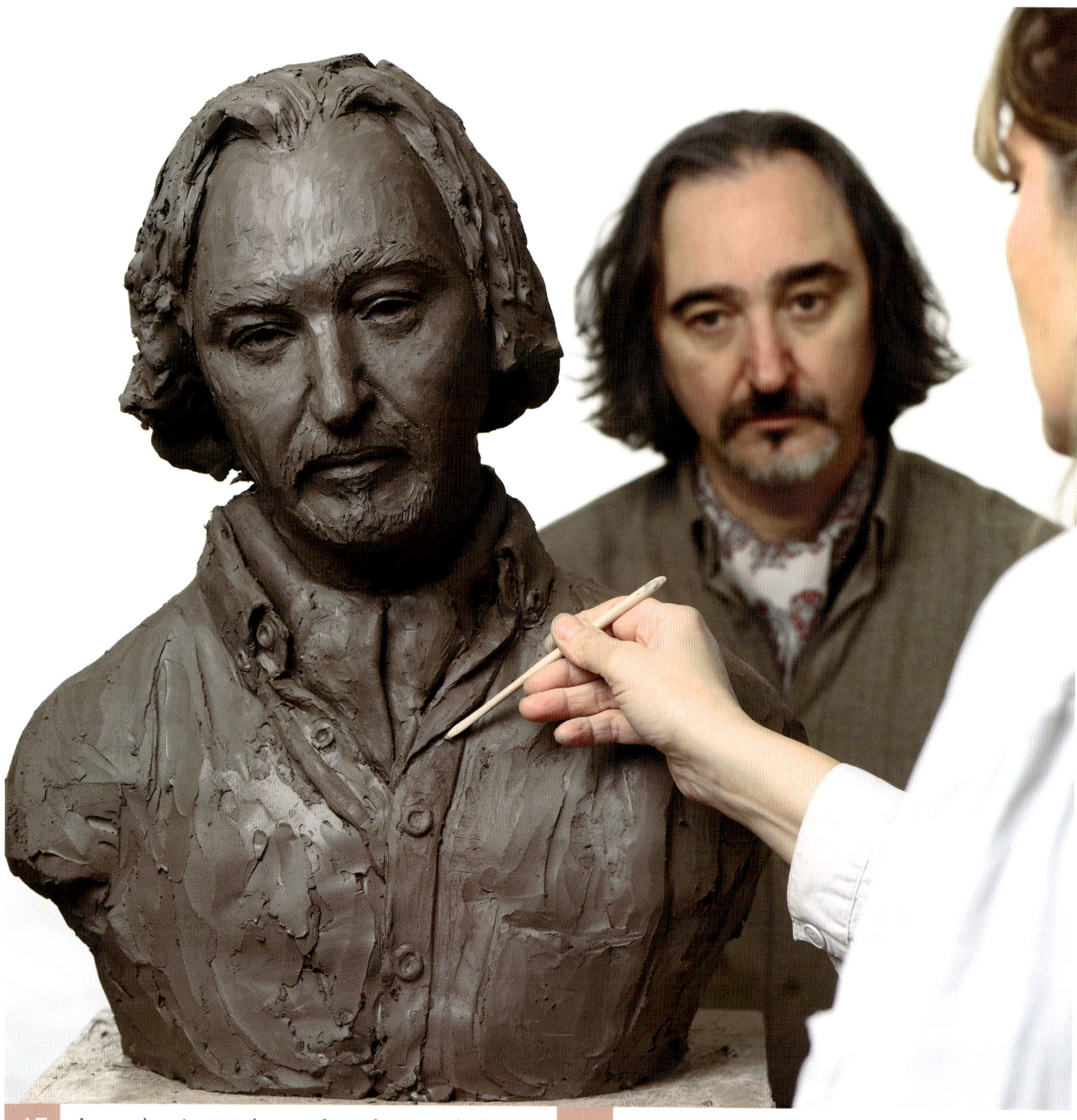

45 Leave the piece to dry out for a day or so before hollowing it out. Start this by the back of the head (see page 27) and then continue on each side of the bust—on a level with the shoulders—until the inside is completely hollow. Its global mass represents 88 lbs. of clay. Once hollow, its mass won't be any more than 33 lbs.

46 You can fire the bust at stoneware or earthenware temperature. The earthenware temperature will take the patina better because the clay is somewhat porous. Stoneware temperature will make the sculpture more solid. No matter which you choose, check the firing temperature of your clay before you fire it.

Patina

1. Mix a large quantity of neat Caparol with burnt umber and gold pigments in a clean bowl. You should make enough to cover the entire bust. Do two coats on the entire sculpture, making sure to fill all the holes. Let it dry. If you have any patina left over, store it in an airtight jar.

2. Using a clean bowl, mix Caparol with a little water and add a point of chrome-green and English green pigments. The mixture should be almost translucent. Dab the entire sculpture with the mixture, using a stiff, short-haired brush, and then let it dry.

3. With the rest of the brown-gold patina and a nearly dry brush, go over the prominent parts to make the reliefs stand out. Let it dry.

4. Then rub a little pencil lead powder on the prominent parts with a soft cloth.

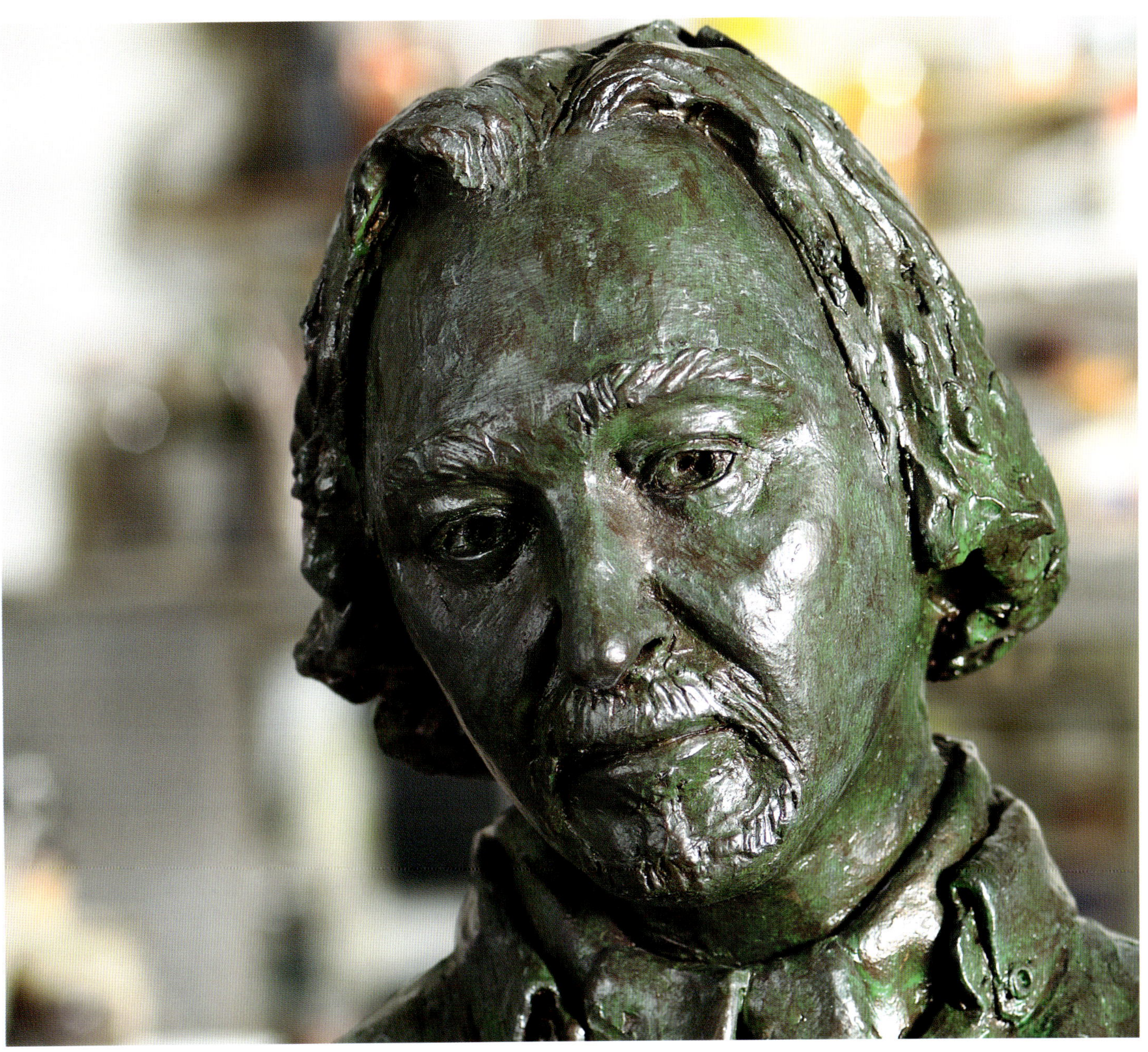

A Child in a Chair

I chose to represent a little girl aged four and a half sitting in a child's chair (Louis XV style). Don't try to make this type of piece if you are a beginner. You will need several years of experience in sculpture before approaching a life-size character, even if you work very hard.

You must be completely familiar with representing the face, the body, the hands, and the feet. Children are more difficult to represent than adults because, lacking wrinkles, their traits are smooth and rounded. This is why it is risky to dive into a work in large dimensions if you haven't completely mastered medium-sized pieces. Defects show up a lot more on a large piece, especially on a realistic representation such as this one.

If you decide to try, start with a medium-sized piece—the imperfections will be more easily excused. Here, the piece was made in impalpable-grogged raku clay and measures 2¾' high, 2' deep, and 17" wide. Its colors were mixed with engobe and painted on after the piece had been hollowed out, on unfired clay and fixed by firing after drying out.

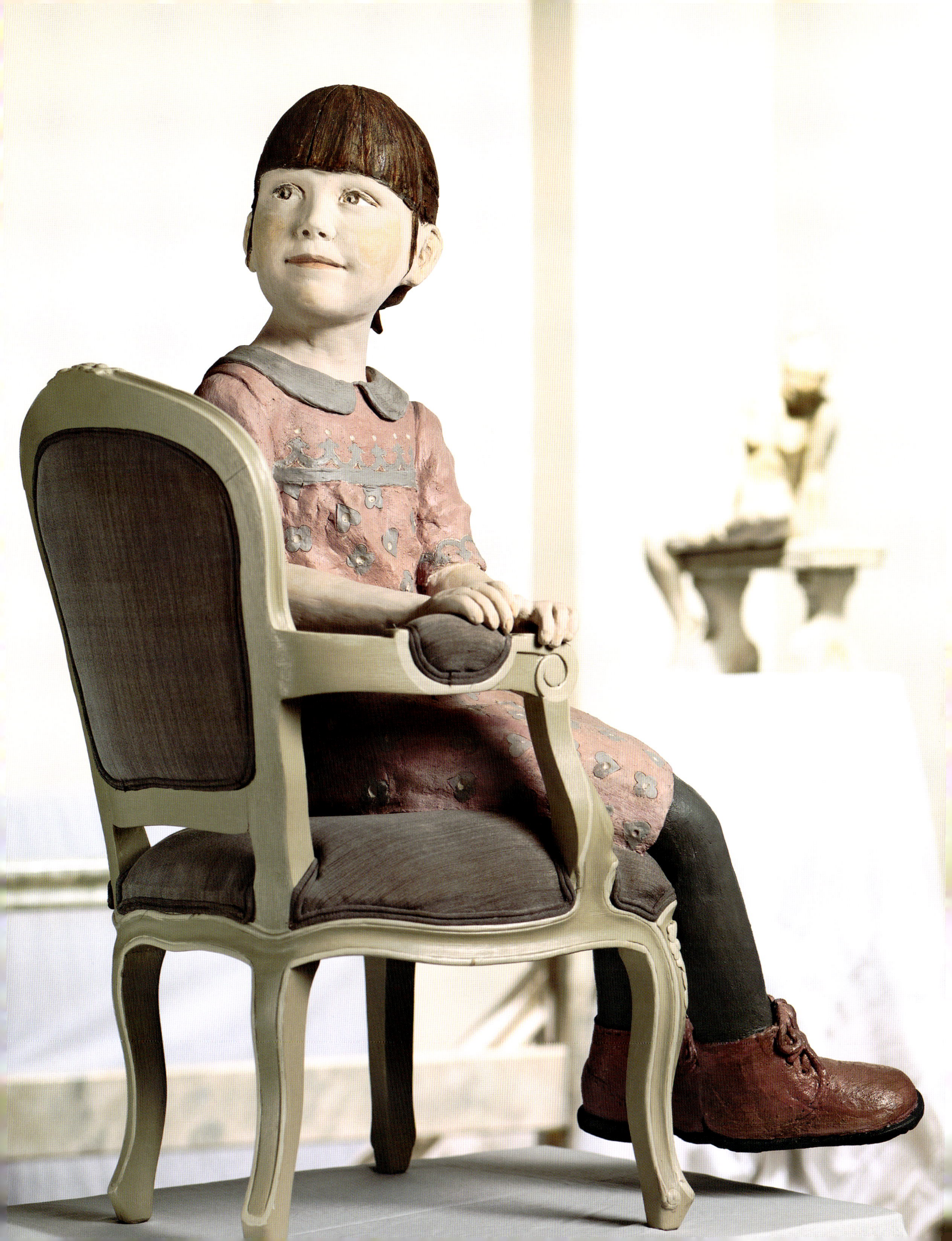

Sit your model on the chair and take photos from different points of view (face on, profiles, three-quarters, back, from above, from below . . .). If you can get the child to pose for a while it's better, but young children have difficulty sitting still. Here, the pose has the torso twisted on the pelvis; the little girl was sitting and turning toward the back of the chair at the same time. It is this position that gives life to the character. Pin the photos on a support close by you.

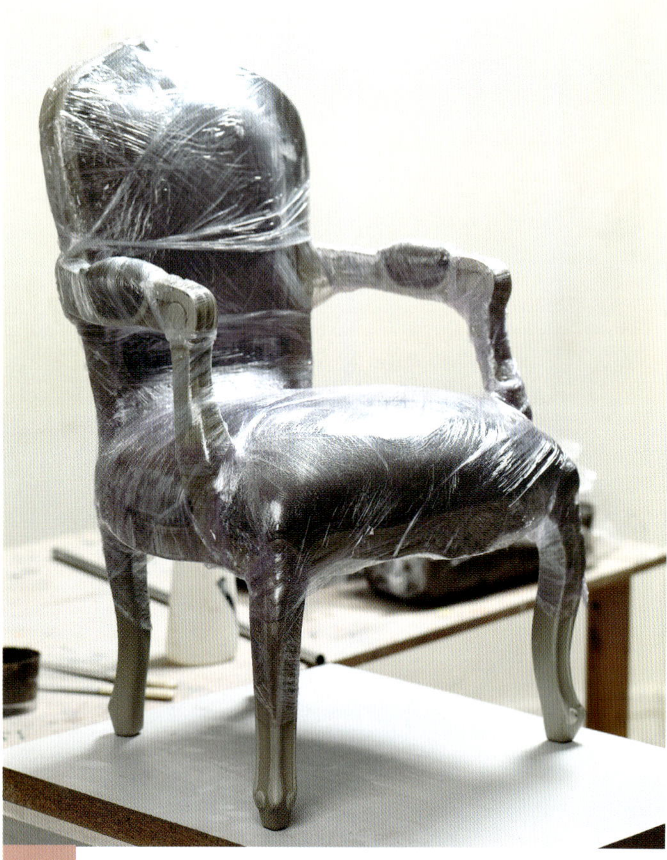

1 Start by protecting your support, taking care to cover the chair (wood and material) with several layers of plastic wrap to avoid damaging it while you are working, since the clay is damp and abrasive.

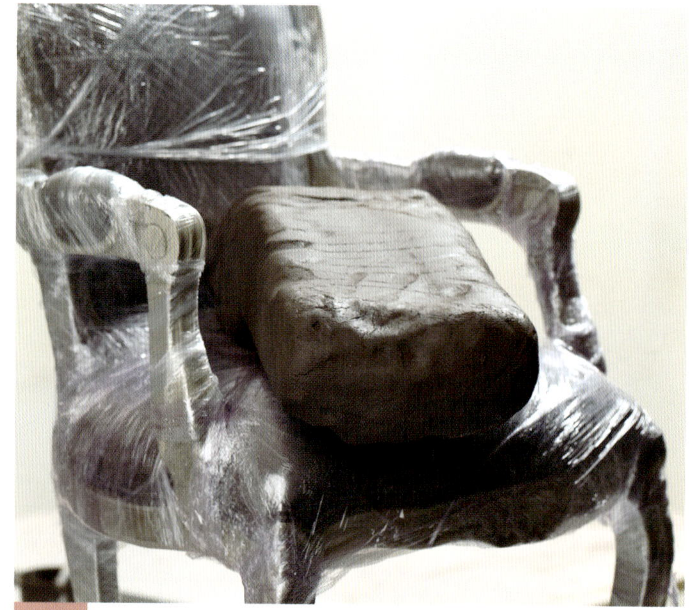

2 The pelvis, thighs, and torso block are going to be made in a very schematic manner. Take two blocks of rather firm clay of around 22 lbs. each (leave them to dry a few hours first to avoid them settling with the weight that will be added later). Place the first block (which includes the bottom part of the pelvis and the thighs) flat and slightly sideways on the chair seat.

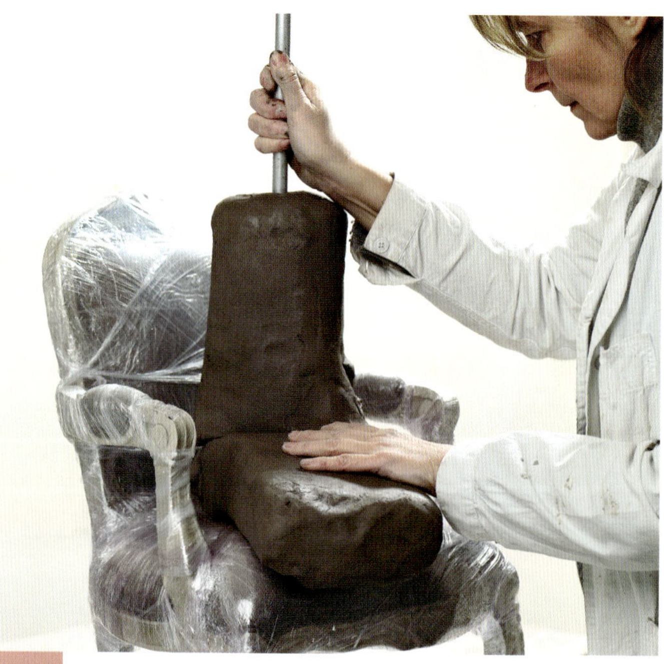

3 Then place the torso block (top part of the pelvis, waist, and rib cage) vertically onto the first, marking the twist of the bust on the pelvis toward the child's right side. In profile the two assembled blocks form an "L" of equal sections. Plant a metal (aluminum) rod through the center of the width of the torso to reinforce the structure and allow the neck and head to be attached to the volume of the torso.

REMARK

A child's proportions aren't the same as those of an adult. At age four and a half, the head represents around ⅕ of the total height. To represent the volume as realistically as possible, check the child's measurements and do a sketch of all sides: total height, height of the head, height and width of the torso and pelvis, length of the upper arms and forearms, length of the thighs and calves, circumference of the head, shoe size, width of the shoulders . . .

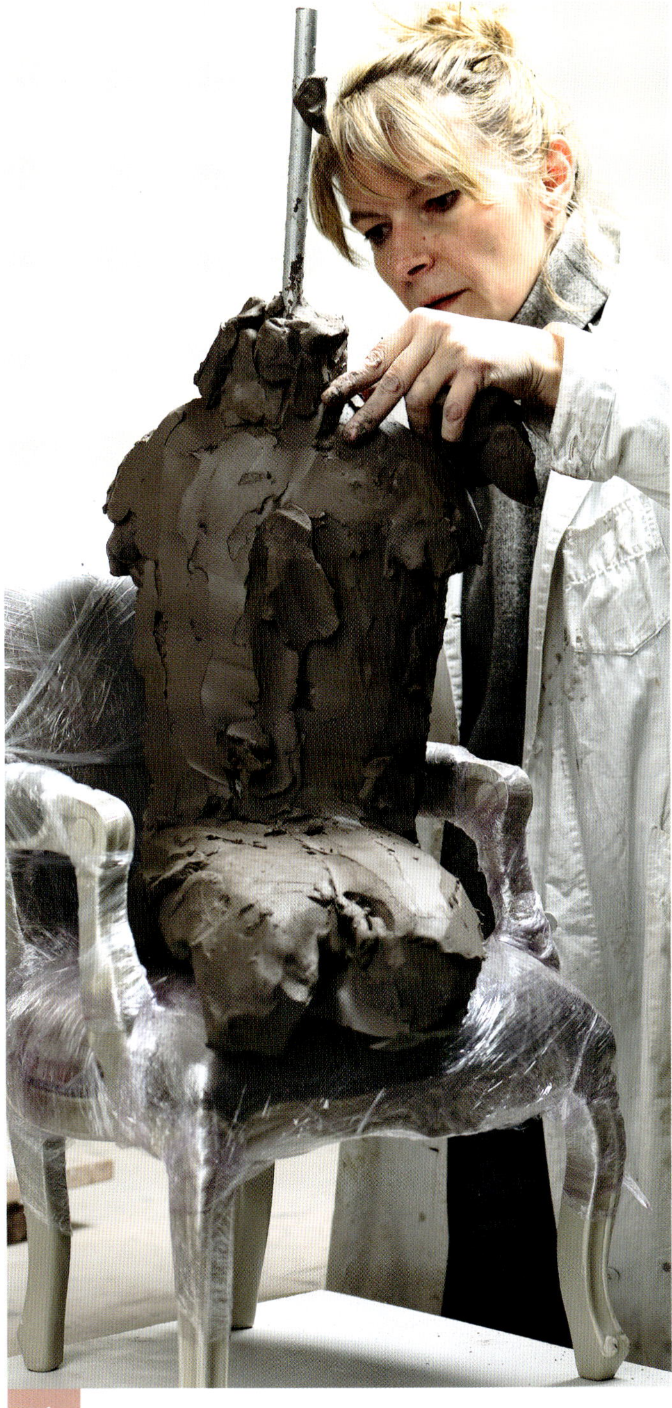

4 Mark the total height of the child by placing a gob of clay at the top of the rod. This will help you master your global mass better. Construct the child by adding pieces of clay to the volume you started with. Start by adding volumes roughly where the shoulders will be, and then the cylinder that will become the neck around the rod.

ADVICE

Remember to regularly check the proportions that you took care to note at the beginning.

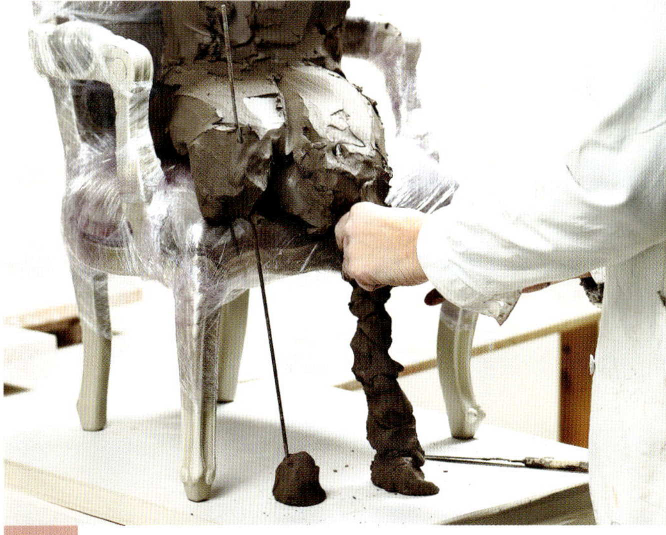

5 Divide the thigh block in two equal parts and plant a thin rod at the tip of each thigh, where the knees will be. These rods should reach the floor. Be careful to orient them in the position of the legs (here, one of the legs is slightly behind the other). At this stage, simply add the volume of clay around each rod, giving it the correct proportion.

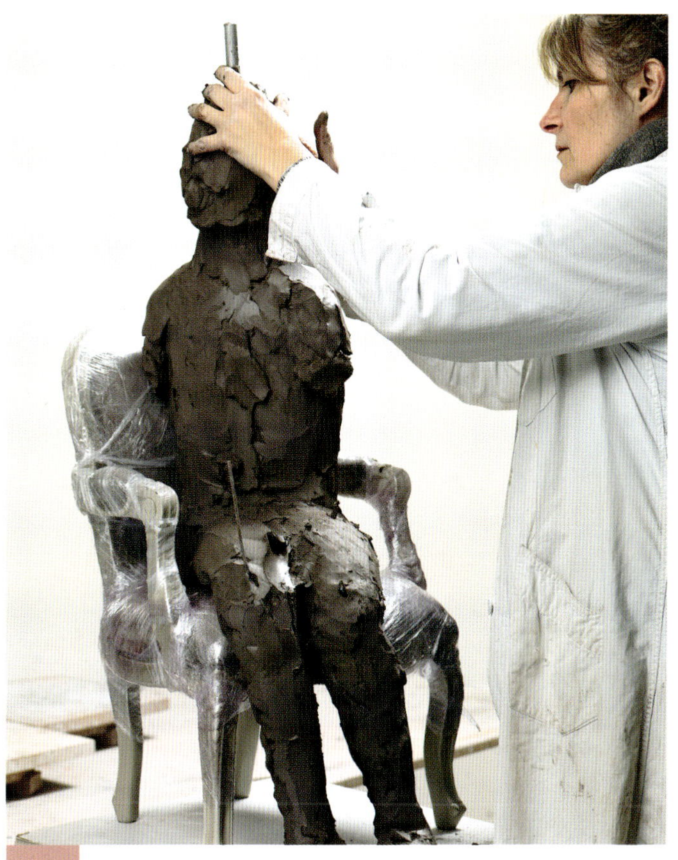

6 Construct the volume of the head, starting in profile to clear the structure of the child's skull, which is particular: half of the skull is situated above the eyebrow arch; the other half is below it.

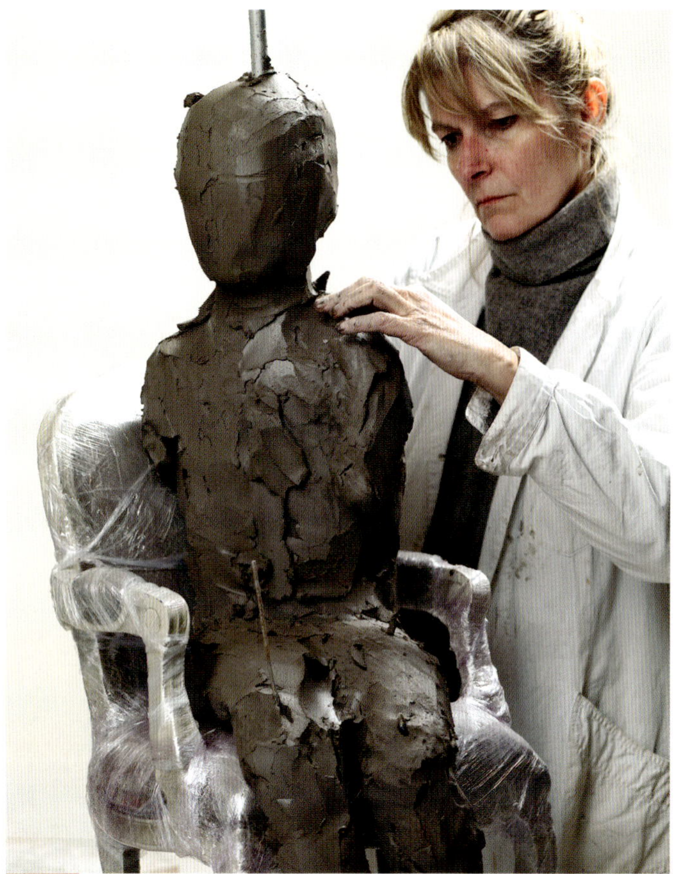

7 Guide your construction, following the contours of the skull's volume that you see in the photos of your model.

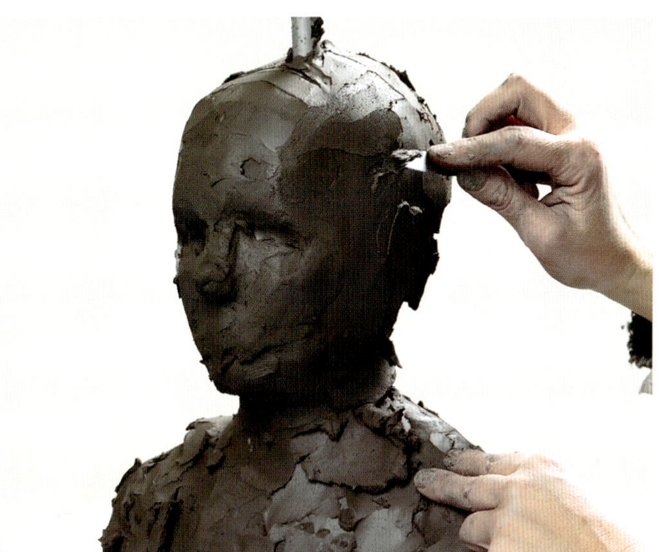

8 Define the proportions of the three different parts of the face (hairline/eyebrows, eyebrow arch / nose, and teeth roots / chin; see "The Face" on page 46) and then clear each side of the eyebrow arch and the eye sockets toward the temple. Plump out the jugal bone and add the volume of cartilage for the nose and the teeth below it. Place the ears.

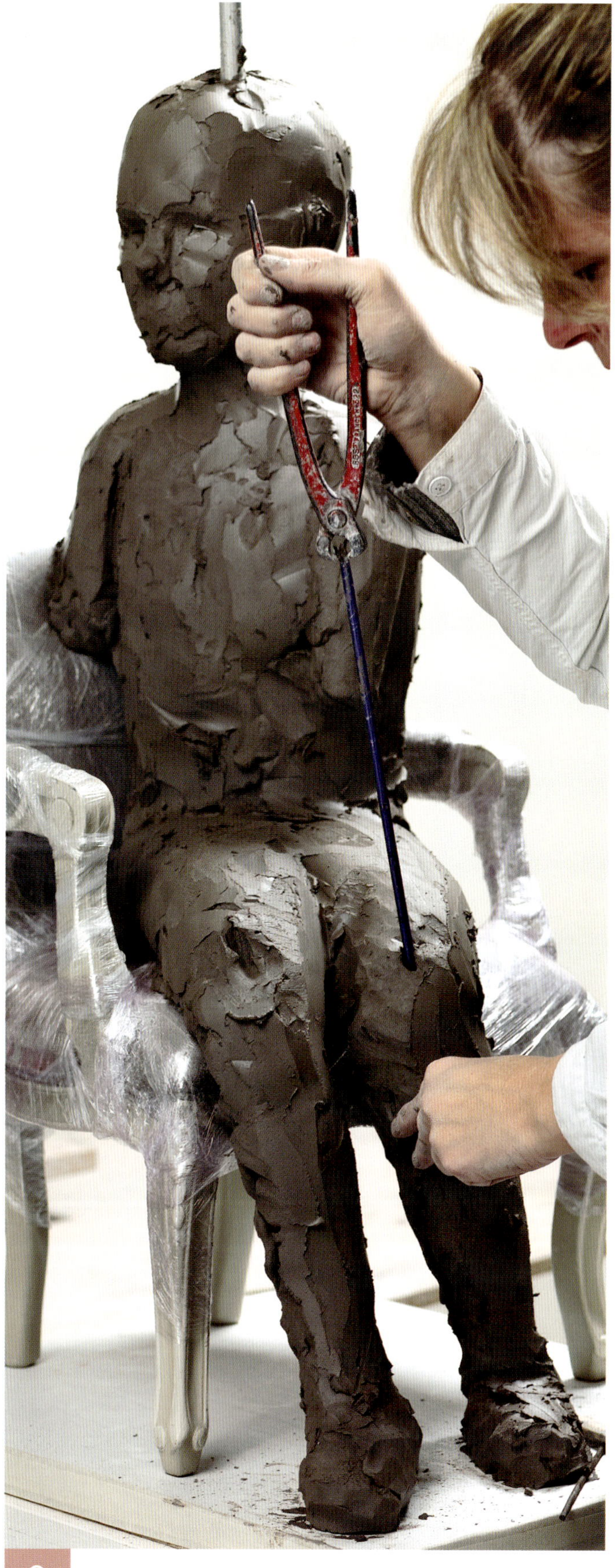

9 Use pliers to pull the rods out of the legs.

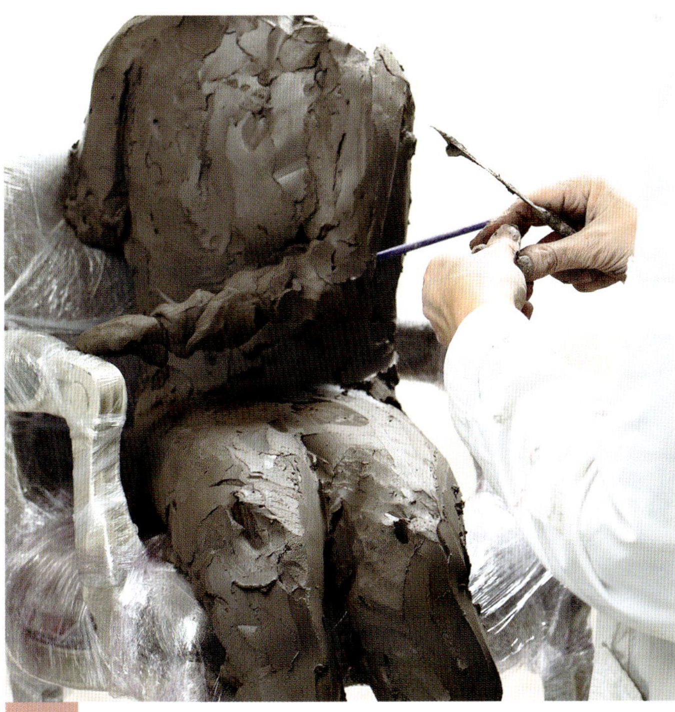

10 Plant a metal rod from the elbow to the arm of the chair, to guide the construction of the child's left forearm.

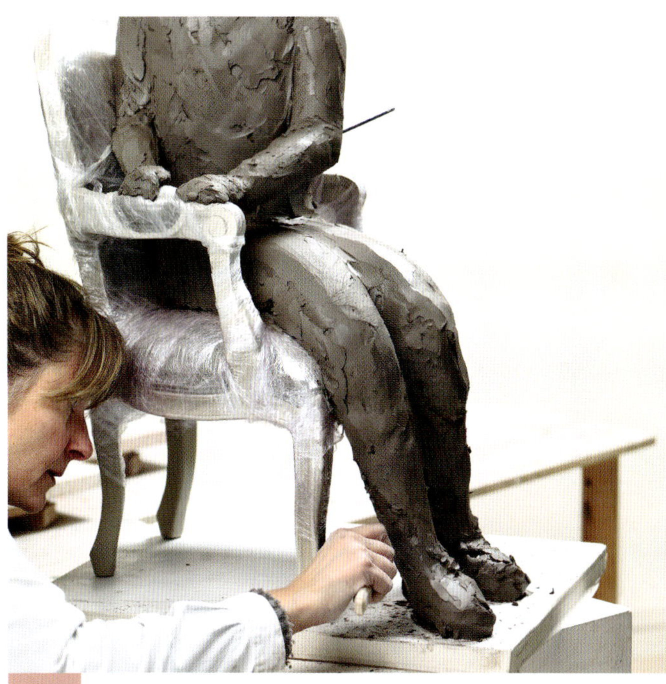

12 Using another metal rod, build the right forearm, which is against the back of the chair. When it is finished, remove the rods from the arms. You now have the global volume that needs to be specified and modeled.

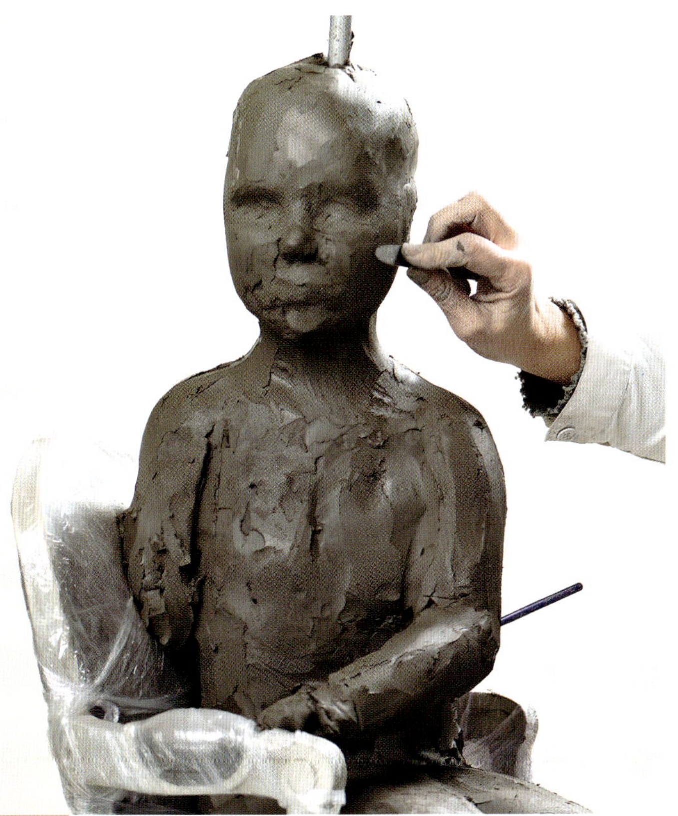

11 Continue to work on the face with small touches and check the proportions. The child's traits gradually take form. The volume of the cheeks is round and develops toward the front.

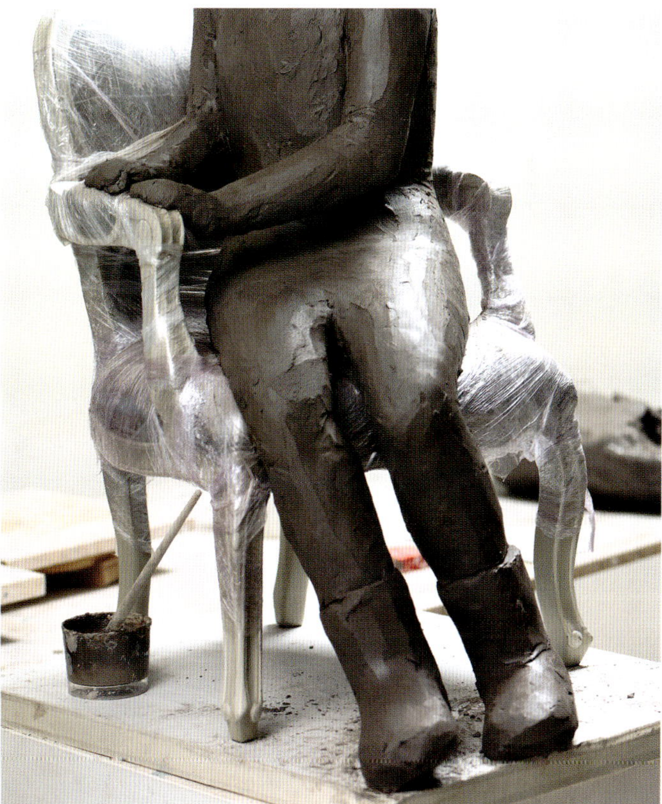

13 Detail the whole: create the volume of the shoes, retouch the arms and forearms, the thighs, the legs, and the roundness of the torso and the back.

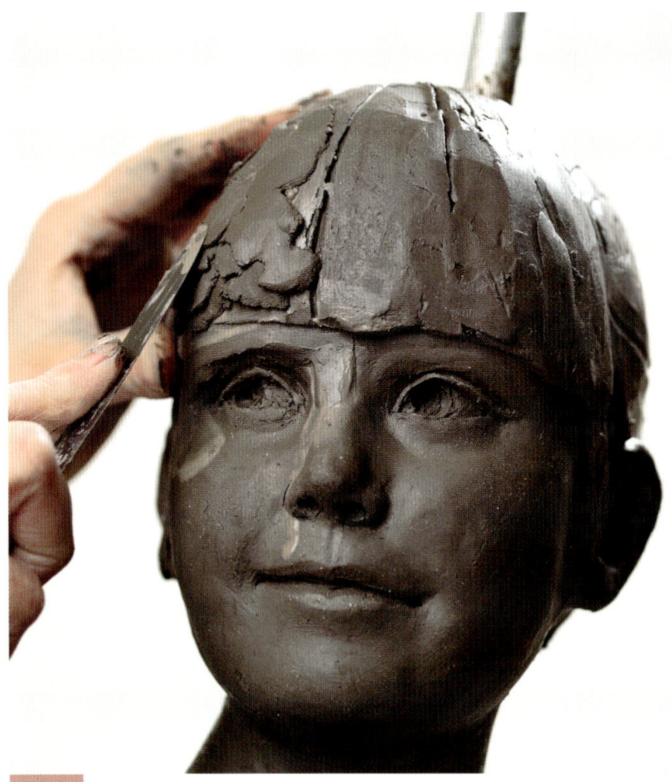

14 Improve the traits of the face (the eyes, the mouth, the ears, and the nose) and add the hair (see "The Face" section, on page 51). Form the regard (page 49).

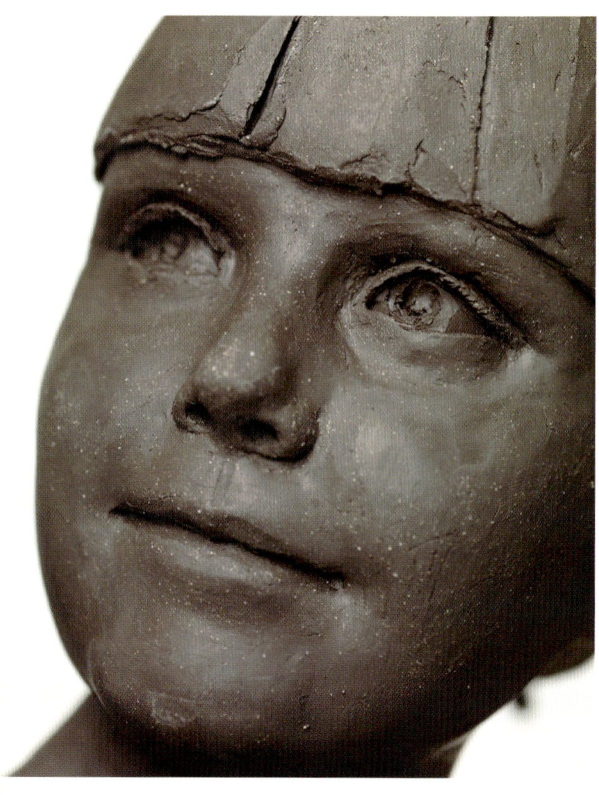

16 You have emptied the pupils and indicated two points of light in the eye: one in the shape of a hollow half moon, and the other in the shape of a hollow point.

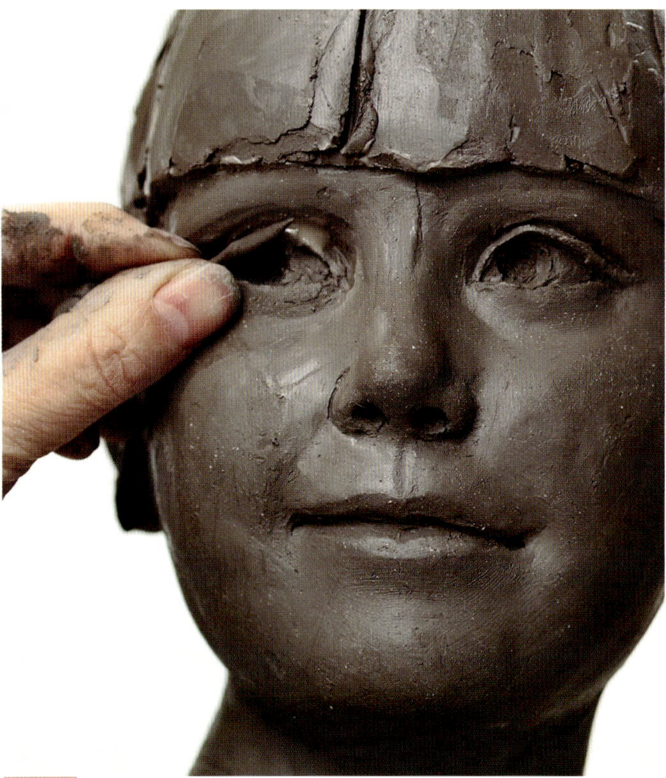

15 Check the symmetry of the traits. Here, the right eyelid is being retouched because it is too sunken in relation to the one on the left.

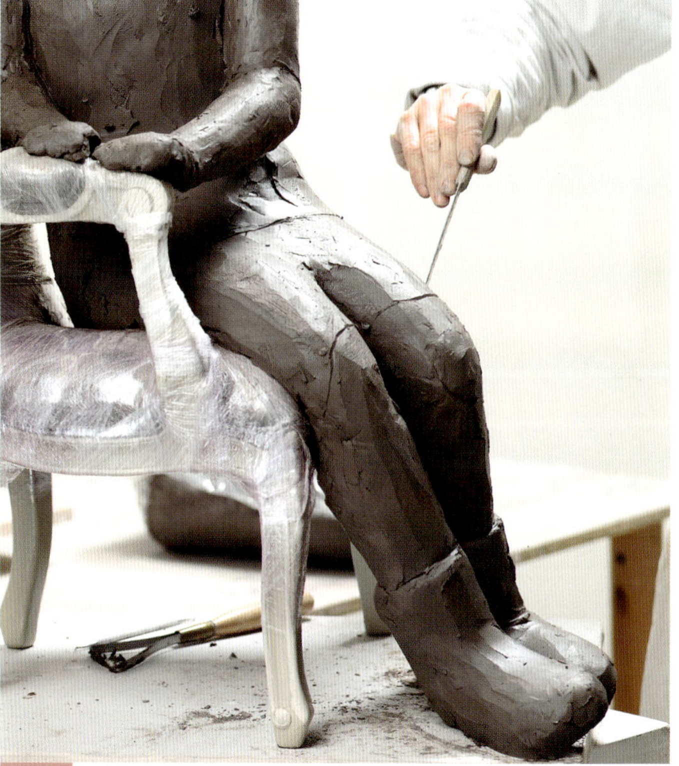

17 Delimit the edges of the cloths, in this case a dress with a Peter Pan collar. Draw the limit of the collar on the neck and that of the dress on the thighs.

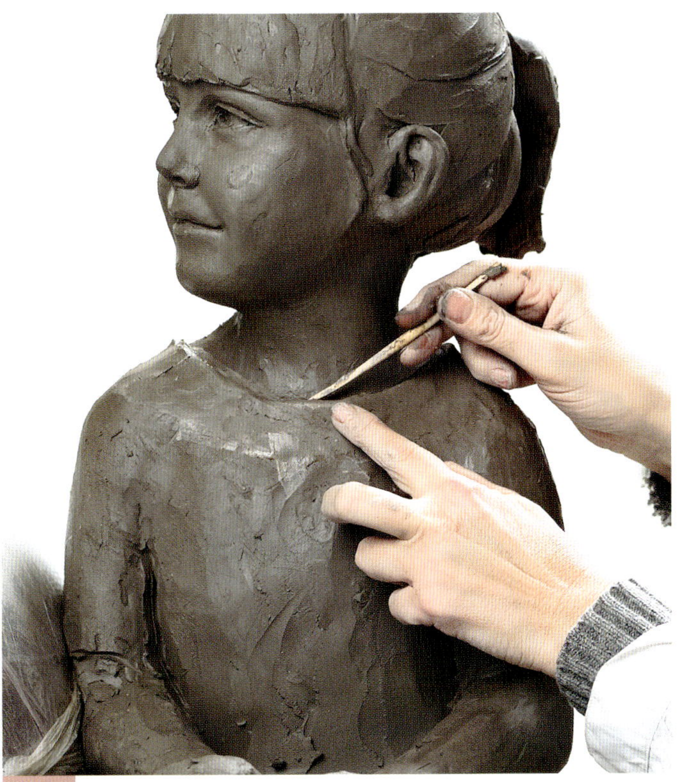

18 Add a clay sausage with slip: this will stand out a little from the neck and give the impression of the thickness of the cloth.

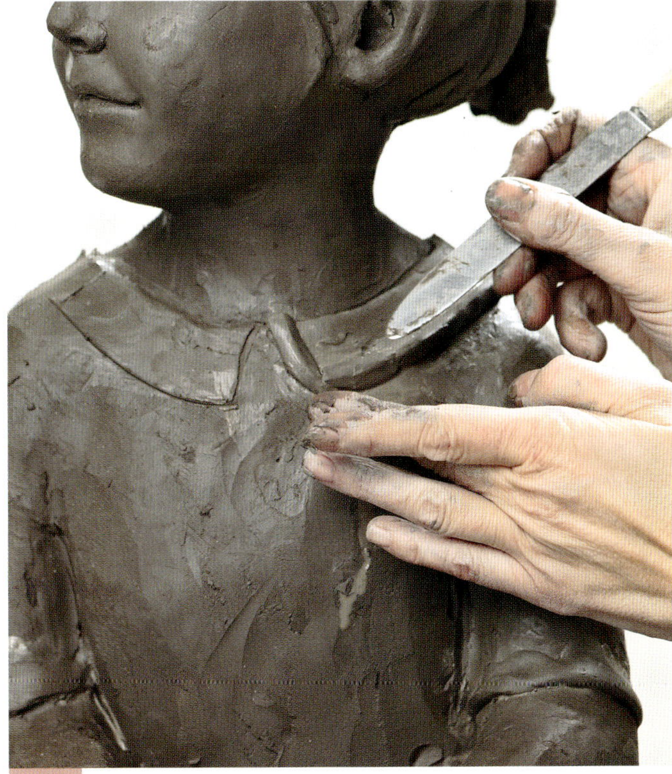

19 Make a slab of clay 2 mm thick and cut out the shape of the collar. Fix it with slip.

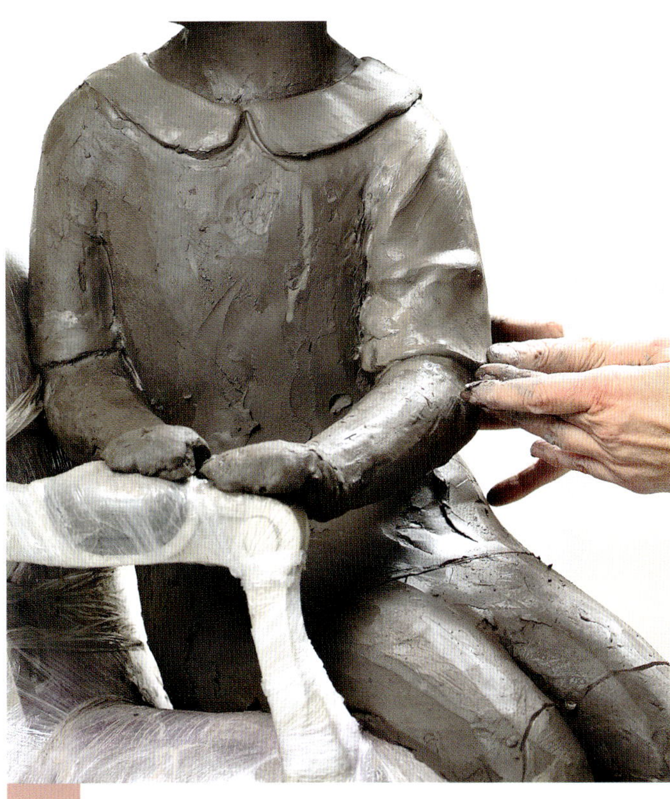

20 To represent the folds in the sleeves, fix on clay sausages with slip. Smooth them into the volume of the sleeve by squashing the edges with your fingers.

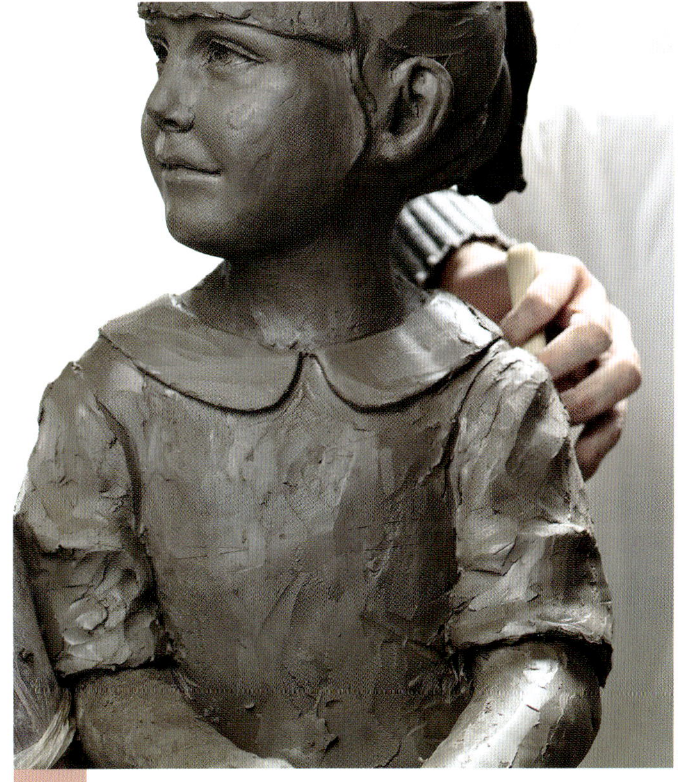

21 Amplify the volume of the sleeves by accentuating the bumps and hollows made by the clay sausages to represent the folds in the cloth.

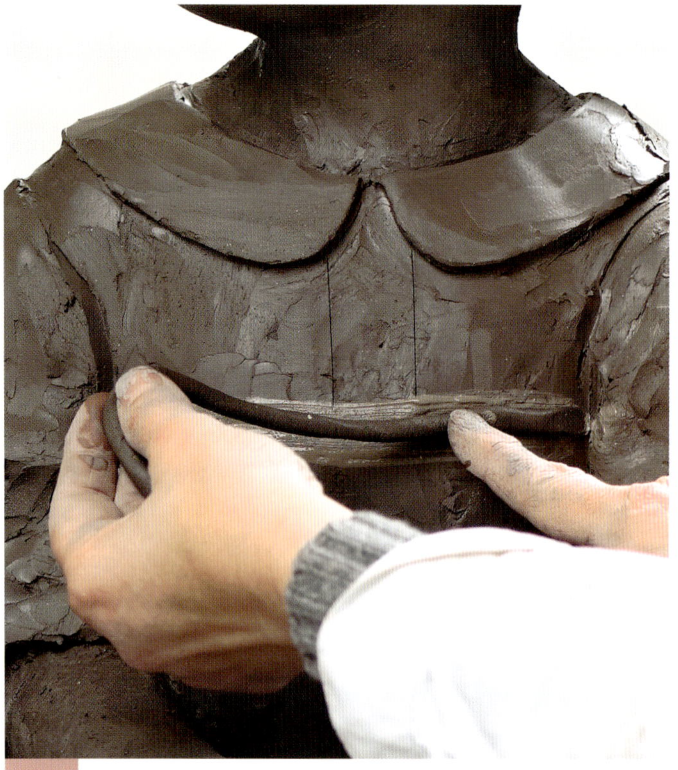

22 Draw the limit of the ribbon on the dress front and use slip to fix a strip of clay 2 mm thick to represent the ribbon.

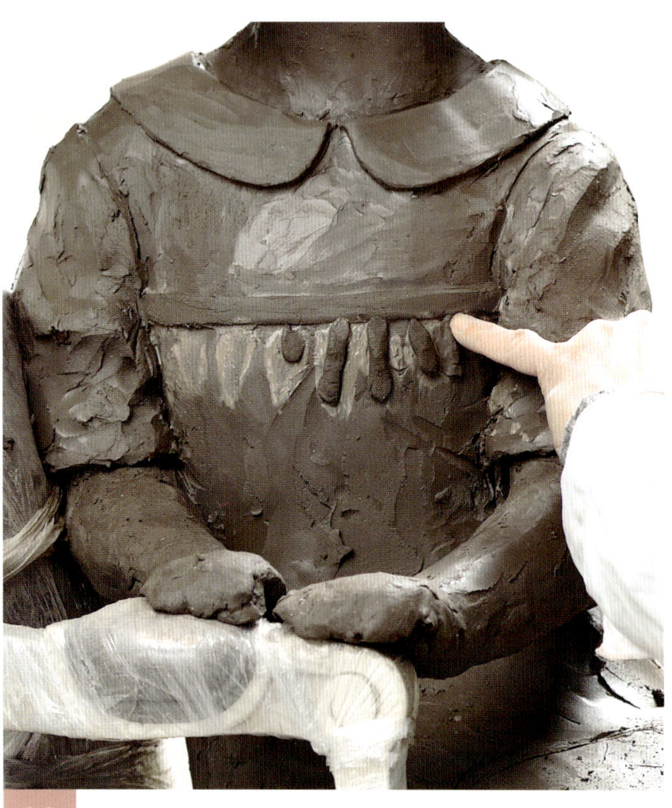

23 Use slip to fix different-length small clay sausages that will represent the folds in the dress underneath the ribbon.

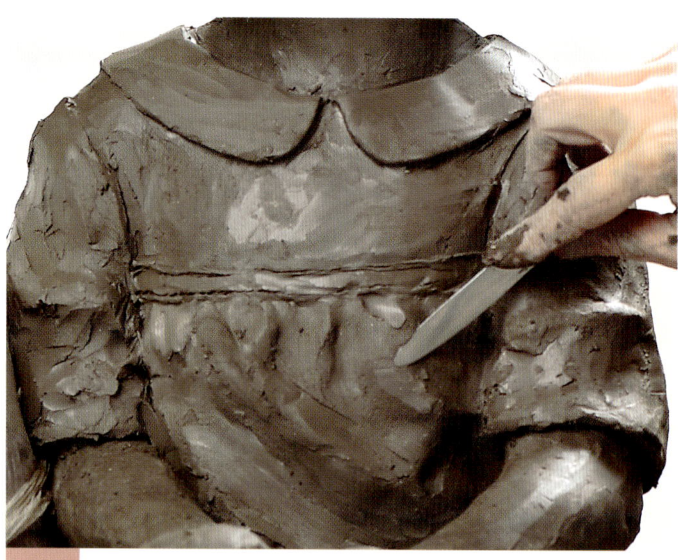

24 Smooth the clay sausage folds into the rest of the dress by squashing the sides with a knife.

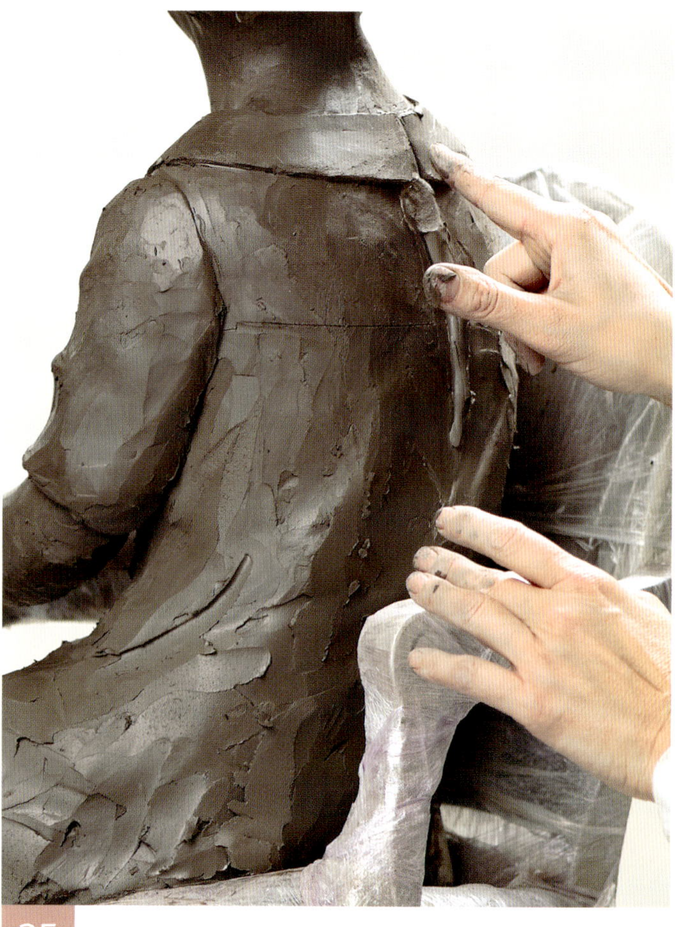

25 Do the same with the back of the child. Draw the ribbon and add a clay sausage to the center of the dress (from the center of the collar to the bottom) to represent the left border of the cloth that folds over the ride border.

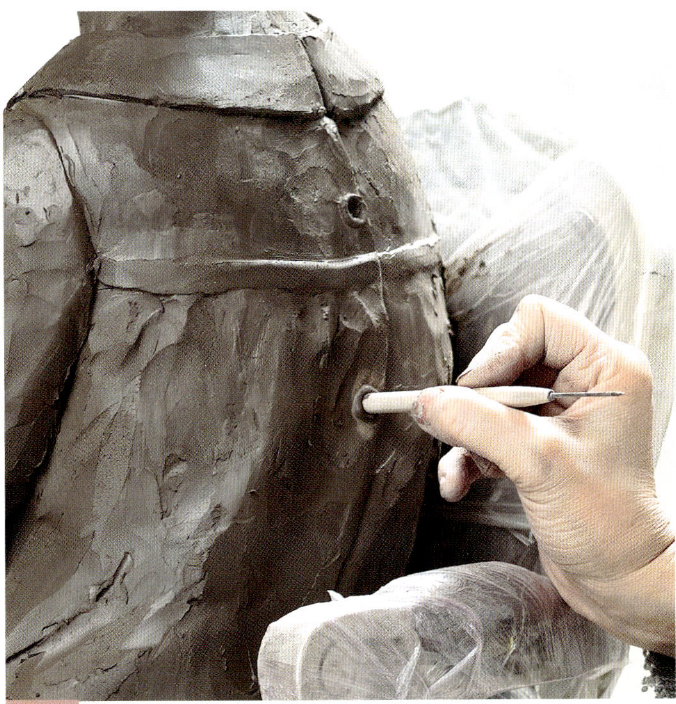

26 Fix on the ribbon with slip, as well as the folds underneath it, and to finish, use slip to fix little balls of clay to represent the buttons. Flatten them with the rounded end of a wooden clay tool, centering it properly to create a hollow in the center and a rim around the edge.

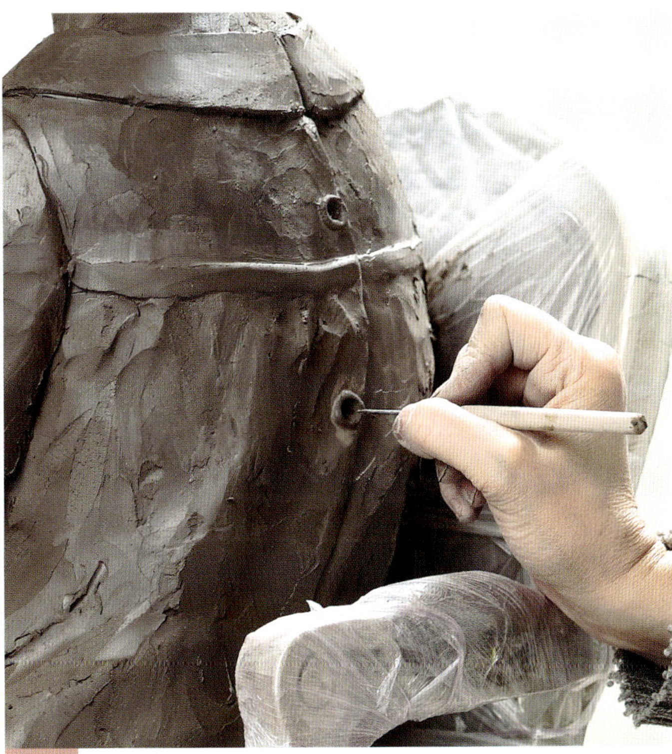

27 Make holes in the buttons with a potter's needle.

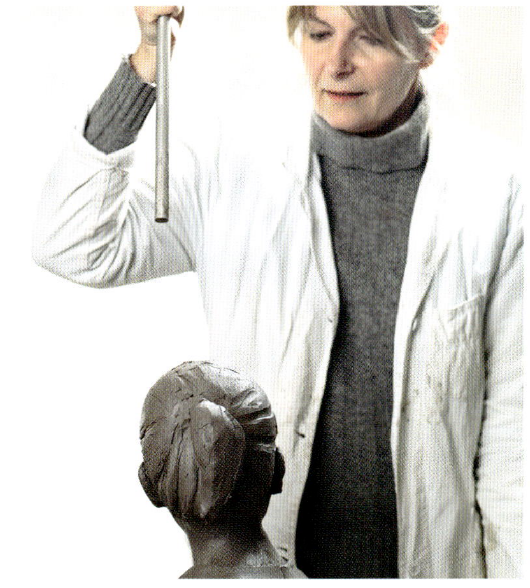

28 You can now remove the metal rod from the head, since your volume is stable and sufficiently dried out.

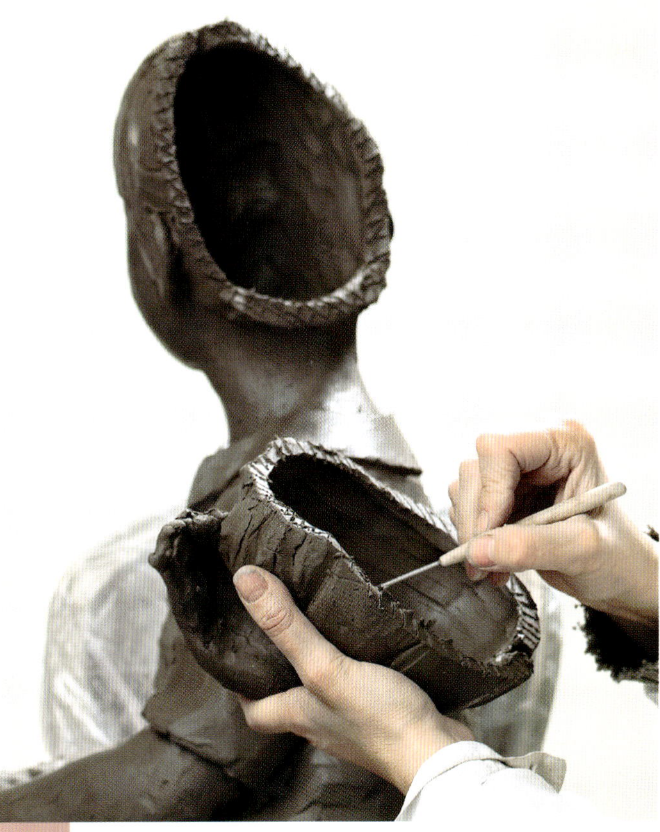

29 At this stage, if you see that the piece has already hardened enough, you can begin to hollow it out, starting with the top of the head (see "Hollowing Out," page 27). If the rest of the body is still too soft to work on after the head is finished, you must fix the head back together before hollowing out the body, and leave the rest to harden and hollow it out later.

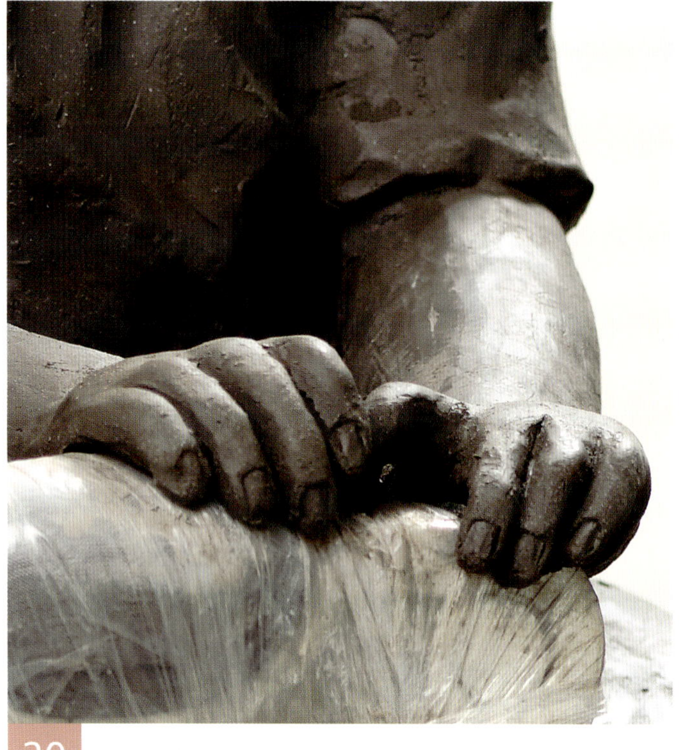

30 Once the head has been hollowed out and put back together, work on the hands. Plump them out and shape the fingers with small clay sausages. Empty the contours of the nails and plump them out (see "The Hand" section, on page 53).

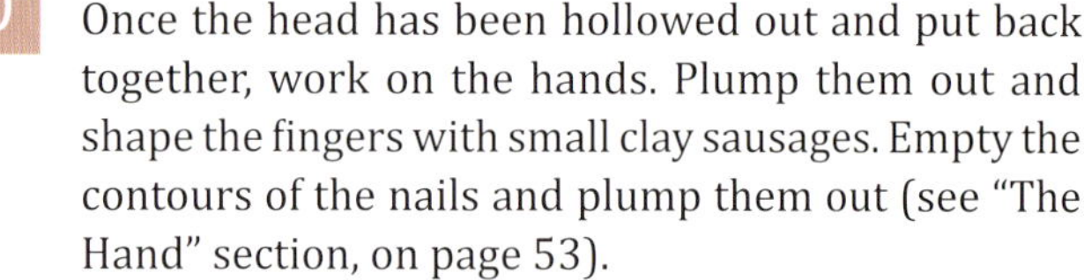

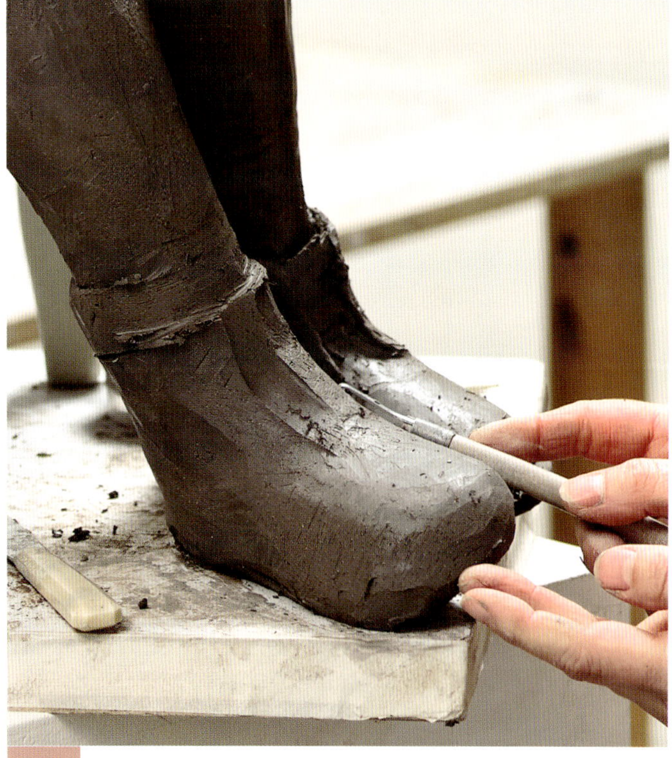

31 Separate the shape of the shoes from the mass.

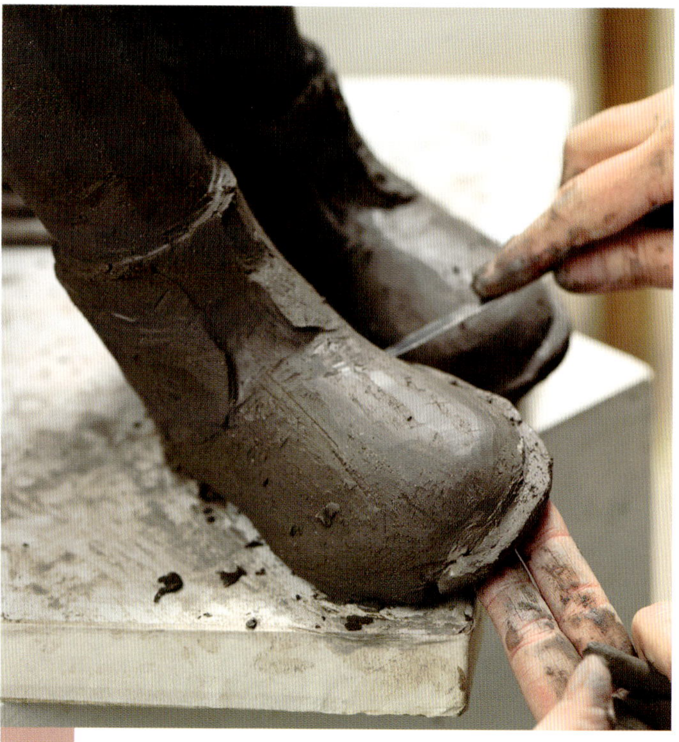

32 Add a clay sausage around each shoe to represent the sole.

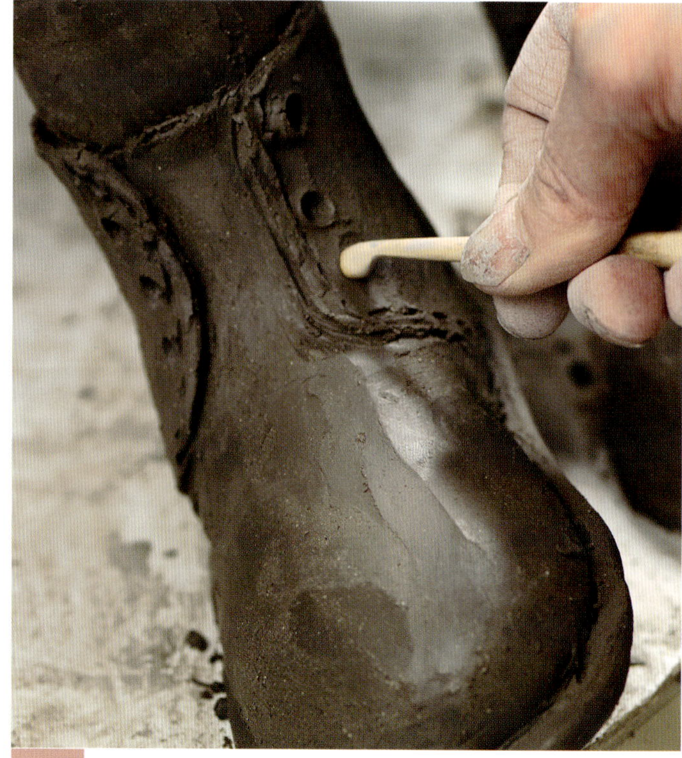

33 Make holes for the shoelace holes with the tip of a boxwood clay tool.

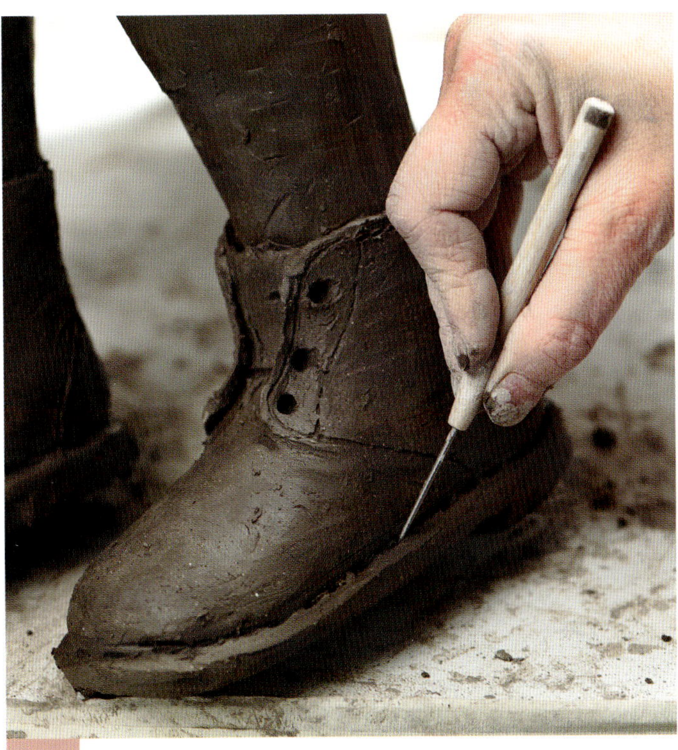

34 Trace the stitch marks around the edges of the soles and shoes, front and back.

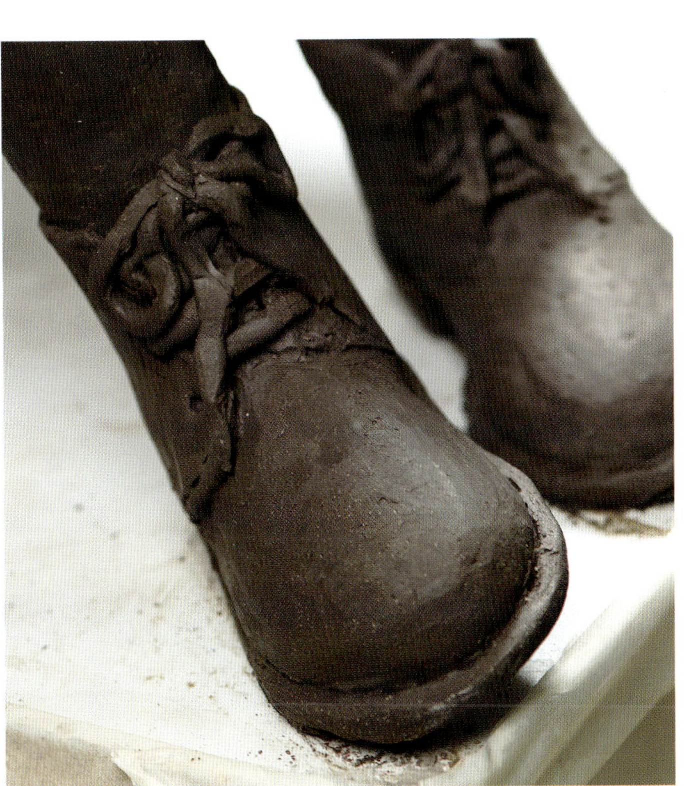

35 Use small clay sausages for the laces and attach them with slip, crossing one over the other. Refine and flatten the ends of the laces.

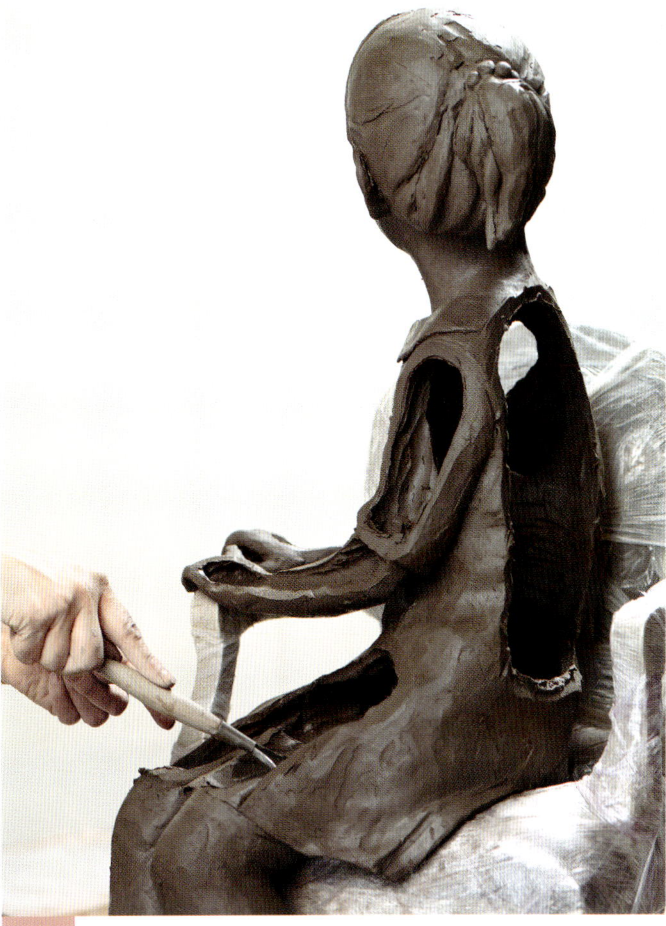

36 Hollow out the rest of the child as soon as the clay is sufficiently firm (see pages 28–29).

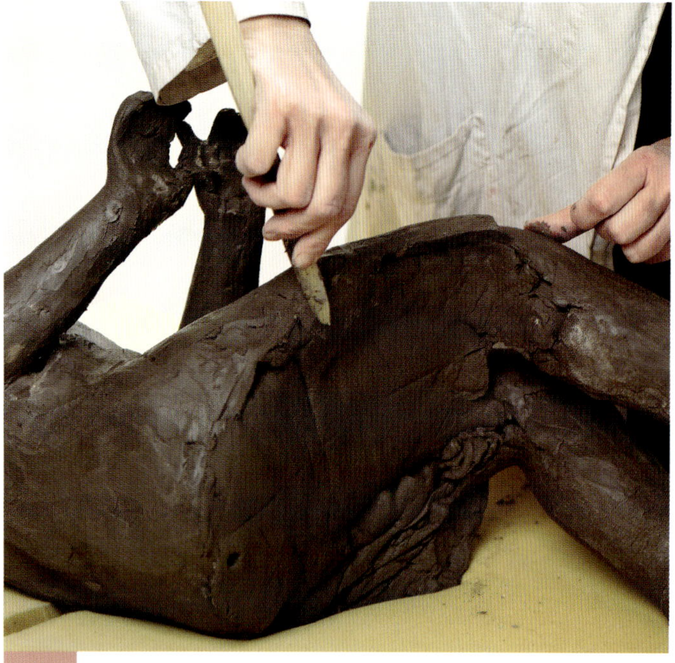

37 You can now remove your sculpture from the chair and retouch the parts that were against the chair: the bottom, the backs of the arms and knees, and under the hands. Place your sculpture carefully onto a piece of foam and use slip to retouch the volumes.

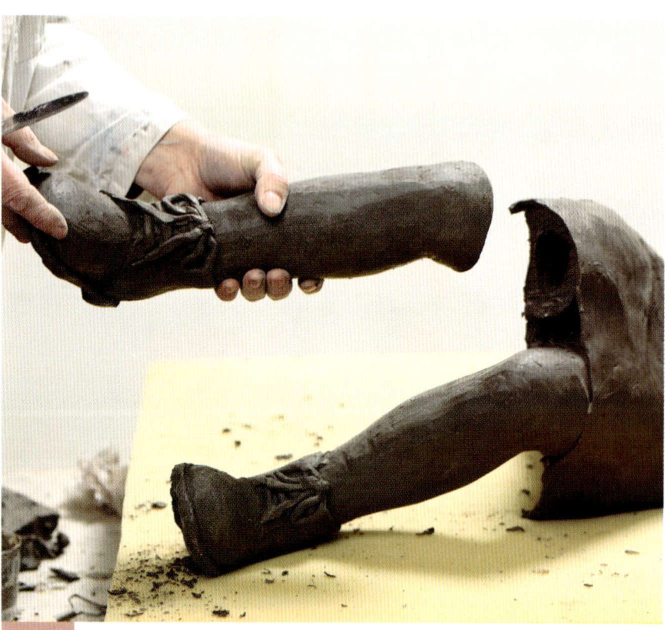

38 The child can't be fired in one piece, so the legs will be cut off above the knee and fired separately. They will be "restored" after firing. Cut the legs in a straight line along the edge of the dress, just above the knees. Score (see page 27) the edges to be restored, to allow the sealant you will use after firing to fix itself properly to the support.

Engobe

Colored Oxides Used:

Golden brown (Peter Lavem CS2201): skin, lips, and locks of hair
Burgundy (Peter Lavem CS2602): dress and shoes
Manganese dioxide G6 (Ceradel) for the black and gray: hair, tights, and the patterns on the collar
Chestnut brown (Solargil P230): pupils
Intense yellow (Solargil PR08): lighter locks in the hair

1 Prepare your different colors in clean bowls as and when you need them. The colors are done before firing, on unfired clay (see "Engobe or Colors on Unfired Clay" on page 32). To mix your colored oxides sand down dry, unfired clay. The clay you used for the child is white and finely grogged, which is perfect for the engobe, except for the skin and the eyes, for which you will use dry white porcelain. To mix the oxide and the clay, see page 33.

Engobe with the Same Clay as the Sculpture:

- Dress : 10% burgundy
- Shoes: 30% burgundy
- Collar and patterns on the dress: 5% manganese
- Tights: 20% manganese
- Hair: 20% manganese on all the hair, 30% golden brown on the locks underneath, and 15% intense yellow on the top locks

Engobe with White Porcelain:

- Child's skin: 5% golden brown
- White of the eye: 100% sanded white porcelain
- Pupils 3% chestnut-brown oxide
- Mouth: 10% golden-brown oxide

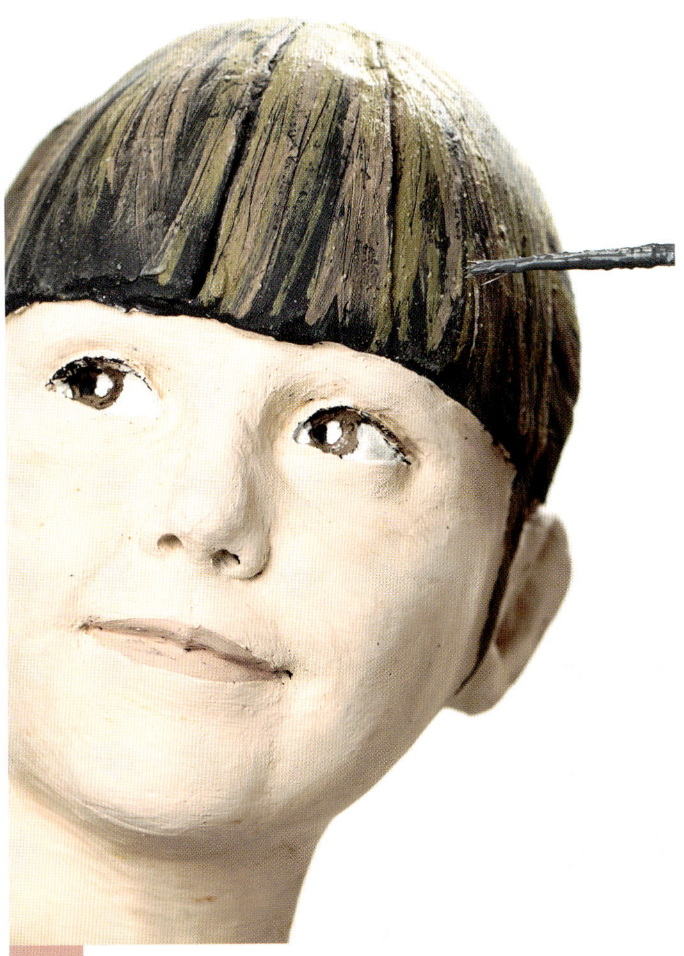

2 Paint on the engobe with a fine-haired brush; the size should be adapted to the size of the surfaces. Start with the face and the hands. Wait until the first coat is dry to the touch, and then do a second coat to make sure the engobe has covered every surface. Leave it to dry and then paint the eyes and the mouth. Now do the hair, beginning with the darker color, and finish with the lighter locks on top. Let it dry.

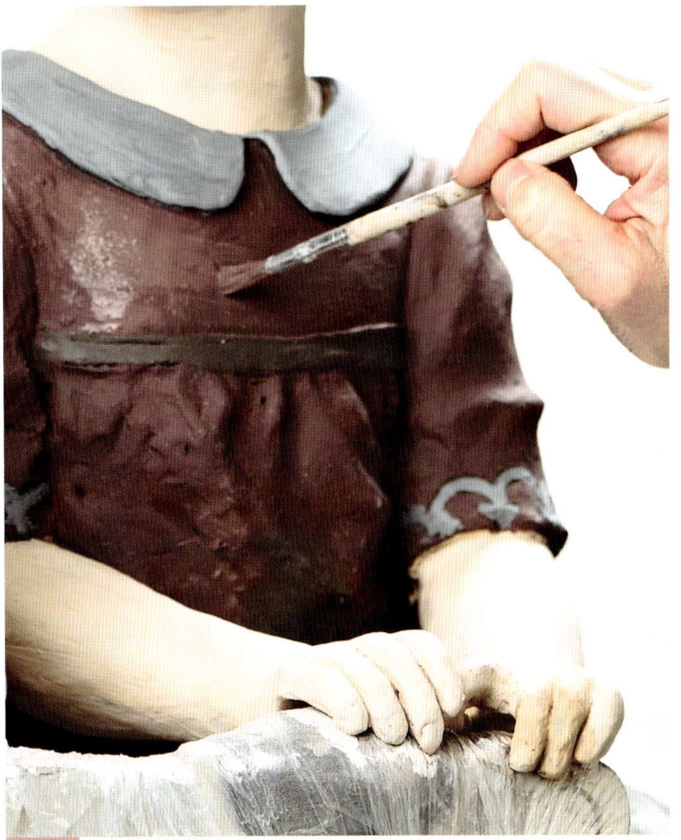

3 Engobe the collar in light gray and then the dress in burgundy. Let it dry.

ADVICE

Cover your bowls of engobe with a lid or plastic wrap so that they don't dry out. If necessary you can rehydrate them with your spray bottle.

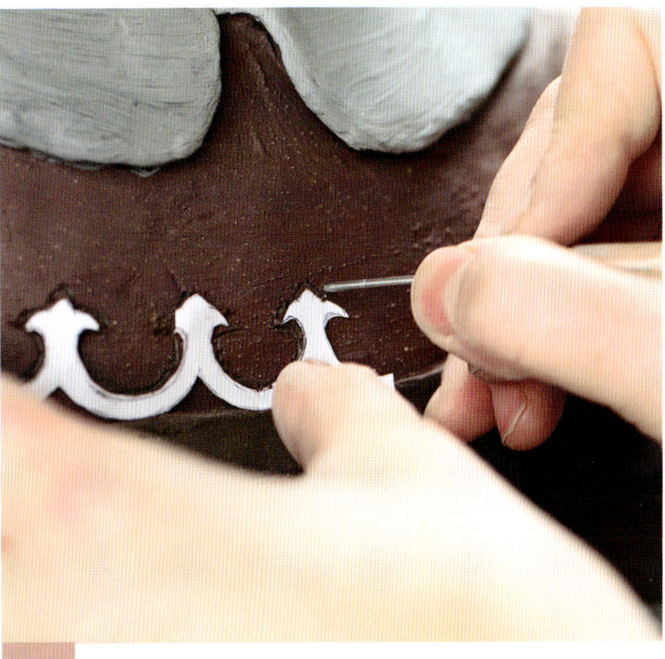

4 Now move on to the legs, which have been cut off; engobe the tights in dark gray and the shoes in burgundy. Let them dry. On the chest and the sleeves, trace patterns with the help of a supple paper stencil and a potter's needle.

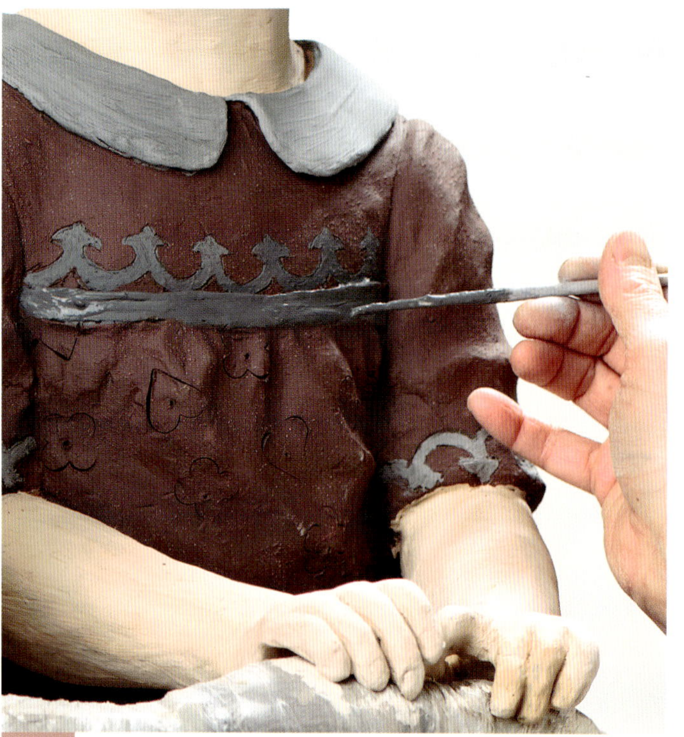

5 Engobe the ribbon and the patterns on the chest and sleeves in gray.

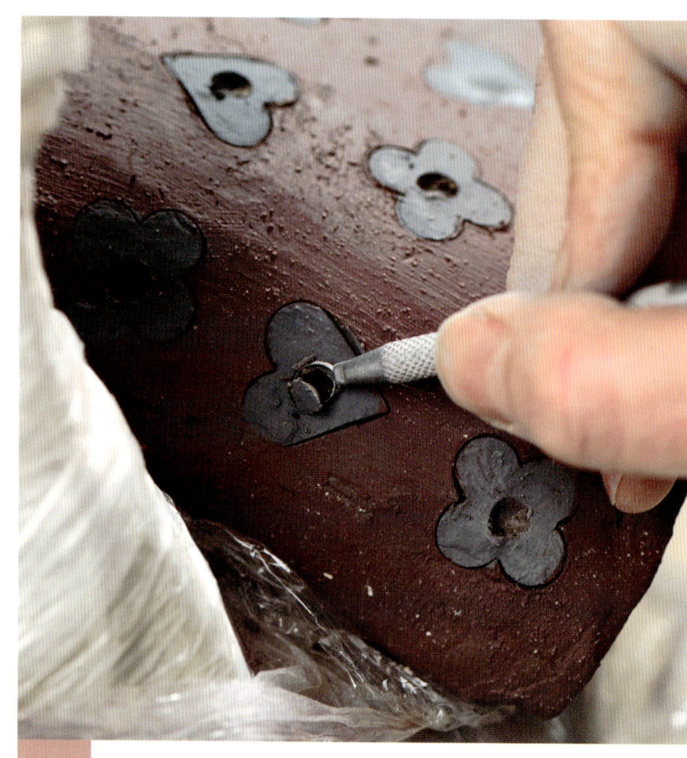

7 Engobe the patterns in gray and wait until they are dry to the touch. Use a small loop tool to empty out the center of the patterns; after firing, these will have the color of the white clay.

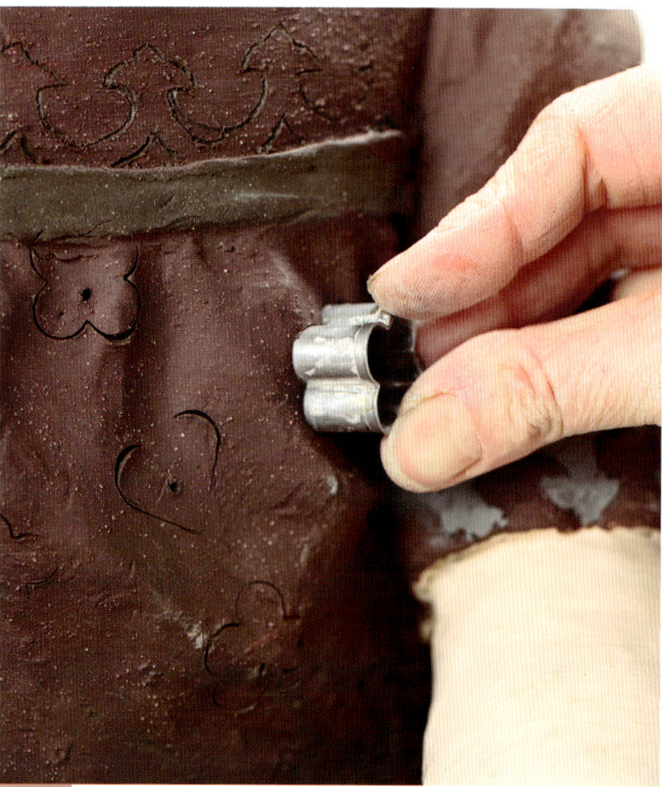

6 Do alternating patterns of flowers and hearts with cookie cutters, which you press carefully onto the entire dress to imprint the patterns.

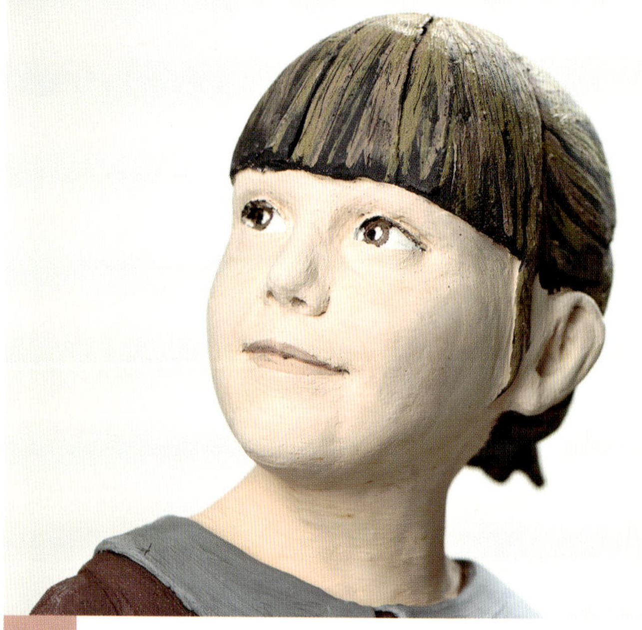

8 Leave the layers of engobe to dry out for at least a day, enveloping your sculpture in plastic bags. Then take the child out of the chair to engobe the parts that were in contact with the chair (under the bottom and behind the right shoulder). Once the engobe is finished and has dried out, sit the child back in the chair and let it dry out for 15 days. Place the legs on a piece of foam to dry out.

9 Remove the child from the chair and fire it and the legs at 1,832°F to preserve the freshness of the colors.

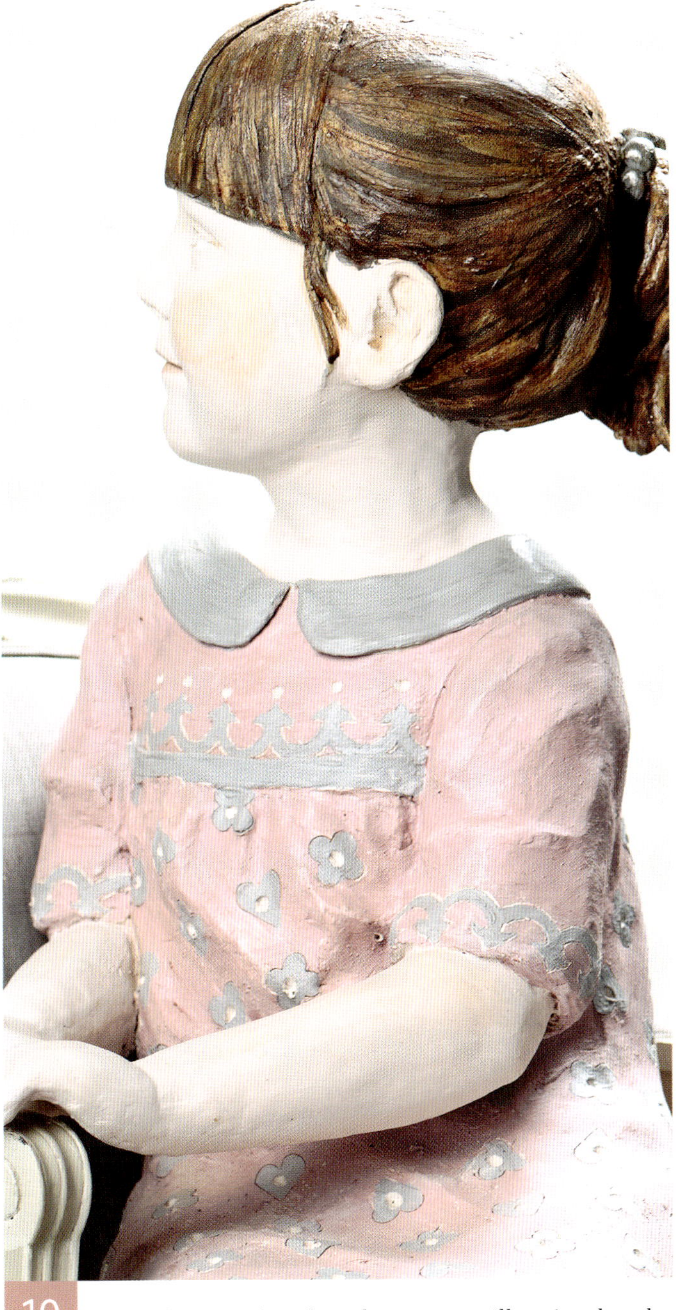

10 After firing and cooling down, you will notice that the colors have a greater pastel tone. However, the color of the hair hasn't mixed enough. You'll have to equalize it by painting on a mixture of Caparol, water, and sienna to harmonize the darker and lighter areas. The slightly satiny result will become matte with time.

Sealing and Restoring the Legs

After firing, you have to reattach the legs and erase the seams by using a sealing and restoration resin that has two components that both fill in and seal ceramic. Replace the child in the chair. You will notice that it has lost 10 percent of its volume: the feet no longer touch the floor if you put the legs in position to be sealed. This detail isn't important, since the little girl will seem more lifelike on her chair with her feet off the floor once you have restored her.

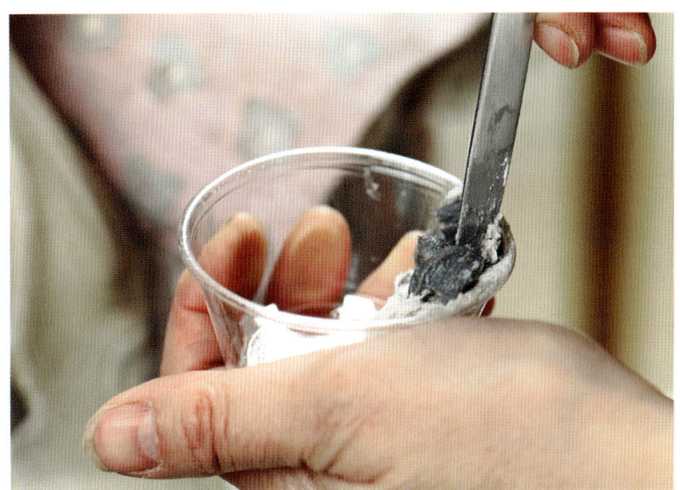

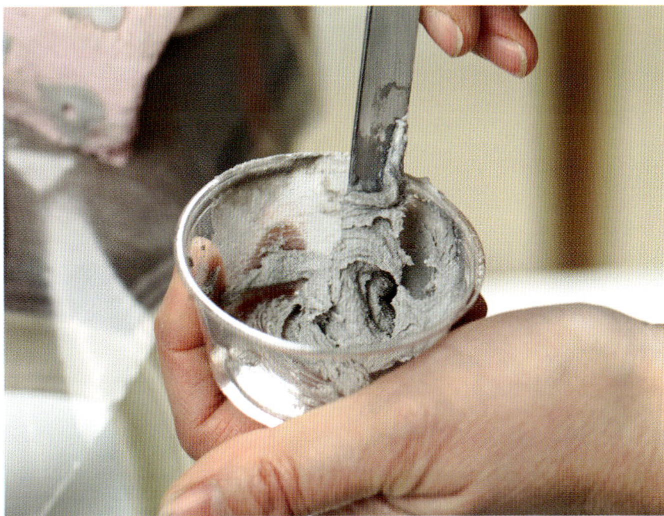

1 Using a knife, mix a little of the sealant in a bowl. The resin comes in two pots: a small one with dark-gray paste, and a large one with light-gray paste. Here, measure $^{2}/_{3}$ of light-gray resin and $^{1}/_{3}$ of dark-gray resin into the same bowl and mix them well. Sealing and drying time is 24 hours. Sticky and difficult to handle at first, this resin becomes firmer after two hours, allowing you to retouch the sealant, remove some, and even smooth out certain parts.

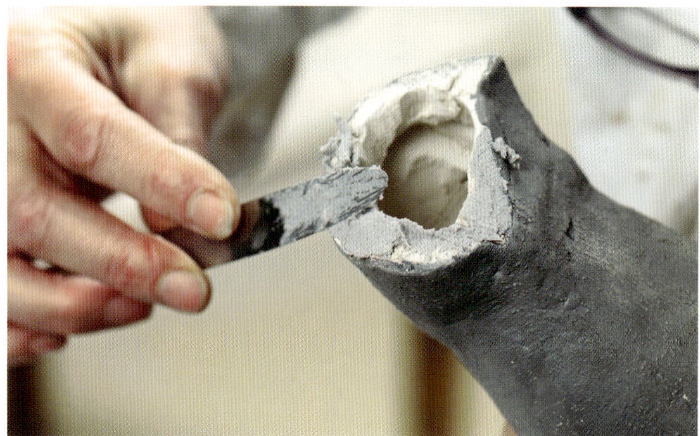

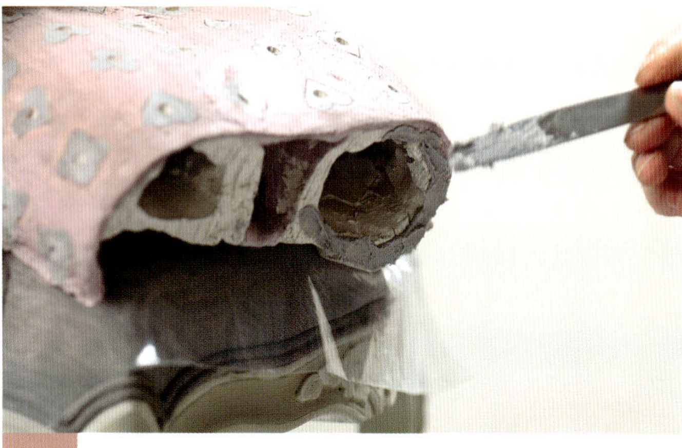

2 Apply a thin layer of sealant onto the edges of the first leg you are going to restore. You need to put the sealant on both parts that will be in contact with each other.

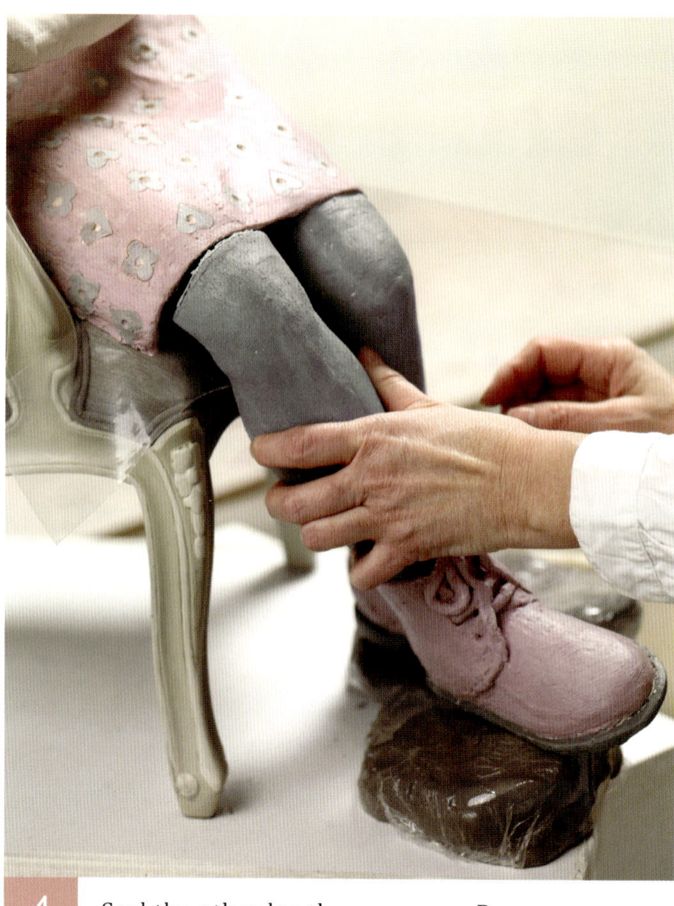

4 Seal the other leg the same way. Do any necessary adjustments before restoring the seams with the same sealant.

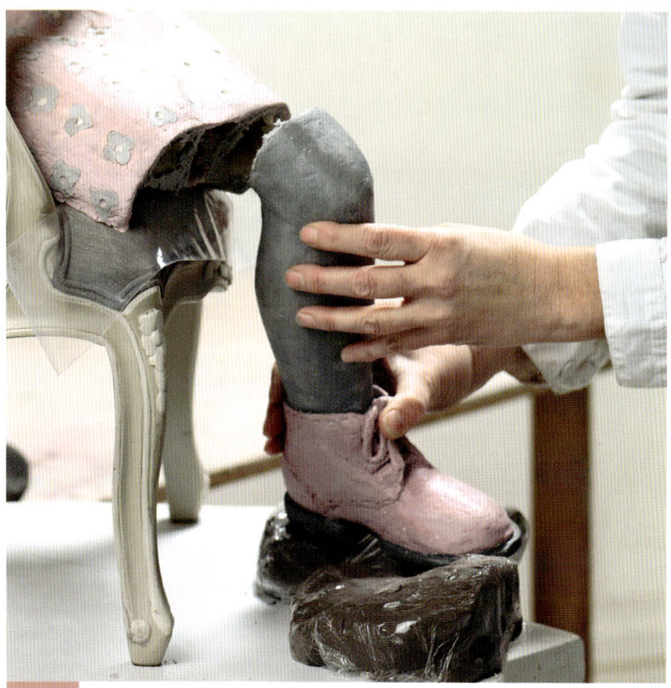

3 Place supports of clay covered in plastic wrap, which will easily adapt to the missing volume under the feet and press the leg into place.

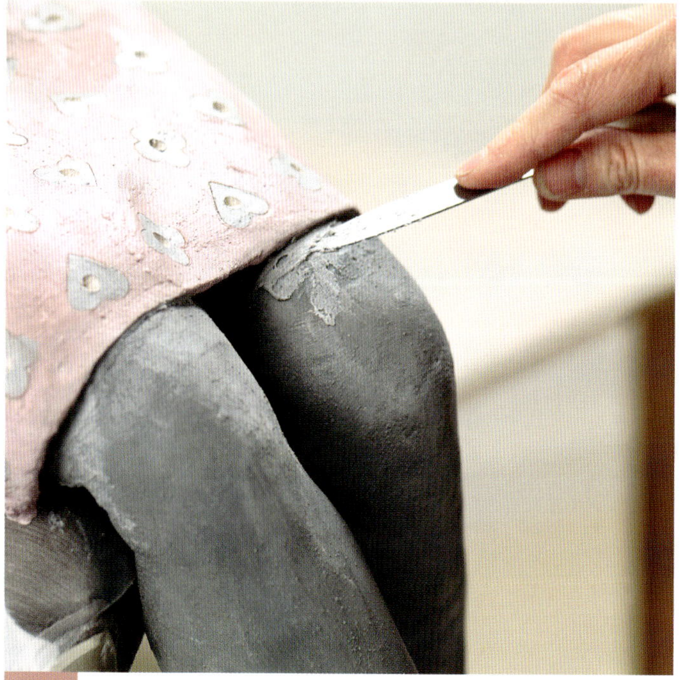

5 Work on the seams with a knife and a spatula. The matter is sticky and greasy, so remove the surplus.

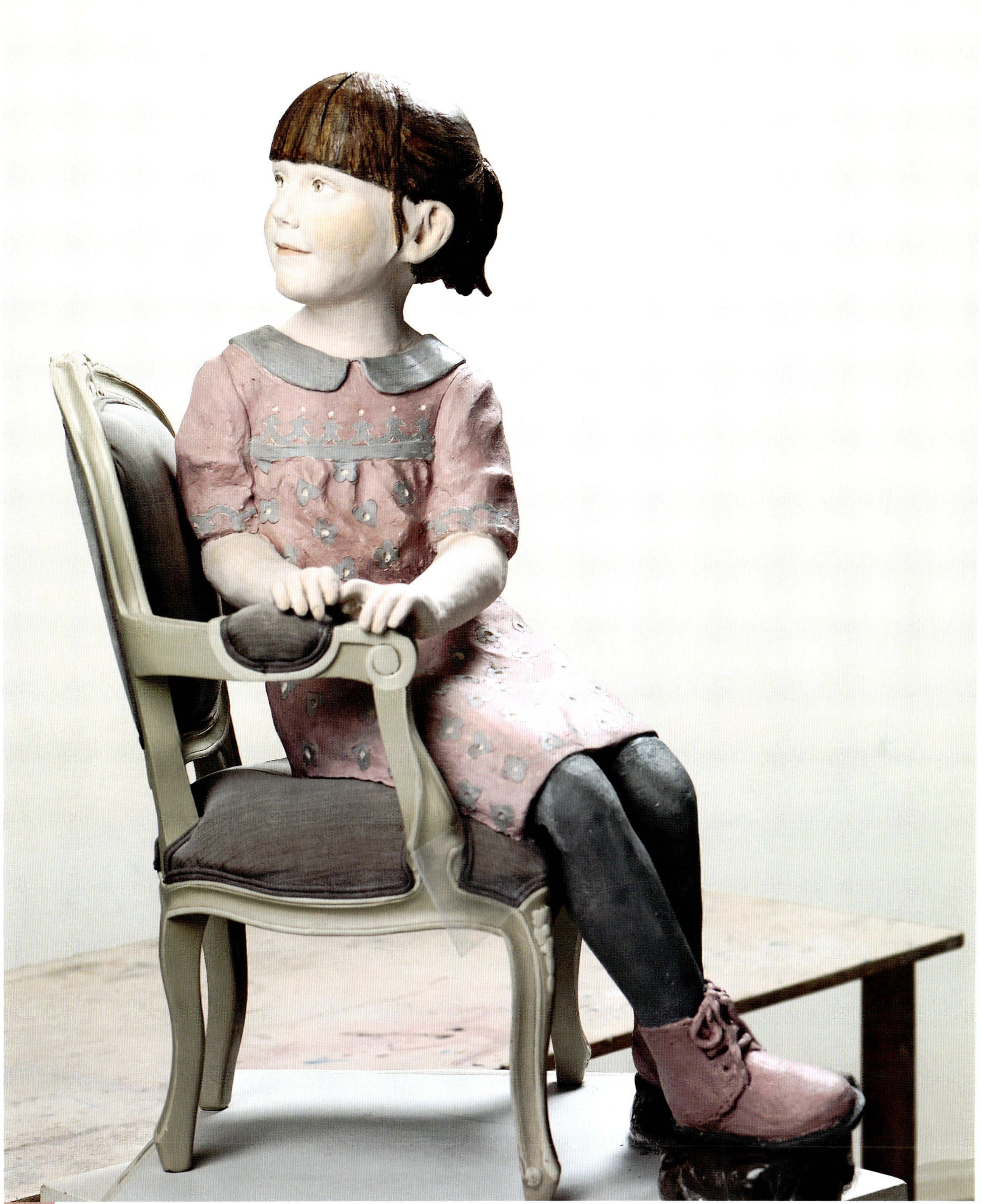

6 The sealant will be dry in 24 hours. You can now sand down the seams and tint them. For this, prepare a small quantity of sealant in the same proportions as before ($^2/_3$ and $^1/_3$). Add a little ethanol (using the screw top as a measure) and a small point of black pigment. The color of the sealant should match the color of the engobe.

The Workshop

Sculpture Lessons

Beginners, amateurs, and professionals hoping to improve their technique have rubbed shoulders in the workshop ever since its creation. I don't fix rules; everyone can work on a personal theme right from the start while learning the structure and the basics of construction in clay at the same time. The sessions are both for learning and for encounters between different personalities. I intervene in a role of technical and esthetical advisor to give coherence to the manner or style desired. I explain while working in front of the student, to guide his regard and help him understand how volume is created. The more the work becomes personal, the less I intervene physically out of respect for the individual style of the piece. Certain students who started out in my workshop have been exhibiting and selling their work for several years now, and I'm very proud of them. Others are already renowned artists who simply want to improve their structures. It's marvelous to work with artists who all have different sensitivities and styles. There is no truth in art, only interior regards looking for a way to express themselves.

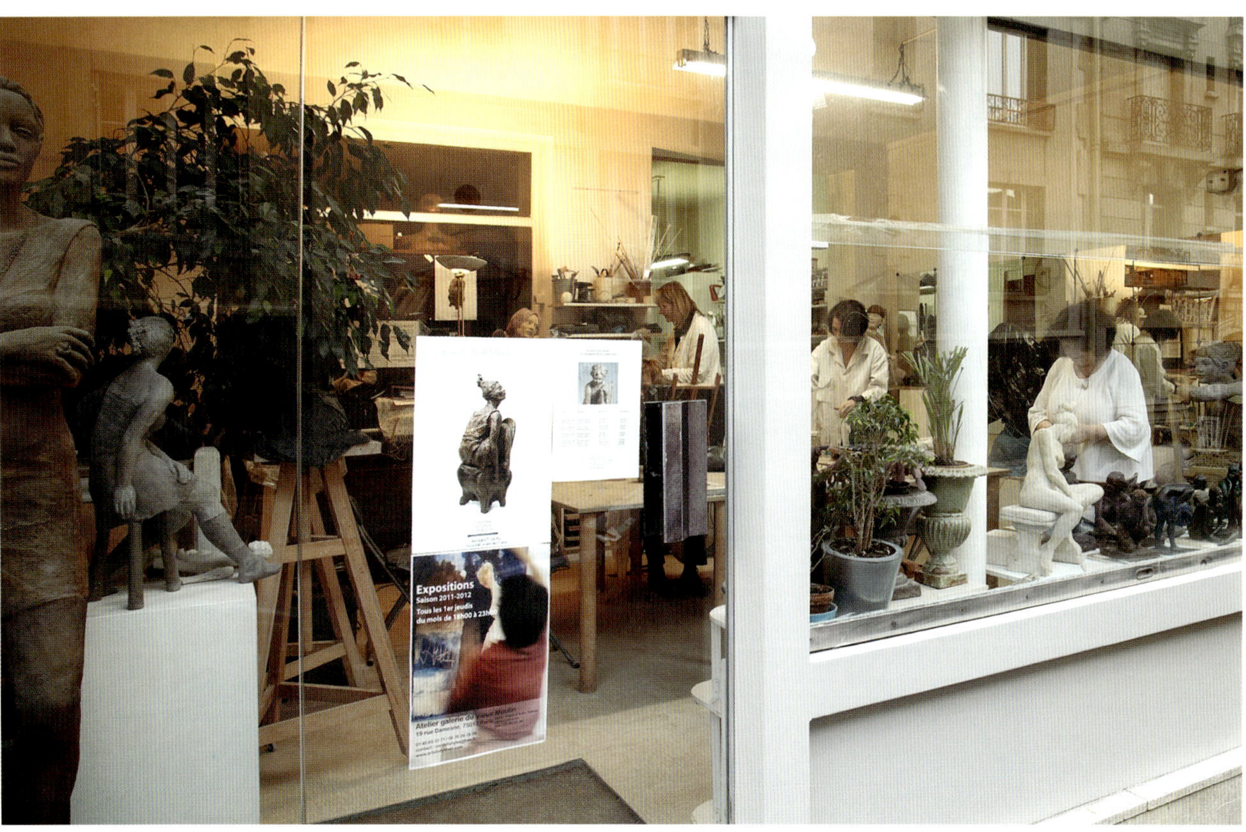

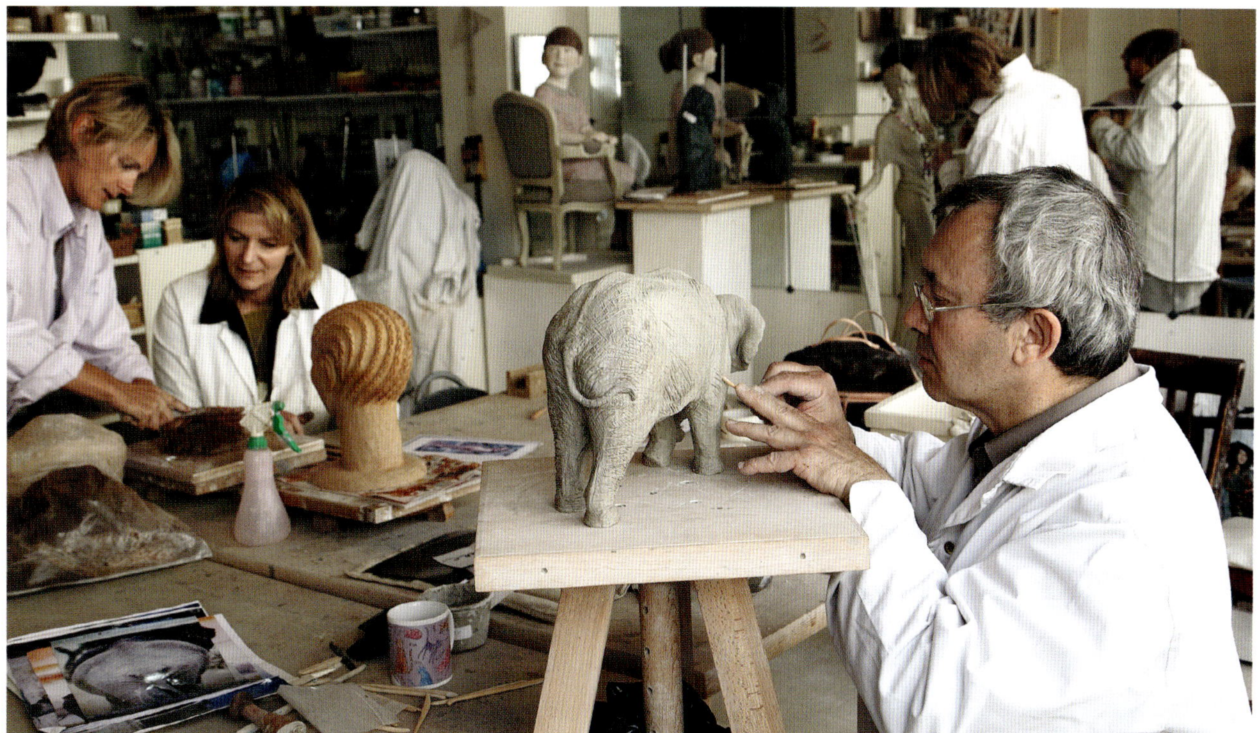

On the left, Nathalie is starting on a large standing nude, and I explain how to begin. In the background, Sophie is polishing her 1930s-style Demoiselle, which will later be molded and thrown in bronze. In the foreground, Pierre retouches his elephant, which is nearly finished.

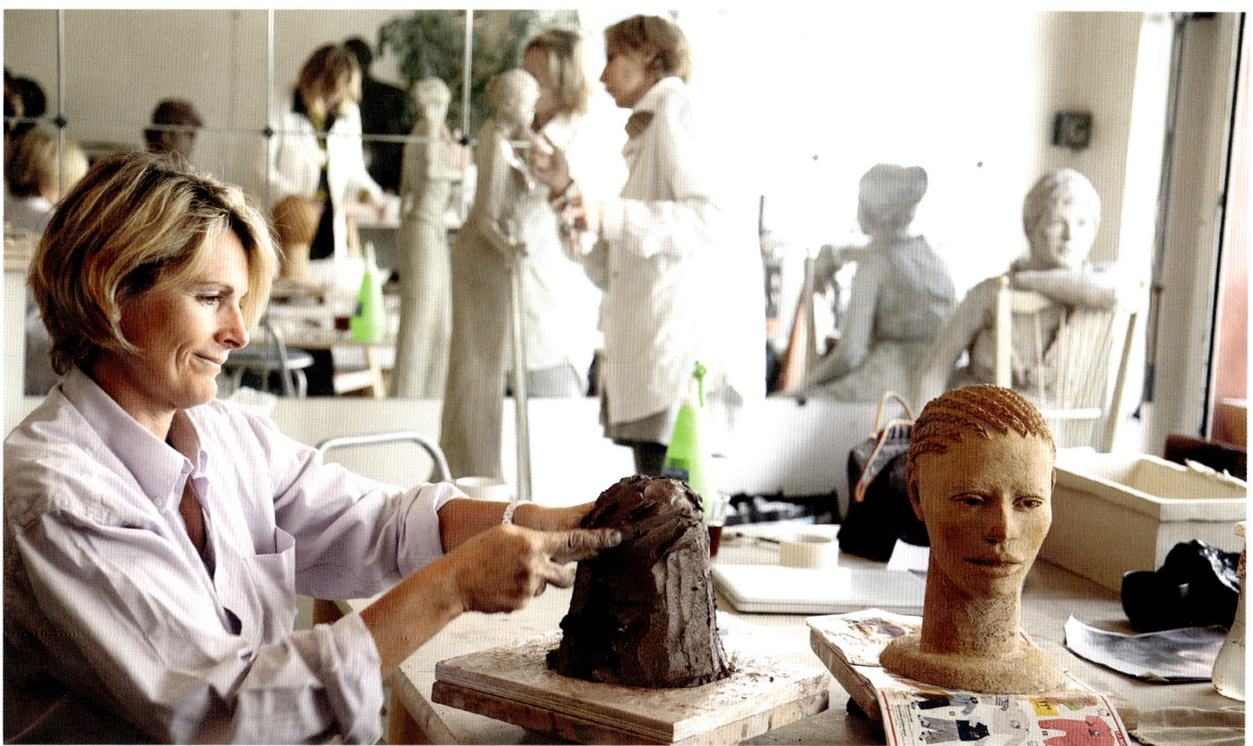

The legs of Nathalie's statue are built by adding on pieces of clay; the volume increases quickly. Sophie is working on the details of the Demoiselle's face.

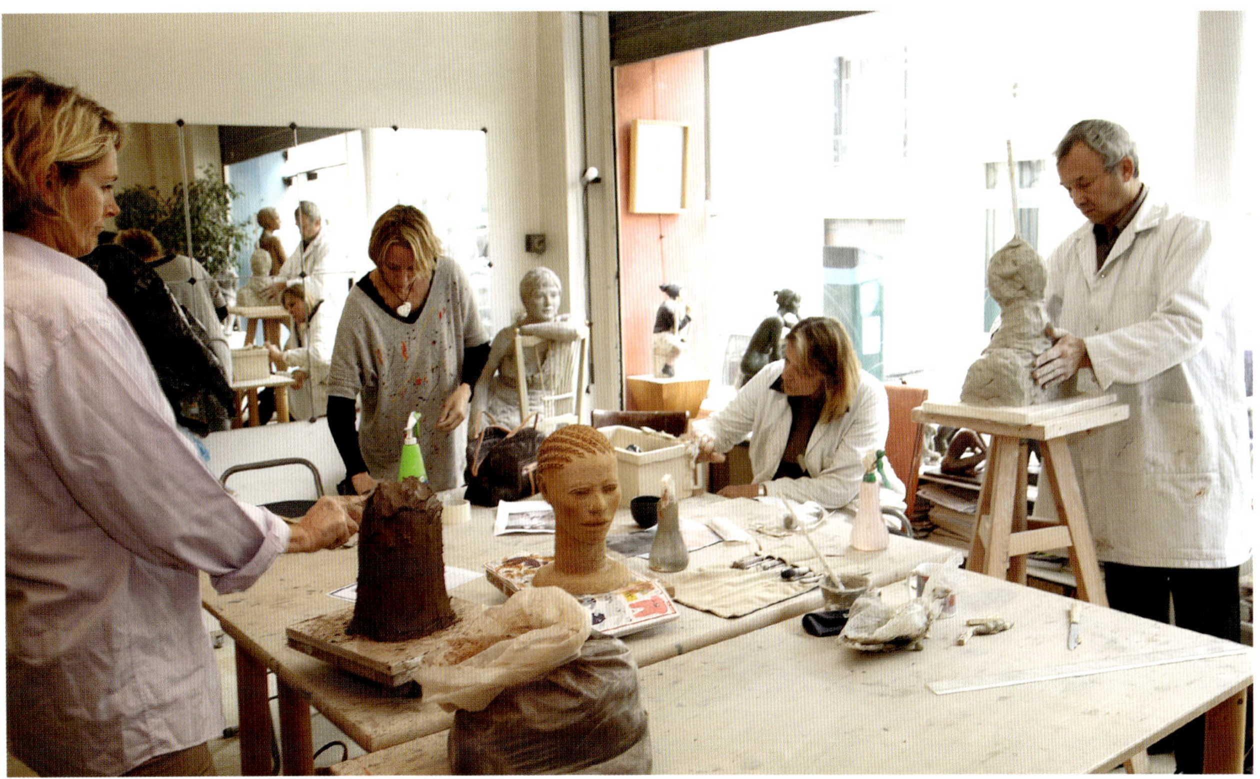

The atmosphere is studious this afternoon.

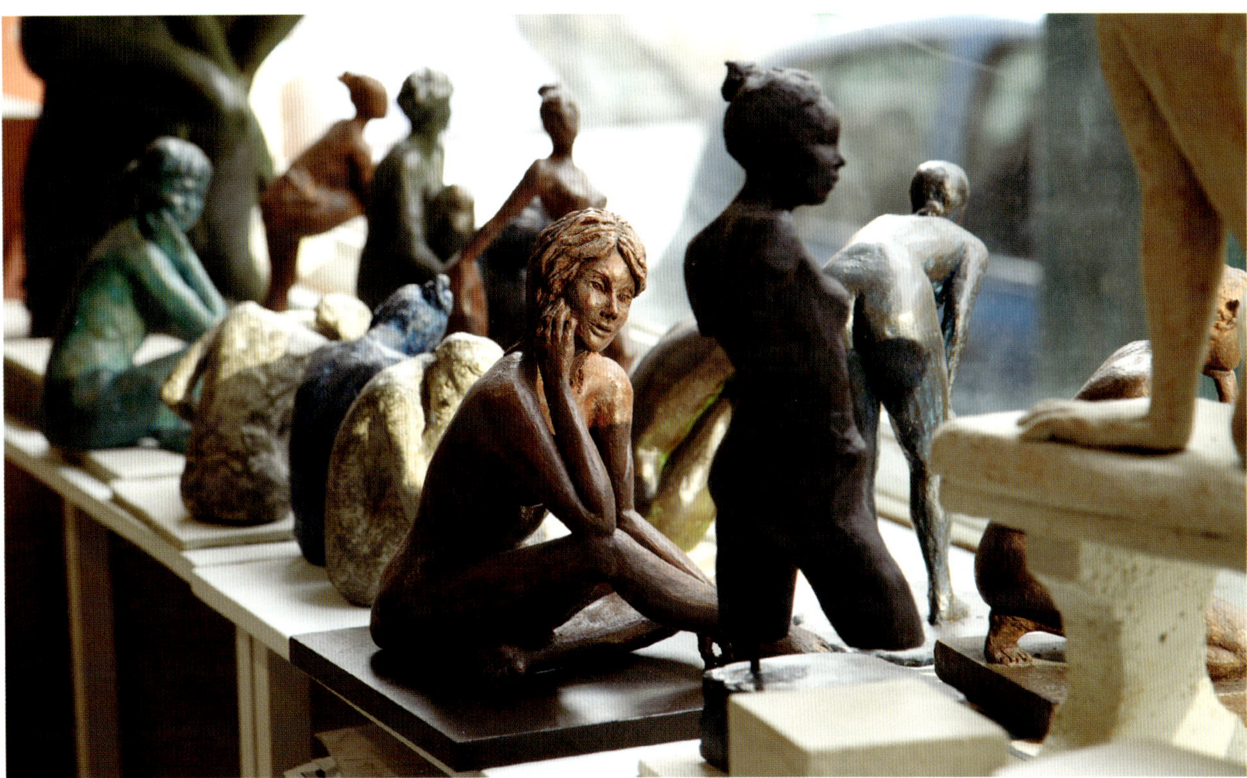

Pieces made by the students, and some personal items together in the workshop's window

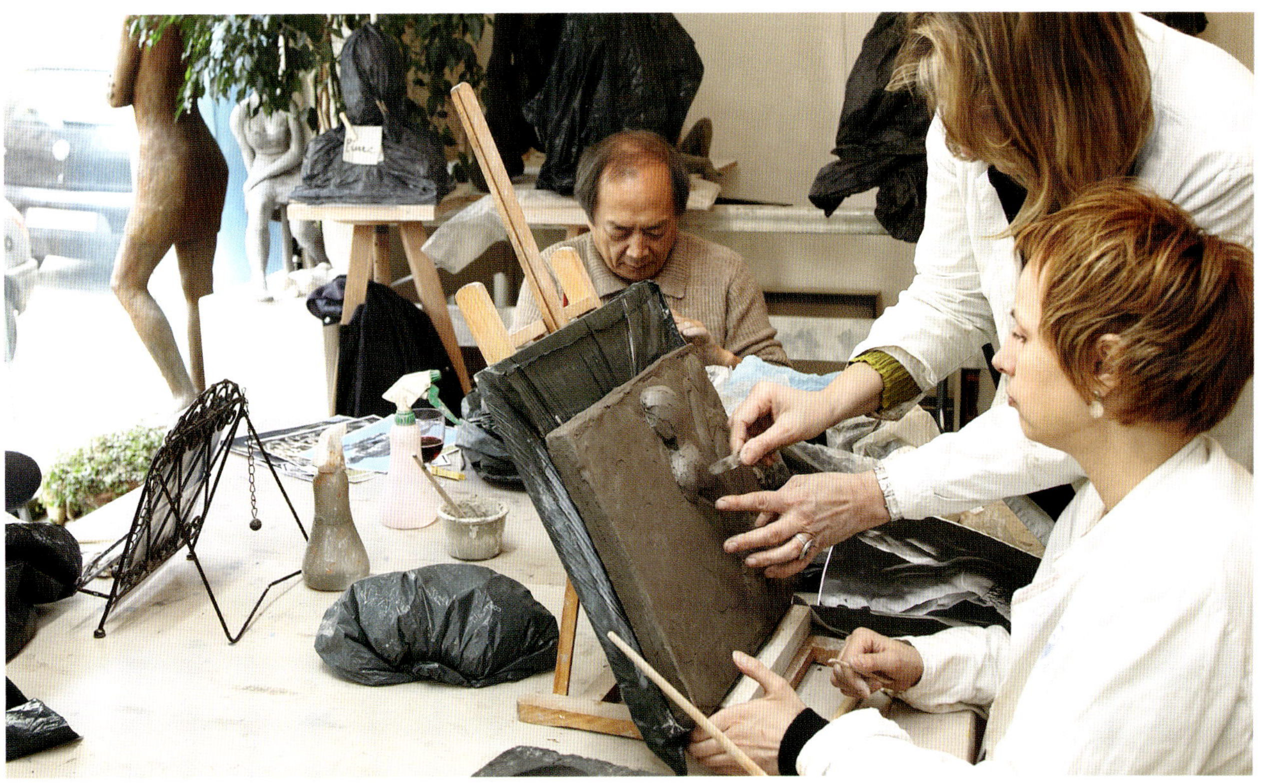

Valerie is working on a bas-relief; I explain how to create the impression of depth.

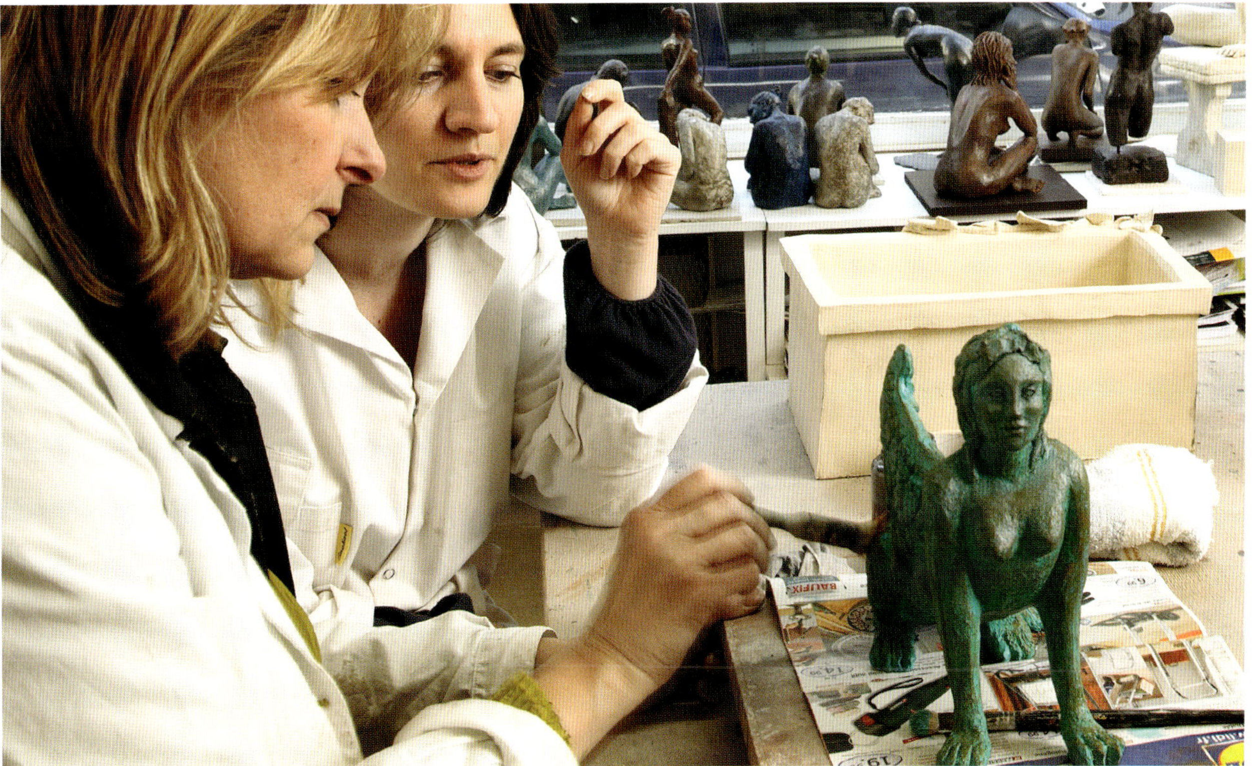

Cecile has chosen a Caparol patina with turquoise and ocher pigments; I show her how to proceed.

Personal Work

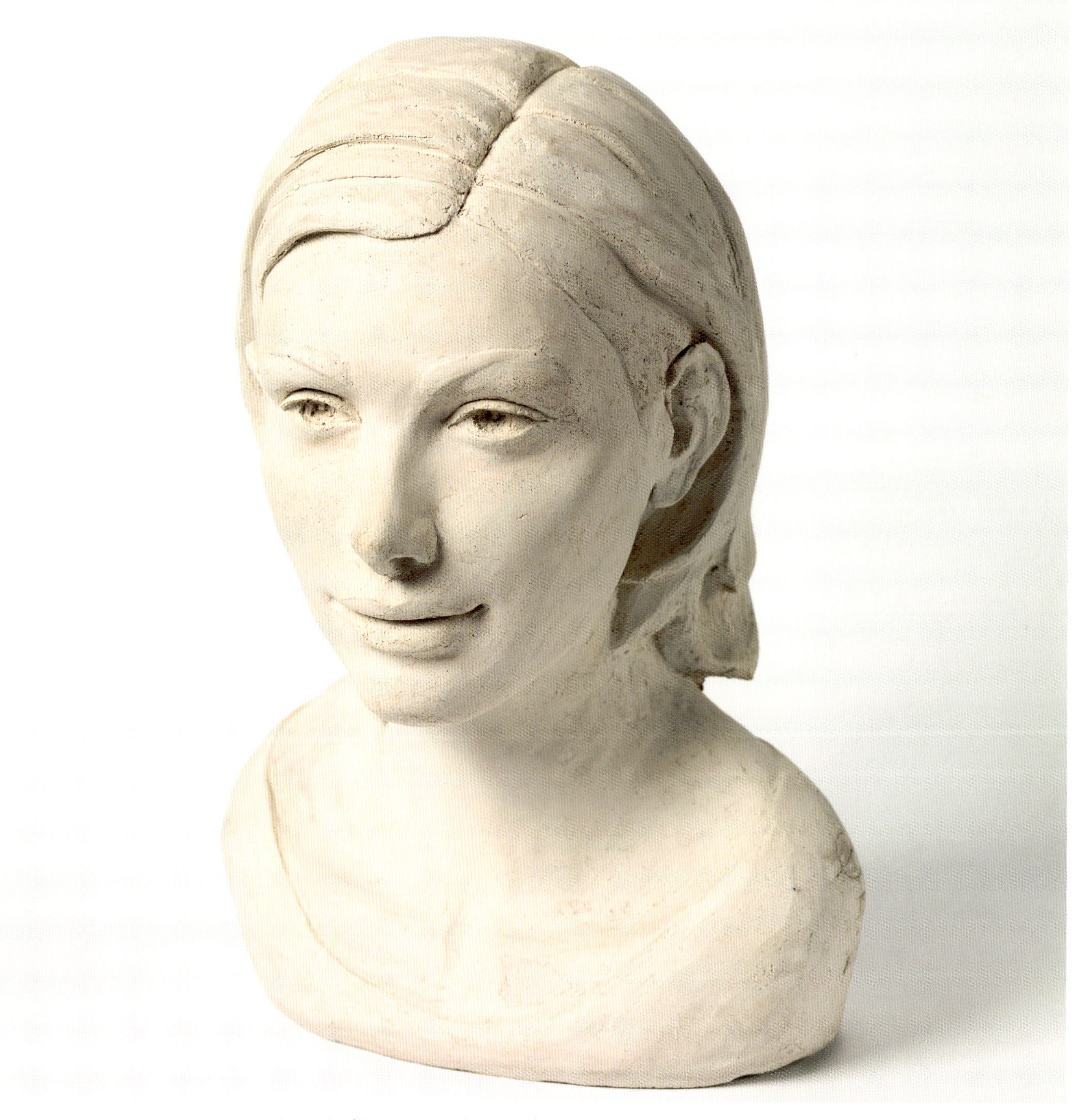

Portrait of Laurette Fugain: natural terra-cotta, height 15¾"

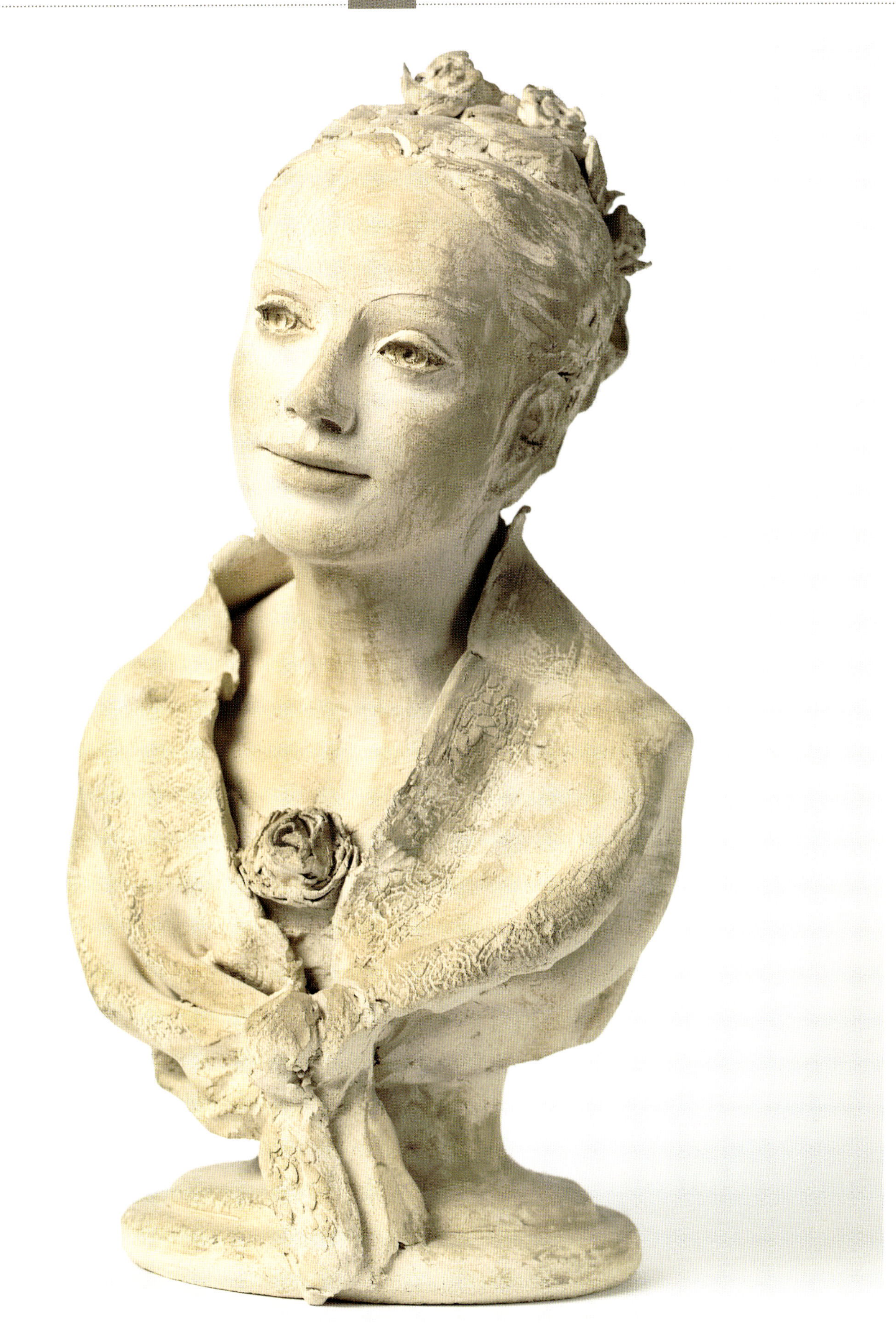

Bust of Claire: finely grogged stoneware with a patina, height 20½"

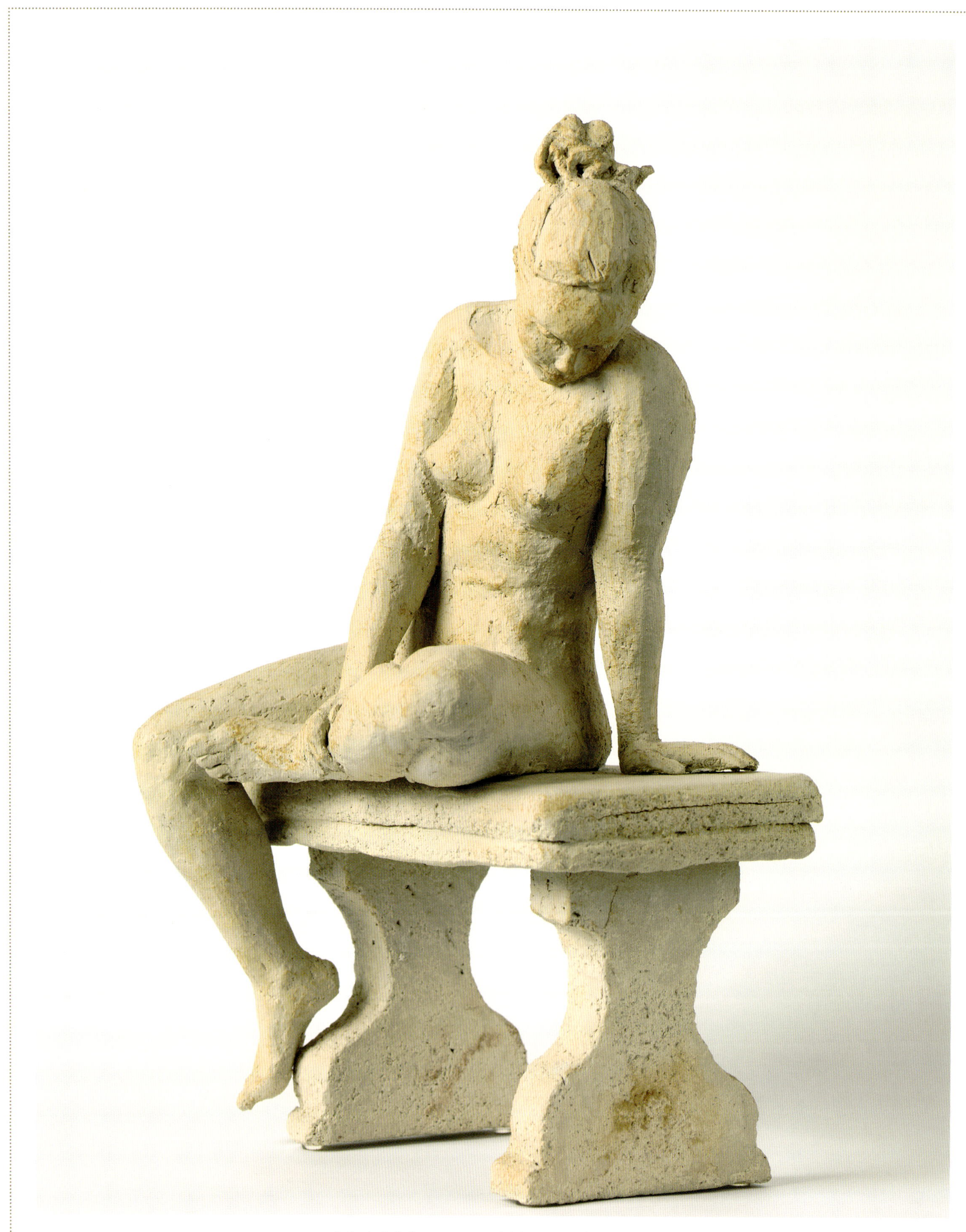

Bain de Soleil: *stoneware with its patina, height 20"*

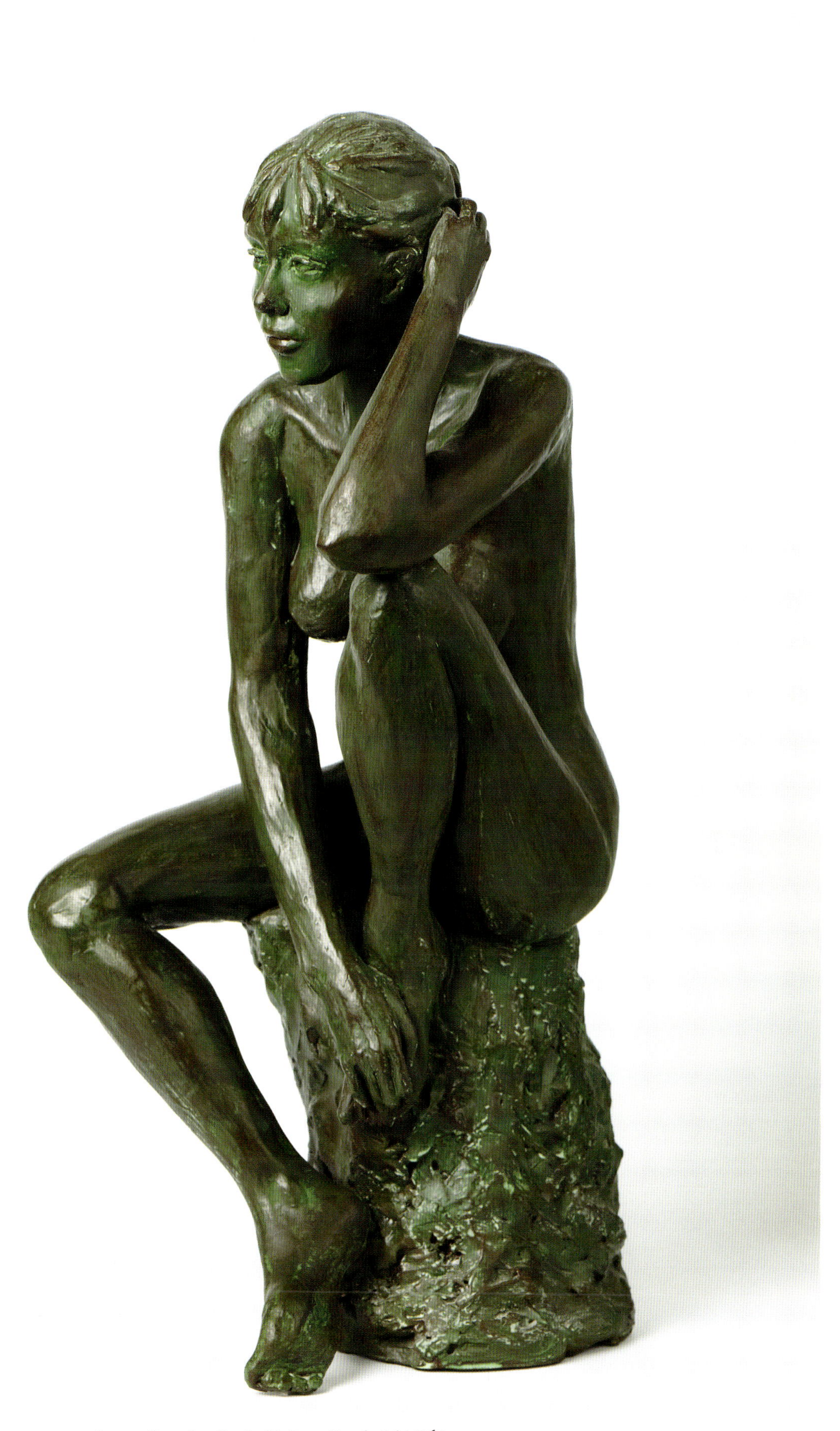

Sensuality: *clay fired with its patina, height 27½"*

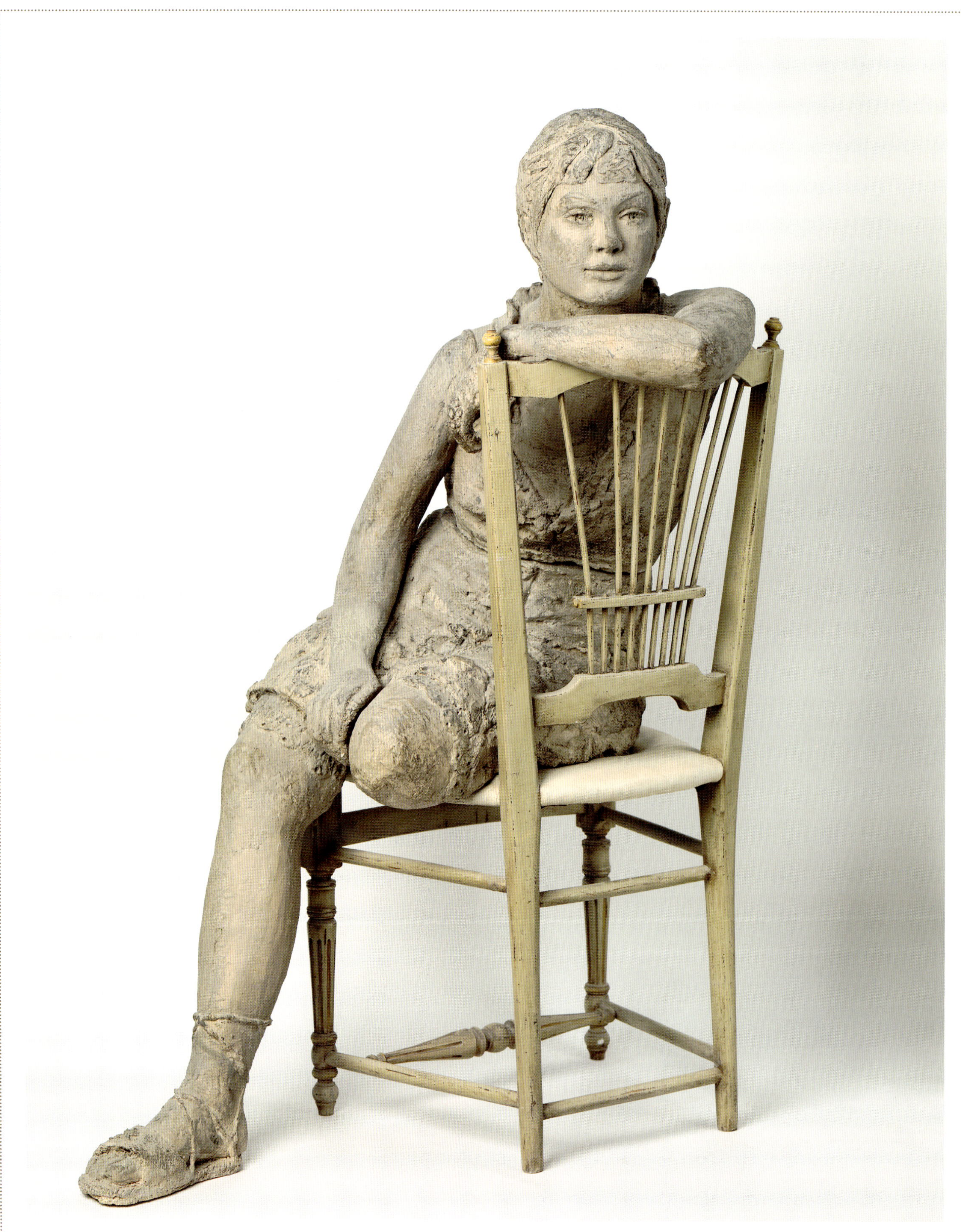

Delphine: clay fired with its patina, placed on a wood and cloth chair, height 4¼'

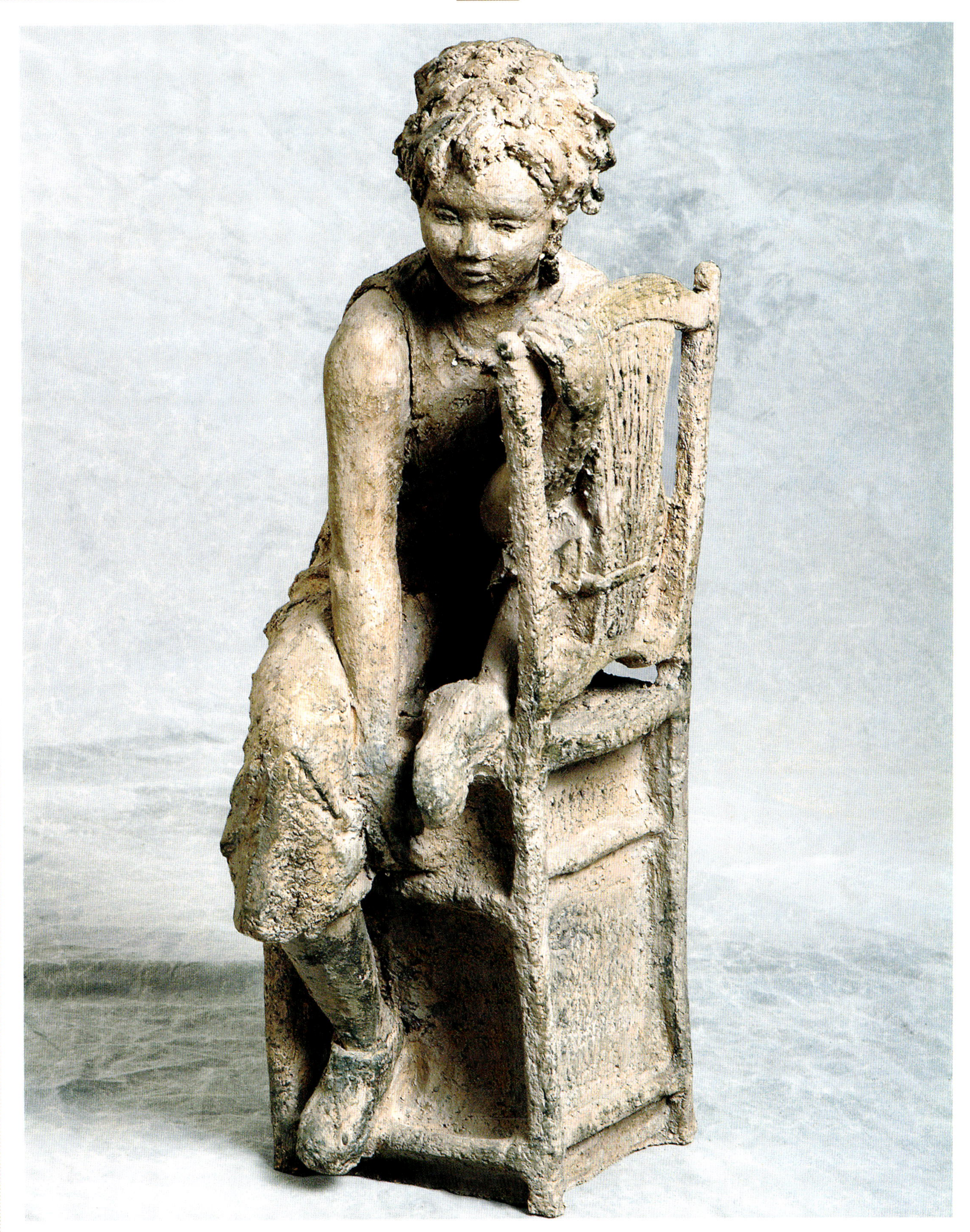

Delphine (1): clay fired with its patina, height 15¾"

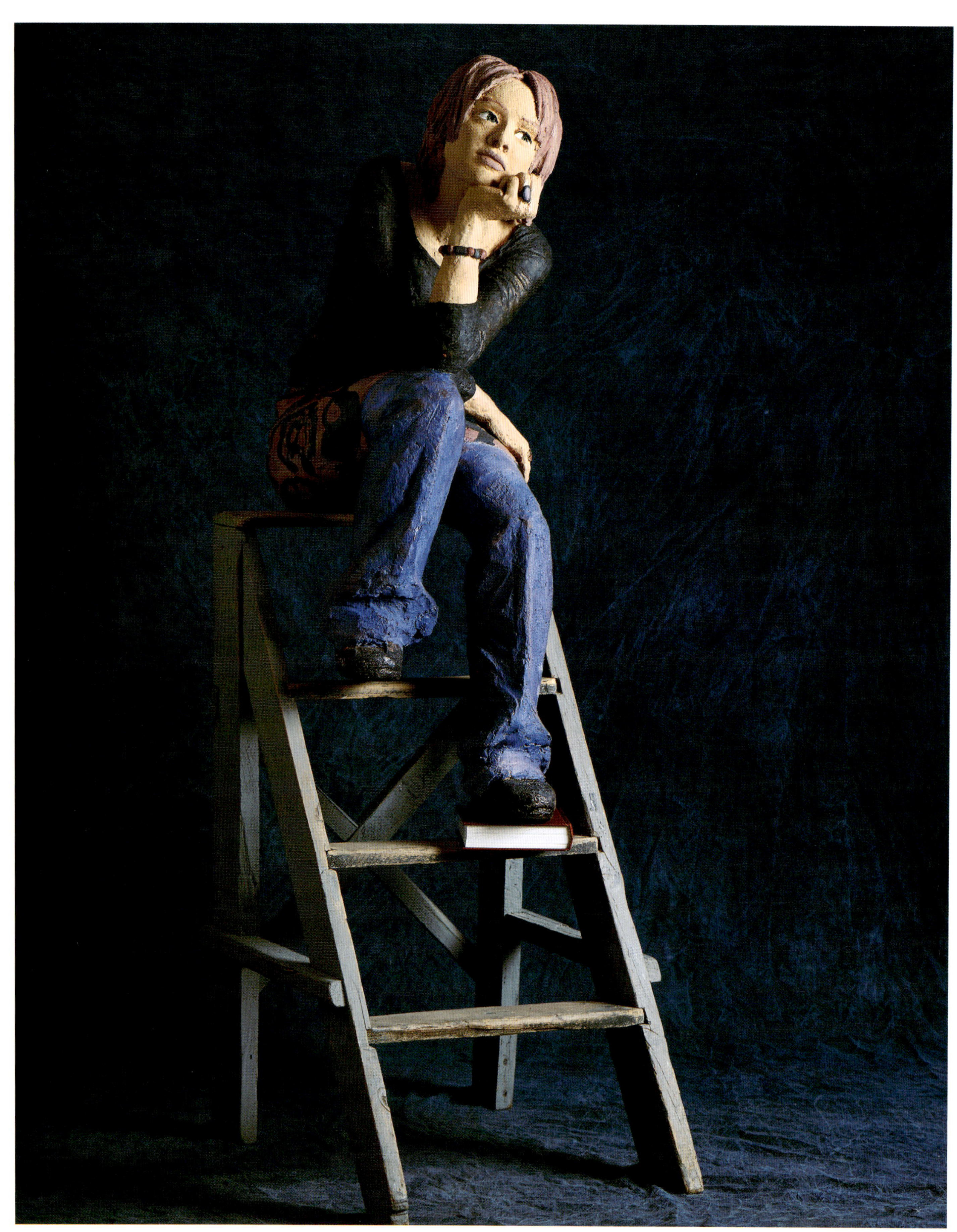

Psyché: *engobe on fired stoneware sitting on a wooden ladder, height 5¼'*

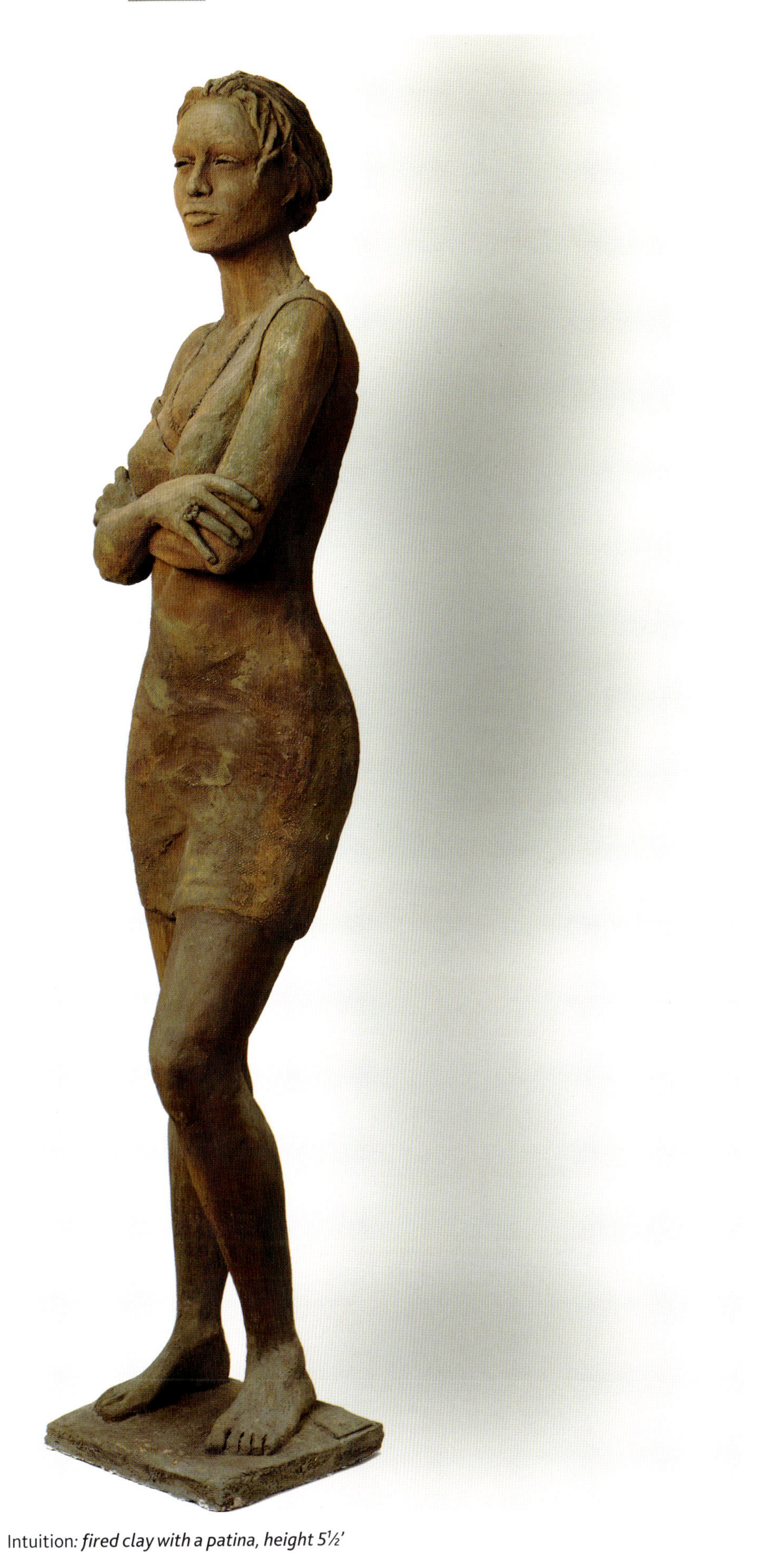

Intuition: *fired clay with a patina, height 5½'*

Glossary

BLISTER
This is the term used when the clay has swellings or bumps after firing. This is due to the quality of the clay, which is rather compact and should be fired at a relatively low temperature for an ideal result. Some stoneware should be fired at a maximum of 2,012°F (instead of 2,336°F), because at a higher temperature it bubbles—its molecules being tightly packed—and it shrinks quicker than classical stoneware.

CAPAROL
Vinyl medium used for painting when mixed with pigments, but also as a patina. It is sold in jars weighing from 2 to 11 lbs.

CERAMIC
This term can be applied to fired clay or clay objects, but also to the art of a sculptor or potter, consisting of giving clay a shape and firing it to solidify it according to the procedure of ceramic firing.

CLAY
Material formed by the decomposition of rocks that is continuously created in nature. These elongated particles accumulate in layers or slabs. The miniscule clay molecule is mainly composed of aluminosilicate, silica, and water.

CLAY MINERALS
Names of clays that have different particularities and have formed in different climates: in cold regions, in hot and humid regions, in temperate regions, or in confined areas (illites, chlorites, kaolinite, smectite and vermiculite).

CLAY SAUSAGE (COLOMBIAN)
A hand-rolled cylinder of clay

EARTHENWARE
A type of clay that is fired at the relatively low temperature of 1,796°F. It is also a term used for the firing temperature of other types of clay.

ENGOBE
Coloration painted onto unfired clay made of a mixture of clay (medium) and metal oxides (maximum 30%)

TO GLAZE
Vitrify at high temperature (2,336°C)

GROG
Grains of fired clay added to unfired clay when it is fabricated, to give it solidity and plasticity; it ventilates and cleans the clay.

LEATHER HARD
Consistency of the clay as it begins to dry out. It gets darker and feels like a piece of leather.

PLASTICITY
When clay contains 40% of water and is easily modeled with your fingers

RAKU CLAY
A highly resistant clay that supports thermal shocks and also a firing temperature. Raku firing consists of raising the clay to

1,832°F in 20 minutes, which is very violent because generally the heat is increased slowly over a period of 8–10 hours to reach this temperature. Then the cone kiln, which is usually outdoors, is opened and the glowing red sculpture is removed and plunged into wood chips, which immediately catch fire; from there the item is put into water (myriad crackles appear on the surface, which will show up once the piece has cooled down and is rubbed with an abrasive sponge). The clay has been subjected to three thermal shocks, so it is important that it is very resistant and grogged.

RESTORE/RESTORATION
Repair of the surface of a sculpture where it had to have parts cut off for firing purposes, or repairing a piece that has cracked or broken. Restoration allows you to erase joining seams or the accidents that a sculpture has had, and leaves the surface as good as new.

SEAM
The visible line where a part of a sculpture has been cut away and later reattached. The seams are erased afterward.

SLIP
A mix of clay and water (70%) that has the consistency of creamy yogurt and is used to fix added or assembled clay

STONEWARE
A type of clay that is fired and vitrifies at the high temperature of 2,336°F. It is also used for other types of clay that don't vitrify but can be fired at stoneware temperature.

SCORING
Scoring the clay with a potter's needle or a thin knife opens the surface and helps it soften up when slip is applied.

SCULPTURE IN THE ROUND
A sculpture you can walk all around

SLAB WORK
Slab work signifies constructing a volume by assembling dried and hardened slabs of clay.

Other Schiffer Books on Related Subjects

The Ceramics Studio Guide: What Potters Should Know, Jeff Zamek, foreword by Steven Branfman, ISBN 978-0-7643-5648-3

Artists Write to Work: A Practical Guide to Writing about Your Art, Kate Kramer, ISBN 978-0-7643-5649-0

Cover design by Molly Shields
Type set in Nevia BT Pro/Cambria
Director: Guillaume Pô
Editorial director: Tatian Delesalle
Book director: Valérie Monnet
Editor: Hélène Raviart
Graphics and layout: Pascal Despeaux
Production director: Thierry Dubus
Production assistant: Axelle Hosten